The FIGHTING CANADIANS

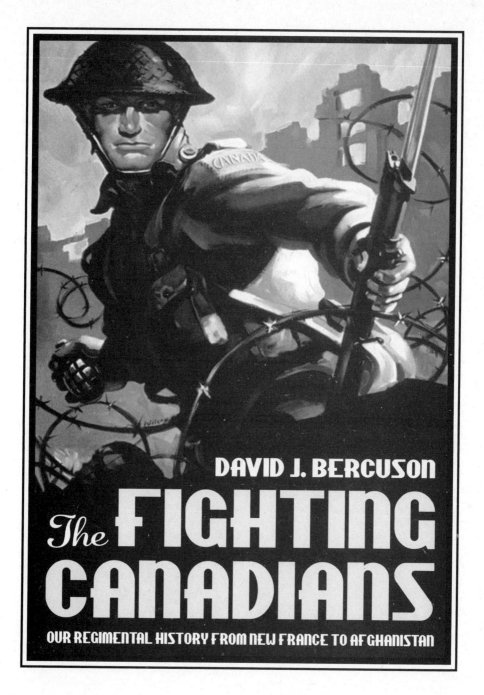

DAVID J. BERCUSON

The FIGHTING
CANADIANS

OUR REGIMENTAL HISTORY FROM NEW FRANCE TO AFGHANISTAN

HARPERCOLLINS PUBLISHERS LTD

The Fighting Canadians
© 2008 by David J. Bercuson. All rights reserved.

Published by HarperCollins Publishers Ltd.

First edition

Grateful acknowledgement is made for permission to reprint the following material:

Excerpt from *The Brigade: The Fifth Canadian Infantry Brigade, 1939–1945* by Terry Copp © 1992 by Terry Copp. Fortress Publications. Reprinted by permission of the author.

Excerpt from *The Canadian General: Sir William Otter* by Desmond Morton © 1974 by Desmond Morton. Adolf M. Hakkert Publications. Reprinted by permission of the author.

Excerpt from "'Contact C'—A Forward Observation Officer with Task Force Orion" by Captain Andrew Charchuk © 2007 *Canadian Army Journal*, vol. 10, no. 2 (Summer 2007). Reprinted by permission of *Canadian Army Journal*.

Excerpt from *Peacekeeper: The Road to Sarajevo* by Major-General Lewis MacKenzie © 1993 by Major-General Lewis MacKenzie. Douglas & McIntyre. Reprinted by permission of the author.

Excerpt from *Red Coats & Grey Jackets: The Battle of Chippawa, 5 July 1814* by Donald E. Graves © 1994 by Donald E. Graves. Dundurn Press. Reprinted by permission of the author.

Excerpts from *The Regiment* by Farley Mowat © 2007 by Farley Mowat. Vanwell Publishing. Reprinted by permission of the author.

Regimental crests appearing on the endpapers courtesy of the Department of National Defence, www.army.forces.gc.ca/lf/english/7_0.asp, reproduced with the permission of the Minister of Public Works and Government Services Canada 2008.

HarperCollins books may be purchased for educational, business, or sales promotional use through our Special Markets Department.

HarperCollins Publishers Ltd
2 Bloor Street East, 20th Floor
Toronto, Ontario, Canada
M4W 1A8

www.harpercollins.ca

Library and Archives Canada Cataloguing in Publication

Bercuson, David Jay, 1945–
The fighting Canadians : our regimental history from New France to Afghanistan / David J. Bercuson.

ISBN 978-0-00-200734-4

1. Canada—History, Military.
2. Canada. Canadian Army—History.
3. Canada—Armed Forces—History.
4. Canada. Canadian Armed Forces—History.
I. Title.

UA600.B468 2008   355.3'10971   C2008-901913-X

HC 9 8 7 6 5 4 3 2 1

Printed and bound in the United States

For F.P.M.

CONTENTS

PREFACE

THERE IS NOTHING more difficult to explain to those who have little knowledge of military history or traditions than what a regiment is. Yet the very concept of the regiment, as well as the nurturing of both individual regimental lore and the broader regimental tradition, is one of the main attributes of soldiering. Thus my immediate reaction to Jim Gifford's suggestion that I write a book on Canada's regimental tradition was to leap at the chance. My second reaction was to wonder exactly how I would explain so complicated a concept. Because I am a historian, I decided to do it through a review of the role that regiments have played in Canadian history from the very beginning to now.

Regiments are first and foremost agglomerations of soldiers that have been created to keep the soldiers steady, focused, and firm in the lead-up to the chaos and bloodletting of battle. Battle lies at the heart of a regiment's history and its traditions. Regiments that are newly minted and have never participated in battle borrow from the regimental lore of allied regiments, which they fashion themselves after and may seek affiliation with. Regiments that have experienced battles place those battles at the core of their identity. The Canadian army inherited its particular regimental tradition from the British army that conquered New France in the Seven Years' War and stayed behind to protect Canada from its enemies. The French army that preceded the British had a regimental tradition of its own, but that line of tradition was broken by the conquest. The First Nations of the St. Lawrence Valley had no regiments as such but, like all societies since the dawn of time, fought wars and established special rituals and traditions to guide warrior conduct. In that, they were not unlike the regiments of the Europeans.

There is considerable controversy among both soldiers and scholars as to the benefits and drawbacks of the regimental system. I have replayed that debate in my introduction, but for the most part there is little theory in this book. In my view, explaining what regiments are means explaining what they did. Since I could not write about every regiment, or even sketch the complete history of a number of regiments—there are, after all, many very good regimental histories on library shelves and in bookstores—I decided to select key events in Canadian military history and examine what selected regiments did on those occasions. My objective was to portray regimental cohesion under the very trying circumstances of war in order to demonstrate why Canada's soldiers still place so much value on the regimental tradition. In doing so, of course, I have traced the history of almost all the regiments of Canada's regular army and many of its reserve regiments.

There is also controversy among soldiers and scholars about regimental antecedents. Regiments have been formed and disbanded throughout Canadian history. New regiments have often claimed to be the successors of preceding regiments, especially when the period between the disbanding of the old formation and the raising of the new one was very short. My own interpretation comes from the authoritative but now very dated *The Regiments and Corps of the Canadian Army,* published under the authority of the Minister of National Defence in 1964. It contains a strict interpretation of regimental precedent and lineage. If an early regiment was disbanded in 1805, for example, and a successor raised in 1807, the guide considers that no official connection can be considered to exist across the two-year gap, even if the successor contained many of the same officers and men, was raised in the same basic area, or claimed to be an official successor.

It is a hard line to draw—and to take—but it is easy to follow, and so I have done. Others are more than welcome to see things differently. After all, it was soldiers who created regiments and soldiers of the British and Canadian (and British Commonwealth) traditions who endowed them with semi-religious characteristics. If the modern Van Doos wish to identify with some famous French regiment of old, or if the Royal Newfoundland Regiment of today wishes to uphold a tradition dating back to the 1803 formation of the Royal Newfoundland Fencibles, who is to say they are wrong?

It is, after all, the men (and now the women too), whose sacrifice has endowed the regimental tradition with the hallowed status it now has, who have made the rules, and they are free to break them or to uphold them as they wish.

David J. Bercuson
Rockyview, Alberta
February 2008

Introduction

BATTLE HONOURS AND MESS DINNERS:
THE REGIMENTAL TRADITION

> These bridges will be held to the last man against any attempt by the enemy to seize or destroy the crossings.
>
> —Major J.L. Love, Officer Commanding,
> Dog Company, Regina Rifles, June 5, 1944

IN THE EARLY MORNING hours of June 6, 1944, the Regina Rifles entered history when they were among the first Canadian units to assault the Normandy beachhead. In the first days of the war, no one would have imagined that the Reginas would have such an auspicious introduction to combat.

When the Canadian army's regular and militia units began mobilizing at the beginning of September 1939, the Regina Rifles were virtually left out. The regiment was only a hundred or so strong in part-time soldiers; most were farm boys from the Regina region and southern Saskatchewan. The Reginas were ordered to provide only local protection in the southern part of the province, which had been one of the hardest hit provinces during the Great Depression. Not only had the farm economy been virtually wiped out by the plunge in wheat prices, but thousands of hectares of prairie topsoil had blown away in the drought conditions of the "dirty thirties." Everywhere across the southern reaches of the province, the wind blew drifting soil over abandoned farms. Thousands of rural families had simply deserted what little remained and moved into the cities, west into the Peace River country of Alberta, or to the Pacific coast. To earn a few extra dollars, some of the young men who stayed joined the militia—mostly the South Saskatchewan Regiment, created in 1920, or the Regina Rifles, created in 1924—mixing with older men, some of whom were veterans of the First World War. They underwent desultory training over the next decade or so, mostly with First World War equipment and uniforms (most of the officers were First World War holdouts). Sports, drilling, and target shooting dominated their preparation.

Then came war, in September 1939, and the mobilization of the 1st and 2nd Canadian Infantry divisions. It appeared that the war would pass Saskatchewan by, but on May 24, 1940, just two weeks after the German invasion of France and the Low Countries, the Regina Rifles were finally mobilized and ordered to expand to full war strength—about 850 men in total. Nine months later they left Canada for the U.K. as a battalion of the 7th Canadian Infantry Brigade of the 3rd Canadian Infantry Division.

The 3rd Canadian Infantry Division was chosen to be Canada's assault force for the Normandy landings almost purely by happenstance. The 1st Division had been sent to fight in the Mediterranean in the spring of 1943, and a lack of ocean transport made it impossible to return the division to France in time for the invasion. Besides, in the spring of 1944 the division was completely tied up in the battle for Rome. Both conditions also applied to the 5th Canadian Armoured Division, which had been sent to Italy in late 1943. The 2nd Division had been decimated at Dieppe in August 1942 and was still rebuilding; no one thought it was in good enough shape to assault another beach so soon, and in fact it did not enter the Normandy fighting until more than a month after D-Day. The 4th Canadian Armoured Division was not ready to fight until early August 1944, so the 3rd Division got the nod for the assault.

The 3rd Division's 7th and 8th brigades were picked to lead the landings on Juno Beach—the Canadian beach. The 9th Brigade would stay in transports on the water, in reserve, until the first two brigades were beginning to move inland. The two other battalions of the 7th Brigade—the Canadian Scottish of Victoria, B.C., and the Royal Winnipeg Rifles—would accompany the Regina Rifles in the first wave. The Reginas' immediate objective was the seaside town of Courseulles-sur-Mer and a bridge in the hamlet of Reviers, about 3 kilometres inland from Courseulles. After that, they and the remainder of the brigade were to try to reach the Caen-Bayeux rail line—about 16 kilometres south of the beach—by nightfall. Able and Baker companies would hit the beach first and capture Courseulles; Charlie and Dog companies were to follow but to immediately drive inland to take the Reviers bridge. Dog Company's commander, Major J.L. Love, instructed his men: "These bridges will be held to the last man against any attempt by the enemy to seize or destroy the crossings."

In the cold dawn of June 6, 1944, the Royal Navy assault transport *Isle of Thanet* pitched and rolled in the rough Channel waters as the Reginas climbed down cargo nets hung over the side. It was approximately 5:00 AM as they clambered into the small assault craft that would take them to the beach. Those who had managed to sleep had been awakened at 4:00 AM for tea and a cold snack before donning packs, grabbing spare ammunition, and taking up their weapons and other tools of war. But once they were in the pitching assault boats, the Rifles couldn't go straight in.

They had to wait for the DD tanks (canvas-sheathed floating Sherman tanks with small propellers at the rear) and the other specialized assault vehicles to lead the way. The floating tanks were especially slow; they seemed always on the verge of foundering and plummeting to the bottom of the Channel. So the Reginas and the other Canadian, British, and American assault formations circled in the heaving sea while heavy bombardment from hundreds of battleships, cruisers, destroyers, rocket-launching vessels, and heavy-gun monitors pounded the beach defences. Fighter bombers and medium and heavy bombers zoomed over, adding to the din. Huge shells rumbled overhead and exploded

with ear-wrenching booms along the line of massive concrete fortifications spaced every few hundred metres at the head of the beaches.
Finally, at about 7:15 AM, the landing craft broke off their circling and
headed toward shore. Most of the men kept their heads down and
tried not to vomit during the rough run to the beaches. Shot and shell
exploded around them as they came within range of the German gunners. If any of the Reginas had looked over the gunwales, he would have
seen dozens of landing craft fanning out to his right as the Winnipegs
and the Canadian Scottish also advanced to the beach.

Able Company nosed up on the sand at 8:09 AM. The ramps dropped
and the men ran toward the German strongpoint that lay ahead. The
tanks that were supposed to accompany them and provide covering fire
were late. Company commander Major Duncan Grosch was hit almost
immediately. Other men were also cut down by the rapid fire of the
German machine guns or by shrapnel from the German 75mm and
50mm guns ahead of them. Some twenty minutes after landing, the
company radioed battalion HQ that it was pinned down and unable to
move. Lieutenant Bill Grayson had huddled beside one of the seafront
houses and managed to avoid the machine-gun fire. Now he crept to
the opening of one of the German pillboxes. He threw his grenade
inside, destroyed the gun, and flushed out the gun crew (he was later
awarded the Military Cross for his heroism). Able Company was now
free to begin pushing forward into the town.

About 400 metres to the left, Baker Company came ashore six
minutes after Able Company. Here the swimming tanks had already
arrived, engines idling as they waited in the surf for the landing craft.
They began to shoot at the German defenders. Most of the German
guns on the beachfront were already firing at Able Company, so
Baker Company were able to scamper from their landing craft into
the front row of houses with almost no casualties. Then, accompanied by a variety of DD tanks and specialized armour, they began
to clear the houses nearest the sea. In the Channel, the two reserve
companies headed for shore. They raced against a rapidly rising tide
that began to flood the beach, covering the thick forest of obstacles,

mostly mined, that were designed to tear the bottoms out of the landing craft or blow them up. Charlie Company hit the beach at 8:35 AM and began to move inland, around Courseulles. Dog Company were late. As they neared shore, some of the landing craft blew up on the submerged mined obstacles. Of the more than 120 men in the company, fewer than half struggled ashore. Major Love was killed.

The survivors pushed ahead under command of Lieutenant H.L. Jones. They began to move cautiously overland beside the Mue River (which was more like a small creek) toward Reviers. They did not know it, but the main line of German resistance beyond the beach lay about 7 kilometres ahead. Before noon, they joined forces with Charlie Company to attack a German position in the town and secure the important bridge. By 3:00 PM, the entire battalion had arrived from Courseulles. They consolidated before pushing on through Fontaine-Henry to Le Fresne-Camilly, about 10 kilometres inland. Before the day was out Major F.L. Peters, Lieutenant G.D. Dickin, and Private A.J. Kennedy had been killed by shellfire in Fontaine-Henry. The battalion dug in at 10:00 PM. In the course of the day 108 Reginas were killed or wounded, including two company commanders, Majors Love and Peters—some 20 percent of their fighting strength. They killed a large but unknown number of Germans and took about 150 German prisoners, and earned the Regina Rifles (now the Royal Regina Rifles) their first battle honour of the Second World War.

—⁓—

THE REGINAS WERE GREEN AS GRASS when they went to war. They were citizen soldiers, despite a few years of sporadic training in Canada's underequipped and undermanned prewar militia, despite even the more intensive training they had received in the U.K. prior to the D-Day assault. In the U.K. they had exercised with tanks and artillery. They had even been exposed to live fire, to inoculate them, as it were, to battle. But the only real inoculation to battle is battle itself. No matter how a soldier is physically prepared for the horrible reality of war—someone out there is trying to kill him (or her)—the moment of truth comes only when the first deadly rounds crack over a soldier's head or stitch the wall beside him or kick dust into her eyes.

How then to prepare soldiers to cope with the sights, sounds, fears of battle? In today's modern armies, training is carried out in sophisticated computer-operated environments such as the U.S. Army's Desert Training Center, the British army's BATUS (British Army Training Unit, Suffield) in Suffield, Alberta, and the new Canadian Manoeuvre Training Centre (CMTC) at Canadian Forces Base Wainwright. On these bases soldiers rehearse for the real thing. They fire weapons at each other using laser gear; hits are recorded by laser sensors. Artillery bombardments, minefields, air attacks, and chemical or biological weapon strikes are all computer simulated. If a soldier is suddenly informed by a signal in his earpiece that "gas" has been dispensed in his vicinity, he must don his gas gear immediately. If a soldier ignores the signal or removes her gas mask—even for a second—a sensor in the mask will relay that data to a master computer. The computer will almost instantly inform her and an umpire nearby that she has been "killed" by a chemical agent, and a beacon she wears will begin to flash. It is all very realistic, especially when combined with days in the field without hot food, showers, or changes of clothing, plagued by sleep deprivation, bad weather, and cranky unit commanders. It is as close to battle as anyone is ever likely to come without actually being in combat, but it isn't battle—it is rough play. And every soldier taking part in this elaborate rehearsal knows in his heart of hearts that no one is deliberately trying to kill him, no lethal rounds are being fired at him, and when the exercise is over, everybody will get to go home unscathed.

What, then, keeps soldiers like the green Regina Rifles functioning under fire—fighting, going into harm's way, making split-second decisions? What enables soldiers to kill other soldiers whom they have nothing personal against (a very unnatural act for the great majority of human beings)? What prompts soldiers to deliberately sacrifice their own lives for their comrades? What prompts a soldier to stay and fight when every instinct in a human who is being systematically shot at, shelled, mortared, gassed, booby-trapped, or attacked by a suicide bomber tells him or her to run? The proponents of what is called the British regimental system believe that it is the regiment that has been most successful in psychologically preparing soldiers to do the most unnatural job in the world—fighting wars.

Whether that is true or not—and the system clearly has its detractors—the regimental system has long been the building stone of soldierly cohesion in the British and Commonwealth armed forces. Soldierly cohesion—no matter how it is developed in a group of soldiers—is absolutely vital to deliver ordinary mortals to the possible place of their death, voluntarily, and even with a sense of determined purpose. If the regimental system does not, in fact, work as effectively as its proponents claim, many nevertheless believe it to work. For those who believe in it, measuring the effectiveness of the regimental system in preparing and bringing soldiers to battle is probably as useful an exercise as measuring the power of prayer, religious symbols, and relics. Indeed, as we will see, there are many parallels between religion and the regimental tradition.

—m—

NO ONE KNOWS WHEN THE FIRST WARS WERE FOUGHT, by whom, or where. The work of archaeologists and anthropologists clearly shows that this very uncivilized form of behaviour paralleled the emergence of civilization itself. From then until now, all wars have had one thing in common—they involve organized groups of persons setting out to kill each other for essentially abstract reasons. In every skirmish, battle, or war, each group of fighters or soldiers, each "army," no matter how small, will usually share a common bond that may be rooted in family, tribe, religion, loyalty, or cause. Rarely do any of the individual fighters actually know, or have anything personal against, any individuals in the opposing army. The man debarking from a landing craft is rarely engaged in a personal crusade—until his comrades around him are shot down without mercy. Then it usually becomes personal, and a factor such as vengeance begins to motivate the soldier. But how are soldiers—the great majority of whom would not deliberately do harm to anyone—brought to that point? How do armies turn loyalty to a cause into an actual will to kill?

Fighting a war causes soldiers to perform two very unnatural tasks. The first is killing other humans for reasons that are rarely personal; the second is deliberately exposing themselves to possible grievous harm, or death, while trying to perform the first. Modern entertainment—especially video gaming—not only glorifies killing, it makes it seem positively easy. But with the exception of the small number of sociopaths and psychopaths who live in any society, most humans abhor killing other humans. Recent research has revealed that some of the post-traumatic stress disorder that affects soldiers returning from combat in places such as Iraq or Afghanistan is actually caused by killing the enemy! Certainly in the heat of battle soldiers will do what they must to preserve their own lives and those of their comrades, but afterwards, few can slough off that killing easily. This phenomenon of deliberately setting out to kill, or deliberately exposing oneself to death, is unique to soldiers and armies. Not even police share the experience. In police work—in democracies, at any rate—violence is the last resort. Police do not set out to purposely kill anyone. When soldiers go into battle, their primary aim is to kill, to destroy the lives of their enemies so as to render them incapable of doing harm.

The exceptional nature of soldiering has created a unique warrior culture that predates written history. The culture differs according to place and time but is marked by a single purpose—to mark soldiers off from everyone else. Whether those soldiers were (and are) part-time "citizen" soldiers, full-time "regular" soldiers, mercenaries, or irregulars, it has always been important to them and to those around them to ensure that they are set aside from society in some fashion. That is because it is they and they alone whom society has sanctioned to kill in its name. This maintenance of separateness is the major function of what is referred to as the regimental system. Secondary functions of the system are to distinguish warriors from everyone else; to differentiate one family of warriors from another in the belief that competition brings out the best; to provide a framework within which soldiers are prepared for war; to make routine the business of killing and of going into harm's way; to ritualize war and battle. The regiment also provides the promise of immortality—of life after death within the bosom of regimental memory—to assuage the very normal fear of death in battle.

The most basic definition of a regiment is simple: it is (or has been) a unit of manoeuvre of so many men and women (from one to five thousand) that is commanded by a colonel, is composed of smaller units such as battalions and companies, and is a part of a division and corps. There is a significant difference between an army composed of regiments and a regimental system. A regimental system is best described as the use of specific, unique regiments to recruit, train, and build cohesion inside an army that is in fact not composed of regiments as units of manoeuvre, but rather of battalions, brigades, divisions, and corps.

In an army that is said to adhere to the regimental tradition, a regiment is not normally a military formation. Regiments instead provide soldiers with extended families, giving them a place in the military order of things and building in them strong bonds with other members of those regiments. Some people assume that those bonds are the basis of unit cohesion, which emerges from the simple reality that soldiers ultimately fight for one another rather than for large abstract causes. Not letting one's comrades-in-arms down is the most important factor that prompts a soldier to endure battle. The research done by American official historian S.L.A. Marshall after the Second World War seemed to confirm this. In a work entitled *Men Against Fire,* based on hundreds of interviews with combat veterans and examination of war diaries, after-action reports, and so on, Marshall found that small-unit cohesion determined the degree to which men would actually fight the enemy.

Marshall's research methods have been questioned and perhaps his conclusions were overstated, but his observations make sense nonetheless. In the large mass of men that make up an army, a fighting soldier cannot possibly know more than a few comrades with whom he regularly sleeps, eats, marches, gets drunk, and fights. Whether he is part of a Greek phalanx, a Roman maniple, a British square, or an American fire team, that soldier's very life will depend on the men who live with him and who will stand beside him to defend him and help him kill the enemy when they are all in peril. Those men will become closer to him than any other people on earth. He will, in a very real sense, love them. He will sacrifice his life for them almost instinctively, as a mother does for her children. He will most definitely not want to appear unsteady or afraid among them. Their very presence nearby as they all approach action will steady him and strengthen his resolve. If he must die, he will at least die in the company of his peers.

All modern militaries are built on these experiences. All higher formations, from the company (about 120 to 200 soldiers) to the division (from 11,000 to 18,000) to the corps (usually 40,000 or more), are built on sections (in the Canadian and British armies) or squads (in the U.S. military) of about ten soldiers commanded by a middle-ranking non-commissioned officer (in the Canadian army, a section is commanded by a sergeant). These squads or sections are the stones upon which all the larger formations are built. The individual personal loyalties that bind the men of these sections are the mortar.

Those who believe that the regimental system is an important key to effectiveness in battle believe that the close bonds these regiments instill in the members of their regimental families are essential to the strength of smaller units, such as the section, platoon, and company, that actually do the fighting. Those who believe that the role of the regimental system in battlefield cohesion has been overblown, for example, in British-inspired militaries, as we shall see, point to the undeniable reality that small units function equally well in militaries that do not harbour regimental systems.

For every argument supporting the absolute necessity of basing an army on a regimental system, there is probably a counter-argument. The basic problem with the system, detractors say, is that it can work properly only if a soldier spends a considerable proportion of his (or her) military career inside a single regiment, entering at the lowest rank and staying in the regiment until retirement. In the modern Canadian army this may be the case for non-commissioned members (privates to warrant officers), but it is not for officers, who leave the regimental bosom no later than after promotion to colonel. In any case, the system is no doubt built—deliberately—on insularity. And this creates problems at both the highest and lowest levels of an army.

At the highest levels, the division of an army into distinct regiments can make career planning very difficult, since it is usually necessary to try to keep soldiers of the same regiment together in their own regimental "stovepipes." Messing, recruiting, and training of individual soldiers can be more difficult. Merging regiments is difficult; tradition dies hard and there is always a retired community that fosters regimental tradition and fights to preserve it. Disbanding regiments is even harder, though a nation's changing demographic profile may well warrant the disappearance of some older regiments and the creation of new ones.

The system is also criticized for its very insularity; the rivalries that arise are not always healthy ones. In the Canadian army it is sometimes rumoured that some failure was caused by a regimental "mafia" taking care of its own. There is fear that soldiers may develop greater loyalty to their regiment than to the army as a whole. In the Second World War it was sometimes charged that, since battalion commanders tended to be promoted from within each regiment, less than able officers were sometimes selected for command. But in some cases good company commanders were transferred from one regiment to another to command a battalion, and thrived in their new positions. In the modern Canadian army, soldiers often move from regiment to regiment as circumstances dictate.

There will probably never be a resolution to the argument. Those who believe in the effectiveness of the regimental system for creating battlefield cohesion are usually those who, quite simply, have never known any other milieu. Fish can always be relied upon to support the thesis that water is the only medium capable of supporting life. Surely the real point is that militaries develop rituals, forms, and traditions that best fit themselves and the societies from which they come, and that history is a very strong determinant of what constitutes a "best fit." If it is a strongly held belief that the regimental system is an effective means of organizing the British or Canadian or Australian or any other army, then that in itself becomes a major argument for its continuation, even if in other armies (the U.S. Army is the best example) the regimental system just doesn't work.

—ᴍ—

THE BRITISH REGIMENTAL SYSTEM actually originated in sixteenth-century Europe, in Germany, France, Holland, and Sweden, when distinct units with their own dress and battle standards emerged. These regiments probably harkened back to the Roman era, when each Roman legion had a distinctive name, standard, and even battle accoutrements such as helmets. The Scots adopted an early regimental form for local defence long before the English did. Regiments emerged in England during the English Civil War, in the seventeenth century. Generally they evolved their own characteristics because they were formed by this duke or that earl, who put his personal stamp on his troops. In periods when Parliament was unable or unwilling to spend large amounts of cash on significant standing forces, wealthy local patrons paid for local standing forces or supported local home-defence troops—the militias that every able-bodied Englishman of appropriate age was obliged to serve in. Since they were paying for the upkeep of the troops, the local patrons bestowed their own colours, uniforms, and philosophies of war upon their soldiers.

When a truly national army began to emerge in Britain in the eighteenth century, it was built on existing regiments. Standardization of much of the British army's uniform in the early 1700s—its kit, its drill, its rank structure—was imposed (and sometimes not very successfully) on regiments that in some cases were already at least a century old. In effect the early British army was a federation of regiments divided into different combat arms (for example, artillery, engineers, cavalry). Regiments were strongly entrenched in its structure, hierarchy, and chain of command, and senior serving regimental members wielded enormous influence in the army. Regiments were often treated as closed entities, with promotion coming only from within regimental ranks, and not always to good effect.

The strength of regiments in the British army has dissipated a great deal since the end of the Second World War with, first, the institution of peacetime national service (conscription) up until the 1960s, and second, the enormous cost of modern recruitment, training, and military equipment. Today many once distinctive British regiments have either disappeared entirely or been amalgamated with other, formerly rival regiments; the higher ranks of the army are selected and promoted almost entirely on the basis of active service experience, not regimental influence.

Historically, British regiments, both regular-force (full-time) and territorial (militia or reservists), were almost entirely geographically based. That is no longer true for the British regular-force regiments. In Canada the history of regiments is somewhat different. Canada's militia regiments were and still are territorially based, as with the Royal Regina Rifles. But regular-force regiments such as Princess Patricia's Canadian Light Infantry (PPCLI) are not. The three current Canadian regular-force infantry regiments—the PPCLI, the Royal Canadian Regiment (RCR), and the Royal 22ᵉ Régiment (R22ᵉR)—are located in specific regions. All three PPCLI battalions (1st, 2nd, and 3rd) are located in western Canada, the 1st and the 3rd at Canadian Forces Base (CFB) Edmonton and the 2nd at CFB Shilo (Manitoba). The RCR's three battalions are in Ontario and New Brunswick, while the three R22ᵉR battalions are located in the Citadel in Quebec City and at CFB Valcartier, north of Quebec. However, personnel assigned to those regiments and battalions come from across Canada. With the advent of bilingualism in the Canadian Forces in the 1960s, francophone Canadians now often serve at least once outside Quebec, while individual anglophone officers are often rotated through French-language units.

In the infantry, battalions are military formations. Each is usually made up of three rifle companies and an administrative company (composition varies over time and circumstances). They, in turn, form brigades—three battalions to a brigade, sometimes with other combat arms such as engineers or artillery as part of the brigade formation. Each of the PPCLI battalions considers itself unique compared to other PPCLI battalions, although they are all part of the larger PPCLI family. By contrast, regiments in the Armoured, Artillery, and Engineering Corps *are* military formations. In the Armoured Corps, the current regular-force regiments all have distinctive names—Lord Strathcona's Horse (Royal Canadians) is based at CFB Edmonton; the Royal Canadian Dragoons is based at CFB Petawawa in Ontario, and the 12ᵉ Régiment blindé du Canada (12 RBC) is based at CFB Valcartier. Unlike the Armoured Corps, the Artillery Corps numbers its units, as do the Engineers—1st Regiment, Royal Canadian Horse Artillery (1RCHA), for example, or 1st Combat Engineer Regiment (1CER). To the uninitiated, the nomenclature can seem very confusing; like the English language itself, there seems to be little consistency, few solid "rules," and too much rote learning necessary to become familiar with all the exceptions. But in spite of the differences in nomenclature across combat arms, each "regiment" in the Canadian army goes about the task of building regimental loyalty in much the same way.

To begin with, each regiment considers itself unique and even superior to all others. History is the key to that uniqueness. A regiment is built on its history and on the lore, traditions, and rituals that have developed as a consequence of that history. Battle is central to a regiment's history, and every significant battle the regiment has fought is marked in regimental lore in a number of ways. The most visible is a battle honour—the embroidered name of a past battle on the regimental guidon, or standard (it is never called a flag). Battle honours for Canadian regiments are awarded by the Governor General in consultation with the Canadian Forces. The battle honour attests that the regiment endured significant action in the face of an enemy in a larger battle that was in itself significant. The more battle honours a regiment has, the heavier with history its guidon will be. The guidon is displayed or carried at all formal regimental occasions, and when not displayed is laid carefully away and treated as preciously as a religious relic. Battles are also marked through paintings, songs, poems, regimental silverware, and accoutrements worn on the formal dress uniforms known as mess kits.

Since battles are the single most important determinant of much of a regiment's lore, mess dinners are normally held once or twice a year to mark their anniversaries, especially in militia regiments. Regular-force regiments generally hold mess dinners to mark regimental birthdays or other such occasions. Regimental marches, toasts at mess dinners, formal induction of new members into the regiment, church parades, and associations of former active members are all intended to keep the regiment's fighting history alive. Virtually all regiments have, at one time or another, commissioned regimental histories, which may vary greatly in quality but are intended as records of the regiment's deeds, especially its battles, campaigns, and wars.

With history as the basis of a regiment's uniqueness, each regiment will normally produce a regimental book that details all its distinctive features, practices, and accoutrements. The regimental book is a template to ensure that the regiment's unique rituals, dress uniforms, accoutrements, order of conducting business, and means of governing will remain unchanged unless formally altered by the regimental senate itself. The regimental senate (sometimes other names are used) is its governing body; it has no place in the military chain of command, but it has everything to do with regimental (as opposed to operational) business. Although a commanding officer (CO) of the senior regimental formation (for example, the CO of the 1st Battalion, PPCLI) will always play a significant role in laying down and maintaining regimental lore, regiments always have an honorary senior regimental officer, one rank higher than the CO, whose main job it is to help guide the regiment in maintaining its own traditions. In militia regiments that senior officer is an honorary colonel. He or she may also have an honorary lieutenant colonel, as will small but still independent units such as an engineers squadron. In regular-force regiments the position is usually known as colonel commandant.

The main task of the regiment is to keep its history alive and guard its uniqueness. This is done to instill in its soldiers a strong belief that their particular regimental family is not only different but also superior. On the face of it, this sense of superiority can seem absurd, especially when most members of regular-force regiments have had absolutely no choice as to which regiments they are assigned to. But this patently manufactured superiority is thought by some supporters of the regimental tradition to be essential to unit identity. Obviously no one is going to serve unit morale by proclaiming to the world that his regiment is, at best, no better than any other regiment! The Mooseville Mighty Mounted Hussars are the best, period. In militia regiments that are geographically based, regional or civic rivalries usually reinforce this sense of superiority. Some residents of Calgary pretend not even to know that their province contains a sister city of approximately the same size some 300 kilometres to the north. How then can anyone expect the Calgary Highlanders to believe that the Loyal Edmonton Regiment is anything but the second-best reserve infantry unit in Alberta?

Everything ceremonial done by a regiment is calculated to extol the differences between it and all others. To better indoctrinate regimental uniqueness (and superiority), regiments maintain their own libraries and reading rooms, museums, archives, and regimental messes—special dining and gathering places where reposes the regiment's collection of art and silver and where the formal mess dinners are held.

A regimental mess dinner is a ritualized meal, not unlike the Jewish Passover seder prescribed in the book of Exodus, or even the

Last Supper. In regular-force regiments, attendance at these dinners is compulsory for all officers. Other guests are usually invited, some civilian, some military. All must wear formal dress. In preparation for the dinner the mess dining room is cleaned and polished and the tables are set with white tablecloths and adorned with the regimental colours. The regimental silver is brought out and shined. Knives and forks gleam; the many glasses for wine, water, and port sparkle. On the table, like silent sentinels, stand regimental candlesticks or other silver mementos—generally in the form of statuettes, cannons, or tanks, engraved to mark some event such as the retirement of a former CO; these are usually gifts from distinguished persons or former officers. The PMC (president of the mess committee), an officer appointed to manage and preside over the dinner, will be the formal host for the evening, not the CO. Seating plans are drawn up according to seniority and precedent; guests normally sit close to the head of the table, near the CO.

A complex, precisely timed schedule of events is followed through the evening. Bugles blow or pipes are played to summon guests to dinner. Anthems are sung. Special hymns or regimental music is played throughout the dinner. Toasts are hoisted to "absent comrades" or to the "allied regiment." Toasts are made standing, even standing on the table, or with one foot on the table and one foot on a chair, according to regimental tradition. No one is allowed to leave the dinner table until after the toast to the Queen, and then only when the PMC announces it is time for a brief pause, sometimes known as "ease springs." When the regimental port is passed from one end of the table to the other, it is never allowed to touch the table. Sometimes a guest will address the assembly, but never for very long. A regimental dinner called for 6:30 PM will rarely end before midnight.

Attending a mess dinner can be an education in regimental diversity. The Canadian Forces provides every serviceman and woman with a daily working and fighting uniform that is virtually indistinguishable from unit to unit. It also provides semi-formal businesslike dress for other occasions. The latter is dark green for the army, light blue for the air force, and navy blue for the navy. In almost all respects (except for the kilts and caps worn by members of Highland regiments) all these uniforms are virtually the same. But the formal mess kit worn by officers and senior non-commissioned officers such as the regimental sergeant major (RSM) must be privately purchased. Generally mess-kit jackets are red with gold embroidery on the sleeves and epaulettes; the cut and design differ, sometimes markedly, from regiment to regiment. Pants are usually black with yellow or red stripes. In some older regiments, mess kit may be of some other colour entirely, such as forest green. The buckles, buttons, embroidery, and accoutrements such as ceremonial spurs also differ. Members of Highland regiments will be kilted, with different kilts for every regiment.

Prior to assembly for dinner, the members of the home regiment and guests from other regiments mingle for drinks. To the uninitiated, the differences between the uniforms are subtle, maybe even indistinguishable, but to those who understand what they are taking part in, each mess kit will stand out. Here is a senior officer of the Royal Canadian Regiment, Canada's oldest regular-force infantry regiment; there is a senior non-commissioned officer of an engineers regiment, or a young subaltern from a distinguished militia regiment that traces its lineage back to the early nineteenth century. Often naval and air force members wearing their own distinctive mess kit will be present. These mess dinners, and the messes they are held in, used to be the centre of regimental life. But in the modern Canadian Forces, the regimental system is eroding somewhat, partly because of modern military transformation and partly because of the social realities of twenty-first-century Canada.

—⚊—

CANADIAN REGIMENTS ARE NOT WHAT THEY USED TO BE. Although regiments as such never dominated the Canadian army to the degree that they did the British army, they were once a vital part of many key aspects of army life. Recruits joined regiments directly. They were largely trained by the regiments, lived in regimental barracks, dined in the regimental mess, and socialized with other members of the regiment. They owed their undying allegiance to the regimental family. And the regiments dominated the process of promotion and selection. Senior regimental officers would look out for their juniors as they climbed through the army hierarchy. Each regiment constituted a "mafia" of sorts, with members watching out for their own regimental interests. Each regiment resented the other regimental "mafias" and did what they could to undermine them. Although regiments had no formal authority over army decisions, such as who would rise up the chain of command and who wouldn't, they strongly influenced those decisions through the pull their senior members enjoyed.

Today, many of the functions that regiments once performed are carried out by the army itself. Recruits join the Canadian Forces through the centralized Canadian Forces Recruitment Group. They receive both basic and more advanced training at sprawling bases such as CFB Gagetown (New Brunswick), CFB Petawawa, or the new Canadian Manoeuvre Training Centre at CFB Wainwright (Alberta). Once they receive basic training, they are finally assigned to their regiments. In the course of their careers they will very often work with other units and regiments, even in the field. An infantry-dominated battle group in Afghanistan will have artillery and engineers, for example, directly under its command. Thus individual artillery officers or combat engineers will actually be embedded with other units and regiments.

In Canada soldiers may live on base in a barracks for a very short time at the start of their army career, but base housing is now increasingly a second choice to off-base housing for quality, price, and location in the larger community. In a standing regular volunteer army such as Canada's, soldiers generally live with their families—the majority are married—and come in to work every day, not unlike civilians in their jobs. They don't hang about the mess on Friday nights or weekends—their spouses don't like it, the children need parenting, and driving home drunk (and getting caught) is a career-killer in today's military. Alcohol abuse is strongly frowned upon. All this applies even more to the reservist, a citizen who temporarily dons a uniform once or twice a week (unless he or she has volunteered for nine months or longer of active service).

The Canadian army began to deliberately erode regimental influence after the Somalia scandal of the mid-1990s. That scandal—which centred on the beating death of a Somali teenager by members of the Canadian Airborne Regiment in March 1993—had many root causes, but one was perceived to be a regimental tradition so strong that the welfare of the army as a whole took second place to regimental pride. One small but highly symbolic move in the weakening of regimental tradition was a decree that when officers moved above the rank of lieutenant-colonel (the highest rank in any regimental formation such as a battalion), they were no longer to be identified on their working uniforms as belonging to one regiment or another, but only to the army in general (this did not apply to mess kit). In addition, the official statement of basic aims, philosophy, values, and ethos that the Canadian Forces formally adopted in 2003—*Duty with Honour: The Profession of Arms in Canada*—makes no mention of the regimental tradition at all.

And yet, in the spring of 2006, a new formation was launched within the Canadian army—the Canadian Special Operations Regiment. This regiment is intended to be an elite fighting formation that will combine all of the training and tactical knowledge that is required by Canada's line infantry formations with the specialized training that marks the world's best special operations forces. The CSOR was given the signal honour of being allowed to wear a tan beret like that worn by the British SAS (Special Air Services). The CSOR will be assigned combat tasks in its own right but will also be the primary pool of manpower for Canada's highly elite special forces unit Joint Task Force II (JTFII). No doubt the new regiment will quickly acquire regimental characteristics of its own, some drawn from predecessor units such as the 1st Canadian Parachute Battalion of Second World War fame and some from allied units such as the SAS. Its birth is proof that despite the rapidly changing nature of the Canadian army today, regiments will continue to occupy a place of pride.

It would be a fitting tribute to Canadian regimental history if, somewhere on its uniform, the Canadian Special Operations Regiment wore a symbol reminiscent of Canada's very first regiment—the "good" regiment that came from France in 1665 to save Quebec from almost certain disaster. This was the Régiment Carignan-Salières, which established the regimental tradition in Canada, setting the pattern for all other regiments that served in North America under the French regime. However, when it arrived it found that the Iroquois and other aboriginal peoples already had long-established warrior traditions of their own—not regiments exactly, but traditions and cultures that in their organization were not so very different from the militia regiments that both the French and British would introduce by the end of the eighteenth century.

Part One

THE BIRTH AND EARLY HISTORY
OF CANADA'S REGIMENTS

Chapter One

FIRST REGIMENTS: THE FRENCH IN EARLY CANADA

All the Canadian population and the clergy, having at its head the renowned Mgr. de Laval, came out to meet M. de Tracy, who carried the title Viceroy of the New France. The reception was imposing; never for the foundation of a country had a similar display of military been seen.

—Contemporary account of the arrival of the Régiment Carignan-Salières, June 30, 1665

THE ABORIGINAL PEOPLES who inhabited what is now Canada prior to its European "discovery" in the 1490s were already well versed in the theory and practice of war, and had developed warrior traditions of their own, long before contact. Although these peoples organized no regiments in the strict sense of the word, those among them who were designated to do both hunting and fighting nurtured specific rituals that were practised by warriors alone. There is no written historical record of these war-fighting practices, so historians and anthropologists rely heavily on observations about the aboriginals made by the earliest European explorers, missionaries, and settlers. They reason that the practices recorded in those very early days are likely to have been in place for some time.

Among the most oft-used early documents are the reports sent by the Jesuit missionaries of New France to their sponsors and benefactors in France. The *Jesuit Relations,* as they were called, paint a very dark picture of how the aboriginal peoples of the northeastern woodlands conducted themselves in war. These accounts portray aboriginal warfare as especially murderous and the treatment of prisoners as extremely cruel. But the sources are coloured by a Eurocentric bias, for example, toward the Iroquois treatment of prisoners, who were beaten and subjected to prolonged torture; some were also burned slowly at the stake and then cooked and eaten. But the actual number of Iroquois victims pales compared to the hundreds of thousands of Europeans slaughtered in periodic religious wars. Cruelty, therefore, can be a matter of perspective and cultural bias.

What we do know about warfare among the Native peoples of the northeast woodlands is that the battles or skirmishes they fought tended to be of very short duration, even though grudges between one people and another might continue for generations. There was a great deal of ritual involved in preparation for war and battle, but the battles themselves were generally very straightforward, involving perhaps two to three dozen warriors at most, with each side trying to kill or capture as many of the enemy as possible while suffering only as many casualties as necessary. Native war leaders were perplexed by all the marching and manoeuvring that prefaced battle among the European formations that came to fight in North America. To them battle was very simple—find the enemy, kill him as quickly as possible, then go home with the spoils (usually prisoners).

In some aboriginal societies of North America, the men designated as fighters were grouped in "warrior societies" that were, in some ways, like militia regiments. These warriors carried on with their normal occupations in peacetime, but when war broke out, a special war chief was selected and the warrior society was activated to serve under that chief's command. This wartime arrangement generally ended when the fighting stopped. Warrior societies as such were unknown among the Iroquoian peoples who occupied what is today most of southern Quebec, southeast and south central Ontario, New England, New York, and the mid-Atlantic region from Virginia and the Carolinas to Tennessee. The Iroquoian peoples planted and harvested crops and lived in semi-permanent villages protected by palisades that were moved only every ten years or so. They built large longhouses, fashioned canoes, and lived in a mixed hunting, farming, and gathering society. They were divided into clans identified by animal or bird totems, tracing their clan affiliations through their mothers. Archaeological evidence indicates that the Iroquoian peoples existed at least as far back as 4000 BC, with little change to their society and culture from about AD 500 until the arrival of the Europeans.

In a sense, virtually every Iroquois male was a warrior who trained from early youth and honed his fieldcraft through hunting, but the entire society became involved in war-making in one way or another, especially in the rituals that accompanied preparation for war and the treatment of captives. Pre-contact aboriginal war in the northeast woodlands, as well as wars that were fought there up to about the late 1630s, had little economic motive. The wars were almost always a form of blood sport—raids to prove the manhood of warriors, to take prisoners, or to exact revenge. One scholar of this early period believes that "warfare was vitally important in the cultures of the seventeenth-century Iroquois and their neighbors." In an article published in 1983, Daniel Richter declares that the Iroquois waged war primarily as a means of mourning their dead and replacing losses among their population. He calls this form of conflict "mourning-war" and explains that it was not simply revenge killing, or vendetta, but a way of warding off or dissipating the sadness of mourning while replacing lost members of the tribe with new blood. Put simply, in mourning their own dead—no matter how those deaths may have occurred—grieving relatives of the deceased would launch raids as an outlet for their anger and sorrow over their loss and as a way of obtaining captives. Some of those captives would eventually be adopted into the tribal family; others would be tortured and killed.

Mourning-war was a significant unifying element in Iroquois society. Women played the major role in determining if such a war ought to be launched. They also provisioned it and participated fully in the beatings, torturing, executions, and cannibalism of the prisoners that ensued. Special war chiefs were chosen to lead the warriors into combat—the regular chiefs or sachems did not exercise any authority over the fighting. The war chief was selected in a highly ritualized procedure aimed at reinforcing his reputation for bravery, fierceness, and wisdom in battle. Relatives of the deceased either joined in the raid or suffered the great dishonour of being accused of cowardice by the matron of the mourning family. The warriors wore body ornaments, face paint, distinctive hairstyles, and feathers to enhance their fierce appearance and as signs of rank. They were armed with bows, knives, hatchets, and clubs and often wore wooden armour or carried wooden shields. They usually attacked only when they had a very good chance of quickly subduing their foe through advantageous position or superiority in numbers. Ambushes were generally quick affairs; the unsuspecting enemy party was rapidly fallen on and hacked, clubbed, scalped, or shot. When two war parties caught each other in the open, the engagement usually started with shouted threats and boasts and a shower of missiles, then hand-to-hand close-quarter fighting with axes, knives, and clubs. There was no dishonour associated with retreat or withdrawal when faced with a superior foe or the possibility of significant losses. Since they were out primarily to replace population, the warriors took great precautions not to suffer numerous casualties of their own.

European armies of this era valued prisoners for the ransom they usually brought, which was one reason why Europeans felt that Iroquois treatment of prisoners was barbaric. The captives taken on a raid—men, women, and children—ran a gauntlet as they were ushered into the village. Male captives were usually severely beaten, and women and children less so. The captives were then stripped and placed in the centre of the village, usually on a raised platform of some kind. Then the torture would begin. Old women would lead by pulling out fingernails or poking sensitive body parts with firebrands and sticks. After a while, the prisoners were allowed to rest and eat. Then they were forced to dance for their captors while their fate was being decided. Headmen apportioned them to families, whose matrons decided to either adopt them or execute them. Those chosen to die were expected to do so with honour despite the immense pain they were subjected to. A warrior in particular was supposed to sing his own death song, detailing his exploits in battle, while the fire was consuming him. The flames were not allowed to grow too quickly, lest death come too fast. After death, the flesh was stripped from the victims' bones, boiled, and eaten. The young Iroquois men who watched and participated in this horrific spectacle learned by example that the warriors they aspired to be were stoic in the face of hardship and pain.

As French, Dutch, and British traders and missionaries began to penetrate the Atlantic coast, the St. Lawrence Valley, and the northeastern woodlands in the early seventeenth century, they formed alliances with the different Native peoples who dominated those regions. These alliances were shaped largely by trade requirements as well as pre-contact rivalries. The Europeans wanted furs, especially beaver. The aboriginals wanted iron cooking and hunting implements, firearms, alcohol, and other goods they could not make themselves. The Iroquois initially aligned themselves with the English in New England and the Dutch in New Netherland (New York and New Jersey). When the English won New Netherland from the Dutch in 1664, their ties with the Iroquois became even stronger. The French in the St. Lawrence Valley aligned themselves with the Huron, another Iroquoian confederacy that dominated southwestern Quebec and southern Ontario as far west as the Huron peninsula. The Huron were historic rivals of the Iroquois. Once the Iroquois, the Huron, and other First Nations from the northeastern woodland regions had begun to participate in the fur trade with the Europeans, economic motives began to influence their decisions for war and peace.

The trade rivalry exacerbated old animosities between the Huron and the Iroquois and between the European powers and one another's aboriginal allies. The ongoing war between the French and the Iroquois was especially vicious, flaring up constantly around French settlements and fur trade posts and along canoe routes. The Iroquois essentially wanted the French to sever their ties to the Huron and stand aside, leaving the Iroquois to monopolize the aboriginal side of the fur trade. The French refused, mainly because of the significant inroads Roman Catholic missionaries had made among the Huron. In the early 1640s, the Iroquois, who were far better armed than the Huron, began a series of attacks aimed at destroying Huron influence in the region. In 1650 they succeeded in wiping out the last of the Jesuit missions in the Huron peninsula, expunging the French presence in the area and putting an end to the Huron Confederacy. Now the tiny settlement of New France, with but 3,500 souls scattered from the western reaches of the island of Montreal to the tiny fishing villages below Quebec, found itself in mortal danger. In 1665 France sent the first major contingent of regular troops to its North American colony. This was Canada's first real regiment, the Régiment Carignan-Salières.

—ɯ—

IN APRIL 1665 the first four companies of the Régiment Carignan-Salières bound for New France mustered on the dock of the Biscay port of La Rochelle in France. Under the command of Colonel de Salières, the unit was a regular line regiment of the French army and one of the first to be issued with a standard uniform. The men on the dock wore broad-brimmed black hats and long grey tunics, with brown pantaloons and matching stockings. They were armed with long-barrelled flintlocks and matchlocks with bayonets. The regimental colours were those of the Prince of Carignan, with a red background and a large blue cross. Although the regiment's antecedents stretched back to 1630, the Carignan-Salières had been raised by the Prince of Carignan in 1644. When King Louis XIV decided in 1664 to send a large contingent of regular French troops to New France to defend the colony, the regiment was well under strength and had to be augmented by some six hundred soldiers from other French army regiments. Although the average age of these men is thought to have been about twenty-six, many of them were veterans of Louis XIV's innumerable wars of expansion.

The dispatch of regular French troops to North America came two years after the Crown had assumed full control over the small French settlements in the St. Lawrence Valley. From the time when Samuel de Champlain founded the village of Quebec, in 1608, until 1663, the French colony had been a private venture. It almost withered entirely, captured once by English privateers in the 1620s and constantly beset by the Iroquois. Few people ventured there and whatever profits were squeezed from the fur trade were insufficient to provide either defence or basic requirements for the handful of colonists. In 1663 Louis XIV and his powerful chief minister, Jean-Baptiste Colbert, decided to throw the full weight of the Crown behind the venture, so they took the colony over and prepared to defend it. In the king's words, the French army was "to carry the war to their [the Iroquois'] doors, to exterminate them entirely."

The contingent sent to Quebec arrived over the summer of 1665. They were joined on June 30 by Alexandre de Prouville, Marquis de Tracy, who had been sent from Martinique with some two hundred soldiers to command the military campaign. Though he was sixty-two at the time—rather old for the rigours of campaigning in the forest and river country of New France—he had been a soldier from his youth, with many significant battles to his credit. Tracy was joined in September by a new governor, Daniel de Rémy de Courcelle, aged thirty-nine, and even more soldiers. Altogether, there were more than 1,200 men in twenty-four companies.

When the first troops arrived, the small contingent of settlers welcomed them joyously as they docked at the lower town. A contemporary wrote: "All the Canadian population and the clergy, having at its head the renowned Mgr. de Laval, came out to meet M. de Tracy, who carried the title Viceroy of the New France. The reception was imposing; never for the foundation of a country had a similar display of military been seen."

After the welcome at the dock, the regiment began the long and somewhat arduous climb to the small fortification high above the river where they were to stay for several weeks. Tracy himself was given an even more signal honour, which he may well have been tempted to refuse. Cardinal Laval led him up the hill to the church and insisted that he take part in a thanksgiving Te Deum, a Mass dedicated to the King of France. Though immensely tired after the long trip, Tracy could hardly refuse, and spent an hour or so kneeling on the stone floor of the small cathedral until it was over. Given that there were only about 500 people living in Quebec, the arrival over the summer of 1,200 soldiers put food and lodging at a premium. Given also that there was a mere handful of women about, the demeanour of the hot-blooded young men in grey tunics and brown stockings must have been constantly tried.

The regiment's first task was to build up the defences of the colony and create a base from which to launch offensive operations into Iroquois country. The Iroquois were a confederacy of five nations—Mohawk, Oneida, Seneca, Onondaga, and Cayuga—who were joined after 1715 by the Tuscarora. It was the Mohawk, whose villages were concentrated south of Lake Champlain, who were the most aggressive of the Five Nations. Their easiest attack route was north along the lake and up the Richelieu River, which connected Lake Champlain with the St. Lawrence about 60 kilometres below the small settlement at Ville-Marie (Montreal). Contingents of soldiers were sent from Quebec to the confluence of the St. Lawrence and Richelieu to build five forts along the Richelieu, starting with Fort Sorel at the north end and ending with Fort Sainte-Anne near the head of the lake. A road was also built from the fort at Chambly, on the Richelieu, to the south shore of the St. Lawrence opposite Ville-Marie. The string of forts would make it much harder for the Mohawk to approach the French settlements, while the road would make it easier for reinforcements to move quickly from Ville-Marie to shore up the defences along the Richelieu.

Tracy and the Carignan-Salières had been sent to Canada to

destroy the Iroquois, but in mid-November, a delegation of Oneida and Onondaga chiefs paddled to Montreal to open talks with the French. To four of the Five Nations—the Oneida and Onondaga chiefs had been authorized to speak also for the Seneca and the Cayuga—the new forts were a clear sign of French determination not to let New France be destroyed. That fact, and internal problems caused both by disease and by an ongoing conflict with the Susquehannock, prompted them to seek some sort of a settlement with the French. But the Mohawk boycotted the discussions, which dragged on for weeks with no resolution. All this time Courcelle was urging Tracy to abandon the talks and attack the Mohawk. In the words of a contemporary, the governor breathed "nothing but war." One historian described Courcelle this way: "he surrounded himself with a considerable retinue and talked incessantly of war, boasting of what lay in store for the Iroquois when they came face to face with French troops and always implying that he would be both the architect of victory and its triumphant general."

In the first days of the new year, Tracy finally decided to attack. He probably had no real understanding of how difficult it would be to campaign in winter. Certainly his regiment was not equipped to march several hundred kilometres through the heavily forested terrain, the land covered in deep snow, in the coldest months of the year, and with but eight or nine hours of daylight. But march they did, setting out from Quebec in mid-month. The contingent consisted of three hundred regulars and two hundred Montreal militia. They were supposed to be accompanied by a number of Algonquin guides, who would also provide game for the expedition, but the Algonquin apparently never arrived for the rendezvous at Fort Saint-Louis, at Chambly. When the expedition left the fort to begin the long trek south, the militia, who were more used to the harshness of a Canadian winter, were instructed to take the lead, which they considered a great honour.

The men were poorly equipped for winter campaigning. Some had moccasins, others mukluks, and few had snowshoes. Almost no one had extra clothes to change into when they got wet. They wore a variety of hats and leggings and carried blankets to protect themselves against the cold, but they had little tentage, few axes to cut firewood, and minimal hardtack rations, since they were counting on their Algonquin guides to provide meat. On January 29, the soldiers departed Chambly for the south, struggling through the cold and snow and, without guides, unsure of where to go. It wasn't long before winter started to take its toll. The soldiers were afflicted with hypothermia and frostbite that froze ears, noses, fingers, hands, and knees. The dazzling sun reflecting off the icy landscape caused snow blindness. The bitterly cold winds drove them to dig shelters in the snow since they were completely unable to dig into the frozen ground. As they struggled south, men began to die of cold, exhaustion, and starvation. They pushed through waist-deep snow by day and slept fitfully in hastily dug snow shelters at night. Day after day for three weeks they pushed south past Lake Champlain and Lake George, across the Hudson River, to the outskirts of the Anglo-Dutch settlement of Schenectady, on the Mohawk River.

On February 20 they spotted a handful of cabins. Courcelle was completely lost and quickly concluded that they had come to a Mohawk village. He ordered an immediate attack. His men lustily fell on the handful of occupants—some women and a mixed-blood boy—and killed most of them. The gunfire drew a party of Mohawk who had come to Schenectady to trade, and battle was joined. This was the first encounter the French regulars had with the Iroquois. It was more of a skirmish, with the French firing from hastily prepared defensive positions at the Mohawk, who were concealed in the trees and who moved about easily on snowshoes. The short engagement ended quickly when the mayor of Schenectady arrived on the scene and told Courcelle where he was and that the settlement was completely undefended. Courcelle decided that if he did not return immediately to New France, his tired and hungry men might desert in droves. The French obtained some provisions, then headed back north. It took them two weeks to struggle back, occasionally harassed by the Mohawk.

The immediate impact of this raid is hard to determine: accounts of Courcelle's losses differ widely. Historian Jack Verney claims that only a hundred or so men survived the ordeal, with the vast majority of deaths caused by starvation and cold. George F.G. Stanley counts only a hundred deaths but agrees that the Mohawk killed very few. From a strictly tactical perspective, then, the expedition was a disaster. However, the Mohawk and their Iroquois allies could not have failed to notice not only the size of the French force but also the sheer determination of the men in the expedition. The largest force the Mohawk could muster would never exceed Courcelle's force, and they knew there were many more French soldiers at the Richelieu forts and along the St. Lawrence.

—◊—

THROUGH THE SPRING AND SUMMER OF 1666, the French gathered their strength and prepared for another, larger attack into Mohawk country. They had learned the hard lesson of how difficult it was to campaign in winter and how much they needed the assistance of the Algonquin, not only to guide them to their objective but also to supply them with fresh meat while they made their way south. This time Tracy would lead the expedition, although Courcelle would command one of three contingents. On September 28, regulars and militia from all the French settlements that stretched from Montreal to Quebec rendezvoused at Fort Sainte-Anne, at the head of Lake Champlain. Tracy had under his command six hundred regulars in twenty-four companies, six hundred militia, and about a hundred Algonquin. But even before he was ready to leave for the south, Courcelle's by now well-known impatience showed itself when he departed several days early with about a third of the contingent.

The troops paddled down Lakes Champlain and George, then headed into the undulating hills at the edge of the Adirondacks, to the southwest of Lake George. Rain, strong winds, and high waves dogged them on the lakes and soaked them as they pushed through woods resplendent with the golds, reds, and browns of autumn. They hastily built skiffs to struggle across the large Sacanda swamp, about halfway through their portage from the southern tip of Lake George to the Mohawk River Valley. Tracy had little hope that an army this size might sneak undetected through the woods. In fact, they had a brief skirmish with a Mohawk scouting party as soon as the expedition penetrated the Mohawk Valley. He therefore decided that his best option was to rush the Mohawk villages before they had a chance to prepare an effective defence. On the night of October 15, his entire column set out on an overnight march, drums beating, to reach the first Mohawk village by dawn.

The village was deserted. The Mohawk had quickly withdrawn into the woods, probably because the French outnumbered them so greatly. But the French were still surprised at what they found—a large palisaded compound with three walls about 2 metres high, and recently harvested fields outside the walls. Inside were a dozen or so longhouses, each with a large storehouse filled to the rafters with enough corn and beans to feed his men for weeks. There were even water casks, likely for fighting fires in the event that the village was attacked. In short order, three other deserted villages were discovered to the west. The last one—the largest—contained the half-burned and mutilated bodies of Indian captives, lying where they had been killed, next to the ashes of a large fire. In each case there were signs that the villages had been evacuated very quickly, just ahead of the French soldiers. Not only were the Mohawk outnumbered, but had they made a stand, they would have been forced to defend four locations, each about 15 kilometres apart. They had long before resolved that there was no shame or loss of honour in refusing to fight a body of men they could not defeat. So, with the odd Mohawk catcall emanating from the woods, Tracy's men systematically looted the villages of everything they could carry, then burned the rest before starting back home. They were welcomed back to Quebec with great jubilation on November 5.

Tracy lost eight men on this expedition, all by drowning. There were no clashes, no battles, and certainly no military victory. But with the growing season now long past, the Mohawk nation faced severe starvation over the coming winter and consequent debilitation of their fighting strength. The French had demonstrated to the largest and most powerful of the Five Nations that they were more than capable of launching a significant sortie of fighting men and projecting their strength hundreds of kilometres to the south and southwest of the St. Lawrence Valley, to strike into the very heartland of Iroquois country. The lesson was not lost on the Iroquois. Before winter froze up the lakes and rivers of the northeastern woodlands, the Iroquois and the French negotiated a treaty that would last for eighteen years.

—⁂—

THE TREATY BETWEEN FRANCE AND THE IROQUOIS ended the immediate necessity to keep a large contingent of royal troops in New France. The bulk of the Carignan-Salières made ready to depart. However, King Louis XIV and Colbert believed that New France needed tough young men, especially those with military experience. Incentives were offered to any officers and men of the regiment who might stay and settle in Canada. Officers were given seigneuries (land grants, or manors) located in some of the more exposed areas of the colony, while rank-and-file soldiers were granted farms within the seigneuries or given cash bonuses. Some 446 members of the regiment stayed, while four companies returned with Tracy to France in 1667. Since some permanent protection was still needed, four companies of the regiment remained in Canada on full pay, two in Montreal and two along the Richelieu River.

The Carignan-Salières had a profound impact on early Canada. New France's life was hanging by a thread when the regiment arrived. Although it is unlikely that the Mohawk by themselves could have expelled the three thousand or so inhabitants of the colony living in widely scattered settlements from Montreal to Quebec, the entire Five Nations might have been able to accomplish that through an ongoing war of attrition. More likely the French Crown could have abandoned the enterprise as a very poor investment. So the mere presence of the regiment—not to mention its two forays into Mohawk country—gave New France a real lease on life. The officers and men of the regiment who stayed in Canada also helped secure the colony. They added roughly 10 percent to the population already there and helped secure land in strategic spots such as the Richelieu River approach to Montreal and Quebec. Not all became seigneurs or farmers—some took to the woods for the adventure and profits of the coureur de bois life, as fur traders, trappers, guides, or scouts. But virtually all of them bolstered the militia, the part-time fighting force that quickly became one of the three supporting legs of the colony's defences.

The militia in New France arose from the inhabitants' obvious need to provide for their own defence, and predates the arrival of the Carignan-Salières by at least a decade. The concept of a militia, or citizen self-defence force, is thousands of years old. The Greek hoplites who fought in the many wars between Athens and Sparta were primarily farmers who kept their swords, shields, armour, and helmets ready for the call-out. As citizens, it was not simply their obligation but also their duty to bear arms in time of need. That was also true of the Roman army during the Roman Republic. By the late seventeenth century the militia was strongly rooted in the British Isles, where it was believed that every able-bodied man had a duty to bear arms in time of danger. Full-time or regular soldiers were often despised by the population as men with no skills, education, or land, who could do nothing but carry weapons for the king or the lord of the local manor and collect taxes.

There was little militia tradition as such in metropolitan France in this era—the strongly entrenched feudal system of master and serf simply did not allow for it. No French seigneur would allow, let alone encourage, his serfs to possess weapons. But New France was a very different place. Although seigneurs in New France were esteemed as members of a social and perhaps financial elite, they were not titled lords. They had no serfs as such; the habitants who worked the seigneuries were essentially free farmers with the right to bequeath their land to their children. They owed their seigneur a few days of labour a year but they kept or disposed of their crops as they wished. They were also free to leave their farms in the winter to trap and hunt to supplement their income and their diet. To do so, they needed to own firearms. Thus the militia of New France was built on an armed population who learned fieldcraft by necessity, who had to be sharpshooters to fill their larders with meat, and who quickly became familiar with aboriginal ways of hunting, trapping, and fighting.

When a New France militiaman campaigned, he wore no uniform. At first, he was dressed in skins and robes like the Iroquois and the Huron. Later, in the 1690s, he was provided with a toque, a breechcloth, leggings, shirts, blankets, and moccasins. He wore moccasins in the summer, snowshoes in the winter. He carried a musket, knives, and a hatchet or axe, and he followed the Indian practices of stealth in the approach and ruthlessness in the fight. He became expert at what was called *la petite guerre*—the almost constant war of raids, ambushes, and atrocities fought in the forests along the borders between New France and the English colonies. As historian Francis Parkman writes, "A skilful woodsman, a bold and adroit canoeman, a willing fighter in time of need . . . he was more than ready at any time for any hardy enterprise; and in the forest warfare of skirmish and surprise there were few to match him."

After the departure of the Carignan-Salières, the king ordered Governor Courcelle to organize what had been up to then a very loose militia into something more formal. Courcelle dallied, but his successor, Louis de Buade, Comte de Frontenac, plunged into the task. With but a few hundred regulars at his disposal, he knew the colony had to bolster its defences as quickly as possible. Peace with the Mohawk could break down at any time and there was always the growing danger posed by the rapidly expanding English colonies to the south. By 1673, the task was well along.

Frontenac did not form the militia of New France into regiments. It was, rather, loosely organized into companies based on the towns, villages, and parishes of the colony. Every able-bodied man was compelled to be in the militia, but actual service in the field was usually voluntary. Each company was led by a captain who was at first appointed by the governor; later, the members of the company elected him. Discharged regular French soldiers who chose to stay in New France, officers or not, were often selected as militia captains. The militiamen simply chose the man best suited to lead them in battle, even though he might not be a high-ranking member of the parish social elite. Periodic musket drill was compulsory but nothing was taught of the European style of marching and close-order drill.

Militiamen were usually physically fit enough from their non-military occupations, so they needed no long marches to get them into shape. They were mobilized by order of the governor, who also determined how many men would be needed for a given campaign. Volunteers then came forward from different companies. In extreme emergencies, the governor might call for a mass mobilization of all militia members. The militia were provided with ammunition but were at first expected to use their own firearms. That soon changed, and the government began to supply them with muskets as well. The militia were not a significant fighting force when measured by numbers alone; as late as 1756 there seem to have been no more than three thousand of them altogether, scattered across the colony. But they were invaluable as scouts and skirmishers, very accomplished at ambushes, and—because of their well-earned reputation for ruthlessness with axe, hatchet, and knife—greatly feared by both the aboriginals and the militia of the English colonies.

—⁂—

TRACY AND THE CARIGNAN-SALIÈRES had been long forgotten by the Iroquois by the early 1680s; warfare returned to New France with raids on outposts and small fur trade forts in 1682. In August 1689, 1,500 warriors launched a surprise attack on the Montreal suburb of Lachine that left twenty-four settlers dead; the Iroquois carried away more than eighty prisoners. The renewed fighting again raised the question of how to protect New France from its enemies. The militia would do its part, of course, and several companies of regulars had been left in the colony after the Carignan-Salières had departed, but these forces were insufficient. Starting in 1683, Paris began to send regular drafts of the Troupes de la Marine to New France.

The Troupes de la Marine were not marines (ship-borne soldiers) as they would later be styled by the British, the Americans, and other countries. Their prime responsibility in France was to guard the ports. Small numbers of them were also occasionally drafted to serve aboard merchant vessels in wartime to provide protection against boarders. They were organized and paid by the Ministry of Marine and Colonies and were completely separate from the regular French army, which reported to the minister of war. For the most part the Troupes de la Marine were poorly trained, physically weak, badly clothed and armed, and somewhat malnourished; they included boys twelve to fourteen years old in their ranks. But along with the militia and the few companies of regulars in the colony, they bore the brunt of the fighting with the Iroquois and the English throughout the remainder of the 1680s. In 1691 they were joined with another force, created in France the previous year by King Louis XIV. This new fighting service was the Compagnies franches de la Marine, or Independent Companies of the Marine.

Like the existing Troupes de la Marine, the Compagnies franches de la Marine served under the jurisdiction of the Ministry of Marine and Colonies. But these men, charged with protecting all overseas French possessions, were far better trained and equipped than their predecessors. Normally from twenty to thirty companies of these troops helped shore up the defences of New France. They formed the backbone of the French military there until the arrival of the *troupes de terre*—regiments of the regular French army—after the outbreak of the Seven Years' War in 1754. The Compagnies franches de la Marine wore distinctive uniforms with a pale grey tunic trimmed with blue, blue breeches and stockings, a black hat, and buckled shoes. Even though the initial contingents were purely French, the officer corps soon came to be dominated by colonists, while the troops themselves were quick to learn Amerindian ways of fighting. As historian George Stanley puts it, "Despite the fact that the marines [*sic*] were regular soldiers and trained according to the European ideas of warfare, they became by experience and example as proficient as the militia in the art of bush fighting with the Indians and the New Englanders."

By the mid-eighteenth century the Compagnies franches de la Marine had become, in effect, the army of the colony; in fact, they were also sometimes referred to as the Troupes de Canada. Although the non-commissioned ranks remained largely French in origin, they identified closely with the population because of their long stay in Canada and the aspiration of many of the soldiers to remain in Canada when their military service was complete. The officers were virtually all Canadiens with strong ties to the colony. The Compagnies knew the country, the terrain, and their enemies well and became a very effective force in both defence and *la petite guerre*. The relatively small size of the contingent—rarely more than 1,100—forced them to integrate their campaigns with both the militia and New France's Indian allies. Even though these "marines" did not officially constitute a regiment as such, their shared heritage, their strong ties to New France, their common uniform and fighting methods, and the cohesive nature of the officer corps strongly resembled many of the classic attributes of a regimental tradition. Nevertheless, there were never very many of them to help defend a growing colony. Between 1683 and 1760, fewer than ten thousand men all told served in the Compagnies franches de la Marine and their rougher predecessor, the Troupes de la Marine.

In 1701 the French and the Iroquois finally concluded a lasting peace, but New France still faced a growing enemy in the ever-expanding English colonies to the south and the English domination of Hudson Bay and the prairie watershed to the west of it. The English presence in Hudson Bay was more of an economic threat; it posed the danger of cutting off New France's access to the western fur trade. Very few settlers from Britain went there until the turn of the nineteenth century, but the Atlantic seaboard colonies were another matter entirely. They grew rapidly and their population pushed the frontier of settlement ever farther westward, threatening to spill over into the Ohio River Valley, block any expansion of New France itself, and cut the link between New France and Louisiana, which the French had established at the mouth of the Mississippi River in the 1680s.

France and England (after 1707, Great Britain) fought four major wars in North America either alone or in conjunction with allies. The first was the war of the League of Augsburg (also known as King William's War), which broke out in 1689 and ended with the Treaty of Ryswick in 1697. The next was the War of the Spanish Succession, waged between 1702 and 1713, followed by the War of the Austrian Succession (1744–48). The final conflict was the Seven Years' War (known in the United States as the French and Indian War), which started in North America in 1754 and ended with the withdrawal of France from virtually all of the continent in 1763. For almost the entire time between the mid-1600s and 1763, a vicious war of raids, ambushes, no quarter and no prisoners, was fought along the border between New France and the English colonies. Throughout that time, a few companies of French regular soldiers, the New France militia, and the Compagnies franches de la Marine (as well as New France's aboriginal allies) constituted the French fighting force in America.

What Britain would call the Seven Years' War began deep in the North American interior in the late spring of 1754, when a small expedition of Virginia militia, led by George Washington, ventured west across the Allegheny Mountains. They were determined to expunge the French presence in the Ohio River Valley as a prelude to both settlement and land speculation. Beginning in the 1680s, French explorers had mapped out a great Y-shaped empire in the interior. In the northeast,

Quebec stood as the major *entrepôt* and military guardian of French interests in America. In the far south, at the mouth of the Mississippi, Louisiana and the post of New Orleans, on Lake Pontchartrain, gave France internal access to the Gulf of Mexico. To the far northwest, Fort Rouge (later Winnipeg) put French traders on the doorstep to the fur-rich lands of Saskatchewan, bypassing the English posts on Hudson Bay. On the southeast coast of Cape Breton, the fortified sea-port of Louisbourg, with its massive stone fort built after the Treaty of Utrecht ended the War of the Spanish Succession, stood guard over the sea approaches to Quebec. New Englanders saw Louisbourg as a mortal threat to their trade and their lives and chafed for opportunities to crush it. And at virtually all the junctions of the great river roads that linked this vast empire in the continental interior stood French forts. They were mostly crudely built and manned by but a handful of regulars or marines. Their major source of strength was not their walls or their soldiers, but the strong ties they had established over decades with the powerful Indian nations who ruled the land from the Great Lakes to the Gulf of Mexico to the Great Plains.

George Washington intended to begin unravelling this network of furs, trade, and Indian alliances at a point he thought vulnerable, virtually at its centre. However, his expedition was a disaster, and the French quickly sent him and his irregulars packing, back across the mountains. Washington and other American colonists had had enough of French border raids, French rule over the interior waterways, French sway over the Indians, and the French threat posed by Louisbourg. They were determined to launch a new foray, this time with considerable support from Britain. Colonial entreaties to London were answered when the British sent General Edward Braddock and a contingent of regular troops to try again to attack the French in the Ohio Valley in the summer of 1755. Braddock led an expedition to take Fort Duquesne, at the forks of the Ohio, but he was killed and his contingent routed. The French then responded to the reinforcement of British troops in North America with reinforcements of their own regular troops from overseas.

In May 1755, four battalions of French regulars arrived at Quebec and two at Louisbourg. These troops were the first formal regiments of the French army to arrive in Canada since the departure of the Carignan-Salières. Over the next three years (war between Britain and France on the European continent officially broke out in 1756) six more regiments arrived, along with Louis-Joseph de Montcalm, Marquis de Montcalm, a professional soldier with long experience in European positional warfare, with its well-drilled infantry, formal approaches to the battlefield, and lines of soldiers engaging in mass volleys of fire. Montcalm and the regulars were sent not so much to bolster the marines and militia of New France, but to take over the war effort. As thousands of redcoats debarked along the Atlantic seaboard and hundreds of Royal Navy warships arrived in Atlantic waters, France was getting the unmistakable message that this fourth war for the continent could well be the last.

—⁂—

THE TWELVE BATTALIONS of *troupes de terre* from the Régiments La Reine, Guyenne, Béarn, Languedoc, Bourgogne, Artois, Royal Roussillon, La Sarre, Berry, Cambis, and Volontaires-Étrangers were the equal of any similar contingent of European regular soldiers of that era. The rank and file were a collection of young adventurers, former serfs, and the dregs of French ports and cities, as well as a handful of the newly emerging middle class, who saw the army as a potential ladder of upward mobility. The officer corps were a mixed bag. Some were young men from noble families whose commissions were largely purchased and whose military skills were minimal. Others had received formal military training and their rank was based on ability and accomplishment. The troops included no cavalry contingent, some artillery, but mostly heavy infantry, armed with swords and muskets fitted with bayonets, who carried heavy packs of hardtack, beer, ammunition, and powder while in the line of march. They were subject to harsh discipline. They drilled, trained, marched, and manoeuvred with but a single objective—to stand shoulder to shoulder at distances as close as 50 metres to the enemy's line and fire mass volleys of lead balls at the men opposite. The nature of the principal weaponry of the day—the long-barrelled musket, made even longer by the bayonet—dictated this tactic. This single-shot flintlock firearm could not be easily reloaded from a prone position, or fired accurately. Besides, accuracy was a moot point so close to the enemy. It wasn't a case of hit or miss but rather of standing in place in the face of withering volleys, firing, reloading, and firing again, without breaking. In such a fashion a line of infantry could shoot thousands of rounds right at the enemy several times in a minute.

The British gained the initial strategic successes on the Atlantic seaboard. British troops captured Fort Beauséjour, in Acadia, in June 1755 and Louisbourg in July 1758. In the latter campaign they mustered 27,000 men, both regulars and colonial militia, and 157 ships to fight 7,500 French soldiers, sailors, and marines. With the fort surrounded and British artillery able to bombard the position virtually at will from surrounding heights, the outcome was inevitable: the French were chased from the Maritimes. But French forces more than held their own in the first years of fighting in the forests and among the lakes and rivers of the interior. In August 1757 they captured Fort Ontario at Oswego, New York, and secured control of Lake Ontario. A year later they besieged and captured Fort William Henry on Lake George, New York, giving them virtual domination over the route from the Hudson River Valley to the St. Lawrence. Although the militia and France's Indian allies greatly aided in the campaign, the brunt of the fighting was done by the French regulars. As late as 1758 Montcalm was pleased with their successes and reported that their discipline was excellent.

But 1758 was also the nadir of French success in the war. Despite their short internal lines of communication, along the great rivers from the St. Lawrence to the Mississippi to the Missouri, and the staunchness and fighting quality of their aboriginal allies, the French were in a precarious position. The Royal Navy ruled the Atlantic and the approaches to Louisiana, Louisbourg, and Quebec. The entire population of New France numbered barely sixty thousand, while the British colonies were already over a million. Even under the best of circumstances the French could never conquer the British in North America, whereas it was entirely feasible that the opposite might happen. Finally, Britain—strongly supported by its colonists—had had enough of the French sitting astride their potential routes of expansion into the west, terrorizing their frontiers, and threatening their trade on the east coast. The British poured tens of thousands of regular troops across the Atlantic, while the colonies raised tens of thousands more. By 1759 an estimated fifty thousand troops carried the British colours in the field, an extraordinary number for North America. No matter how well the French fought, no matter how good they were, superior numbers created a strategic advantage all its own.

In 1758 British forces captured and destroyed Fort Frontenac, near present-day Kingston. France's aboriginal allies in the Ohio country decided to make a separate peace with the obviously superior British army, forcing the French to abandon Fort Duquesne. With the interior cleared and Louisbourg gone, the British launched three major attacks on the heartland of New France—the area between Montreal and Quebec—in 1759. One army captured Fort Niagara, another drove up the Lake Champlain–Richelieu River route toward the St. Lawrence, and the third besieged Quebec City. Although both the morale and the fighting ability of the French-Canadian militia and the marines remained high, the state of the French regiments had deteriorated markedly. There were constant arguments between Montcalm and the colony's Canadian-born governor Pierre de Rigaud de Vaudreuil de Cavagnial, Marquis de Vaudreuil, who was nominally in charge of all military forces in the colony. Vaudreuil had little patience for or knowledge of the apparently stiff European style of warfare, and he and Montcalm rarely agreed on either strategic objectives or tactical preferences. Because of British control of the seas, few reinforcements reached the French regiments, and the constant fighting and movement through the hilly and often cold and rainy forests of eastern Canada and northern New York and New England wore them down. Discipline began to deteriorate; desertion increased; performance under fire declined.

By the spring of 1759, Montcalm's hold was precarious. He could muster only some five battalions of regulars in defence of Quebec itself—2,900 troops—together with about 8,000 militia from Montreal, Trois-Rivières, and Quebec, 600 garrison troops, and a number of his aboriginal allies. But because of serious disagreements between Montcalm and Vaudreuil, the French neglected to build blocking positions downriver of Quebec to forestall the Royal Navy besieging the town or landing troops.

On June 26, 1759, a British fleet of 168 ships under Admiral Charles Saunders anchored off the south shore of the island of Orléans and began debarking 8,500 troops under the command of General James Wolfe. The French did not directly contest the landings; in fact, Vaudreuil, who as governor was in overall command of the garrison, withdrew his troops from the entire south shore of the river. The British set up artillery on the south shore of the narrows, directly opposite Quebec, and began to bombard the town and the citadel. They also established major encampments at Point Lévis and on the eastern bank of the Montmorency River. The French manned the citadel and entrenchments along the north shore of the river from the tidal flats off the mouth of the St. Charles River, east of Quebec, to the western bank of the Montmorency River. On July 31, Wolfe tried to cross the Montmorency in an effort to roll back the French left flank to the flats below the citadel, but the attack was beaten back with heavy losses.

As the summer waned, Montcalm and Wolfe weighed their prospects. Montcalm's position was even more precarious than it had been when Wolfe and Saunders arrived, a result of the surrenders of Forts Niagara, Carillon, and Saint-Frédéric (at the northern end of Lake Champlain) at the end of July. Even so, he knew that if he could hold out until October, the British would have to withdraw their fleet before the onset of winter and the freezing over of the St. Lawrence. Wolfe was well aware that he did not have unlimited time to bring the siege to a successful conclusion, but he was unsure how to get at the French positions. Finally, he and his officers decided on an indirect approach—to put men and ships upriver of Quebec, cross the river at a point to be determined, and threaten to cut Montcalm's supply lines to Montreal from the French rear. That could force the French to come out and fight.

On the night of September 12/13, 1759, British troops from ships anchored in the river rowed stealthily, with muffled oarlocks, from midstream to the small cove of Anse-au-Foulon, at the foot of a cliff about 3 kilometres above Quebec. A small guard at the top of the cliff was quickly overcome, and for the next several hours the British troops quickly scaled the cliffs, dragging cannon, stores, and munitions with them. They then assembled on the Plains of Abraham and moved north, toward the road that connected Quebec with the small settlement of Sainte-Foy and, beyond it, to Trois-Rivières and Montreal. Not long after daybreak, the French spotted Wolfe's advancing lines, 4,800 strong. They were taken completely by surprise. Montcalm did not learn of the British deployment until mid-morning. When he did, he raced from his headquarters at Beauport, about halfway between Quebec and the Montmorency River, and ordered his troops to muster opposite the British. Some 4,500 regulars and militia answered the call and, to the roll of drums, began to deploy in front of the walls of Quebec, facing the British.

Montcalm was not greatly outnumbered by Wolfe, but his troops were a mixed bag. History has recorded that he had about five battalions of regulars but gives little detail about their composition at this stage of the war. The well-trained regiments that had arrived with Montcalm four years earlier still existed in name and still flew their regimental banners, but by now many of the soldiers in their ranks were former militiamen or marines. They had not been trained in the severe firing discipline of the regimental troops; instead they instinctively sought cover in the rolling terrain, the tall grass, or the bushes on the battlefield as soon as the shooting started. As the lines approached each other, shots rang out from the flanks as French snipers and skirmishers fired at the redcoats, who came steadily on. The French line fired several volleys at the British but the British did not return fire. Instead, they continued to advance, seemingly oblivious to the gaps in their ranks that opened every time one of them fell dead or wounded.

Some of the French riflemen—those not trained in European-style warfare—threw themselves to the ground to reload. This increased the confusion in the French ranks. Were these men dead or wounded? Was it time to dive to the earth or even to run back to the citadel? Gaps opened in the French line, rendering their firing discipline much less effective than it might have been. When the two lines were at the astonishingly close distance of 12 metres or so, the British stopped, then opened a withering fire at the French, cutting the troops down like mown wheat. After a few volleys, the kilted Highland regiments drew their large claymore swords and charged the French. The French line broke and, with few exceptions, ran in panic back to Quebec and even past it, to Vaudreuil's encampment. Both Wolfe and Montcalm were mortally wounded in the encounter. Vaudreuil then led the surviving French troops around the British and on to winter in Montreal. British forces entered Quebec six days later.

The Battle of the Plains of Abraham, as it is called, did not end the war in Canada. Over the winter the French regrouped and reorganized in Montreal, then marched on Quebec in late April 1760. The French commander, François-Gaston de Lévis, Duc de Lévis, led a combined force of 5,000 men against British commander James Murray's 3,900 men at the Plains of Abraham. This time the French won the encounter and the British retreated to Quebec, where they were put under siege. Within weeks, however, the ice broke on the St. Lawrence and the British fleet reached Quebec first. Lévis broke camp and retreated to Montreal. The British, now reinforced, followed him, and other British columns advanced on Montreal from Lake Ontario and Lake Champlain. On September 8, 1760, Vaudreuil surrendered New France to the British commander, General Jeffery Amherst. The surrender was confirmed by the Treaty of Paris, which formally ended the Seven Years' War on February 10, 1763. This ended the era of Canada's French regiments, and the British regimental tradition in Canada was about to be born.

Chapter Two

THE REDCOATS: BRITISH REGIMENTS OF FOOT AND CANADIAN MILITIA

It is the essential Property of a free Government to depend on no other Soldiery but it's [*sic*] own Citizens for it's [*sic*] Defense; so in all such Governments, every Freeman and every Freeholder should be a soldier.

—Massachusetts ordinance, 1758

IN THE COURSE OF THE SEVEN YEARS' WAR, Britain sent some twenty thousand regular troops to North America. They were augmented by a bewildering variety of local volunteers raised throughout the Thirteen Colonies. These "provincials," as they were known, made a significant difference in the war, especially where they were deployed in large numbers, such as at the battle for Louisbourg in 1758. But the provincials played virtually no role in the siege and capture of Quebec. The mix of regular British regiments of the line and colonial troops that together expelled the French from America presaged the mixed force of British regulars and Canadian militia that was to provide defence for British North America for more than a hundred years.

The British army had been a standing army since 1660. Prior to that, English forces had consisted of regiments maintained by wealthy, usually noble, individuals; royal soldiers—paid by the king—such as the Household Cavalry; and militiamen, who were obliged by law to maintain arms and periodically muster for training. The standing regiments, consisting of officers, non-commissioned officers (NCOs), and other ranks, were named for the individuals who raised and commanded them. Those notables normally paid the entire bill for uniforms, weapons, barracks, provisions, halters, saddles, and boots and shoes. The regiments changed their names when one commander stepped down and another took his place. After the consolidation of the standing regiments and the royal regiments into a single army, the concept of the "regiment of the line" evolved. Each of these regiments was supposed to be a standard size, with a fixed establishment (set number) of officers, NCOs, and other ranks. They represented a variety of different arms—cavalry, engineers, and artillerymen, for example—but most were infantry. The infantry regiments were called regiments of foot and were numbered according to the order in which they became part of the regular army. Thus the 1st Regiment of Foot was the Royal Scots, which was counted as the oldest, having been formed in 1633. Some regiments consisted of two or more battalions of roughly eight hundred men each, one of which would serve somewhere in the British Isles and the others overseas in the colonies.

In the early 1750s a system of two colours (regimental guidons, or standards) was promulgated for these regiments. Each was assigned a "King's colour," an almost square Grand Union flag with a gold Roman numeral in the top left-hand corner (the number signified its precedence) and a symbol of historical importance to the regiment at the centre of the flag. There was also a "regimental colour," which differed in background for each regiment, usually according to the facing of the regimental uniform. Each had a small Grand Union flag in the fly, and the same symbol at the centre of the flag as on the King's colour. The older regiments, such as the Royal Scots, the Queen's (the 2nd Regiment of Foot, formed in 1661), and the Buffs (the 3rd Regiment of Foot, established in 1672), already had a history and traditions stretching back decades, and in some cases perhaps even a century. But for most of the regiments of foot, "tradition" was rather instant—a large number were established in 1702, at the start of the War of the Spanish Succession (also known as Queen Anne's War), which pitted England against France. It is unlikely that anything resembling what we know today as regimental cohesion actually existed in those units.

Britain was no democracy in the late seventeenth and early eighteenth centuries, but it was most certainly a constitutional monarchy in which government revenues were wholly derived from taxes levied by Parliament. In times of peace the military shrunk; in times of war it expanded, sometimes rapidly. Beginning in 1703, a series of recruitment and conscription measures was adopted by Parliament in a desperate attempt to rebuild the army for the war against France. The legislation gave local magistrates wide powers to release prisoners from jails for enlistment and to conscript any able-bodied man who was unemployed and had no apparent means of support. Recruiters who brought in such men were paid a bounty. The system was ripe for abuse, and abused it was. Regimental commanding officers such as Lieutenant-Colonel Robert Killigrew of the 8th Dragoons, stationed in Barcelona, Spain, wrote that he had returned several recruits "wich ware either lame, or to old, or Blind . . . and thare wos amongst them severell Boyes." Doctors were supposed to attest to the fitness of these men, but should a bribe pass from recruiter to doctor, an otherwise wholly unsuitable specimen might find himself classified as ready for army service.

It is no wonder that the British army of those years was an institution sustained largely by a very harsh regimen of drill and punishment. First of all, the individual redcoat had to be thoroughly schooled in the many intricate steps required to manoeuvre on the battlefield and to prepare and fire his weapon. He had to be so completely trained as to perform these functions automatically, with no thought given to anything else, no matter how fatigued, how wet, how dirty, or how close to enemy fire. He had to be, in other words, transformed into an automaton. For example, about 120 orders might be used by a field formation commander to place his troops in just the right location to pour a withering fire on the enemy. And when those troops were in position, they had to be able to carry out the twenty-one different steps needed to fire their weapons and then clean, prime, aim, and fire again. Four moves were required just to fix a bayonet. The aim of the training was to ensure that their smoothbore, single-shot "Brown Bess" or Tower muskets could be fired at the rate of about two rounds per minute. The overall objective was simple—to ensure that the regiment could shoot about 1,600 rounds per minute at an opposing force that might have been as close as 40 to 50 metres.

It was all very rote, but very necessary. For example, the cavalry were required to learn six basic sword cuts to be used against the enemy with sword in one hand and pistol in the other—there are authenticated cases of neophytes killing their own horses during such training. Artillery was no less complicated. The numbers in a gun crew varied according to the size of the gun, and the heavy old field pieces were far different from today's artillery. They were smoothbore, muzzle-loaded, and completely unequipped with any means of absorbing recoil. Their barrels had to be swabbed out after every shot to lessen the danger that a new charge of powder be ignited by burning residue of just-fired powder or wadding that might still be in the barrel. Guns had to be quickly dragged back into position after every shot and "laid" over open sights before the next one. The loader, the spongeman, every member of the crew had to be trained thoroughly to each perform his function in turn, quickly, and with as little risk as possible of having the gun fire when a crewman was too close to the muzzle, or a misstep that would result in explosion in the breech or barrel.

The less than sterling character of many of these soldiers and the training required to turn them into unthinking robots seemed to cry out for harsh discipline, and the British army was probably a much harder environment for the individual soldier than the Royal Navy of the period has often been made out to be. The standard instrument for meting out punishment was the cat-o'-nine-tails, which was usually made up of nine lengths of whipcord, about 60 centimetres long, attached to a wooden handle. Each cord had from three to nine knots spaced along it. It was the perfect instrument for tearing away flesh when applied vigorously to a soldier's back. Sentences of up to two thousand lashes were not uncommon. When King George III limited punishment to a thousand lashes in 1807, it was considered a step forward in army reform.

Some of the colonists who had served the king's cause in the Seven Years' War joined British regiments stationed in or transferred to North America—an estimated eleven thousand recruits. Some even joined British regiments that had been founded in the Thirteen Colonies, such as the 60th Regiment of Foot, the Royal Americans, established in 1755, which fought at both Louisbourg and Quebec. The soldiers were largely colonials, the officers mostly British, and the training and discipline no different than in any other British regiment of foot. After the Seven Years' War the 60th was transferred to the West Indies, where it was stationed throughout the American Revolution, although four of its battalions were sent to Georgia to defend Savannah against the congressional troops. Afterwards the 60th was assigned postings in the same fashion as any other line regiment in the British army, serving from Canada to India and in many other colonial stations. But the Thirteen Colonies also raised a somewhat bewildering variety of local or "provincial" units ranging from independent ranger companies to militia to provincial regiments that resembled British regiments of foot in all but name.

Rangers were lightly equipped troops who were supposed to be well trained to live off the land, travel quickly through the forests of the northeast, and fight like Indians. They could be used as reconnaissance troops or scouts to seek out the enemy, as light skirmishers to keep the enemy pinned down until heavier troops arrived, or as harassing troops whose task it was to snipe at and ambush heavier columns of enemy soldiers moving through the forests. Their tactics were to hit fast and withdraw into the woods. One of the most famous of these companies was Rogers' Rangers, commanded by Robert Rogers in the Seven Years' War, who did a fine job of harassing both Indians and French in the central New York area. Although the reputation of

Rogers' Rangers as an effective fighting force has ebbed and flowed through the years, Rogers' creed of moving quickly, travelling lightly, living off the land, and building close comradeship is still the basic philosophy of ranger-type units in both the U.S. and Canada today.

Each of the Thirteen Colonies also raised regular regiments for defence of the colony or to be used in other parts of America if conditions warranted it. These provincial regiments were equipped and trained as British regulars, and were often placed in the order of battle with British regiments. But since none of them were permanent organizations and contracts lasted only as long as nine months, they rarely had as much battle experience and were thought by the British to be not nearly as effective. Nonetheless these units were exceedingly popular in times of war because the pay was much better than that of the British regiments, the discipline was usually less harsh, and a system of bonuses, bounties, and sharing of plunder acted as a strong inducement to sign up. Although the British reserved their own regiments of foot for the two key battles of the war—Louisbourg and Quebec—the provincials won many important victories, especially in the interior, at places such as Fort Frontenac and Fort Duquesne.

Each colony also raised its own militia. The colonial militias were modelled on the old English militia that stretched back to the Tudor period. By law every male between the ages of sixteen and sixty was required to own a firearm, powder, ammunition, and a hatchet and to muster at set times of the year—depending on the imminence of danger, this could be from once a week to once a year. Once or twice a year the militia also gathered for a modicum of close-order drill and target shooting, usually followed by a massive drinking bout. Service in the militia was hardly an imposition, but it was the duty, as well as the right, of every free male citizen to present himself to take part in the defence of his government. A 1758 Massachusetts proclamation put it succinctly: "It is the essential Property of a free Government to depend on no other Soldiery but it's [*sic*] own Citizens for it's [*sic*] Defense; so in all such Governments, every Freeman and every Freeholder should be a soldier."

—m—

ALL THE COLONIAL OR PROVINCIAL REGIMENTS and most of the British regiments of foot departed Canada immediately after the French surrender. About two thousand British troops remained in scattered locations from Halifax to the Great Lakes. Those among the French-speaking population who wished to remain French were given eighteen months to leave Canada after the signing of the Treaty of Paris on February 10, 1763. The vast majority of French officials and regular soldiers did leave but most of the population stayed put, as did most of the captains of the militia. Some British soldiers of the disbanded 78th and 80th Regiments of Foot chose to stay in Canada and were given farmland as a sort of pension.

The first governor of the new British province of Quebec, which was defined by the Royal Proclamation of October 7, 1763, was former Major-General James Murray. He was given all necessary power to defend the colony, including mustering the militia, which was, of course, virtually all French-Canadian Roman Catholics. Since the colony was not threatened in any way that he could perceive, Murray was unwilling to risk alienating the Canadian population by reminding them that their militia forces were now under overall British command. There also existed the not inconsequential problem that under British law no Roman Catholic could be an officer in the British forces. Thus the captains of the militia would have to serve under English Protestants.

Besides, what use was there for militias or even regular troops? After the French had formally surrendered at Montreal on September 8, 1760, the eastern half of the continent faced the prospect of its first long peace since the early seventeenth century. The French were vanquished, the British were masters of Hudson Bay, the St. Lawrence Valley, and the eastern seaboard of North America as far south as Florida, and there were no ongoing disputes anywhere between the aboriginal nations and Euro-Canadians or Americans. But the British were quick to learn that real peace was as elusive as ever.

Only weeks after the finalization of the Treaty of Paris in 1763, the Ottawa chief Pontiac launched a guerrilla war against a number of western British outposts at the head of a mixed group of Ottawa, Potawatomi, and Ojibwa. They first attacked Fort Detroit, killing forty-six British soldiers, then went on prolonged frontier raids, taking eight British garrisons and killing an estimated two thousand settlers. At the end of July, Pontiac's fighters ambushed a 260-man column of British troops and colonial militia en route to Detroit and overran them. When the campaigning season drew to a close in the fall, Pontiac was left in virtual control of the land between Lake Huron and Lake Michigan.

Over the winter of 1763–64, General Thomas Gage, the British commander-in-chief in North America, who was stationed in New York, determined to raise a force of both regulars and militia to extinguish Pontiac's rebellion. He called on Murray for a contribution from Quebec. In early March 1764 Murray called for a battalion (three companies) of volunteers, offering as inducements a bounty of "twelve piastres in money . . . a capote, two pairs of Indian shoes and a pair of gloves" in addition to arms, ammunition, rations, and "six pence per day English money." He authorized a Catholic priest to accompany the volunteers, but there were few takers. By the end of the month Murray had to warn the captains of the militia that he would invoke a militia call-out under the still standing laws of the old French regime; if that did not produce the desired results, he would seize the men's firearms. That got results. In early April a battalion was formed and left Montreal for the west. It did little fighting, since most of Pontiac's followers deserted him when the large British contingent approached. The Canadians received much praise, according to G.F.G. Stanley, but their reluctance to take up arms under British command did not bode well for the future defence of the colony.

Murray departed Quebec in 1766 and was replaced by Guy Carleton, who had served under Wolfe at Quebec. Carleton sensed the maelstrom that was building in the Thirteen Colonies and was determined to ensure that whatever happened to the south, Quebec

would remain politically and militarily secure under British rule. He
had few resources and only a handful of troops, but he did what
he could to renovate some of the old defences and fortifications that
the French had used to secure New France. He understood that the
most important of these was Quebec City itself, and that even if
rebellion engulfed the colonies, Britain's hold on Quebec City might
well determine the future of Canada. Carleton also successfully urged
the British government to adopt the Quebec Act of 1774, which,
among other things, gave to the Roman Catholic Church and the
old seigneur class powers and privileges they had never enjoyed under
the *ancien régime.* Carleton believed that such a step would bring the
people to Britain's side, but he misunderstood the social and political
realities that had governed Canada in the French regime, and the key
roles that the captains of the militia—not the seigneurs—had played
in the defence of New France.

The storm that Carleton had foreseen broke in April 1775,
when colonial militia loyal to the Continental Congress then meeting in Philadelphia skirmished with British troops at Lexington
and Concord. Not long after, a small force of rebels (or Americans,
as we shall now refer to them) attacked and captured the poorly
defended but important British posts at Ticonderoga and Crown
Point, opening up the possibility of invasion of Montreal from the
south. Then, at the end of June, the Congress authorized attacks
on both Canada and Nova Scotia. Nova Scotia very much reflected
the political and social makeup of the Thirteen Colonies that were
in rebellion to the south. Some community leaders felt strong ties
to the rebels, but Nova Scotia was dominated by the Royal Navy,
based in Halifax. The Nova Scotia legislature declined to join in
with the other rebellious colonies or even to send official delegates
to the Continental Congress; no one knew how long that situation
would last. Canada, with its overwhelmingly French and Catholic
population, was another matter entirely, especially since a number
of southern colonists had arrived and settled in both Montreal and
Quebec since the Treaty of Paris.

Carleton estimated that he needed at least ten thousand regular troops to defend Canada; he had fewer than nine hundred scattered from Lachine, on the south shore of the island of Montreal, to Chambly, downriver from Quebec. In early June an appeal to loyal British subjects in the Mohawk Valley brought in some four hundred volunteers who eventually formed the core of two battalions of the Royal Highland Emigrants, likely the first Highland regiment ever formed in Canada. One battalion was sent to Nova Scotia and the other was deployed to the vicinity of Montreal to shore up the small British detachment there.

The American attack on Canada developed from two directions. From the Crown Point area, Generals Philip Schuyler and Richard Montgomery advanced on Montreal with more than two thousand men. From Maine, General Benedict Arnold marched overland with just over one thousand men up the Kennebec and Chaudière rivers, a very difficult route. Carleton failed to rally enough Canadian militia to fill in the ranks of Montreal's defenders, and the town fell to the Americans on November 11, 1775. Carleton then fled to Quebec, arriving on November 19, just five days after the town's defenders first caught sight of Arnold's troops approaching from the south.

Carleton acted quickly to consolidate Quebec's defences. He had a rather motley complement to work with. Accounts differ but it appears that the defenders numbered from 1,100 to 1,800, with 300 to 550 French militia, 200 to 339 English-speaking militia, about 200 Royal Highland Emigrants recruited from Newfoundland, 480 seamen and marines from ships in port, and a small contingent of 60 to 70 soldiers from the 7th Regiment of Foot. The French were not enthusiastic at first. Major Henry Caldwell, a British half-pay officer and new seigneur, observed: "The Canadians [the French militia] were at first very luke-warm and said if the English inhabitants would defend the town, they would; and the British subjects, to their eternal honour, not only set an example on that, but on every other occasion during the siege." At times during the long and very cold winter nights English-speaking guards "submitted with greatest cheerfulness to the command of the [French] Canadian officers, whom they held cheap, and who were in reality their inferiors, both as to education and fortune," Caldwell wrote.

Carleton faced a force almost as ragtag as his own. By the time Montgomery arrived to join Arnold, he had only about 300 soldiers with him to add to the 650 or so who had survived the long trek from Maine. The Americans mounted the most serious of their assaults in the early hours of December 31, 1775, with a double attack from the west aimed at enveloping the citadel by capturing the lower town. In cold and blinding snow, Montgomery's forces were spotted coming from Cape Diamond and were fired on from close range. Montgomery was mortally wounded and his troops driven back. The defenders then rushed to the other flank in time to meet Arnold's forces attacking from St. Roch, and defeated them too. Arnold was wounded and more than 450 Americans were taken prisoner.

Although the attack failed, the siege continued, as the Americans remained in control of the river above Quebec. They fired the odd cannon volley into the town but Carleton's men matched their cannon fire about ten to one. Smallpox, cold, and near starvation thinned the American forces. Some simply went home when their enlistment expired. The longer they stayed, however, the more their relations with the local French deteriorated. Finally, in May 1776, the Royal Navy ended the siege, just as it had in the spring of 1760, as the ice broke up on the St. Lawrence. The Americans under Arnold retreated upriver. By the second half of June they had abandoned their last positions in and to the south of Montreal and crossed back into New York. The invasion was over.

Subsequently the British poured thousands of troops into Canada in a buildup aimed at attacking south along the traditional Lake Champlain route and cutting the rebellious colonies in half, but the British commander, John Burgoyne, was defeated at Saratoga in October 1777. Among Burgoyne's contingent was a sullen handful of French-Canadian militia, recruited as labourers under Lower Canada's first militia act, which was approved by the legislative council at Quebec in late March 1777.

Carleton and the British were sorely disappointed by the failure of the French-Canadian militia to show any enthusiasm for a cause they considered to be a family quarrel among the English. The French were quite willing to sell supplies to the Americans, as long as the Americans had specie. In some instances they even appeared ready to muster militia companies to help maintain order in occupied Montreal and Trois-Rivières, but none went so far as to actually fight against the British. Carleton reported to London after the siege of Quebec was lifted that as far as the French Canadians were concerned, "there is nothing to fear from them, while we are in a state of prosperity, and nothing to hope for when in distress; I speak of the People at large; there are among them [some] who are guided by Sentiments of honour, but the multitude is influenced only by hopes of gain, or fear of punishment."

The British position in Halifax had been somewhat desperate when the revolution broke out in the summer of 1775. Governor Francis Legge had only three companies of the 65th Regiment of Foot in Halifax and another in Newfoundland. Worse, he was unsure of the loyalties of many of the new settlers who had arrived in the western reaches of the colony after the end of the Seven Years' War. They were almost all from New England and could be expected to harbour revolutionary sentiments. In July 1775 some sympathizers living in Halifax tried to burn down a military storehouse, forcing Legge to organize a few light companies of militia volunteers. He did not have an easy time of it: rumours had spread through the colony that men raised in Nova Scotia were to be shipped off to fight in New England against the revolutionaries, some of whom were actually kinsmen. Legge was forced to issue reassurances that local recruits would be used only for local defence in the event of an invasion. The regiment thus formed, the Loyal Nova Scotia Volunteers, had a total complement of around 240 and never did any fighting. Legge was also reinforced from Boston, by two companies of British regulars and the newly formed Royal Fencible Americans. Fencibles were troops raised for colonial defence who were trained and equipped as regular British soldiers but who could not be deployed outside British colonial territory in North America. In the far west of the province it was, surprisingly, the local remnant of the Acadian population, the survivors of the expulsion by the British in 1755, who assumed the primary role in defence of the Crown.

British reinforcements arrived in Halifax through the winter of 1775–76, but the Americans mounted an attack against the strategically placed Fort Cumberland (formerly the French Fort Beauséjour) in November of 1776. Had they succeeded they might have cut off the isthmus of Chignecto. However, the fort was defended by about two hundred Royal Fencible Americans under Joseph Goreham, an experienced fighter who had once commanded a ranger company. The defenders were low on provisions and rations and their uniforms were in rags. The fortifications themselves had never been restored after the French defeat. Nonetheless, they had held off three American attacks by the time a Royal Navy warship arrived on December 28 carrying a detachment of Royal Highland Emigrants and Royal Marines. Thus ended the American threat to Nova Scotia.

The American Revolution was henceforth played out in the Thirteen Colonies to the south. No further efforts were made to take Canada, as George Washington (who had opposed the invasion of Nova Scotia in the first place) convinced the Continental Congress that the success of the revolution depended almost exclusively on his ability to sustain a continental army in the field. Pitched battles were fought at a number of locations from the southern swamps of Virginia to the vicinity of New York as Britain used its overwhelming seapower to try to blockade the rebellious colonies. British troops also chased Washington's army from the New Jersey uplands to the valleys of Pennsylvania. Eventually both France and Spain took advantage of the revolution to strike a blow at their old nemesis. French troops arrived to support Washington while the French navy effectively neutralized the British at sea. The surrender of a besieged British army under Lord Cornwallis at Yorktown, Virginia, in 1781 struck a final blow at a war-weary London. Many opposition politicians and businessmen were already clamouring for an end to the fighting, while the British, ironically and belatedly, had conceded to the main demand of the colonists—no local taxation without representation—in the conciliatory act passed in 1777. It only remained for the diplomats to bring down the curtain, which they did on September 3, 1783, with the Treaty of Paris, by which Britain recognized the independence of the new United States.

—⁓—

THE BIRTH OF THE UNITED STATES had immediate repercussions for Britain and what remained of British North America. About forty thousand Loyalist refugees made their way to British territory during and immediately after the war, with some thirty thousand settling in western Nova Scotia and about ten thousand establishing themselves north of the Quebec–Vermont and Quebec–New York borders and along the north shores of the St. Lawrence, Lake Ontario, and Lake Erie. Many of those who settled had at some time or another carried arms against the revolution, although many others were simply victims of circumstance. In any case, those who came to Nova Scotia soon clamoured for a colony and a legislative assembly all their own, and the colony of New Brunswick was created in western Nova Scotia in August 1784. Those Loyalists who settled in western Quebec chafed under the appointed government established by the Quebec Act, and their demands (and those of the loyalists in Quebec proper) were satisfied with the passage of the Canada Act in 1791, which created the provinces of Upper and Lower Canada, both with elected legislatures.

The arrival of these tens of thousands of loyal English-speaking settlers completely altered the social and political situation that had faced the British at the end of the Seven Years' War. Now, only eight years after the end of the American Revolution, a new British North America stretched westward thousands of kilometres from Newfoundland to the Detroit River. How was this territory to be defended? The Americans, a boisterous and expansionist people, could be counted upon to challenge British sovereignty in the western reaches of Upper Canada at least, if not also in other contentious places along the boundary such as the Maine–New Brunswick border.

The British North American colonists could of course rely on some British protection. Immediately after the Revolutionary War there were about two thousand British regulars scattered across a frontier of some 1,800 kilometres, with major concentrations at Halifax and Quebec. But there were strict limits to the amount the British Parliament was prepared to spend on permanently stationed troops for defence of its possessions in North America. This was especially true because the conciliatory act of 1777 had put virtually the entire burden of this cost on the British themselves. Clearly the colonists were going to have to shoulder arms to defend the Crown. Within a few years of establishment of the new Loyalist settlements, local regiments began to appear from Nova Scotia to Upper Canada.

One of Canada's longest-running regimental traditions began in 1793, when Major Thomas Skinner of the Royal Engineers sought permission from London to establish an infantry formation to protect British interests in Newfoundland in the wake of the recent outbreak of war between Britain and France. Britain declared war on France on February 1, 1793, after the execution of Louis XVI—four years into the French Revolution. This war was the beginning of what became known to history as the Napoleonic Wars, which continued with but two interruptions until 1815. Newfoundland had once been a French possession. Originally Britain did not want permanent settlement on the island, but fishers moved there with their families and eventually so too did merchants, shipwrights, and others connected with the seaborne and fishing businesses. At first the inhabitants set up their own militia to fend off French attacks. A local volunteer regiment was organized for defence of the island during the American Revolution, but disbanded in 1783. Many Newfoundlanders also volunteered to join the Royal Highland Emigrants and helped to defend Quebec in the winter of 1775–76.

Thomas Skinner's effort was rewarded with the founding on

April 25, 1795, of the Newfoundland Regiment of Fencible Infantry (Skinner's Fencibles), later called the Royal Newfoundland Regiment. Fencible regiments were raised only for the duration of hostilities— they were not intended as line regiments in the British army and were to be deployed within North America only as needed until the end of the war. Skinner's unit was disbanded in 1802, when the Treaty of Amiens brought a temporary respite from the war, but when the Napoleonic Wars broke out again in 1803, a successor formation— the Newfoundland Fencible Infantry—was established. This regiment was given "Royal" designation in 1806 and served in both Lower and Upper Canada in the War of 1812 against the United States. It was disbanded in 1816.

The Queen's Rangers, also known as the Queen's York Rangers, was one of the most colourful regiments founded in the early Loyalist period. The Rangers were the brainchild of John Graves Simcoe, who had joined the 35th Regiment of Foot in Britain in 1770 at the age of eighteen. Simcoe was posted to Boston in 1775, at the outbreak of the American Revolution, where he pushed hard for creation of a ranger-type fighting unit along the lines of Rogers' Rangers. He was eventually assigned to command the successor to Rogers' Rangers (which had been renamed the Queen's Rangers) in 1777. He returned to Britain after the revolution and was elected to Parliament in 1790. But Simcoe's heart remained in America. He supported the division of Quebec into Upper and Lower Canada in the Canada Act of 1791 and eagerly accepted appointment as Upper Canada's first lieutenant-governor.

Simcoe knew that Upper Canada was going to be especially vulnerable should war break out between Britain and the United States, and he had reason to worry. Although the revolution had formally ended in 1783, several issues remained unsettled, especially in the reaches to the south and west of Lake Erie. The new U.S. government was dragging its heels on settlement payments to the Loyalists, and the British refused to relinquish some of the key western posts they held at the end of the war, even though they were located in American territory. The British were especially reluctant to give up long-established ties with the First Nations of the Ohio River Valley, whom they saw as valuable potential allies in any future confrontation with the U.S. Eventually Jay's Treaty of 1794 eased the tensions as the British began a two-year withdrawal from most posts within the boundaries of the United States. But, until then, the distinct prospect of a nasty little frontier war remained.

Simcoe was also well aware of the serious lack of both settlements and infrastructure in Upper Canada. So, in late 1790, before departing for his new post, he proposed the creation of a new ranger-style regiment, raised in Britain, that would not only help defend the colony but also establish settlements and build roads and fortifications. As a student of Roman history, he wanted to set up military outposts in the tradition of the old Roman Empire, which had formed the basis of so many great settlements on the Roman frontier. They had been built by active soldiers and peopled by retired ones who were given generous land bounties upon retirement. Royal approval of this new regiment—to be called, once again, the Queen's Rangers—was given on August 29, 1791. The new unit was charged with the task of "assisting in the erection of public buildings, the construction of bridges, forming roads of communication, and in any other civil or military duties, either within or out of that province which his Majesty's service may require." The first contingent of the regiment left for Upper Canada in the spring of 1792. When Simcoe arrived in Kingston, Upper Canada, on July 1, 1792, he was, in the words of the unit's history, "pleased to see the neat orderly rows of tents of the Queen's Rangers, encamped about a quarter of a mile from the house appointed for the Commanding Officer." In keeping with their ranger background and tradition, the Queen's Rangers were directed to wear forest green uniforms, setting them well apart from the traditional red of both British and provincial units.

The outbreak of the Napoleonic Wars brought reinforcement of the British Army in North America and establishment of several other provincial regiments aside from the Queen's Rangers and Skinner's

Fencibles. All the British colonies had adopted militia acts by 1794 that obliged eligible males of appropriate age to be armed and to train for militia service on a regular basis. In addition, the 1st and 2nd battalions of the Royal Canadian Volunteers—the 1st battalion made up of French-Canadian volunteers—were raised in Upper and Lower Canada. In the Atlantic colonies, the Royal Nova Scotia, King's New Brunswick, and His Majesty's Corps of St. John's regiments were also raised to supplement the regular British regiments, naval troops, and Royal Marines. In March 1802, the Peace of Amiens appeared to bring an end to the Napoleonic Wars, and all of the units raised since 1792 were disbanded. Thus, officially, no Canadian (or Newfoundland) militia regiments established after the Seven Years' War can be said to have survived the start of the nineteenth century.

Chapter Three

THE WAR OF 1812: SAVING CANADA

The 26th has been a glorious day for me and those of my troops engaged. The American army commanded by Gen'l Hampton and another general has been repulsed by a little band—all Canadians—and yesterday that army commenced its retreat.

—Lieutenant-Colonel Charles-Michel d'Irumberry de Salaberry,
October 26, 1813

ON OCTOBER 26, 1813, on the Chateauguay River, about 40 kilometres southwest of Montreal, Lieutenant-Colonel Charles-Michel d'Irumberry de Salaberry stood behind the breastworks that his men had built on the north bank of the river and waited for the approaching Americans. Local farmers and Indians loyal to the British cause had kept Salaberry well informed of the enemy's progress from the time the Americans had crossed the border in September. The American forces consisted of some five thousand troops with ten cannon. They were led by General Wade Hampton, whose original intent had been to march quickly from Plattsburgh, on the western shore of Lake Champlain, north to Montreal by the most direct route. At the same time another, even larger American force under Major-General James Wilkinson was moving down the St. Lawrence from Lake Ontario to join with Hampton and overwhelm the British and Canadians at Montreal.

That would cut off Upper Canada from Lower Canada and from the main British garrisons at Quebec and Halifax. It might end the war in Canada; it most certainly would cause Upper Canada to fall like a ripe fruit into the hands of the United States. The only "British" troops standing in Hampton's way were Canadians. This was a mixed force under Salaberry's command: two Canadian regiments—the Canadian Fencibles and the Voltigeurs Canadiens—with about a hundred local militia and fifty Indian warriors from the nearby Kahnawake reserve.

Salaberry was a legendary figure even then. He was born on a seigneury at Beauport, in Lower Canada, in 1778; his father, the seigneur, had fought alongside the British against the Americans in 1775. The entire family had a long tradition of military service in both New France and with the royal army of France that went back several generations. After the British conquest of New France, they decided to stay and serve their new political masters; Charles joined the 44th Regiment of Foot when he was fourteen. He served in both the West Indies and Europe and rose rapidly in the ranks because of his leadership qualities and fighting ability. Salaberry seemed to take a special interest in the welfare of his troops even though he was a bear for both training and discipline. His men respected him for his impartiality, his honour, and his fairness.

In 1810 Salaberry was recalled to Canada as a lieutenant-colonel in the British army. Britain was then in a difficult state: the Treaty of Amiens, which had temporarily ended the Napoleonic Wars in 1802–3, had quickly broken down and the war had resumed. The British army and the Royal Navy were being rapidly expanded at great expense, causing a major drain on British manpower. At the same time, however, friction between Britain and the United States had also started to increase. The deterioration in Anglo-American relations was due to growing calls in the American south and west to annex Upper Canada—especially the rich farmland between the Niagara and Detroit rivers—and also increasing incidence of British warships stopping American vessels at sea and impressing (seizing) sailors, claiming they were British subjects who had deserted from the Royal Navy.

Most British military commanders and governing officials in Canada thought it was only a matter of time before the Americans attempted to seize Canada. But with the Napoleonic Wars raging, Britain had little to spare for the defence of its American colonies. A man like Salaberry—Canadian, French, and with a solid military record—would be invaluable in Canada. In 1812 he was appointed to command a new Canadian regiment—the Voltigeurs Canadiens— a "formed" regiment authorized by the government of Lower Canada and composed entirely of militia volunteers, who were to be outfitted and trained as if they were a British regiment of foot. Salaberry trained these men well and even paid for some of their equipment out of his own pocket. One contemporary observer noted that the regiment "presented a serviceable effective appearance—pretty well drilled, and their arms in perfectly good order, nor had they a mobbish appearance." Now, on this cool fall day with the brilliant foliage of the forest as a backdrop, Salaberry and his men awaited the enemy.

Salaberry's men had felled trees and built barriers of brush and logs perpendicular to the river on its north bank, between the river and a marshy thicket of trees, brush, and very soft ground. There were three barriers, each constructed behind a small river or stream that flowed into the Chateauguay. Salaberry commanded from behind the first barrier, accompanied by about three hundred Voltigeurs and Canadian Fencibles. The rest of his force waited behind the second barrier, about 1 kilometre to the rear. The least-trained men—the local militia—were in reserve about another kilometre beyond the second barrier. About 160 militiamen had been deployed to the south of the river, across from the third barrier, to cover a ford. The reserve forces were under command of Lieutenant-Colonel "Red George" Macdonnell.

As he approached the Canadians, Hampton divided his troops; he led the larger column along the north bank of the river and sent a smaller detachment along the south bank. The southern force of about 1,500 men was supposed to advance to the ford during the night of October 25–26, then cross the river in the morning and attack the Canadian rear, but they got lost in the thick woods in the dark. In the morning they were spotted emerging helter-skelter from the trees, considerably short of their goal, and were subjected to withering fire from Salaberry's troops. The Americans tried to continue the advance but ran into the militia guarding the ford. Under heavy fire, they began to retreat. In the meantime, Hampton's column advanced on Salaberry's position. One American officer walked ahead of the troops to demand surrender, but he was not carrying a white flag and was promptly shot dead. Some witnesses later reported that Salaberry himself did the shooting. Then Salaberry's men opened fire. On both sides of the river the Americans fell back. Soundly beaten, Hampton returned to Plattsburgh. Later Salaberry penned a note to his father:

> The 26th has been a glorious day for me and those of my troops engaged. The American army commanded by Gen'l Hampton and another general has been repulsed by a little band—all Canadians—and yesterday that army commenced its retreat. . . . I was in the first line during the whole of the action and afterwards, with a small reserve, beat off a large body of Americans. . . . We are all very much harassed and I am not well.

Salaberry recovered quickly and became a folk hero in French Canada. After the war he served as a justice of the peace and a member of the legislative council for Lower Canada before succeeding his father as seigneur of Saint-Mathias.

Salaberry was a Canadian officer, albeit thoroughly trained and with much experience in the fighting doctrine of the British army of Napoleonic times. Yet he was Canadian, and so were his men. Most were French-speaking but about 20 percent were from Lower Canada's English-speaking population. They were trained and equipped like British troops—they were even paid for by the British army—but the Voltigeurs had been formed under the provisions of the Militia Act of Lower Canada and were, in effect, the army of that province. They were only one segment of a much larger Canadian contingent that fought beside the British, and pro-British Indians, in holding back the Americans in the war of 1812–14. The very few Canadians—only a handful of French, rather more who were English-speaking—who had first helped beat back the Americans in 1775–76 had almost all been irregulars or militiamen; they had not constituted standing formations, equipped and trained as soldiers, fighting alongside the British regiments. But the Voltigeurs and Canadian Fencibles who took part in the Battle of Chateauguay were, and so were a number of other Canadian units that fought in the War of 1812. Those units were the first-ever Canadian fighting regiments, and they were instrumental in saving Canada.

—⁜—

WASHINGTON, D.C., was an awful place to live and work in the late spring of 1812. It was an artificial city of streets laid out in a grid pattern intersected by broad diagonal avenues, originally designed by the French-born architect Pierre Charles L'Enfant in the early 1790s. It lay on the north bank of the wide Potomac River at the south end of a 10-square-mile (26 square kilometres) capital district carved out of the state of Maryland. In May 1812 many of the large stone-faced, classical-style federal buildings of the new city were still under construction, including the White House—the president's official domicile. The city sat alongside river flats and near mosquito-infested swamps. It was hot and muggy in late spring, and constantly smelled of outdoor privies and cesspools. Yet here there gathered in late May of 1812 the gentlemen of the American Congress, to debate the weighty issue of whether or not the United States should declare war on Great Britain and, if so, what kind of a war it would be.

The young republic's political leadership was incensed over the Royal Navy's violation of U.S. territorial waters and its stopping of American ships on the high seas to inspect cargoes bound for Europe or to impress alleged deserters among the American crews. The Napoleonic Wars were approaching their climax. Britain and France had declared boycotts, blockades, and embargoes against each other on traffic to and from the Continent; the neutral Americans were caught in between. Since the Royal Navy effectively controlled the Atlantic after the Battle of Trafalgar in 1801, it was the British whom the Americans most often encountered. But there were also politicians, former president Thomas Jefferson among them, who believed that the time had come to complete what Arnold and Montgomery had attempted in 1775–76—the conquest of Canada. It would be merely a matter of marching, Jefferson believed, and others agreed. Together these politicians were known as the War Hawks. Only in New England was there consistent opposition to war, among merchants who believed that such a war would severely damage American trade—and their livelihoods.

On June 1, President James Madison sought the guidance of Congress. Madison did not actually ask Congress to declare war, but his message was a damning indictment of British conduct at sea that also alleged that the British were continuing to stir up trouble with the Natives in the northwest. Madison didn't actually want all-out war with Britain, but he did appear to desire a conflict restricted to the high seas, in essence to make a statement about the right of Americans to resist British encroachments on their freedom of navigation. For the next two weeks the House of Representatives and the Senate debated what to do. There was significant disagreement among those who wanted all-out war, a war only at sea, or no war at all. Finally, on June 17 Congress voted a full declaration of war against Britain. Madison agreed and signed the declaration, and preparations began almost immediately for a land invasion of Canada.

On paper the Americans were a formidable foe. The United States was at that time a nation of more than seven million people, and at the end of June 1812, Congress voted to pay for a regular army of almost thirty-six thousand. More than six hundred thousand other young men were capable of bearing arms and thus being mobilized into state militias. But the reality was different. Many of the men in the regular army were very poorly trained, virtually all of the U.S. commanders were old and hesitant, and the men in the state militias were not subject to federal authority. In Canada the commander-in-chief of military forces, who was also the governor, Lieutenant-General Sir George Prevost, had at his disposal only 5,720 regulars. These men were organized into two British regiments of foot and four Canadian fencible regiments scattered from Nova Scotia to Amherstburg, on the Canadian side of the Detroit River (the Voltigeurs Canadiens, the fifth Canadian fencible regiment to fight in the war, had not been formed when the war broke out). There were also some fifty thousand militia of various types spread across the colonies, but many of the militiamen in Upper Canada were American-born, and their sympathies were suspect. No one knew how the predominantly French population of Lower Canada would respond to the danger. Prevost's biggest worry was that a successful American thrust anywhere from the eastern end of Lake Ontario to Montreal would isolate Upper Canada and render it vulnerable to invasion from the west. Prevost and his chief military commander in Upper Canada, Major-General Isaac Brock, both knew that Quebec was the key to Canada, but, after spending some time in Upper Canada, Brock concluded it could be defended by bold action at the outbreak of a war.

On June 24, 1812, a courier from New York reached Montreal with the news that the U.S. had declared war. Across the British colonies, the ponderous process of raising, or calling out, the militia began almost immediately. Prevost, Brock, and other British military leaders knew that there were not enough British regulars to defend the colonies and that, with the Napoleonic Wars still raging in Europe, there was little chance for any relief from the U.K. Canadians themselves would have to fight effectively if Canada was to be saved from the Americans.

Virtually all the historians of the War of 1812 write of the three military forces that defended Canada: British regulars, Indians, and the Canadian militia. The British regulars were the regiments of foot, artillery, engineers, and other British troops—led by British officers, raised in Britain, and trained and equipped to fight in the European style of the day—who had been assigned to garrison the colonies and who would now fight in their defence. The Indians were First Nations, such as the Shawnee under Chief Tecumseh and the Six Nations of the Grand River near Brantford, who sided with the British and deployed warriors to fight mostly on the flanks of British formations. Sometimes these warriors were used to snipe at American formations from behind cover; sometimes they were let loose to pursue them after a battle. Their very presence terrified the Americans.

The Canadian militia are not so easy to define. The Canadians who took part in the War of 1812 can be placed into four main categories. The most important and effective Canadian force eventually consisted of five regiments of fencible infantry. These regiments were the Royal Newfoundland Fencibles, the New Brunswick Fencibles, the Canadian Fencibles, the Voltigeurs Canadiens, and the Glengarry Light Infantry Fencibles. The men in these regiments had signed on for a fixed period of service, usually with a bonus paid on signing and a promise of land to farm after their military service was completed. They could be deployed anywhere in British North America, were paid by the British army, and were subject to British military law and regulations. They were issued essentially the same uniforms, weapons, and other equipment as regular British regiments and they were drilled, trained, and expected to fight like regular British regiments, and alongside them. They are sometimes referred to as "provincial" or "incorporated" troops.

Although on paper the Voltigeurs Canadiens were supposed to be a militia unit, they were paid for by the British army (as were the other four fencible regiments), but they were subject to the laws and regulations of the Militia Act of Lower Canada rather than those of the British army. In the words of military historian John Grodzinski, these units "were to all intents and purposes the closest approximation to a professional Canadian force" raised in the War of 1812 (Grodzinski is referring to the units raised in or serving in Upper Canada, but the Voltigeurs were indistinguishable from them). These regiments added about two thousand to three thousand well-trained troops to the ranks of the British army in the opening stages of the War of 1812.

—⁓—

HIS MAJESTY'S NEW BRUNSWICK REGIMENT of Fencible Infantry was authorized in July 1803 as part of the regular establishment of the British army, even though it was a fencible regiment. In 1808 the regiment's officers and men volunteered to change their status from fencible to general service, that is, they agreed to allow themselves to be sent to any British garrison or theatre of operations. The offer was not accepted at first, but it was taken up in 1810, when the unit was renamed the 104th (New Brunswick) Regiment of Foot. When the War of 1812 broke out, detachments of the 104th were posted throughout New Brunswick. In the early winter of 1813, the head-quarters and six companies were dispatched overland from Fredericton to Quebec. They set out on February 16, 1813, and reached Quebec after a grueling twenty-four-day march in sub-zero temperatures. They stayed at Quebec for only two weeks before they were sent on to Kingston, where they arrived on April 14 after having covered 1,125 kilometres since February. Different companies of the 104th served in a number of the key campaigns of the war, including the Battle of Sackets Harbor on May 29, 1813.

The Royal Newfoundland Fencible Infantry was authorized on June 7, 1803, for service in North America. It was to consist of ten companies and, although a fencible unit, it was to be paid, equipped, and trained as a British regiment. By Christmas 1803 the regiment was 385 strong; by June 1805 it had 683 officers and other ranks. In that month it sailed for Nova Scotia to begin a decade of service in Nova Scotia and Canada. In September 1807 the regiment was moved to Quebec. As war loomed in the spring of 1812, it was ordered to form five companies of marines for service aboard naval vessels operating on Lake Ontario; 360 men were dispatched to Kingston, where they joined detachments of the Upper Canadian Provincial Marines. After the war began, companies of the regiment were dispersed to Quebec, Kingston, Prescott, Fort George, and York. One detachment serving with the Provincial Marines was brought ashore to join Brock's forces marching on Detroit in mid-August 1812. Another detachment saw action at the Battle of Mackinac in 1814.

His Majesty's Canadian Regiment of Fencible Infantry was placed on the British army establishment in 1803. The British had planned to raise the regiment in the Scottish Highlands for service in Canada, but when recruiting began, rumours spread that the regiment had been purchased by the East India Company for service in India. Many Scots were eager to migrate to and settle in Canada; very few were interested in India. In late 1803 open rebellion broke out among those who had volunteered, and the regiment was disbanded. However, the officers and non-commissioned officers sailed for Canada, where in 1805 they started over, recruiting mainly in Lower Canada. Recruiting was slow, partly because of the incompatibility of Highland traditions with those of French Canadians and partly because of competition from another fencible unit, the Glengarry Light Infantry Fencibles. By the outbreak of the war in 1812, the Canadian Fencibles had more than six hundred officers and men from both Upper and Lower Canada in their ranks. The Canadian Fencibles were the most active of the five provincial regiments in the War of 1812. Units of the regiment accompanied Brock on his march to Detroit and took part in the battles of Red Mills (October 7, 1813), Chateauguay (October 26, 1813), Crysler's Farm (November 11, 1813), and Lacolle Mills (March 30, 1814). Troops from the Canadian Fencibles were also employed as marines on Lake Champlain.

The Glengarry Light Infantry Fencibles were raised in Glengarry Township, Upper Canada, from among a mainly Scottish immigrant population, in the autumn of 1811 at the express direction of Sir George Prevost. Prevost's intention was to have at his disposal a light infantry fencible formation, based at York (now Toronto), that might be rapidly deployed anywhere it was needed in the event of war with the United States. The men signed on for three years or "until six months had elapsed after authentic intelligence of the conclusion of peace." No French Canadians were allowed into the regiment, nor were immigrants from the United States. Since many of the men had already seen service with Highland regiments in the British army, it was first proposed that they be a kilted regiment. However, a large amount of dark green cloth being available and time being of the essence, the Glengarries were outfitted with the dark green with black facings of the British army's Rifle Brigade. They did not, however, carry rifles, but instead were armed with the venerable Brown Bess musket that was still the main weapon of most British and Canadian regiments. The Glengarries saw action at Stoney Creek (June 6, 1813) and Lundy's Lane (July 25, 1814).

In the spring of 1812, the Assembly of Lower Canada decided to raise a light infantry regiment of volunteers and four line infantry battalions. The light infantry regiment was named the Voltigeurs Canadiens and was placed under the command of Charles-Michel d'Irumberry de Salaberry. Six companies of Voltigeurs were raised made up of men between the ages of seventeen and thirty-five; the Assembly had instructed Salaberry to recruit among "the most respected Families in the Province." The men were outfitted in grey uniforms with black facings, Canadian short boots, and light bear-skin caps. The *Quebec Gazette* waxed euphoric on April 23, 1812, as it described the recruiting campaign:

> This Corps now forming under Major de Salaberry is complet-ing with a dispatch worthy of the ancient warlike spirit of the Country. . . . The young men move in solid columns towards the enlisting officers, with an expression of countenance not to be mistaken. The Canadians [i.e., the French-Canadians] are awak-ening from the repose of an age, secured to them by good govern-ment and virtuous habits. Their anger is fresh; the object of their preparation simple and distinct. They are to defend the King, known to them, only by acts of Kindness, and a native country long since made sacred by the exploits of their forefathers.

But in some parts of the province, recruitment dragged: there were only 309 other ranks (non-officers) as late as June 5. Although the Voltigeurs were raised as a militia regiment by the Lower Canada assembly, they were treated as a provincial unit throughout the war and paid for by the British army. The regiment was instrumental in the victory at Chateauguay and played a key role at the Battle of Crysler's Farm (November 11, 1813).

The five fencible regiments were for all intents and purposes "regulars," but most Canadians who took part in the War of 1812 were not part of these units. Instead they belonged to militia formations that were either "select embodied militia" or "sedentary militia." Select embodied militia were county- or town-based battalions of local volunteers, with ranks filled out by conscripts selected by lot or by ballot. The various militia acts of the different colonies spelled out the obligation of every eligible male to provide military service in defence of the colony, so anyone who tried to sidestep his obligations by refusing to serve if selected was subject to fines or imprisonment. However, if a man selected for militia service could find a substitute—usually by paying him—then his military obligation was considered fulfilled. The local units that constituted these battalions, such as the Dorchester Provincial Light Dragoons and the Quebec Volunteers, were required by law to form up and train, or "muster," on a regular basis, sometimes as often as once a month, to practise drill and marksmanship. Impending danger might require them to assemble as often as once a week. They were usually uniformed, in whatever manner the regimental colonel would decide according to what cast-offs were available. By the end of the War of 1812 virtually all these formations wore the traditional red coat and were reasonably well equipped.

The sedentary militia comprised all the other able-bodied males of the colony who were liable for military service. They were obligated to take up arms—even if those arms were barely able to inflict harm on the enemy—and they were required to assemble at least once a year to drill and practise. More often than not those assemblies were an occasion for precious little training and a day (and night) of drunken shenanigans in the town centre or on the parade field. The sedentary militia were also organized into local regiments, usually "commanded" by a colonel whose only real qualification for the position was that he could afford to pay for some of the accoutrements or uniforms that the men might don when needed for service.

The sedentary regiments provided the "flank companies" that were authorized by the legislature of Upper Canada in March 1812 at the urging of Isaac Brock. These flank companies were formed of men from sedentary regiments who volunteered for additional training and drill. They were fully equipped and paraded eight days a month for up to six months. As Brock explained it, the role of the companies was "to have in constant readiness, a force of loyal, brave and Respectable Young Men, so far instructed to enable the government, on any emergency, to engraft such portions of the militia as may be necessary." The men were formed into independent companies to fight alongside other units—provincials, militia, or regulars—or to fight independently. Many Upper Canadian regiments, such as the Lincoln Militia, formed flank companies, as did a number of regiments in Lower Canada and the Atlantic colonies. The sedentary militia were usually not uniformed, although officers and sergeants were expected to acquire uniforms similar to those worn by the British, and they encouraged their men to at least dress alike. Although few took the Canadian sedentary militia seriously as a fighting force, these soldiers did occasionally surprise both the Americans and the British with displays of courage and fighting ability.

—m—

UPPER CANADA WAS IN A FRIGHTENINGLY VULNERABLE POSITION at the outbreak of the War of 1812. The war would have been quickly lost had it not been for two men: the incompetent Brigadier-General William Hull, in charge of the U.S.'s westernmost forces, and the daring Major-General Isaac Brock, commander of the British and Canadian forces in Upper Canada. Brock was born on the island of Guernsey in 1769, the eighth son in his family. He followed three older brothers into the army in 1785, joining the 8th Regiment of Foot as an ensign. In 1797 he purchased a lieutenant-colonelcy and command of the 49th Regiment of Foot. In 1802 Brock's regiment was transferred to the Canadas. As fighting broke out once again between Britain and France after the collapse of the Peace of Amiens, Brock tried desperately to get himself back to the Continent. He grew increasingly frustrated and discouraged in Canada, but he was needed in the colony, and was given rapid promotion to major-general and command of the all-important garrison at Quebec. There he also became Sir George Prevost's chief military commander. When the lieutenant-governor of Upper Canada, Francis Gore, was called back to England in 1811, Brock was sent to Upper Canada to replace him as chief administrator, thus giving him both military command and civil authority.

Brock first thought that defence of Upper Canada was impossible, but he was a good tactician and a charismatic leader. He decided that in the event of war with the United States, a well-prepared defence and a quick foray into the U.S., south or west of Lake Erie, might completely frustrate American ambitions. He set about rebuilding or strengthening fortifications and military structures that dated back as far as the Seven Years' War. He organized the militia flank companies and also cultivated relationships with Indian leaders such as Tecumseh, knowing how vital their support was going to be.

His chief opponent in the west was William Hull, whose headquarters were in Detroit. Hull had been reluctant to take the assignment in the first place, and this became obvious in his hesitancy during the first weeks of the war. On July 12, 1812, he and two thousand of his men crossed the Detroit River and occupied Sandwich (now Windsor). He issued a declaration calling all who favoured the republican cause to his side and warning all others not to take up arms against him. The occupation and this declaration disheartened some of the Canadian militia in the region, who melted away in the face of a supposedly superior force. But Hull did little else except wait for surrender.

Brock quickly seized the initiative, ordering Charles Roberts to attack the American post at Michilimackinac. Roberts mounted his little expedition with about six hundred British, Indians, and Canadian militia. The fort's defenders were not even aware that war had been declared and so were taken completely by surprise. The move succeeded in both cutting American supply lines to the upper Great Lakes and emboldening the Indians and Canadian militia in western Upper Canada. Tecumseh and his warriors then cut Hull's supply lines and forced him back across the Detroit River. Brock decided to strike quickly. With three hundred men of his own and six hundred of Tecumseh's, he crossed after Hull, laid siege, and forced Hull and his two thousand men to surrender. This quick victory and the massacre of an American garrison at Fort Dearborn severely undermined American morale while greatly boosting the British cause in Upper Canada.

Hull's effort to roll up the British and Canadians from west to east flew in the face of all military logic and the entire history of warfare on the Great Lakes and in the St. Lawrence Valley. What the Americans ought to have done at the very start was to try to cut Upper and Lower Canada off from each other, via the Niagara frontier, at Kingston, or at Montreal. In early September 1813 they finally tried the first of these options. U.S. General Stephen Van Rensselaer was a militia man who had been placed in charge of the American troops on the Niagara Peninsula. His appointment had been a cause of great dissatisfaction among U.S. regular officers, who resented having a part-time soldier in command. And Van Rensselaer was as ponderous and hesitant as Hull. He took weeks to build up his forces on the eastern bank of the Niagara River, earning the subtle rebuke from his commanding officer, General Henry Dearborn, that if he did not get on with an attack across the Niagara River, the Americans could not "calculate on possessing Upper Canada before winter sets in."

Throughout the fall Brock watched the American preparations. He had about 1,500 regulars and Canadian militia from Lincoln and York counties and 250 Indians to Van Rensselaer's 6,300, of whom

3,650 were regulars. Brock's command was located at Fort George, in present-day Niagara-on-the-Lake, near Lake Ontario. He seems to have thought that the main American attack would be directed at that point, but on the night of October 12, the Americans tried to cross the river below Niagara Falls. The attempt was a disaster of disorganization made worse by the rough waters of the roiling river as it emerged from the Niagara Gorge. But Brock remained fixated on the notion that the American crossing would take place near Lake Ontario. He was wrong. The next night the Americans tried again, this time north of the falls, at Queenston.

Queenston was defended by about 350 men under Captain James B. Dennis. When American boats suddenly appeared out of the dark, British cannon at Vrooman's Point, near Queenston, opened fire on them. Dennis and his men rushed to the riverbank. Badly outnumbered, they lost their cannon to the Americans and were pushed back to the village. The Americans scrambled up the heights overlooking Queenston. The skirmishing between Dennis's men and the Americans continued as Brock, alerted by the cannon fire, galloped toward Queenston with as many men as he could quickly gather. The remainder of the Fort George garrison followed under the command of Major-General Roger Sheaffe. When Brock arrived at Queenston, he immediately took command and gathered a small force of Dennis's men for a desperate charge up the heights to recover the British guns. Brandishing his sword, he was immediately spotted by an American sharpshooter, who shot him dead.

After Brock was killed there was a lull in the fighting. The Americans were atop the heights, but they had suffered heavy casualties and were running low on supplies. The New York State militia, who were supposed to reinforce the original attackers, refused to cross the river, as was their right under state law (the militia of each state was governed by the laws of that state). On the British side it took several hours for Sheaffe to gather the men from Fort George and those streaming in from adjacent counties and villages. When his forces were strong enough, he led them up the slopes to confront the

Americans. A British charge against the by now completely demoralized Americans killed and wounded about five hundred. The rest, close to a thousand, surrendered. Brock was dead, but there would be no American takeover of Upper Canada—until the spring at least.

—⁂—

FOR THE MOST PART the Canadian fencible regiments saw little action during those early battles in 1812. The great bulk of the troops fighting in Canada in the first year of the war were British regulars, helped by their Indian allies and contingents of both embodied and sedentary militia. The Indians, especially those under Tecumseh, were very effective, but in the British effort to capture Fort Meigs in January 1813, they proved to have little patience for siege warfare, and the effort failed when most of Tecumseh's men melted away. The experience of the Glengarry Light Infantry Fencibles in the first year of the war was perhaps typical of the engagements that the Canadian regiments were involved in.

The Glengarries, headquartered at Quebec in the summer of 1812, were still in the process of recruiting when word arrived that war with the Americans had broken out. The recruiting parties were immediately recalled and the regiment began to concentrate while planning began for a move to Upper Canada to take part in its defence. On October 16, the regiment—now eight companies (about six hundred strong)—left Quebec for the long march westward. During the march the Glengarries successfully dislodged a small force of about forty New York Volunteers who had settled into a blockhouse on the south bank of the St. Lawrence River not far from Cornwall. After a brief fight on the night of November 22, 1812, the Americans surrendered and were taken prisoner. They suffered at least three killed, while the Glengarries took no casualties. The Glengarries then settled in for the winter with detachments near Cornwall, Prescott, and Kingston guarding the river and the road that connected Upper Canada with

Montreal. By Christmas the regiment had lost some 125 men, with 31 dead from disease or accidents, 66 desertions, and 25 discharged as unfit for service. The effective strength of the regiment as the year ended was 550, all ranks.

The second year of the war opened with minor British victories at Frenchtown (in present-day Ohio) on January 22 and at Ogdensburg, New York, on February 22. There the Glengarries joined the Newfoundland Fencibles, a detachment of the British 8th Regiment of Foot, and local militia in the attack. In the course of the action one company of the Glengarries, led by Captain Jenkins and accompanied by Upper Canadian militia, assaulted an American battery of seven heavy guns guarded by two hundred infantry. The history of the Glengarries describes the subsequent action this way: "advancing as rapidly as the deep snow and the exhausted state . . . of his men would admit, he [Jenkins] ordered a charge, and had not proceeded many paces when his left arm was broken to pieces by a grape shot." Jenkins forged ahead, then was shot again, in his right arm. He kept going until the pain and exhaustion overcame him and he fell, badly wounded but not dead. His company kept going but the steady fire of the Americans took its toll and they soon turned back, having suffered two killed and twelve wounded.

The Americans now began to take the war much more seriously. Changes in command, including promotion of General William Henry Harrison (governor of Kentucky) to command of the U.S. troops in the west, further mustering of trained troops and supplies, and a new strategy aimed at capturing Kingston, led to a reinvigorated American offensive in the spring of 1813. On April 27 an American force of 1,700 men commanded by Dearborn and Zebulon Pike (the discoverer of Pike's Peak in the Colorado Rockies) invaded York (Toronto). The British garrison, commanded by Sheaffe, withdrew to the east with his regulars, while the Canadian militia dispersed into the countryside. The British blew up their ammunition dump inside the fort and burned a ship being built in the harbour. Pike was killed in the explosion and the angry Americans burned the town in reprisal. One company of the Glengarries was present at York. It saw no action, but when the main magazine was blown up, two men were killed and most of the regiment's weapons were lost.

On May 27 a force of 7,000 Americans easily captured Fort George, forcing British commander John Vincent and his 1,700 men to retreat westward along the south shore of Lake Ontario toward Burlington Heights, near the site of present-day Hamilton. The Glengarries were among the troops that General Vincent selected to cover the British withdrawal. He later wrote: "This movement was admirably covered by the Glengarry Light Infantry, joined by a detachment of the Royal Newfoundland Regiment and militia, which commenced skirmishing with the enemy's riflemen who were advancing through the brush-wood." The cost was high: the three companies of the Glengarries at Fort George lost more than half their number and much of their equip-ment, and when they mustered three days later at Forty Mile Creek, they could count only five officers and fifty-eight other ranks.

The Americans were slow to follow the retreating British and Canadian forces, so Vincent halted at Stoney Creek and waited for them to advance. It took the Americans the better part of a week to get organized and on the road. They encamped near Stoney Creek on June 5 with two brigades totalling more than 3,500 men, but Vincent's adjutant, Colonel John Harvey, learned of the American disposition and even their password from a local scout. Harvey convinced Vincent to allow him to make a risky night attack. At 2:00 AM Harvey's men broke into the middle of the American camp and bayoneted dozens of sleeping troops. They captured the American field guns and took both brigade commanders prisoner before the Americans rallied. As dawn broke, Harvey and his men withdrew. They had suffered heavy casual-ties—23 killed, 134 wounded, and 5 missing—while the Americans had lost 155 killed, wounded, or missing, but the American drive had been halted and they withdrew to Fort George.

The most important American victory of the year came at Moravian Town on October 5, 1813. The engagement followed the defeat of a British naval force at Put-in-Bay, on Lake Erie, on September 10 by American naval commander Oliver H. Perry. The American victory gave the United States complete control of Lake Erie and rendered untenable British General Henry Proctor's position at Detroit. Proctor and his troops, accompanied by Tecumseh and his warriors, burned the fort at Detroit and withdrew across the Detroit River toward Niagara, pursued by the Americans commanded by William Henry Harrison. Proctor's mixed column of Indians, civilians, British soldiers, and Canadian militiamen and their families made the best time they could through the rough country along the Thames River. But Harrison had three thousand troops reinforced by five hundred Kentucky cavalrymen. He caught the British and Indian forces at Moravian Town and shattered them. Tecumseh was killed; Proctor took flight toward Niagara. The British forces lost more than 600 killed or wounded for just 29 American casualties. The way east lay open to Harrison, but instead of taking advantage of this decisive victory, he merely burned Moravian Town and returned to Detroit.

Harrison's victory set up a two-pronged American assault on Montreal. From the south came General Wade Hampton, while General James Wilkinson, with eight thousand men, set out from Sackets Harbor to march down the St. Lawrence. Hampton's forces were turned back by an all-Canadian force led by Salaberry at Chateauguay on October 26. Salaberry then rushed westward with the Voltigeurs and the Canadian Fencibles to block Wilkinson's men from advancing on Montreal. Wilkinson, unaware of Hampton's withdrawal, was himself being pursued by a force of some 1,200 British regulars consisting mostly of the 49th and 89th Regiments of Foot under the command of Lieutenant-Colonel Joseph Morrison. Morrison fought a short and indecisive engagement with a rearguard of the Americans at Hoople Creek, near Morrisburg, Ontario, on November 10 before joining up with Salaberry's troops. The following day Morrison drew up his forces at Crysler's Farm and waited for the Americans to come on. They did, in wave after wave, but even though they outnumbered Morrison's men about three to one, they were committed piecemeal to battle and suffered heavy casualties.

The battle itself was a saw-off, but after three hours the Americans withdrew across the border. They had lost about four hundred men killed, wounded, or taken prisoner; more importantly, they had abandoned their drive on Montreal. The Canadian Fencibles paid a heavy toll that day, with about a third of their men killed or wounded. The Battle of Crysler's Farm put an end to the American threat to Montreal in 1813 but it did not end the year's fighting. Skirmishing continued across the Niagara River until December 18, when five hundred British troops crossed the river, captured and destroyed Fort Niagara, and then burned a number of American settlements, including Buffalo.

What were these battles like for the soldiers fighting them? The relatively small size of the engagements of the War of 1812—never more than ten thousand protagonists in any one battle—makes them pale in comparison to the massive clashes of arms that the Napoleonic Wars had produced in continental Europe. But for the individual soldier, the sights, sounds, smells, and fear of battle could not have been much different from what his counterparts were exposed to at Austerlitz or Waterloo. One of the best descriptions is given by Donald E. Graves in his book about the Battle of Chippawa, which took place on July 5, 1814:

> [T]he soldier often entered combat hungry, and usually tired after a long march. Blinded by powder smoke, packed in tightly crowded ranks, watching round shot bouncing towards him but unable to move, suffering from raging thirst brought on by tension and the necessity of biting into cartridges containing bitter black powder, seeing men killed and maimed around him, the infantryman stood, fought and died. Not the worst of the business were the unnerving sounds peculiar to battle: the deadly "hissing," "whizzing," "sighing," or "whistling" of passing round shot; the "rattle" of canister bullets on rows of bayonets; the ominous "thud" of musket balls impacting on human flesh, followed by the screams, moans, and pleas of the wounded and dying.

At the end of the year, the Americans might have taken stock of the campaigning in Upper Canada since the outbreak of war eighteen months earlier. Essentially they had gained nothing—all efforts to take and hold vital ground had failed. They had captured and burned York, but without naval control of Lake Ontario they had been forced to withdraw. They had cleared the British and the Indians from Detroit but had failed to take advantage of the victory at Moravian Town. Hampton's hesitant thrust toward Montreal had been stopped by a handful of Canadian regulars and militia, and Wilkinson had chosen to abandon his advance on Montreal after the draw at Crysler's farm.

Now thousands of British regulars began to pour into Quebec with the close of the Peninsular campaign in Europe; Napoleon's collapse after his disastrous march on Moscow had given the British an opportunity to send even more troops to America. In the meantime, the Royal Navy's mastery of the Atlantic was wreaking havoc on American trade and undermining what little support the war had in the first place in New England. Hesitant commanders, reluctant state militias, and the fierce defence of Upper Canada by British regulars, Canadian fencibles and militia, and their Indian allies offset the Americans' two main advantages—numerical superiority and proximity to Canada.

In the spring of 1814, the Americans renewed their effort to take Upper Canada. American Major-General Jacob Brown, based at Sackets Harbor, built up a large force of well-trained and disciplined troops over the winter of 1813–14 and then set about to attack Kingston. The U.S. secretary of war instructed him to make a direct attack across the lake, but Brown was reluctant to do so because of British naval strength. Having been given two plans—one for a direct attack on Kingston and the other for an expedition via the Niagara frontier—Brown chose the latter and set out in late June with a force of more than 3,500 troops. The Americans easily captured Fort Erie, on the Canadian side of the Niagara River. But British Major-General Phineas Riall rushed forward with 1,500 regulars, 300 militia, and 300 Indians from the

Grand River Reserve and attacked the Americans at Chippawa, on the Canadian side of the river about 3 kilometres south of Niagara Falls. In the past the Americans had usually fallen away when facing a large agglomeration of British regulars, but not this time. Riall suffered a stinging defeat and was forced to withdraw toward Fort George. Brown then ordered General Winfield Scott to push ahead with a brigade toward Queenston; two other American brigades followed. Unknown to Brown, a force of British regulars under the command of Lieutenant-General Gordon Drummond had rushed from Kingston to reinforce the contingent at Fort George. Drummond had brought the 8th and 89th Regiments of Foot and the Royal Scots. Another group of five hundred British regulars based at Fort Niagara also headed for the area while Riall reinforced his men with contingents from the Glengarries, the New Brunswick Fencibles, and a battalion of local militia.

The British set up their defences on Lundy's Lane, a road running westward from the portage road along the river. In the late afternoon of a hot July 25th, with the thunder of the nearby falls as a back-drop, the two armies clashed. The battle, close and bitter, raged until almost midnight, with first one side, then the other holding sway. Just after midnight the Americans broke. Brown pulled back to Fort Erie, Drummond close on his heels. But the British were unable to drive the Americans across the river, and they remained in possession of the fort until the end of the war. In early January 1815, word arrived from Europe that a peace agreement had been reached on December 24, ending the war. The Treaty of Ghent stipulated that the status quo ante bellum would prevail—the boundaries between the U.S. and the British colonies would return to where they were at the outbreak of war. Canada would remain Canada, and British, for now.

—ᴍ—

THE WAR OF 1812 was Canada's most important war. Although the young country was not even a country, technically speaking, but five

British colonies scattered along the northern boundary of the United States, its population (for the most part) did not want to be forced into the new republic. In the English-speaking colonies a strong Loyalist tradition still existed, and with it a belief that British life and politics had much to offer Canada if the colonies were to enjoy a stable and prosperous future. In Lower Canada the dominant feeling was probably that here was another war among *les anglais* that French Quebecers ought to avoid. But other French Canadians feared that an American conquest would quickly negate the rights of language and religion that the British had conceded in 1774. Better the devil you knew than the devil you didn't! As for the Americans who had settled in Upper Canada, the war forced them to choose between a sullen neutrality and expulsion to the U.S. Most chose the former.

The largest number of the colonists—both English- and French-speaking Canadians—fought, and some died, to maintain their ties with Britain. They fought in the regular Canadian regiments—the Canadian Fencibles, the Royal Newfoundland Fencibles, the New Brunswick Fencibles, the Glengarry Light Infantry Fencibles, and the Voltigeurs Canadiens—formed immediately before and just as the war commenced. They also fought in the embodied and sedentary regiments that stood alongside both the British and Canadian regulars. Throughout, their Indian allies helped immensely, though more at the start of the war than at the close. At all times, steadfast and well-trained British regular troops and British commanders provided core strength for the resistance against the invaders.

There is much discussion among Canadian military historians about the birth of the "militia myth" in the War of 1812. The myth alleges that it was the Canadian militiaman, grabbing his rifle and mustering to his cause, who drove the Americans out. That is certainly not true. But what is true is that large numbers of Canadians who either served in or aided the military made it very clear that they did not want to become American. And that is no myth at all.

It is hard to know what the War of 1812 contributed to the regimental tradition in Canada. All of the regular Canadian regiments were

disbanded within just a few years of the end of the war. Succeeding decades of peace with the Americans created an opportunity for thorough
revision of Canada's military forces, but Canadians then, as now, were
very reluctant to spend money on defence when there was no obvious
threat. Thus no regiment today can trace an unbroken line back to the
stalwarts of 1812. But when Canadians began slowly, even ponder-
ously, to rearm to meet the new threats posed by the Crimean War and
the U.S. Civil War in the late 1850s and early 1860s, some of the more
permanent regiments created then sought to draw on the history and
traditions of the earliest Canadian regiments of the War of 1812. It was
obvious to them that an effective fighting force should be built on the
by then well-established convention of unique units bringing local men
together, each under their own banner, with uniforms, traditions, and
customs designed to engender regimental pride.

CHAPTER FOUR

BRITANNIA DEPARTS: CANADA'S NEW REGIMENTS EMERGE

[The] fire of the now pursuing Fenians became hotter than ever, and the [Queen's Own Rifles] volunteers being crowded up in a narrow road, presented a fine mark to their rifles, causing our poor fellows to fall on all sides. . . . For the first two or three hundred yards it was a regular panic. . . .

—Account of the Battle of Ridgeway, June 2, 1866, from the official history of the Queen's Own Rifles

THE STAGGERING COST OF THE NAPOLEONIC WARS placed immense burdens on the British treasury; after 1815 one of the U.K.'s main objectives was to save money through drastic cuts to its army and navy. Spending on the colonies had never been popular at Westminster and was even less so in this time of extreme parsimony. Britain began to pull its troops from North America almost immediately after Waterloo and aimed to seek accommodation with the United States wherever it could. When a British commission was appointed in the mid-1820s to examine the costs of building a truly effective defence in the Canadas, the elaborate scheme it came up with would have cost billions of dollars in today's funds. The idea was "laughed at by Parliament," in the words of historian John Grodzinski. The magnificent Rideau Canal was built, connecting Kingston, on Lake Ontario, to Ottawa, but that was all. When uprisings by rebels in both Upper and Lower Canada in 1837–38 were put down with relative ease by a handful of British regulars, aided by some local militia, the Colonial Office began to adopt an accommodating position toward political reform in the Canadas. By 1849 the Canadian colonists were electing their own governments and seeing to their own internal affairs. Britain was then moving seriously toward completely free trade; colonies became even more burdensome in the minds of large numbers of liberal British thinkers both inside and outside Parliament. In 1851 there were only 8,800 British troops in both Canada and the Maritime colonies, and the outbreak of the Crimean War with Russia in 1853 prompted the British to withdraw even more troops. By 1861 there were only about 3,300 redcoats in North America. Canadians were finally forced to take their own defence somewhat more seriously than they had since 1814.

The Canadian militia system that was in place in the 1830s and early 1840s was fundamentally unchanged from the pre–War of 1812 era. Even though Upper and Lower Canada had been joined together by Westminster in 1840—and a new Militia Act passed for the new United Province of Canada—the colonial defences still depended on a sedentary militia (which existed more in imagination than in reality) and a formed militia virtually untrained and equipped with obsolete weapons. In the mid-1840s changes to the Canadian Militia Act called for the establishment of an "active" militia, to consist of some four thousand volunteers who would be trained and equipped to modern standards, but almost nothing was done to follow through. Then, with the outbreak of the Crimean War, the Canadian legislature established a commission in late 1854 to examine the state of the colonies' defences. It recommended that an active militia be established with a strength of four thousand men, with cavalry, artillery, and infantry, and modern weapons and equipment, who would follow "a course of prescribed training."

This time there were major changes to the militia system. The Militia Act of 1855 divided Canada into eighteen militia districts, nine in Canada West (Ontario) and nine in Canada East (Quebec), which were themselves divided into regiments. Battalion and company divisions were set within the regiments. All males between the ages of eighteen and sixty were deemed to be part of a compulsory-service militia (the old sedentary militia). A voluntary or active militia was also created with sixteen troops of cavalry, seven field troops of artillery, and fifty companies of riflemen, not to exceed five thousand men in all. Each of the volunteer units was allotted twenty days of annual training with pay. No provision was made for uniforms, which were to be purchased by the volunteers themselves. As Grodzinski puts it, "the volunteer movement was the foundation of the modern Canadian Militia." It was also, in a very real sense, the birth of the Canadian army of today, since most of the regiments that emerged from the reforms of 1855 are still alive in one form or another.

In early 1861 a major political convulsion rocked North America and led to a renewed burst of military preparedness in the British American colonies. Republican Abraham Lincoln was elected president of the United States in November 1860, and talk of secession in a number of southern states broke out almost immediately. By the late spring of 1861 the United States was at war with itself. Britain sided with the Confederacy for reasons almost solely rooted in power politics and economics. A southern raid into Vermont from Quebec, the stopping of the British packet *Trent* by the Union Navy in 1861, and the arrest of two Confederate agents on board that ship greatly increased tensions along the border. In the Maritimes and in Canada, new regiments of active militia units began to appear in large numbers.

In Nova Scotia, the Halifax Volunteer Rifles were formed on May 14, 1860. They were a forerunner of today's Halifax Rifles, a reserve infantry regiment. The New Brunswick Regiment of Yeomen Cavalry, established on January 3, 1866, is the ancestor of the 8th Canadian Hussars, an existing reserve armoured regiment. In Canada East seven new regiments appeared, the oldest being the 1st Battalion Volunteer Militia Rifles of Canada, founded on November 17, 1859, and perpetuated today by the Canadian Grenadier Guards. Only one of those seven, the Voltigeurs of Quebec, established on March 7, 1862, and perpetuated today by Les Voltigeurs de Québec, had a substantial Francophone contingent. In Canada West nineteen new regiments sprang up between 1860 and 1866. The first was the 2nd Battalion Volunteer Militia Rifles of Canada, founded on April 26, 1860, which shortly after became the 2nd Battalion, Queen's Own Rifles of Canada.

—m—

THE FIRST OF THESE NEW MILITIA REGIMENTS (originally labelled the First Battalion Volunteer Militia Rifles of Canada) was established on November 17, 1859, in Montreal. It had a strength of thirty-seven officers and six hundred other ranks. Drill parade was held once a week over the winter and more often in summer. Sometimes in summer, the battalion turned out to drill at 4 and 5 AM, the men then going off to their jobs for the rest of the day. When the Prince of Wales (who later became King Edward VII) visited Montreal in 1860, the battalion's name was changed to the First (or Prince of Wales) Regiment of Volunteer Rifles of the Canadian Militia, now the Grenadier Guards. The regiment saw no action during the Fenian crisis of 1866, though it was called out several times. On one occasion the regiment was sent to Ormstown, southwest of Montreal. The regimental historian recorded:

> The men were in heavy marching order, the roads were deep in mud all the way; but eighty wagons with breakfast awaited, and the village was agog with a rumour that the Victoria Rifles had been engaged and literally cut to pieces (it was only a rumour!). . . . The Battalion finally reached its destination, Ormstown, between seven and eight in the evening, tired and soaked to the skin, for the rain had persisted all day.

Mud, filth, and fatigue are the inevitable lot of anyone who chooses the infantry as a vocation, part- or full-time. But the experience of these militia men from Montreal, and similar ones elsewhere in the budding military formations of Canada, began to shape the regimental traditions of the new Dominion.

Ironically, government parsimony also played a role. New regiments such as the 13th Battalion, Volunteer Militia of Canada, forerunner to the Royal Hamilton Light Infantry, were given licence to decide for themselves what they would wear in the field, because although the government authorized these volunteer units and armed and paid them while on service, they would not pay for much else in the early years. Thus the officers of the new formations—sometimes the commanding officer himself—designed their own uniforms, caps, badges, a regimental colour, even their own "web gear" (straps or vests that soldiers wear to carry canteens, extra ammunition, etc.). Designs were usually chosen that might allow them to lay claim to the military traditions of their county, town, or parish, or that identified them with a historical regiment or soldier who had fought in their region.

Almost always, these strictly local symbols were combined with imperial antecedents so that a connection might also be claimed to ancient British military customs as well. It was tradition by association, although in reality it was instant history. And as the British Empire reached its heyday around the world—an empire of "God, gold, and glory"—creating and maintaining a British-rooted regimental tradition was a tangible way in which otherwise dull Canadians might share in that great and glorious adventure. In seeking to make themselves unique in some way, the local militiamen attempted to emulate the traditions of some of Britain's oldest and most famous regiments. Like the aspiring Highlanders of Montreal, they emphasized their distinction from one another and—most importantly—from the Americans by creating traditions partly rooted in local history, partly in long-ago struggles such as the American Revolution and especially the War of 1812, and partly in famous British campaigns.

All the Canadian militia regiments were at first styled as rifle regiments, and indeed they were eventually all equipped with rifles instead of smoothbore muskets. In Britain the Rifle Brigade, which was not a brigade formation but the proper name of a venerable regiment, was outfitted in green uniforms instead of the traditional red. Thus a few Canadian regiments—the Queen's Own being one—adopted green jackets (and still use green mess dress). In Montreal the 5th Battalion of the Royal Light Infantry of Montreal, established in 1862, had a strong Scottish component among its officers and many of its soldiers. Over the next four decades it evolved as a Highland or kilted regiment in reaction to the desire of its members to link with the fighting traditions of those Scottish clans who had maintained strong ties to the British monarchy during the eighteenth century. By 1900 the regiment had adopted the full uniform of the U.K.'s Black Watch, including kilt and tartan, jacket, and bonnet. Only the badges and sporran were different.

Battle always lies at the heart of regimental tradition and most Canadian militia regiments saw virtually no action at all until the Northwest Rebellion of 1885. A very few, such as the Queen's Own, were first blooded fighting to defend Canada from the Fenians.

—m—

THE IRISH REVOLUTIONARY BROTHERHOOD—the Fenian Brotherhood, or simply the Fenians—were virtually all battle-hardened veterans who had fought in the Union armies during the American Civil War. They were usually led by officers who had command experience under fire. Their initial aim was to raise a volunteer force to fight the British in Ireland, but given the strength of the Royal Navy, this plan was completely impractical. The Fenians then decided to invade Canada instead. Their aim was twofold—to force the British government to reinforce British garrisons in Canada, thus possibly withdrawing troops from Ireland, and even to capture Canada, or enough of it to trade for Irish independence. The Fenians were not officially supported by the American government, but even without such backing there were enough of them—potentially several tens of thousands in large northern cities such as Boston, New York, and Chicago—to pose a significant danger to Canada. The Fenians struck their first blow in April 1866 with a small raid on New Brunswick. On the morning of June 1, 1866, they returned, this time to the Niagara Peninsula.

John O'Neill had been an officer in the Union forces in the U.S. Civil War. He now styled himself a lieutenant-colonel in the Fenian army. In the early hours of June 1 he led eight hundred to a thousand men from Tennessee, Kentucky, New York, Indiana, and Ohio across the Niagara River in four scows towed by hired tugboats. They landed on the Canadian side of the river near Frenchman's Creek, not far from Fort Erie. They quickly entered the little town and coerced the mayor and the town council into providing provisions; within hours the alarm went out across the Niagara region and as far as Toronto.

A Fenian incursion had been expected for some weeks; in late May a warning was telegraphed to militia units from Kingston to Windsor. By the time O'Neill's men crossed into Canada, a large force consisting of two British regiments—the 47th at Toronto and the 16th at London—and several Canadian militia regiments was ready for action under the overall command of British Major-General George Napier. On the news of the invasion Napier deployed his forces in two groups. One contingent, commanded by Lieutenant-Colonel Alfred Booker, a British regular officer, consisted of the 2nd Battalion of Toronto's Queen's Own Rifles with 480 men, the Caledonia Rifle Company, the York Rifle Company, and the 13th Battalion from Hamilton. They would confront the invaders directly. The other—the British regulars and a collection of militia regiments under Colonel George Peacocke, another British regular officer—would act as a secondary blocking force should O'Neill succeed in breaking out of the Niagara Peninsula.

Booker took his forces by rail to Port Colborne, on the north shore of Lake Erie, about 12 kilometres west of the small town of Ridgeway.

There he met a messenger from Peacocke who was superior to him in rank and who ordered him to proceed by rail directly to Ridgeway; Peacocke's plan was to rendezvous with Booker at Stevensville, then close in on the Fenians. Booker and his men boarded the train for Ridgeway, arriving at about 6:00 AM on June 2. He did not then know that Peacocke's force had been delayed by provision and supply problems. But O'Neill had caught wind of the plan for a hookup of the two forces and decided to attack Booker's column before it could reach the meeting point. He marched his men southwest and took up a position along a ridge north of Bertie Road, which ran at right angles to Booker's line of march.

The Fenians were well placed to block Booker's advance. O'Neill put the main body of his riflemen at the base of the ridge, with lookouts on top and skirmishers on both flanks and forward of Bertie Road. As the sun rose in the sky, the new day got hotter. Keeping still, the Fenians waited in the grass and behind trees and bushes as Booker's men walked on. Booker's men were in high spirits, but they were not prepared for a real fight. Their heavy woollen uniforms were completely unsuitable for a warm June morning, and they were short of food and wagons to carry provisions and supplies.

Booker was the only man with a horse. He rode at the front with the Queen's Own right behind him. Local farmers warned him that O'Neill's men were close by but he ignored them. After marching about 3 kilometres north from Ridgeway, Booker's scouts reported that they had spotted O'Neill's force. In classic Napoleonic style, Booker ordered the Queen's Own to extend itself into a line of battle while the reserve companies stayed behind on the road. The Queen's Own then began to move forward abreast in a line astride the road. As they closed with the Fenians, the first shots rang out. The Queen's Own pressed on. They drove the Fenian skirmishers from their positions along Bertie Road back toward the main Fenian force. But the Fenian rifle fire was fierce and the Queen's Own began to run out of ammunition. Booker ordered them to pull back and the 13th Battalion to replace them. The advance continued. Booker ordered the 10th Highland Company of the Queen's Own into the woods east of the Fenian positions to clear out snipers and skirmishers and perhaps to outflank the Fenians.

Thus far in the battle, the green Canadian militiamen, many of them students, were performing very well. In fact, the Fenian skirmishers were taking flight. But then someone spotted a handful of Fenians in the woods on stolen horses and mistook them for cavalry. A shout went up: "Prepare for cavalry." The eight companies of the Queen's Own, now in the second line, stopped their advance and tried to form a hollow square, a time-worn tactic for infantry to defend itself against cavalry. As they did so, some men from the 13th came running back in a panic, fearing a cavalry charge. But there were no cavalry.

As the Fenians realized what was happening, they turned on the Canadians and poured a devastating fire into their ranks. The Canadian formations quickly began to disintegrate. Some men thought a retreat had been ordered, others began to run in panic. Booker tried to rally his force but the momentum was gone. The official history of the Queen's Own records the next few minutes: "On re-forming, the reserve being too close to the skirmish line, [it] was ordered to retire, the left wing of the 13th who were in our rear, seeing our men retire and thinking that we were retreating, broke and retired in a panic, on seeing which our men also broke and ran." Fear ran through the ranks like a highly contagious disease. "On seeing the reserve in disorder, [1 and 2 companies of the Queen's Own] became demoralized and fled. The fire of the now pursuing Fenians became hotter than ever, and the volunteers being crowded up in a narrow road, presented a fine mark to their rifles, causing our poor fellows to fall on all sides. . . . For the first two or three hundred yards it was a regular panic, but after that the men fell into a walk, retiring in a very orderly manner, but completely crestfallen."

O'Neill and his men, hard-pressed until only a few moments before, pursued the Canadians back to Ridgeway. Some of the Canadians stood and fought, but it was O'Neill who called off the attack within sight of the Ridgeway railway station. He and his men headed back to Fort Erie, where, after a skirmish with less than a hundred militiamen from Welland and Dunnville, he returned to the U.S. the following day. Booker's men suffered ten killed overall, with some thirty-six wounded; seven of the dead were Queen's Own, as were twenty-one of the wounded.

The Toronto *Globe* recorded the regiment's return to Toronto by steamer late on June 4, 1866:

> Owing to unavoidable delay and an adverse wind, the steamer did not reach her landing as early as was expected. Towards five o'clock, however, several hearses, and stretchers borne by soldiers of the 47th Regiment, were brought to the wharf. Several members of the medical profession were in attendance to render any service in their power to the wounded soldiers. Before ten the steamer hove in sight, and shortly after came to her moorings. At one end of the vessel lay arranged together the rough coffins containing the dead. They were formed of rough pine timber, the name of the occupant being chalked on the cover.

The war between Canada and the Fenians was not a very large war, and no real threat to the newly emerging country. But the dead of that campaign were no less dead. Their blood nourished not only the roots of the soon-to-be Dominion of Canada but also the traditions of those regiments who had borne the brunt of the action.

—∾—

THE FENIAN THREAT OF 1866 was but one factor in a long list of political and economic reasons behind the final success of an initiative that was launched at the Charlottetown Conference, held September 1–9, 1864, to unite the British North American colonies. The new political entity—the Dominion of Canada—came into existence on July 1, 1867. The Militia Act adopted by the new Parliament of Canada in 1868 did not fundamentally alter the structure of the militia, it simply consolidated all of Canada's military forces under the new Dominion Government at Ottawa. Within eighteen months of the passage of that act, ten more militia regiments were added to Canada's defences. Thus, by the end of the 1860s, there were at least thirty-eight active militia regiments in Canada. This was not an insubstantial number, but the quality, training, leadership, and equipment of these regiments varied widely.

Initially Canada included only Nova Scotia, New Brunswick, and the United Province of Canada. One of the major aims of this unification was to annex the vast Hudson's Bay Company lands, which stretched from northern Ontario to the Great Divide, before the Americans could somehow grab them. But the plans of Canadian prime minister John A. Macdonald went awry when the Métis population of the Red River area, led by Louis Riel, rebelled against the annexation in a largely bloodless coup in early December 1869, which delayed the transfer of the Hudson's Bay lands. Macdonald had no military means available of putting the rebellion down. There was no Canadian militia at Red River, while the militia in Ontario, Quebec, and the Maritimes were fundamentally untrained and did not have the logistical capability of getting themselves to Red River from Canada without using U.S. rail links to Minnesota. That the Americans would not allow. In fact, the Americans would not have been unpleased if the rebellion had succeeded. Macdonald was forced to ask Britain for help from its fast-shrinking regular garrison in Canada. The British agreed, but only if Macdonald entered into serious negotiations with Riel.

Macdonald had no choice, and in early 1870 those discussions began. At the same time, British Colonel Garnet Joseph Wolseley and the 60th Regiment of Foot, augmented by about three hundred Canadian militia from Ontario and Quebec, set out for Red River in May 1870. Travelling by lake and river and using difficult portage routes when necessary, the troops finally reached Red River at the end of August. Riel and some of his men fled before the red-coats could take control of the colony. Riel had won his main points when Macdonald agreed to most of his demands; as a consequence the province of Manitoba was joined to Canada by the Manitoba Act of May 1870, which had many of the Macdonald–Riel provisions built in. Wolseley and his men returned to Canada almost immediately after they arrived in Red River and joined the last contingent of British troops that left in 1871 (except for a small garrison that stayed to guard the Royal Navy base at Halifax). The Canadian volunteers who stayed at Red River were augmented by another two hundred or so militia from Canada in the fall of 1871. This group, known as the Manitoba Force, was responsible for all law and order in the Red River area until the arrival of the North West Mounted Police in 1874.

—⁓—

THE DEPARTURE OF BRITISH TROOPS FROM CANADA in 1871 caused the Canadian government to finally begin to seriously examine the question of how Canada might defend itself in the ever-decreasing likelihood of an attack from the United States. It was ever-decreasing because both Britain and the U.S. were eager to mend fences after the Civil War, especially since the United States was rapidly beginning to rival, and in some cases even outstrip, Britain as an industrial and trading power. Both countries sought to settle all outstanding diplomatic claims in the negotiations leading to the Treaty of Washington in 1871 (at which John A. Macdonald acted as one of the British commissioners). Nonetheless, some military prudence was necessary; as a result, two batteries of garrison artillery were established at Kingston and Quebec City in the fall of 1871. These were permanent batteries, artillery schools, in fact, designed not simply to guard these two important garrisons but also to instruct the militia in the "science" of artillery. These two batteries were the tiny beginning of the "permanent" or "regular" force—today's professional, full-time Canadian Forces. In 1893 they would become known as The Royal Canadian Artillery.

Gunners, engineers, and armoured corps personnel are as much a part of the Canadian regimental tradition as infantry, but in a slightly different way. When the British army adopted the battalion as its basic infantry fighting unit in the late nineteenth century, regiments ceased to exist as actual military formations but continued as the family framework of individual battalions. For the other branches of what is today called the "combat arms"—artillery, cavalry, and engineers—the regiment continued to be an actual military formation. Thus in Canada the 1st Combat Engineer Regiment (1CER) and 2nd Regiment, Royal Canadian Horse Artillery (2RCHA) retain the term "regiment"—with all its traditional connotations—while also being organized as a regiment for both administrative and operational purposes.

By the mid-1870s the Canadian militia consisted of about four dozen battalions or regiments across Canada. Thus several thousand Canadian men would meet once a week at a local armoury or drill hall, sometimes at night, sometimes on a Saturday afternoon. They donned ill-fitting uniforms and undertook some rudimentary marching, drilling, and target shooting with obsolete rifles or even muskets. They learned when, where, and how to salute. Then they went home, back to their often mundane civilian occupations. City armouries were usually built of brick and concrete, generally close to downtown, and contained a drill hall, an indoor rifle range, offices, and separate messes for officers and other ranks. In small towns or rural areas the local drill hall was usually built by public subscription and was far less imposing. But their purpose was the same as for the more ornate structures in the cities—to store the weapons, provide a place for training and practice, and serve as the centre for regimental social functions.

Like the buildings that housed them, the regiments also differed in the state of their uniforms and accoutrements, their bands, and the frequency and quality of their social gatherings. Simply put, those regiments fortunate enough to have a wealthy patron, usually the regimental commanding officer himself, fared far better than those that did not. Whatever the government would not pay for—usually everything that was not a military necessity such as arms and ammunition—was purchased for the regiment by the CO, from funds pooled by the officers, by local supporters, or by some combination of the three. If there were no funds for these extras, the regiment went without them.

Commanding officers were usually selected by the Department of Militia and Defence for their loyalty to the government party. They were not paid (other than the small stipend all militiamen received for their actual days of service, including the annual summer encampment), but the position was much sought after anyway because it carried a certain amount of prestige. In their appointment there was almost no thought given to military ability, leadership style, knowledge of tactics or weapons, and so forth. After all, what wars were the militia intended to fight? Young men joined the local regiment to have something to do in their spare time, or to attend the regiment's many balls or sporting events, especially shooting, or for the annual summer exercise, which promised shooting, marching, sleeping in tents on warm summer nights, and as much carousing as the more enterprising could organize. Militia life was especially glamorous over the Christmas holiday season, with Christmas parties, balls, skating parties, snowshoeing, sleigh rides, and New Year's levées. All these occasions bonded the men, built strong regimental ties, and established the local regiments as important institutions in their communities. None of them provided serious military training.

One of the best descriptions of the annual summer training exercise has been provided by historian Desmond Morton:

> At camp, militiamen slept in long lines of bell tents, each under his own greatcoat and a couple of the notoriously thin, moth-eaten militia blankets. Men were issued the traditional pound of beef and pound of bread, supplemented by a few ounces of tea, sugar, salt, vegetables, and whatever the colonel had the wealth

and generosity to purchase. No wonder camp canteens were popular and profitable. Training was simple and repetitious. Battalions drilled their men, mounted guards, marched to the ranges to fire thirty rounds from the well-worn Snider-Enfields and occasionally indulged in a sham battle.

With the exception of a very few officers and men, no one took the militia very seriously. Canada's defence against the Americans was sustained by being unobtrusive and accommodating. And who else was there to fear?

As early as 1880 Canada's minister of militia and defence Adolphe Caron began to consider a small but permanent force. In his mind there were two good reasons to do so. First, a permanent force would provide needed instruction to the part-time militia, and second, it created a whole new opportunity for patronage appointments. The model would be the artillery schools in Kingston and Quebec City that had been set up in 1871. In 1883 the government finally acknowledged that some sort of permanent, professional military force ought to be established, and a new Militia Act founded an Infantry School Corps (now the Royal Canadian Regiment)—consisting of three companies, one at Fredericton, New Brunswick, one at St. John's, Quebec, and one at Toronto—and a Cavalry School Corps (now the Royal Canadian Dragoons), based at Quebec City. Command of the Infantry School Corps was given to William Otter, a popular Canadian soldier who had seen action with the Queen's Own Rifles at Ridgeway and who had later commanded that regiment. The new units were created fundamentally as schools of instruction; but within less than two years, they would be at war.

CHAPTER FIVE

REBELLION AND WAR: CANADA'S REGIMENTS IN SASKATCHEWAN
AND SOUTH AFRICA

> We dared not return the fire as it would give us away. To lift one's head
> would mean sure death.
>
> —Royal Canadian Regiment soldier at Paardeberg Drift

AFTER THE RED RIVER REBELLION of 1869–70, Louis Riel fled Canada
to begin a new life among the Métis of Montana. But in the summer of 1884 a group of disaffected residents of central Saskatchewan,
including Métis, white settlers, and Indians, called on Riel to return
to Canada to lead them in pressing their several grievances against
Ottawa. Riel obliged. But instead of organizing a political protest
movement, as many of his followers had expected, he decided to repeat
the strategy he had used successfully to win concessions from John A.
Macdonald in 1870. On March 19, 1885, he proclaimed a provisional government in the North-West with its capital at Batoche. Two
days later he demanded the surrender of the North West Mounted
Police detachment commanded by Superintendent L.N.F. Crozier at
Fort Carleton, about 32 kilometres from Batoche.

This was an open rebellion against the legitimate authority
of Canada, and Crozier decided to act. On March 26 he left Fort
Carleton with a force of ninety-eight Mounties and volunteers from

nearby Prince Albert and headed to Batoche to put down the rebellion. At Duck Lake, Crozier's force was ambushed by Métis led by Gabriel Dumont, who was effectively Riel's war chief. Twelve men were killed on the government side and six rebels. Crozier was at one point almost surrounded. The slaughter might have been much greater but for Louis Riel, who was watching from a distance; he convinced Dumont to let Crozier and the survivors of the Mountie force withdraw. Crozier's men then beat a hasty retreat to Prince Albert and abandoned Fort Carleton, their largest post in the area.

This was the first skirmish in what is known to history as the Northwest Rebellion of 1885. Riel's secession was based mostly on the premise that the government of Canada would negotiate with him in 1885 as it had in 1870 and that he might then force Ottawa to make concessions regarding treaties, land rights, and better services for white farmers. He was dead wrong in his assumption. Three things were very different in 1885: Canada had no intention of negotiating anything and now had sufficient military force of its own to put down the rebellion; the Canadian Pacific Railway was virtually complete from Ontario to the Rocky Mountains, with only three gaps of about 150 kilometres in the main line north of Lake Superior; and the telegraph now provided instant communications between the major settlements in the Northwest and eastern and central Canada. The Canadian militia in 1885 may not have been a significant military force on a world scale, but it was larger, better trained, and better equipped than it had been in 1869–70, and it now had a core of competent professional soldiers in the artillery, cavalry, and infantry schools. It could also rely on the Hudson's Bay Company to provide ready stores in the west, and on wagon teams and steamboats to provide transportation.

The general officer commanding (GOC) of the Canadian militia was Frederick D. Middleton, a former British army officer who had taken over the post in 1884. Macdonald had sent Middleton west to size up the situation even before the Mounties and Dumont's men clashed at Duck Lake. By the time he arrived on March 27, the news of the Duck Lake fight had swept the Dominion. Middleton sent word to mobilize the militia and dispatch the small regular force while he made arrangements with the CPR to transport his men over the gaps in the rail. From Winnipeg the 90th Rifles and the Winnipeg Field Battery immediately answered the call and were sent west to Qu'Appelle. They were the first of some three thousand western Canadians from the Lakehead to the Rocky Mountains who volunteered. The militia units from Manitoba eventually included three battalions of infantry from the Winnipeg area—the 90th, the 91st, and the 92nd, also called the Winnipeg Light Infantry. Local companies were raised in Birtle, Battleford, Qu'Appelle, and Calgary; also participating were the Rocky Mountain Rangers, the Moose Mountain Scouts, and Boulton's Scouts.

Many of the western militia units were completely new, with very limited experience in the regimentation of army life. But the four thousand or so who came from Ontario and points east were somewhat better prepared. They included the Governor General's Body Guard, the 10th Royal Grenadiers, the Queen's Own Rifles, and all three companies of William Otter's Infantry School Corps. The Midland Provisional Battalion, from central Ontario, combined eight companies from seven battalions. From London, Ontario, came the 7th Fusiliers, and the Governor General's Foot Guards mobilized at Ottawa. The Halifax Rifles came from faraway Nova Scotia; the Voltigeurs de Québec, the Carabiniers Mont-Royal, and the Cavalry School Corps were dispatched from Quebec. On Monday, March 30, the first of Otter's contingent left Toronto for the west. By April 10 a sizable force was beginning to assemble along the rail line just east of Regina. They came armed with several batteries of artillery, a Gatling gun purchased from the United States, and tons of provisions and stores. Crowds gathered to see the men off at dozens of embarkation points throughout central and eastern Canada as the excitement of Canada's first real war moved the people to a patriotic fervour. Here was Canada's own little imperial adventure, right inside its own backyard.

Those Métis who were in the rebellion were vastly outnumbered. Many English-speaking Métis had refused to join the insurrection. The white farmers would have nothing to do with the rebellion, and most of the Plains Indians, as disaffected as they were by the government's failure to abide by its treaty commitments, decided to steer a wide course around Riel. Only a few hundred Cree warriors under Chiefs Poundmaker and Big Bear joined in. But the rebellious Métis still had certain advantages; their leader, Gabriel Dumont, was a skilled leader of many hunts and a born tactician who knew every trail, every ford, every coulee and wash in central Saskatchewan. His riflemen used a motley collection of firearms, some of which dated back to the days of the long-barrelled Hudson's Bay Company flint-lock trade muskets, but they could shoot, and they could ride. Their supply lines were short. They were fighting for home and family—in their minds, for their very existence. And they knew the land well. Middleton's militiamen would not have an easy time of it.

Middleton's initial plan was straightforward: concentrate his force at Qu'Appelle, just north of the CPR main line and just east of Regina, and march them directly to Clarke's Crossing, not far from Batoche. A second column, under Otter, was to march from Swift Current to Clarke's Crossing. When the two columns met, they would go on to Batoche, moving on each side of the river as they approached the Métis capital. After crushing the Métis, Middleton intended to relieve Prince Albert and Battleford while at the same time dealing with the Cree chief Poundmaker. After that he would join a third column (the Alberta Field Force), which would proceed north from Calgary under the command of Thomas Strange, a rancher and former British officer. The combined force would attack Big Bear near Fort Pitt and stamp out the last sparks of rebellion.

On March 30, two hundred Cree under Poundmaker attacked Battleford and forced the settlers there to take refuge in the nearby Mounted Police post, while another Cree band, nominally under Big Bear's control but led by a member of the warrior society named Wandering Spirit, killed nine settlers and took three prisoners at the small settlement of Frog Lake on April 2. Middleton was forced to alter his plan in order to take back Battleford and Frog Lake as quickly as he could. On April 6, after the arrival of the batteries with their 9-pounder guns from Kingston and Quebec, Middleton began his advance toward Batoche. He had 800 men with him. Otter marched on Battleford from Swift Current with about 550 men, while Strange began his foray from Calgary with 600 men, eventually to join the others at Fort Pitt.

The advances did not go smoothly. Although Otter easily relieved Battleford on April 24, Middleton's force was engaged that same day at Fish Creek by a large body of Dumont's riflemen. It was a mistake for Middleton to divide his men into two columns and send them up both sides of the South Saskatchewan River. Dumont's men ambushed the column on the east side of the river and, using the ravines and brush as cover, managed to kill eleven men and wound forty-eight before withdrawing. Middleton was unnerved and decided to rethink his plans and consolidate his force before resuming his advance on Batoche. Several days later Otter pushed out of Battleford and headed west toward Poundmaker's encampment at Cut Knife Hill. But the Cree were waiting for him too. They surrounded him and killed eight and wounded fifteen of his men before he managed to withdraw.

Despite these setbacks, Middleton believed that he could take Batoche with his superior force and that the rebellion would quickly collapse when he did, so after languishing near Fish Creek for almost two weeks, he resumed his march on Battleford on May 9 with about 850 men. Middleton devised a scheme to take Batoche quickly: he secured the paddleboat *Northcote*, fortified it, and placed several hundred men aboard with orders to run by Batoche (on the east bank of the river), land to the north of the settlement, and then attack in coordination with a drive to be launched from the south side. Dumont's men stymied the plan by raising a ferry cable that ran across the river to the height of *Northcote*'s smokestacks, knocking them off and causing the boat to lose power and drift downriver. Middleton's own force was held back by steady fire from well-positioned rifle pits that Dumont's men

An officer of the Régiment de Carignan-Salières, the first regiment to fight in Canada, 1666.
—Robert Rosewarne/Library and Archives Canada/C-010368

French-Canadian militia and *troupes de terre* storm Fort Oswego during the French-Indian War, August 1756.
—Steele & Co./Library and Archives Canada/Acc. No. 1992-462-2

The Battle of Fish Creek, the first major deployment of Canadian regiments without the support of British regulars, April 1885.
—Fred W. Curzon/Library and Archives Canada/C-002425

A contingent of the Black Watch (RHR) in Quebec prepares to depart for the Boer War in South Africa, October 30, 1899.

—Reproduced with permission from the Black Watch (RHR) Regimental Museum and Archives.

The Royal Canadian Regiment (RCR) at the battle of Paardeberg during the Boer War, February 1900. The RCR was the only Canadian regiment present at the battle, distinguishing itself with a night-time manoeuvre that gained it the high ground above the defending Boers.

—Arthur Hider/Library and Archives Canada/Acc. No. 1983-38-2

Soldiers of the PPCLI advance under German machine-gun fire during
the First World War.
—Reproduced with permission from the PPCLI Regimental Museum and Archives/59.10-1II.

The 22nd Battalion of the Canadian Expeditionary Force going over the top at the Somme, September 1916. The 22nd Batallion would later become the Royal 22ᵉ Régiment, better known as the Van Doos.

—Musée du Royal 22ᵉ Régiment, Fonds Première Guerre Mondiale, Ph/172/111, Canadian official war photograph/Library and Archives Canada/PA-648

A German shell bursts close to an advanced Canadian dressing station, September 15, 1916.

—Musée du 22ᵉ Régiment, Fonds Première Guerre Mondiale, Ph/172/86, Canadian official war photograph/Library and Archives of Canada/PA-625

At Vimy Ridge, Canadian machine-gunners from the 22nd Battalion dig a foxhole to protect themselves against shrapnel, April 1917.

—Musée du Royal 22ᵉ Régiment, Fonds Première Guerre Mondiale, Ph/172/129, Canadian official war photograph/Library and Archives Canada/PA-1017

Canadian artillery supports an infantry advance by the 10th Battalion during the battle of Drocourt, September 1918.

—Reproduced with permission from the Calgary Highlanders Regimental Museum and Archives/52-25.

The Black Watch (RHR) on parade in Mons, Belgium, on the last day of the First World War, November 11, 1918.

—Reproduced with permission from the Black Watch (RHR) Regimental Museum and Archives.

Officers toast King George VI at a regimental dinner held by the Black Watch (RHR) Regiment.

—Reproduced with permission from the Black Watch (RHR) Regimental Museum and Archives.

The Calgary Highlanders victory parade in Amsterdam, circa 1945. Canadian regiments fighting on the left flank of the Allied armies were instrumental in freeing the Netherlands.

—Reproduced with permission from the Calgary Highlanders Regimental Museum and Archives/P100-33.

had dug on the slopes leading down to the river from above Batoche. Well hidden in the brush, the Métis snipers took a steady toll.

Middleton's hesitation sparked dissent among the ranks. The men, virtually all volunteers, had now been in the field for many weeks. At home, jobs, wives, and sweethearts awaited, while here there were clouds of blackflies and mosquitoes, long, sharp grass, bad food, and persistent Métis snipers. Everyone worried that thousands of Plains Indians such as the Blackfoot and Cree might jump into the fray on Riel's side. It was time to put an end to this.

Two militia officers, Colonel Arthur Williams of the Midland Battalion and Colonel Grassett of the Grenadiers, seized the moment on May 12 when they detected a slackening of enemy rifle fire. Major Charles A. Boulton would later describe the scene as the Canadian skirmishers finally rose, almost spontaneously, and advanced toward and over the Métis rifle pits:

> The whole line, stretching upwards of a mile from the river bank, now advanced steadily but rapidly through the brush to the open space which lay between us and the village. Before getting through the brush we came to a gully, at the bottom of which lay a number of the enemy. I shouted to the men not to hesitate, but to rush down, as it was dangerous to stand in the exposed position they had gained. At this moment poor Ted Brown, who had only lately been promoted to his captaincy, and was a universal favourite, became a mark for the enemy and was instantly killed. . . . This exasperated our men, who, with the 90th on the left, rushed furiously down the gully and drove the enemy before them. As they ran from us, five of them dropped under the fire of the now excited men, and pit after pit was cleared in front of our skirmishing line as we took them on the flank.

For all intents and purposes, the Battle of Batoche and the Northwest Rebellion ended with that charge. Riel was soon captured, tried for treason, and hanged in November. Dumont escaped to the United States. The militia regiments and the small regular force returned home. The west had been saved for Canada and fourteen militia regiments received their very first battle honours: "North West Canada, 1885," "Batoche," and "Fish Creek." Otter's Infantry School Corps received its first battle honours for "North West Canada, 1885" and "Saskatchewan," while the Cavalry School Corps received an honour for "North West Canada, 1885." In the British tradition, and subsequently the Canadian, neither artillery nor engineers—who are supposed to be "ubiquitous" (that is, on every battlefield and in every clash of arms)—received honours.

The Northwest Rebellion of 1885 further entrenched the regimental tradition in the Canadian military. Regiments that had served purely as sports, social, or hunt clubs had been blooded in battle. Not all the regiments had distinguished themselves, but hundreds of men had been exposed to real campaigning, real field operations, real combat, and real moments of life and death. The absolute importance of military effectiveness had been proven. More important, regiments had further bonded together under adversity. History had been made, leaders had been tested, and the regiment as a form of military family had proven itself in the minds of the men who were there and of the civilians who had cheered them on. The militia victory in the Northwest Rebellion can hardly be counted as one of the great triumphs of modern times, but it did preserve the west for Canada and demonstrated that large numbers of Canada's volunteer soldiers and the regiments that nurtured them could and would step forward in time of need. For many of Canada's venerable regiments of today, it was the first real test of war. For some, the next test would come half a world away.

—⚏—

ON OCTOBER 11, 1899, Transvaal and the Orange Free State, two Boer (Dutch-speaking) republics in what is now South Africa, declared war

on Britain. They claimed they were doing so to forestall a British invasion of their territory to be launched from the two British colonies
in South Africa, the Cape Colony and Natal, with the aim of seizing
the enormously rich gold fields that lay within Transvaal. The British
claimed that they had been making preparations for a military inter-
vention in the two Boer republics to protect the rights of non-Boer
immigrants, who had been pouring into the Transvaal ever since the
discovery of the vast Witwatersrand gold fields a few years earlier.

It is highly doubtful that many Canadians had even heard of these
two obscure states, let alone followed the events leading up to the declaration of war. But within a short time, a clamour arose from within
Canada, by people who believed that the British Empire was always
in the right, for Canadian troops to be sent to join in an imperial
mission to vanquish the Boers. The Liberal government of Sir Wilfrid
Laurier had little choice but to agree. The Boer or South African War
thus became Canada's first overseas military conflict.

Most Canadians probably knew very little about the causes of the
South African conflict. French-speaking Quebecers certainly appeared
to believe, en masse, that the war had resulted from the mighty British
Empire trying to impose its will on a beleaguered minority—the white,
Dutch-speaking South Africans—not unlike their own situation. They
were not far wrong in their assessment. The most vocal Quebec opponent of the war, Liberal MP Henri Bourassa, attacked his own government for even contemplating sending Canadian soldiers to a faraway
conflict that, in his view, had nothing to do with Canadian interests.
But the English-speaking Canadian elites of Montreal, Toronto, and
the other large cities, strongly backed by the newspapers, overwhelmingly supported the war. They believed that, as an integral part of the
Empire, Canada must come to Britain's aid.

The British, personified by colonial secretary Joseph Chamberlain, agreed. The British army did not appear to need any help from
the so-called white dominions—Canada, Australia, and New Zealand—at that stage of the war, but Chamberlain believed that it was
important for Britain to show the world that its empire, especially

the self-governing part of it, supported the war. Behind the scenes, and without the permission of the government, the general officer commanding (GOC) the Canadian militia, General Edward Hutton, secretly prepared a contingency plan for dispatch of a Canadian contingent to South Africa. That was completely improper, but Laurier caved in to all the pressure and agreed to send a Canadian contingent. It would consist of a single battalion of infantry that would serve together as an identifiable Canadian unit. Ottawa would pay to recruit, equip, and transport the battalion if Britain would assume financial responsibility for it upon arrival in South Africa and for the duration of the war. To command the Canadian contingent, the minister of militia, Frederick Borden, turned to William Otter, by then fifty-six but arguably the best Canadian-born officer available; the basic element of Otter's contingent would be provided by the Infantry School Corps.

In May 1892 the Infantry School Corps had received the designation Canadian Regiment of Infantry. One year later it was renamed the Royal Regiment of Canadian Infantry. Now it was decided that the contingent to be raised for South Africa would be designated as the 2nd (Special Service) Battalion of the Royal Canadian Regiment of Infantry. This was the first time in Canada's history that a regiment would generate a second battalion and that one of the battalions would serve somewhere other than with the original regiment. Almost everyone referred to the Royal Canadian Regiment of Infantry as the Royal Canadian Regiment, and thus the name was officially (and for the last time) changed on November 1, 1901. Today the Royal Canadian Regiment is Canada's senior infantry regiment. Regimental headquarters and the 1st and 3rd battalions are based at CFB (Canadian Forces Base) Petawawa, in Ontario, and the 2nd Battalion is stationed at CFB Gagetown, in New Brunswick.

With astonishing speed, hundreds of volunteers began filling the ranks of the 2nd Battalion. Some were civilians right off the street; most were members of eighty-two different militia units across Canada. Just over seven in ten were Canadian born and 25 percent were from Britain. There weren't very many from French Quebec. Surprisingly, most came from cities, probably because city-dwellers could sign up more easily at their local armoury. Later contingents—particularly a regiment of cavalry and mounted infantry raised by Lord Strathcona—would have more farm boys and cowboys. Only one in twelve of the 2nd Battalion listed his occupation as soldier.

While the volunteers poured in, arrangements were made to clothe and equip the men. They were to wear rough khaki uniforms supplied by a Hamilton clothing maker—they would later complain that the khaki was too stiff when first worn and rotted when too wet. Their white pith helmets would have to be stained brown. They were to have a field service cap, two pairs of boots, blue serge puttees, and leather leggings. Their basic weapon would be the British Lee-Enfield Mark 1 .303, a superb repeating rifle that, in different versions, would equip Canadian troops up to and including the Korean War. A hundred thousand residents of Toronto turned out to cheer the contingent that left by train on October 25. Other groups departed from different cities, and all gathered at the Citadel at Quebec or were housed in close-by immigration sheds. The battalion of 1,061 all ranks left Canada aboard the former Allan Line cattle boat *Sardinian* on October 30, bound directly for Cape Town. The voyage was long, the ship crowded, hot, and terribly unsanitary, the food barely edible, and fresh water at a premium. Discipline suffered, men got sick, horses died and were thrown overboard. On November 29 the ship finally docked at Cape Town.

For the most part the RCR sat and did little for the first month of its tour in South Africa; it was almost as if the British had forgotten the Canadians were there. Broiling under the hot summer sun by day and soaked to the skin when it rained heavily at night, the men grew bored and browned off. They were almost glad to hear that, for the most part, the Boers had whipped the British in the early months of the war. As hopes for a quick British victory faded away, the chances that the war would last long enough for the Canadians to see action increased. Their first skirmish came at the side of a number of British and Australian troops at Sunnyside Kopje, a quick and painless victory over a small Boer contingent on January 1, 1900. Their first real battle took place in February as the British began to besiege Boer General Piet Cronje at Paardeberg Drift, on the banks of the Modder River. Pursued by two British divisions, Cronje decided to stand and fight.

The British 19th Brigade, to which the Canadians were attached, mounted an assault on well-entrenched Boer positions and took heavy losses, with eighteen dead and sixty wounded. The attack gave the British pause; they decided to wait Cronje out. With each passing day, the British tightened the cordon around Cronje. Then, on the night of February 26–27, the Canadians were ordered to advance under cover of darkness and get into the Boer trenches if possible. If not, they were to dig in as close as they could. Six companies set off after dark on the 26th, with Otter in command of the attackers in the centre.

The plan was simple: move as far forward as possible and try to take the Boer positions by storm. After they had advanced slowly and stealthily for some 600 metres, the Boers heard something in the dark. A few shots rang out from their trenches, followed by a fusillade. The Canadians hit the dirt as the Boer riflemen fired, mostly over their heads. "We dared not return the fire," one Canadian private wrote, "as it would give us away. To lift one's head would mean sure death." Other Canadians did fire, however, until someone called out for the whole regiment to retire. Afterward, no one was sure who it was, Boer or Canadian, but the net result was that five of the six companies scrambled back to their starting positions. One company of Maritimers did not hear the shout, and stayed put. As dawn broke, they and the Boers realized that these remaining Canadians had entrenched themselves on a vantage point that completely dominated the Boer positions. They began to fire into the Boer trenches, a white flag went up, and the battle of Paardeberg Drift was over. It was the RCR's first major victory, at an eventual cost of thirteen Canadian dead and thirty-two wounded.

After the battle, the British resumed their march on Pretoria, the Boer capital in Transvaal. Again the appalling conditions of heat, dust, thirst, sand, and disease took their toll. After only a hundred days or so, the RCR has lost about 25 percent of its men through disease or physical breakdown alone. Finally, on June 5, 1900, Pretoria fell to the British. This, however, was not the end of the war, but only the end of a first phase in which Boers had fought British with standing armies in set-piece battles or in sieges. From there on in, the Boers began to resort to guerrilla tactics, hit-and-run raids by mounted riflemen, dubbed commandos, who roamed the veldt when on the attack, then melted back to their farms or villages when chased by the British.

This new phase of the war demanded cavalry, scouts, and mounted riflemen, and by sheer coincidence Wilfrid Laurier's government had decided to send such troops to South Africa even before the Royal Canadian Regiment arrived at Cape Town. This time men with a rural background were preferred, good shots and good riders. They would form the 1st Battalion, Canadian Mounted Rifles, an entirely new formation created solely for the South African War. The heart of this battalion was the old Cavalry School Corps, which had gone through name changes and consolidation with other units before emerging in 1893 as the Royal Canadian Dragoons. Here too volunteers from militia cavalry units or right off the farms and ranches of the west were to form around a core of permanent-force cavalry. When the battalion arrived in South Africa in August 1900, the unit requested, and was granted permission, to rename itself the Royal Canadian Dragoons (RCD). It took part in the advance to Pretoria and in the guerrilla war that followed. Although the first battalion had renamed itself, subsequent battalions of mounted riflemen sent to South Africa went under the label of Canadian Mounted Rifles. Detachments from the Royal Canadian Artillery—the old Artillery School Corps—also fought in South Africa.

While the RCR and the RCD fought their way toward Pretoria in the spring of 1900, yet another famous regiment was being created back in Canada. Donald A. Smith had been a Hudson's Bay Company factor in the Red River country at the time of the first Riel rebellion in 1869–70. John A. Macdonald had asked him to act for the government in secret negotiations between Ottawa and Riel that were forced on the Canadians by the British. After the rebellion ended and Manitoba was admitted into Canada as a province, Smith was elected as a Conservative Member of Parliament. But Smith rebelled against Macdonald when the prime minister was caught taking money from American railroaders in 1872 (the Pacific Scandal), and helped bring the government down. He was also on his way to becoming a rich man through business and investment. In the 1870s he partnered with other investors to launch the highly profitable Minneapolis, St. Paul, and Minnesota Railway, and in 1880 he was one of the four main investors who launched the Canadian Pacific Railway. It was Smith who drove the last spike on the CPR in November 1885.

At the outbreak of the South African War, Smith had already become Lord Strathcona and Mount Royal and was Canadian High Commissioner in the United Kingdom. On January 10, 1900, he approached the British government with an offer to raise an entire cavalry regiment for service against the Boers. The offer was accepted; the venture would eventually cost him close to $600,000—roughly $18 million today—a major fortune. A famous Mountie officer who had been responsible for law and order in the western railway construction camps in the mid-1880s, Sir Samuel B. Steele, was named to command the unit, which would be known as Strathcona's Horse.

Under Steele's command—and because of his sterling reputation among the Mounties—many Royal North West Mounted Police volunteered, as did hundreds of western cowboys. In fact, almost all of the squadrons of the new regiment were recruited in the west. Although the unit was supposed to be part of the British army, it was equipped by the Canadian government, quartered in Lansdowne Park in Ottawa before departure, and paraded on Parliament Hill. After a long and difficult voyage in which many men grew sick and hundreds of horses died and were thrown overboard, Strathcona's Horse arrived in Cape Town on April 10, 1900—the third Canadian contingent in a war that Laurier had been reluctant to enter. In June it joined the

Natal Field Force and engaged in long-range scouting and fighting the Boer commandos. It gained a reputation for fierceness in combat, and rumours circulated that the Strathconas took no prisoners. The unit returned to Canada in January 1901 but stopped in London for presentations of medals by King Edward VII. Lord Strathcona attended the ceremonies.

The war ended with a Boer surrender on May 31, 1902; 8,372 Canadians had enlisted to either fight in South Africa or to replace British units that were. Of these, 89 were killed in action, 135 died of disease, and 252 were wounded. The fighting experiences of Canada's permanent-force regiments—the RCR, the RCD, and the Royal Canadian Artillery—strengthened regimental bonds and added to regimental tradition. After the war Strathcona's Horse was also absorbed into the permanent force, eventually receiving the designation Lord Strathcona's Horse (Royal Canadians) on May 1, 1911. It is today stationed at CFB Edmonton and is one of three regular-force Canadian armoured regiments along with the RCD (based at CFB Petawawa) and the 12e Régiment blindé du Canada, which is based at CFB Valcartier.

By 1901 the regimental tradition had sunk deep roots into Canadian soil. The tradition was British in origin but Canadian by experience, stretching back to the fencible regiments of the War of 1812. Regiments such as the Queen's Own at Ridgeway or the RCR at Cut Knife Hill had learned the reality of war, but on a small enough scale to be able to learn without incurring too much loss. Most of the time, however, Canada's militia regiments were simply having a good time. Led by political appointees chosen for their local influence and their help to the governing party, they held dances and field days, mess dinners and rifle shoots, and marched with their bands playing the regimental march on Dominion Day or Victoria Day or other public holidays. New Year's Day levées were especially crowded affairs, cold outside and warm with good cheer and "camel's milk" (a rum-laced drink) inside. The regiments of the permanent force, now called the permanent active militia, had been blooded in South Africa and, in the years that followed, tried to make some sense of what they had experienced. But the patchwork of militia regiments that covered the country—they were now called non-permanent active militia—seemed simply to carry on after South Africa. They were all about to learn, very quickly and at great cost, what war was really about.

PART TWO

THE FIRST WORLD WAR

Chapter Six

YPRES: THE PATRICIAS AND THE 10TH BATTALION

> I looked back across the field we had crossed the previous night and I could
> see what havoc had been wrought on our boys. . . . All around were the
> dead bodies of men who, a few hours before, had been singing Canada's
> national song. . . .
>
> —Sergeant, 10th Battalion, Canadian Expeditionary Force,
> April 23, 1915

WHEN BRITAIN DECLARED WAR ON GERMANY on August 4, 1914, Canada
was a self-governing dominion in the British Empire; thus, constitu-
tionally, Canada was automatically at war when Britain was at war.
As it was self-governing, the extent of Canada's participation in the
war would be decided in Canada, by Canadians, acting through their
elected government. Prime Minister Sir Robert Borden and all of
his Cabinet, especially the minister of militia and defence, Sir Sam
Hughes, decided without hesitation to make a major contribution of
troops—at least a full infantry division—the largest commitment of
Canadian soldiers in any war to date.

Hughes had been a strong political supporter of the prime minister
during the long years he spent in the Opposition; his appointment to
the Cabinet after Borden's victory in the 1911 election was his reward.
He was a stalwart believer that any man who enjoyed the benefits of

citizenship owed military service to his country when needed. As far as Hughes was concerned, the part-time citizen-soldier, the reservist, or, in his day, the militiaman made the best soldier material. Unlike full-time professionals—who Hughes considered to be mostly incompetent bumblers who had chosen military duty out of laziness or inability to do anything truly useful—the militiaman was motivated by patriotism and equipped with the skills and successes of his private life. Hughes had served with distinction in the South African War. A nationalist and an imperialist at the same time, he believed in the British Empire and was proud to be part of it, but he also believed that Canadians were unique members of the Empire who were, quite simply, better at most things than the British were. He was tough, gruff, self-centred, and manly. In his own mind, he represented the heroic and stalwart men who had built the Empire and Canada and who would guard both with their lives if necessary.

At first there was almost no opposition to the war or to the commitment of troops, even in French-speaking Canada. In English-speaking Canada there was, in fact, great enthusiasm, wild outbursts of imperial patriotism and jingoism, and a rush to the colours by both civilians and members of the militia. Across the nation scenes were played out over and over again of departing troop trains filled with eager volunteers, cheered on by family and friends, pulling out of stations and heading for the great concentration point at Camp Valcartier, near Quebec City. It would be months before any of these men got near the front, and the brutal reality of this "war to end all wars" was that when they did, memories of the cheering crowds and the waving banners quickly faded against the backdrop of mud, disease, and violent death in many forms.

Princess Patricia's Canadian Light Infantry was the first Canadian formation raised specifically for the war. In fact, the idea for the new regiment was conceived even before Britain declared war on August 4. Fighting had first broken out in Europe on July 28, when the Austro-Hungarian Empire invaded Serbia in response to the assassination of Archduke Franz Ferdinand of Austria in Sarajevo in late June. Montreal businessman and community leader Hamilton Gault anticipated that the British Empire would soon be involved in the fighting and decided to follow the example set by Lord Strathcona at the outbreak of the Boer War. Gault had served in the South African War and was a staunch Empire patriot. After overcoming initial objections from Hughes, he was given permission to go ahead with the new regiment. The conditions agreed upon were that he would pay the government $100,000 and the government would in return provide equipment, transportation to a place of concentration in Canada, and transport overseas. Gault wanted the new regiment to consist entirely of veterans of the British army living in Canada. That way, he thought, much training could be dispensed with and the PPCLI could be rushed overseas to be inserted into the British army's order of battle.

Gault was helped immeasurably by Lieutenant-Colonel Francis Farquhar, military secretary to the Governor General and a veteran of several imperial wars, who became the PPCLI's first commanding officer. Gault himself became the senior major and second-in-command. The Governor General—the Duke of Connaught—was asked permission to approach his daughter, Princess Patricia of Connaught, to lend her name to the new regiment. She not only agreed but sewed a camp colour, which the regiment carried throughout the war. The colour symbolized the princess and her ties to the regiment—Princess Patricia's Canadian Light Infantry. It was not in any way a true light infantry battalion, as Gault himself admitted, but he thought the name gave added dash to the formation, and so it did.

Within days of the agreement's being signed between Hughes and Gault, posters and recruiting notices began to appear across the country and men headed toward the Lansdowne Park exhibition grounds in Ottawa, where the new regiment was to be formed. The recruiting campaign eventually brought some three thousand volunteers to Ottawa; only about one of every three was eventually selected to go overseas. The Patricias had a decidedly western flavour from the very beginning, with large numbers of volunteers coming from the Prairie provinces and even British Columbia. For one thing, men of British birth proved to be the most eager group to serve, and many thousands of them had arrived in Canada since the turn of the century to try their luck in the west. For another, these farm hands, cowboys, and miners were more likely to be younger and single than the veterans of imperial wars who had settled in Ontario and started to raise families.

By August 19 Farquhar had completed his selection; 1,098 men were chosen. Fully 1,049 of them had seen military service of some kind and 456 of them had been in a war. They collectively held 771 decorations or medals for courage or meritorious service, and every British army regiment but one was represented among their ranks. The vast majority (over 90 percent) of the "Originals," as they were soon called, were British-born, an even higher ratio of British- to Canadian-born than in the contingent gathering under Hughes's direction at Camp Valcartier.

The Patricias sailed from Canada on September 27 and arrived in the U.K. on October 18. On January 6, 1915, the battalion was inserted into the 80th Brigade of the British 27th Division and sent to hold a stretch of line to the east of the Belgian town of Ypres. The PPCLI thus holds the honour of being "first to the front" in the First World War, as it was also during the Korean War and in the war against the Taliban and al Qaeda, when Canada sent its first combat troops to Afghanistan in early 2002.

On the night of March 19–20, Farquhar took the commanding officer of the 3rd Battalion of the King's Royal Rifles—the unit about to relieve the PPCLI in the front trenches—on a short tour of his battalion's positions. PPCLI sergeant Louis Scott watched the two men proceed: "Colonel Farquhar was with the Colonel of the Rifle Brigade. They came up on an inspection tour to observe what was going on. He moved out just a little ahead of me, talking to the Rifle Brigade Colonel, when suddenly we heard him go down. He was shot with a stray bullet." Farquhar was buried on the evening of March 20 in the growing PPCLI cemetery at the nearby crossroads of Voormezeele.

—m—

THE FOUNDING AND MOBILIZATION of the PPCLI went almost without a hitch, especially when compared to the gathering of the 1st Canadian Division at Valcartier. When Canada went to war, the Canadian army consisted of a permanent active militia (i.e., full-time soldiers) of about 3,100 men. There were a variety of artillery and engineer units along with the Royal Canadian Regiment, Lord Strathcona's Horse—which had remained on strength as a full-time unit after the Boer War—and the Royal Canadian Dragoons, as well as about 55,000 non-permanent active militia (part-time reservists) in 226 units across Canada. A mobilization plan was in place that aimed at creating an overseas force of one division and one cavalry brigade totalling some 24,000 men.

The plan basically called for the militia districts and divisions (districts in western Canada; divisions in Ontario, Quebec, and the Maritimes) to order the militia regiments in their jurisdictions to recruit and equip enough volunteers to create a battalion from each regiment. Each battalion would recruit up to the war establishment of approximately one thousand men each. The battalions were then to gather at Camp Petawawa, northwest of Ottawa, before going overseas. Senior officers for the battalions and brigades (and other smaller units) would be selected by the Militia Council in Ottawa, which had been established in 1904 to administer the army without political interference.

But there was a significant hitch to the mobilization plan: the Militia Act did not give the Government of Canada legal authority to send serving members of the non-permanent active militia out of the country. Almost all those who had fought in South Africa—with the exception of the permanent force—had been volunteers off the streets. Militiamen who had gone to war had joined new formations authorized specifically for South African duty. This meant that with war quickly spreading in Europe, the government had two choices for quick action. Either Parliament would have to quickly change the

Militia Act to allow the battalions to be sent to the U.K., or entirely new militia units could be formed, composed of volunteers (former militia or not), that would have no formal connection to existing regiments. Both processes would be very time-consuming, and both Hughes and the government were anxious to get Canadians overseas as soon as possible.

Hughes's solution was to assign the infantry volunteers (militia or not) into brand-new numbered battalions created only for overseas service. The existing regiments would be ordered to recruit for these new numbered battalions, most of which would spring up in their own communities. That meant that in many cases the new numbered battalion would consist mostly of members of the original regiment anyway. In other words, a regiment like Montreal's Victoria Rifles of Canada would not simply go overseas or send a battalion of Victoria Rifles overseas; it would instead send its own men and recruit others from off the streets to join a numbered battalion (or more than one) being raised locally. In fact, during the war the Victoria Rifles recruited men for the 24th, 60th, and 244th Canadian battalions. The first two of these battalions saw action on the Western Front, but the third was broken up in the U.K. and its men were used as reinforcements (or replacements) fed individually into battalions that were already in action.

No matter how strong Hughes's allegiance was to the militia, he was ready to mix members of different regiments together when necessary. Some of these battalions—the 10th Battalion is a good example—contained men from at least three different regiments from three different communities. Here is a strong indication that Hughes did not believe the regimental system to be the only means—and maybe not even a necessary means—of creating loyalty and cohesion in a fighting force. Any opposition that might have arisen from denizens of the regimental system was clearly overridden in the urgency of the moment. The future of the regimental tradition would remain in doubt until after the war.

Hughes caused great chaos in the raising of the overseas contingent. Virtually all of the major decisions he made were ad hoc and some were made with no real thought as to consequences. The very selection of Camp Valcartier, which did not even exist when Hughes chose the site (it belonged to an associate of Hughes and was purchased by the government at a very handsome price), created unimaginable confusion. There was no rail line to it, there were no roads, no structures, no training fields or parade grounds, no rifle ranges, not even latrines or fresh water. It was all being built as volunteers poured in from across Canada and tried to live in conditions of indescribable filth and mud. Why did Hughes do it? His biographer, Ronald Haycock, puts it this way: "the best explanation for his action remains the fact that Sam Hughes was an egotistical and grand improviser, led on by an archaic war concept and encouraged by a particular view of a citizen's martial responsibilities, by existing military moods and by his own experience."

Though Hughes's mobilization was deeply flawed—and would later produce significant difficulties for the Canadian Expeditionary Force, or CEF, as it was called—the failures were initially swept aside by a tide of enthusiastic volunteers. A large percentage of the tens of thousands who poured into Valcartier were British-born, as with the Patricias, or the sons of British immigrants, even though a significant number of officers were Canadian. One of the sixteen battalions in the first contingent was the 10th Battalion of the 2nd Brigade. The battalion consisted mostly of men from Calgary and southern Alberta and Winnipeg. The largest part of the Alberta detachment came from the 103rd Calgary Rifles, while most of the Manitobans had volunteered via the 106th Winnipeg Light Infantry. But other men from all over Canada filled out the battalion's establishment of just over a thousand. That was because, as with all the other battalions, many of the men who had signed up were right off the street and had never served in the militia. Many of these volunteers could not break into the battalions that were being filled by particular militia regiments, so they were put wherever there was room—with little regard for the impact this might have on unit cohesion.

There were so many volunteers in the first two months of the war that when the Canadian Contingent, as it was called, embarked from Gaspé Harbour for the U.K. on October 3, it contained thirty-two thousand men and needed thirty-one transport ships. It took three hours for the massive convoy to exit the harbour and steer downstream toward the Gulf of St. Lawrence. The contingent—which would form the Canadian Division—was organized into four brigades, each of which consisted of four battalions. Most of the small permanent force, which had been mobilized by the end of August, was included in the contingent, except the Royal Canadian Regiment, which was sent to do guard duty in Bermuda, relieving a British unit that went home to fight. The fleet began to enter England's Plymouth Sound on October 14. From there the men proceeded by train to Salisbury Plain, a 90-square-mile (234 square kilometres) military camp and training ground in south-central England, where bell tents were pitched in the midst of a growing city of tens of thousands of armed men from Britain and much of the Empire.

The fall was cold and rainy, turning much of the ground into a muddy quagmire. Sickness spread through the camp like wildfire. There was little training and much trying to find warmth and dryness. The Canadian government wanted the troops moved to the front as quickly as possible, but much of the equipment they had brought with them was completely unsuitable and had to be replaced with British-pattern kit. However, the Canadian-built Ross rifle, a hunting firearm that was totally unreliable under combat conditions, was retained. It, like much of the other useless kit, had been especially selected for the CEF by Sam Hughes. In the first days of February 1915 the transfer from Salisbury Plain to the front began. By February 16 the Canadian Division (later referred to as the First Canadian Division) had reached France, and its units entered the lines that formed the Ypres Salient.

THE BELGIAN CITY OF YPRES had been the centre of a thriving cloth trade for half a millennium before the war. The stylish buildings that faced the central market square were the equal of any in Europe; the spires of Ypres, the cathedral, and the famous Cloth Hall could be seen for miles around. Ypres was also an important crossroads town connecting Flanders with the Channel coast. Whoever held the city would dominate movement for hundreds of kilometres in all directions. The Germans captured Ypres for a brief period in late October 1914 but were then forced from the town by the British Expeditionary Force (BEF). In the First Battle of Ypres—October 31 to November 17, 1914—the British fought off heavy German attacks and managed to hold the town but were forced to give up much of the surrounding ground, including the heights of the ridges to the north, east, and south. The British-held territory formed a salient in a trench line that, by the end of November, ran from the North Sea to the Swiss border. The salient, surrounded on three sides, was subject to steady fire. In early 1915 the Germans began to use massive railway guns to destroy the cathedral and the Cloth Hall and to carry out a steady, systematic destruction of the rest of Ypres. Then, in mid-April, they attacked Ypres again, this time with a terrible new weapon—poison gas. Thus began the Second Battle of Ypres.

—※—

THE 10TH BATTALION OF THE CANADIAN DIVISION was under the command of Lieutenant-Colonel Russell Lambert Boyle. It re-entered the trench lines around Ypres early on the morning of Thursday, April 14, 1915, after a brief respite behind the lines. The area it was assigned to was in deplorable shape. The battalion adjutant described the trenches there as "extraordinarily filthy . . . Actually they were paved with dead Germans. When you'd move, bubbles would come up from the dead men. And it was very smelly." The trenches were shallow and narrow and had been hastily dug and fought over numerous times.

The barbed wire in front of the trenches was laid thinly and easy to get through. Boyle wrote of his situation on April 16: "I am writing in a dug-out just in [the] rear of the front line trenches. It certainly is a hot corner. The artillery on both sides shell at intervals both night and day. However, this battalion has earned the reputation of being able to hold its own and I guess that we will be able to live up to it."

It was not long before Boyle's prophecy was tested. On Thursday afternoon, April 22, the Germans threw an entire corps at the northern flank of the Ypres Salient. The attack began with chlorine gas, released from thousands of cylinders that had been secretly brought to the German trenches north of Ypres and buried, waiting for an opportune moment and a southerly wind. On April 22 the wind was favourable. The gas valves were opened and a massive green cloud drifted toward the Allied lines along a 6-kilometre front, to the immediate left of the positions occupied by the Canadian Division. The gas engulfed most of two French divisions, one of reservists and the other of colonial troops. They broke, tearing a huge hole in the lines and leaving the Canadian left flank hanging. Some of the gas drifted into the Canadian positions; with stinging eyes and breathing through urine-soaked rags, the Canadians held their part of the line against the advancing Germans as shellfire and machine guns raked their torn-up trenches.

The 10th Battalion was not near the direct German line of attack, but it was obvious to the soldiers of the battalion that something ominous was going on to their west. They could see "a queer sky" and hear the sounds of intense shell-, machine-gun, and rifle fire. Boyle quickly summoned his adjutant, Major Dan Ormond, and his company commanders to battalion headquarters, where word soon arrived that the battalion was to be ready to move out at 6:00 PM. There was "nervous excitement" as the men assembled. Some sang "O Canada" or "The Maple Leaf Forever" as they began marching from their positions toward Mouse Trap Farm, the HQ of 2nd Brigade, under the command of Brigadier-General Richard Turner. Although the battalion's full strength was 1,022 all ranks, 200 men were left out of battle in the event of a disaster, so that a core of the battalion might remain. As darkness fell, the road was crowded with fleeing remnants of the French formations and civilian refugees, but the battalion pushed through the chaos, closer to the front. When Boyle reached 2nd Brigade headquarters he found that his battalion and the brigade reserve battalion—the 16th Battalion, formed from men of regiments from Victoria, Vancouver, Winnipeg, and Hamilton—were going to mount a counterattack to capture and hold an oak plantation known as Kitchener's Wood. The orders had come directly from Divisional HQ in response to a French request to take the pressure off the collapsing French lines.

The jump-off point for the attack was just a few hundred metres to the east of Turner's HQ. As his men prepared for the attack, Boyle visited his lead sections and platoons. "We have been aching for a fight," he told them, "and now we are going to get it." The men assembled about 500 metres south of the wood waiting for the 16th Battalion to form up. It was light enough to see the wood, but not light enough to see the ground between them and the edge of the plantation. Effectively, they were about to advance over unknown ground in the dark, in the hope that no Germans were standing watch and that they could get to the edge of the wood unheard and unseen. At 11:48 PM, the advance began. They moved forward, line abreast on a two-company front, just as they might have done in the War of 1812. At first, all was well. "Not a sound was audible down the long waiving [*sic*] lines but the soft pad of feet and the knock of bayonet scabbards against thighs," Ormond later wrote. "The lines went steadily ahead as if they were doing a drill maneuver," one of the other officers remembered. But then they ran into a hedge, about 200 metres from the wood, that had a thick tangle of barbed wire running through it. They tried to get through with as little sound as possible, but it was not possible; a flare went up from the darkened wood and they were engulfed in a storm of rifle and machine-gun fire. Almost everyone went down immediately, some for good. Others rose and charged the German positions. Captain D.L. Redman, a former officer of the 103rd Calgary Rifles, recalled, "The wood seemed to be literally lined with machine guns. . . . They played these guns on us with terrible effect. Our men were dropping thick and fast. It was almost impossible to be heard." The bullets sounded "like a hailstorm on a zinc roof," an NCO remembered. "Somehow a few of us were missed, while other fellows were cut in half by the stream of lead."

Men were falling by the dozens, but those who pressed on reached the German trench at the edge of the wood and engaged its defenders in hand-to-hand combat with bayonets, rifle butts, brass knuckles, grenades, and studded trench clubs. The battle went on only until midnight but it must have felt like hours. Then, suddenly, it seemed as if the fighting had ended. The 10th and 16th battalions had punched through to the north side of the wood, almost a kilometre into the German lines. It was after midnight and they would have to consolidate their gains or lose the wood at dawn. The men fanned out to clear the remaining Germans. Then, in the southwest corner of the wood, they came up against a strongly held German redoubt. Ormond organized a frontal assault; it was a complete failure. Another attack was led by Lieutenant William Lowry—another bloody rebuff. Word came to Ormond that Boyle had been seriously wounded and that Ormond was now in command; he decided that they must withdraw.

The two battalions were ordered to fall back to the trench on the south side of the wood before crossing back to the Canadian lines. As the 10th re-formed in the trench, Ormond found that only 193 of his men were still fit to fight out of the 816 who had started the attack six hours before; the rest had been killed, wounded, or taken prisoner. The 16th Battalion had lost about two-thirds of its strength. The Canadians retreated from Kitchener's Wood. A sergeant later recalled: "I looked back across the field we had crossed the previous night and I could see what havoc had been wrought on our boys, for all around were the dead bodies of men who, a few hours before, had been singing Canada's national song." Boyle died of his wounds two days later. In 1934 the militia regiments that perpetuated the 10th and 16th battalions—the Calgary Highlanders, the Winnipeg Light Infantry, and the Canadian Scottish Regiment—were authorized to

wear a special shoulder badge with an oak leaf and an acorn to com-
memorate the counterattack of April 22–23, 1915, on Kitchener's
Wood. That patch commemorates the first significant trial by fire
of two Canadian battalions and the regiments that preserve their
memory.

After the attack on Kitchener's Wood failed, the fighting continued all the next day as British units were rushed forward to
plug the line, while German artillery reduced Ypres to a heap of
ruins. Then, on April 24, the Germans attacked again using gas,
this time directly against the 2nd and 3rd Canadian brigades in the
line near St-Julien, about a kilometre east of Kitchener's Wood. As
the Germans advanced, the Canadians at first held to their positions despite the thick, choking gas and the constant jamming of
their Ross rifles (the Ross was finally replaced by the British Lee-
Enfield in 1916). The jamming weapons, the heavy fire, and the gas
eventually wore the Canadians down and drove them back. They
withdrew in fighting order, taking even more casualties, but they
did not break. Again the 10th Battalion saw heavy action as fighting for control of St-Julien continued for two more days. When the
Canadian Division was pulled out of the line on April 26, the 10th
Battalion could muster only 119 men from the original 1,022; all
the rest were dead or wounded or had been taken prisoner.

The German attacks did not break through to Ypres, thanks in
part to the tough resistance of the once-green Canadians, but the
British and French were forced to pull back. By the time their lines
were consolidated on May 4, their trenches (to the north and east of
Ypres) were some 3 kilometres closer to the town than they had been
when the German attacks began on April 22. The Canadian Division
as a whole suffered more than six thousand casualties. The 10th
Battalion, which is perpetuated today by the Calgary Highlanders
of the Canadian army reserves, received one of its first major battle
honours for its role in the fight for St-Julien.

—✕—

ON MAY 8, 1915, Princess Patricia's Canadian Light Infantry was entrenched about 3 kilometres east of Ypres, just north of the Ypres-Menin road on Bellewaerde Ridge, when the Germans resumed their offensive against Ypres, this time from almost due east. The German plan was to attack the line from north to south with three entire corps. The southern-most of those corps—the German 15th Corps—would attack between Bellewaerde Lake and Zillebeke Lake, about 2 kilometres to the south of the PPCLI positions. The Patricias realized that something big was up when the normally sporadic shelling of the early morning suddenly increased into a torrent of shells ranging over the entire Patricia front.

W.J. Popey was in the No. 2 Company position when the heavy shelling began. "We were rudely awakened the morning of the 8th by a shell bursting in our lean-to artillery dugout," he later remembered. "One man, I forget his name, sat with his head off. He had been cleaning his rifle. Most of us had been hit by fragments of shrapnel. We all rushed out and got into the trench. A piece [of shrapnel] had cut through my belt and was rubbing my side. Wright dug it out and I helped some of the others."

The German guns virtually wiped out the No. 1 Company posi-tions and left the No. 2 Company positions in little better shape. Half the Patricias' effective machine-gun strength (two out of four guns) was silenced almost immediately. Shrapnel killed and maimed men, high explosives destroyed positions and blew away wire. Machine-gun fire swept over the PPCLI like driven rain. Hamilton Gault, now in command of the regiment he had founded, ordered every able-bodied man who could fire a rifle into the support trench and sent a brief message to brigade HQ over the still-uncut wire. It read simply, "very very heavy shelling." He followed that up with a written mes-sage detailing the situation, announcing his intention to hold and even counterattack if necessary, and asking for two machine guns to replace those he had lost. By the time the message reached its destina-tion, the first German infantry advance had started.

The Germans climbed up out of their forward positions and advanced against the Patricia front lines. They were convinced that none of the defenders could possibly be left alive. They were wrong. Private T. Richardson was handling the machine-gun rangefinder in one of the PPCLI positions: "I had a splendid view of the German advance. We couldn't miss them. Our machine guns did terrible execution. But still the Germans came on. Their ranks seemed inexhaustible. It became a sort of nightmare of slaughtering wave after wave of Germans and seeing fresh waves advance over the bodies of the dead." Sergeant Louis Scott was with No. 2 Company: "After a severe bombardment which depleted our very frail trenches and destroyed 75% of our personnel, the Germans advanced. . . . They came forward in fan formation carrying their full equipment, evidently intending to stay. . . . We had a splendid field of fire for a while and were enabled to hold the Hun in position. But not for long." Private Vaughan was wounded by a shell splinter: "I was just laying there in the trench, what there was of it and Lieutenant [Talbot] Papineau came along. . . . One of my buddies had already ripped my puttees off and slit my pants down because I was hit in the leg and my leg had started to swell. Lieutenant Papineau looked at it and he shoved a cigarette in my mouth and lit it and said 'Don't worry Vaughan, we'll get you out just as fast as we can.' I said, 'That's fine, sir.' But I lay there for six hours."

Gault had also been badly wounded, hit by shellfire in his left arm. He was hit again in the left thigh, much more seriously, about a half-hour later. Hustled to a position in the support trench, Gault passed in and out of consciousness as the battle raged around him. He refused any suggestion that he be evacuated ahead of any other of the wounded. With Gault out of action, Major Agar Adamson took command. He too was soon hit, in the left shoulder. Still he carried on, reorganizing the Patricia defences on the left flank, with rifle and machine-gun fire covering the gap left by the collapsing 83rd Brigade. At the same time he struggled to help bring ammunition to his beleaguered men: "Even today I can see Major Adamson with one arm hanging down getting ammunition from the dead and dying and handing it to us," one Patricia would remember many years later.

With sustained rifle and machine-gun fire the survivors of No. 2 Company drove back the first German attack and gave as much fire support as they could to their comrades on the right. But No. 1 Company was too shredded to offer anything like firm resistance and was forced to give way after a few minutes. The Germans came on, firing and throwing grenades and killing anyone in their path: "they reached our trench and the dogs bayoneted our wounded," one survivor later remembered. On the left flank of the Patricia positions, the scene was even grimmer as the 83rd Brigade of the 28th British Division took the full force of the attack and began to collapse. By 10 AM or so, the Germans had swept close to a kilometre beyond Frezenberg, turning the PPCLI's left flank. With the lake at their backs and stiffened by their own spirit and the strong will of their leaders from Adamson down, the Patricias fought back. As one Patricia would later put it, "With Hamilton Gault there, nobody could think of retiring." Was this simply loyalty to an honoured CO? Or was it loyalty to the man who had created this new and unique regiment? Whatever was behind the refusal to withdraw as long as Gault lay wounded among them, it was at least as much a raw expression of regimental tradition as anything else, and it kept the Patricias focused in the most trying of times.

At about 10:30 AM a PPCLI counterattack succeeded in driving the Germans back from the No.1 Company positions, while men firing from the support trenches and the survivors of No. 2 Company sent a firestorm of machine-gun and rifle bullets into the Germans. But the situation of both forward companies was getting more desperate by the minute. No. 2 Company was open on both flanks and virtually isolated because of the all-but-impassable condition of the support trench; No. 1 Company could never hold, even against a weak German thrust. Adamson ordered both companies back. With a handful of officers providing covering fire, the survivors of No. 1 Company crawled back over open ground. Then No. 2 Company followed, making its way down the corpse-choked support trench.

At noon came some salvation. A company of the British Rifle Brigade regiment worked their way forward to the PPCLI, bringing two machine guns and carrying thousands of rounds of small-arms ammunition, struggling under their load as they moved up. Adamson deployed the machine guns and most of the Rifle Brigade men on the PPCLI's left flank, then ordered a counterattack to attempt a link-up with British troops on the other side of the gap. But there weren't enough reinforcements to carry that off and the drive stalled very quickly. "Orders came to get in touch with the unit on the left, the Monmouth Regiment," W.J. Popey later recalled. "Crawling over the dead and dying I couldn't find anyone from whom I could get information. I reported to either Lt. Clarke or Sgt. Beaton (am not sure which) that Germans were going over to the rear."

Adamson could not close the gap with men, but he sited the machine guns to dominate the open ground with fire while at the same time adding to the firepower of the riflemen in the support trench. No one can say how many more German assaults were turned back over the next few hours by the dwindling number of able-bodied Patricia riflemen in that support trench, nor how many Germans were killed or wounded in the process. But when a platoon from the Shropshires went forward to reinforce the PPCLI at about 3 PM, the Germans launched their last major attack of the day. One PPCLI runner met the Shropshires just below Bellewaerde Lake, some 200 metres from the PPCLI positions. As they passed him, they doffed their hats and said, "Goodbye, Princess Pats, we are going to our deaths like you." The runner—Pte. G.W. Candy—remembered being "overwhelmed and could not suppress [his] tears."

Adamson quickly broke up the Shropshire platoon and placed the men wherever they were needed in the PPCLI trench. Then, as the German attack petered out and the fighting slackened off—and weakened by his wound—he turned command over to Lieutenant Hugh Niven, who held the Patricias in position until after dark. They were relieved by the 3rd Battalion, King's Royal Rifles, at about 11:30 PM. As Niven led the Patricias out, the camp colour made by Princess Patricia came back with them: "The Colour had been buried in a dug out," Popey later recalled. "We were marching away when someone thought of the Colour. Charlie Palmer and I were sent back to recover [it]." The banner had been shot through, possibly when Regimental Sergeant Major William Jordan had uncased it during the thick of the morning action and waved it from atop a parapet until shot in the head. Jordan was badly wounded but survived to receive the Distinguished Conduct Medal for his courage and leadership in the day's heavy fighting. Adamson received the Distinguished Service Order (DSO). Most Patricias did not survive the battle. Niven led only 4 officers and 150 men out of the support trench and back along the Ypres-Menin road on the night of May 8–9, 1915; 392 had been killed or wounded or gone missing in the day's fighting.

CHAPTER SEVEN

ST-ELOI AND THE SOMME: THE 28TH BATTALION
AND THE NEWFOUNDLAND REGIMENT

> They advanced, almost sideways with their chins tucked into their shoulders, as they might have headed into a blizzard of blinding snow, instead of the hail of bullets that buzzed past them like angry bees.
>
> —Witness to the attack of the Newfoundland Regiment, July 1, 1916

THE HEAVY FIGHTING OF THE FIRST THREE MONTHS of the war came as a shock to the Canadian government, as it did to almost everyone else involved. By the time the first Canadian contingent had ensconced itself on Salisbury Plain in England at the end of October, the British Expeditionary Force of only six divisions had been virtually wiped out in fighting in Belgium. Whitehall struggled to replace it with a force six times the size. In Canada, Ottawa quickly authorized a second division to be commanded by Brigadier-General Richard Turner, with Brigadier-General Arthur Currie taking over the 1st Canadian Division. The two divisions would fight together as the Canadian Corps, commanded by a British officer, E.A.H. Alderson, who had been the commander of the Canadian Division at Ypres. The 2nd Division consisted of the 4th, 5th, and 6th Canadian brigades, with each brigade having four numbered battalions. The 6th Brigade was an all-western unit consisting of the 29th Battalion from Vancouver, the 31st from Alberta, the

27th from Winnipeg, and the 28th Battalion, a mixed unit with men from Winnipeg, Regina, Moose Jaw, Saskatoon, Prince Albert, and the Lakehead cities of Fort William and Port Arthur, under the command of Lieutenant-Colonel J.F.L. Embury.

The 6th Canadian Brigade gathered at Winnipeg over the winter of 1915, then embarked for the U.K. It arrived in June 1915 and trained at Shornecliffe Camp before it entered the trenches on the night of September 26, 1915. The 28th and 29th battalions relieved battalions from the British Highland Brigade at Kemmel, south of Ypres. For the next several months the 28th Battalion endured the usual rotations into and out of the front trenches, taking casualties in trench raids, from enemy artillery and sniper fire, and, on the night of October 8, 1915, surviving a mine explosion underneath them that killed a number of Saskatoon men. The mine was actually a tunnel dug under the Canadian lines by the Germans, then packed with explosives and detonated.

In August 1915 British tunnellers sank three deep shafts behind their lines, then dug six galleries forward toward a German position known as "the mound," near the hamlet of St-Eloi. By March 1916 they were under the German positions. They placed six caches of ammonal, a powerful explosive, ranging in size from 600 to 31,000 pounds (1,320 to 68,200 kilograms), in each of the tunnels. At 4:15 AM on March 27, they blew the mines, immediately wiping out two German companies. As soon as the dirt had settled, the 9th British Brigade of the 3rd British Division rushed to occupy the badly smashed ground. The British infantry on the right flank quickly overran three of the six craters (craters 1 to 3) created by the explosions and penetrated all the way to the German reserve positions. On the left, they captured one of the new craters (crater 6), but because the ground was so badly torn up by the explosion and by previous shellings, they occupied two more craters that they thought were new craters 4 and 5, but which were not. These two craters were, in fact, old craters in no man's land. Thus the British attackers inadvertently opened a large gap in their own lines, a gap that included two of the six new craters.

As the Germans recovered from the shock of the huge explosions and the subsequent British rush, they began to counterattack. One group of Germans entered and took new crater 5, from which they poured an overwhelming fire into the British positions. It took the British a week, and hundreds of dead and wounded, before the Germans in crater 5 were dislodged. By then, the British 3rd Division was worn out. Turner's 2nd Canadian Division was ordered in to relieve them on the night of April 3–4.

Turner gave the job to the 6th Brigade. The Brigade commander, Brigadier-General H.D.B. Ketchen, sent the 27th and 31st battalions to take over the right flank of the line, with the 29th Battalion in support and the 28th Battalion in reserve at the hamlet of Dickebusch. For the first time in the war, Canadian troops wore the now-famous tin hat—the flat-brimmed steel helmet they would use for the next forty years—but only fifty were available per company! It was dark and wet, the roads were muddy and narrow, and the reserve and support trenches were in very bad shape. One Canadian staff officer wrote: "Our front line is no line at all. The men are unprotected and in mud and filth and have to be relieved every twenty-four hours." In fact, as the Canadians would soon find out, they had inadvertently occupied the wrong craters, leaving the Germans in their front line with an unequalled opportunity to dominate the Canadian positions with shell- and machine-gun fire and to strike back. Both Turner and Ketchen bore the responsibility for not catching the error. The Canadians might have had a chance to hold the positions so dearly bought by the British 3rd Division, but the craters the Canadians had taken over were virtually indefensible. To make matters worse, the deep water that lay at the bottom of the craters made movement in them almost impossible, and any wounded man who slipped to the bottom of a crater was sure to drown. All day long on April 5, German shelling made a living hell for the Canadians; early the next day, the Germans counterattacked.

The 28th Battalion was still in reserve at Dickebusch when the German assault began. The shelling was so heavy that the battalion was forced to move closer to the front in order to escape some of the bombardment. The battalion's "bombers" (grenade-throwing specialists) were sent to support the 31st Battalion while A Company moved into the line to support the 27th Battalion. As one member of the 28th Battalion would later remember, "The old front line around St-Eloi was found to have been entirely obliterated and A company had to improvise a line as best it could. The proceedings of the day were so badly involved as to be incapable of being detailed with any hope of coherence." Throughout the day and into the next, men fought in small groups, sometimes even alone, trying to hold their positions against the German attacks. Lieutenant F.A. Howlandson "ventured into no man's land only to have his covering party killed or wounded." Lieutenant Gerald D. Murphy was separated from his men by shellfire and wandered the shell holes and craters for hours, fired on by both sides. Captain L.M. Bidwell led a small party forward under heavy fire, found what he believed to be one of the craters that the Canadians had to reoccupy, and held it for two days with no relief and food, water, and ammunition running out. One of the most heroic actions of the day was carried out by Lieutenant Murphy, a young bank clerk, who led a band of bombers forward, reached three of the craters, established machine-gun posts in them, and held them until ordered to withdraw.

The 28th was relieved on the morning of April 8, but the fighting for the craters continued for eleven more days. In the end, the 2nd Canadian Division could not hold. German counterattacks, supported by massive artillery fire, wore them down. The battlefield was a sea of mud broken by craters and mounds; everything looked the same, and no one seemed to know who was in the next crater; attackers were often mistaken for work parties or reinforcements and not identified until too late. On April 15, the Canadians began to construct new defensive positions short of the craters. The battle was effectively lost: the original six mine craters recaptured by the Germans, the original German line restored. St-Eloi was no field of glory; it was an opportunity lost because of faulty intelligence and poor communication, especially at 2nd Canadian Division HQ. Perhaps this is why "St-Eloi" does not appear on the guidon of the Royal Regina Rifles, the major successor of the 28th Battalion. Lost battles are seldom honoured. If so, its absence is no reflection on the individual acts of heroism of a green battalion caught in a terrible battle it could not possibly win, through no fault of its own.

—⁓—

WHEN BRITAIN DECLARED WAR ON GERMANY on August 4, 1914, Newfoundlanders quickly formed the Newfoundland Patriotic Association to organize an island-wide, all-out war effort. The famous Royal Newfoundland Fencibles, which had fought in Canada in the War of 1812, were now a memory, although many Newfoundlanders had served in both the British army and the Royal Navy in the almost hundred years since the Fencibles were disbanded. Nevertheless, the Patriotic Association undertook to raise five hundred men for service with the British army and a thousand for the Royal Naval Reserve. A proclamation was issued on August 22, 1914, and by the end of September, nearly one thousand volunteers had signed up for army service. About half were turned away for physical or medical reasons, while the other half were equipped with locally manufactured khaki uniforms. Slouch hats of the Australian variety were planned but never arrived, nor did Canadian-supplied Ross rifles—a blessing in disguise. There wasn't enough cloth of the right colour for regulation puttees, so a local manufacturer supplied blue ones, giving the first contingent of five hundred the nickname "the Blue Puttees."

The Newfoundlanders sailed for the U.K. on October 3, 1914, and joined the convoy taking Sam Hughes's Canadian Expeditionary Force overseas. When the Newfoundlanders arrived, they were sent to Scotland for training. There, in May 1915, the 1st Newfoundland Regiment was officially stood up as a unit in the British army. Not long after, the regiment was selected to deploy to Gallipoli, in Turkey, to replace a battalion of the Royal Scots Regiment that was badly in need of relief. The Newfoundlanders went by sea to Egypt and then directly to Suvla Bay, on the Aegean coast of the Gallipoli peninsula, to join the 88th Brigade of the 29th Division in an ill-fated campaign that had commenced several months before.

The Gallipoli campaign began in April 1915 when British and Australian and New Zealand (ANZAC) forces landed on the European side of the Dardanelles strait in an effort to force open the waterway and free up a naval passage from the Mediterranean to Istanbul. The notion, thought up by First Lord of the Admiralty Winston S. Churchill, was then to besiege Istanbul and force Turkey—which was allied with Germany and Austria—to surrender. Churchill hoped this might allow Britain and France to come directly to the aid of Russia and bypass the stalemate on the Western Front. Brilliant in its strategic conception, the plan proved impossible to accomplish against Turkish resistance. The British and ANZAC troops were able to get ashore, but the Turks rallied and held them close to the water's edge for nine months, in a bloody stalemate that ground up tens of thousands of casualties on both sides.

Sanitation was almost non-existent, supplies came up from the ships off the beaches in a trickle, and food and medicine were always in short supply. Here too the machine gun and barbed wire forced both sides into massive trench works—a bizarre reproduction of the Western Front on a smaller, dustier, and generally hotter scale. The occasional attack against the Turks, entrenched on the heights, usually ended quickly and with tragic consequences. Or men simply died by ones or twos from constant sniper and shellfire, or from disease.

The Newfoundland Regiment endured Suvla Bay for three months before pulling out in January 1916; thirty men were killed in action or died of their wounds, but dozens more suffered from dysentery, typhoid fever, trench foot, and other diseases. Summer was hot and dry, but in late November and through December the waterlogged trenches occasionally froze. More than 150 members of the regiment were afflicted with frostbite and exposure. Still, the Newfoundlanders were relatively fortunate; they were never called upon to participate in one of the major useless assaults on the Turkish positions that could chew up an entire regiment in only a few hours. When the British government finally decided that Gallipoli was a dead end (after Churchill had been relieved of his Cabinet post in a change of government), the Newfoundlanders accompanied the 29th Division to France to prepare for a major British and French offensive on the Western Front astride the Somme River.

—⁊⁊⁊—

THE BATTLE OF THE SOMME was originally conceived at the end of 1915 as a war-winning British and French attack of massive proportions designed to smash through the German lines and end the war. The Somme River Valley was chosen as the focal point for the attack for no better reason than it was the place where the British and French armies came together on the Western Front, with the British to the north of the Somme and the French to the south. It was not otherwise a particularly good place to launch a major attack. In the original plan, both allies were to contribute a similar number of corps and divisions, but in February 1916 the Germans launched a major offensive of their own at Verdun, about 200 kilometres south of the Somme. The French were forced to pull most of their troops away from the Somme to Verdun, and the plans were altered to provide for only five French divisions attacking south of the Somme and twenty-seven British and Empire divisions attacking to the north of the river. Fourteen of those were to go "over the top" on the very first day, which was eventually designated as July 1, 1916. One of the attacking divisions was to be the 29th.

The 29th Division consisted of the 86th, 87th, and 88th brigades. At the end of June 1916, it was deployed on the left flank of the British Fourth Army about 6 kilometres north of the town of Albert on a front of about 2 kilometres. The division's section of trench ran along the forward slope of a series of spurs that extended from high ground to the west. Between the division and the German lines lay a shallow valley. The German defences were on the high ground across this valley, about 400 metres from the British wire. The Germans had incorporated both the ruined village of Beaumont-Hamel and a long Y-shaped ravine in their defences. One arm of the Y Ravine lay behind the German front trench. It was honeycombed with dug-outs and caves that the Germans had deepened into bunkers capable of holding close to a thousand defenders. Thick barbed wire lay in belts in front of the first line of German trenches, which could not be seen from the British positions. To the left of the 29th Division, anchoring the German line in that sector, lay a low ridge—dubbed Hawthorn Ridge on British maps—with a German redoubt atop it and just behind the German front trench.

The plan for the attack itself was relatively simple: after a massive bombardment lasting several days and designed to kill or incapacitate the German front-line defenders, and ten minutes after a massive mine had been exploded under the German redoubt on Hawthorn Ridge, the attacking troops would advance from their trenches, in the words of the General Headquarters instructions, "in successive waves or lines, each line adding fresh impetus to the preceding one when this is checked, and carrying the whole forward to the objective." In other words, lines of infantry would cross no man's land and simply take possession of the German first and second trench lines. The attackers were specifically instructed not to break up into small groups in order to leapfrog toward their objectives, protecting their comrades as they moved forward. They would not need to do this, in theory, because the preceding bombardment would have destroyed the German defensives, including the many belts of barbed wire, the machine-gun posts, the artillery observation positions, and anything else that might impede the advance.

The attackers were to carry extra ammunition, rations, entrenching tools, wire cutters, Lewis machine guns, and anything else they would need after taking possession of the German trenches. The load amounted to approximately 30 kilos per man. In preparation for the attack, lanes were cleared in the barbed wire in front of the British trenches. For weeks prior to the attack, the 29th and the other assaulting divisions rehearsed over ground that was taped and marked to replicate the areas they would attack over and the German positions they were assigned to capture. As it turned out, however, the Newfoundlanders would assault a part of the front they had not practised for and were unprepared to deal with.

The divisional commander, Major-General H.B. de Lisle, deployed the 86th and 87th brigades in the front line, with the 88th Brigade in reserve. The two attacking brigades were to go over the top at 7:30 AM, capture the first German trench line, and move quickly to the second line. When they had secured their objectives, they were to pass the battalions of the 88th Brigade through and onto the German third line. Those two battalions, the Newfoundland Regiment and the 1st Battalion of the Essex Regiment, were to move into the British front trenches as soon as the initial wave of attackers had pushed off, then move out themselves when the first wave reached the German wire. De Lisle had arranged for the first troops to cross the German trenches to send up flares as a signal for the 88th Brigade to attack.

The plan went wrong from the very first moments of the attack. The massive British barrage did little damage to the German wire, while the German defenders stayed safe in their deep bunkers along the Y Ravine, moving back into prepared positions as soon as the barrage lifted. The explosion under the Hawthorn redoubt served to give them ten minutes' warning that the attack was about to be launched. They recovered so quickly that they were able to reoccupy the large crater caused by the explosion almost as soon as the dirt settled. As the British troops rose from their trenches, the Germans opened an intense machine-gun and rifle fusillade as their artillery began to churn up the area between the trench lines.

The German machine-gunners aimed at the open lanes in the British wire and began to cut the attackers down by the score. The dead and wounded choked the lanes all along the front. The official history of the Royal Newfoundland Regiment—*The Fighting Newfoundlander,* by G.W.L. Nicholson—quotes a German account of the opening minutes of the attack: "This explosion [on Hawthorn Ridge] was a signal for the [British] infantry attack, and everyone got ready and stood on the lower steps of the dug-outs rifles in hand, waiting for the bombardment to lift. In a few minutes the shelling ceased, and we rushed up the steps and out into the crater positions. Ahead of us wave after wave of British troops were crawling out of their trenches and coming towards us at a walk, their bayonets glistening in the sun." Nicholson then describes what came next: "The volume and accuracy of [the German artillery] fire, together with the hail of machine-gun and rifle bullets that swept No Man's Land, disorganized the 29th Division's attack at the very outset."

On the 87th Brigade front—the division's right flank—a very few Inniskilling Fusiliers got through the German wire and into the front trench before they were shot down. The rest of the battalion was held up by uncut wire. To their right, the 2nd South Wales Borderers, attacking the Y Ravine, were cut down within five minutes. The brigade's reserve battalions, the King's Own Scottish Borderers and the Border Regiment, were gunned down practically at the British front trench by shellfire and machine guns. It was the same story on the left flank of the division. There, according to the "Report on Operations" of the British army's General Staff Headquarters, the 86th Brigade's 2nd Battalion of the Royal Fusiliers "immediately came under heavy cross machine gun fire. A few reached the mine crater, but none got as far as the enemy's wire."

Heavy German shellfire, and the large number of casualties so soon after the attack began, unnerved commanders and caused near chaos in brigade and divisional headquarters across the entire front. The word came down from corps to divisions to reserve brigades— delay the follow-up attacks! No one was sure what was happening as runners were killed, telephone wire was cut by the German barrage, and smoke and shell masked the ground. In the sky, observers tried to make sense of the action; so did forward observation posts. Many of the conclusions they drew were wildly optimistic; literally thousands of men were being killed but some reports seemed to indicate a smashing success.

The Newfoundlanders waited in the reserve trench dubbed "St. John's Road," a quaint reminder of home. They could see nothing, but they could hear the steady roar of shellfire and the incessant chattering of the German machine guns and rifles. And there were delays. First one deadline for their attack passed, then another. As the official history puts it, "This postponement and the persistent sound of the great volume of machine-gun fire coming from the enemy's lines made it apparent to the waiting troops that all was not going according to plan. Soon the sight of casualties streaming back emphasized the gravity of the situation." At his divisional headquarters, de Lisle was told that white flares had been seen coming up from the 87th Brigade's right front. That was the pre-arranged signal that the Brigade's leading elements had taken their initial objectives and were preparing to pass the reinforcements from the reserve brigade—the 88th—through to the German rear positions.

When de Lisle heard about the white flares, Nicholson writes, he decided "to make another attempt to capture the front line" and support the 87th Brigade's troops, who he thought were already in the German trenches. But he was wrong. The flares had been German flares, the 87th Brigade had been stopped cold, no British soldiers were anywhere near the German trenches, and the 88th Brigade was about to attack right in the teeth of fully alert German defenders who were pouring thousands of rounds into the open lanes of British barbed wire, already choked with the bodies of the dead and badly wounded.

At 8:45 AM Brigadier-General D. Cayley, commanding the 88th Brigade, issued orders to Lieutenant-Colonel A.L. Hadow, CO of the Newfoundland Regiment, to attack the German positions immediately in front of the Y Ravine "as soon as possible." Hadow asked if that meant he was to wait until the Essex Regiment was ready to join the assault (that was the plan), and was told that his men were to go as soon as they could move, and not wait. Had the German front line been taken? Hadow asked. "The situation is not cleared up," Cayley replied. Time was of the essence. Hadow now realized that the communication trenches between his reserve position and the British front trench were clogged with wounded men. He decided that instead of the regiment's making its way forward through the jammed communications trench, they would attack from where they were. This meant, in effect, the regiment would have to cross 250 metres of open ground before they could even reach their own front trench. Then they would still have to pass through the cleared lanes of barbed wire, where casualties were piling up by the minute, before proceeding across a bullet- and shell-swept battlefield toward the Germans.

What did the men feel in those last minutes before climbing to the lip of the trench and joining battle? Nicholson tells his readers that "the resolve and determination of each man remained firm. His chief concern seemed to be how could a man burdened with sixty pounds of baggage hoist himself up on to the parapet when the order came. . . . In spite of all cheerfulness abounded, and the traditional sense of humour went unchecked, particularly when it was recalled that the awards awaiting them were not confined to the honours of battle." (Nicholson was referring to the charms of waiting Newfoundland girls.)

Possibly. More likely many said a silent prayer and hoped their courage would survive; the silent terror of what they were about to undergo struggled within them against an intense desire not to fail—to do so would be to let their buddies down. In moments like these was it "the regiment" that sustained them? Does it really matter whether their cohesion was born of regimental tradition or of a desire not to shame themselves in front of those who had become, in the closest sense, their brothers in arms? Whatever it was, the two leading companies—A and B—waited as Hadow climbed up and over the edge of the trench, walked forward about 20 metres, then signalled the two company commanders to follow. They did, and so did their men.

As one witness described, "From each corner of every traverse men came pouring. . . . The rear sections stood on the parapet waiting for the leading ones to gain their proper distance (40 paces). They advanced, almost sideways with their chins tucked into their shoulders, as they might have headed into a blizzard of blinding snow, instead of the hail of bullets that buzzed past them like angry bees. As they advanced, they began to drop, first by ones and twos, then as they neared the lanes in their own wire, by the dozens." "Where two men had been advancing side by side," Nicholson writes, "suddenly there was only one—and a few paces farther on he too would pitch forward on his face." Private Anthony Stacey later remembered how the "men were mown down in waves"; the gaps in the wire were "a proper trap for our boys as the enemy just set the sights of the machine guns on the gaps in the barbed wire and fired." The survivors struggled on toward an isolated tree about halfway down the slope. That tree went down in history as "the danger tree," which few men reached and even fewer passed. All too soon, Stacey could see "no moving, but lots of heaps of khaki slumped on the ground." The Newfoundlanders were the only British troops moving in the open on that sector of the front, and every German rifle, machine gun, and artillery piece was aimed directly at them. In less than thirty minutes, the Newfoundland Regiment almost ceased to exist. The badly wounded lay out in the sun all day; those who tried to crawl back were shot by German snipers. The full count of the tragedy wasn't compiled for several days—233 killed or dead of wounds, 386 wounded, 91 missing. Every officer was killed or wounded. It took four days to bury all the dead.

The opening day of the Battle of the Somme was a ghastly failure. On that day alone the British suffered 57,470 casualties, 19,240 of them dead. Even so, the battle dragged on for months at the insistence of Sir Douglas Haig, the British army's commander-in-chief on the Western Front. The Canadian Corps itself entered the battle on September 15, 1916, at the Battle of Courcelette. From then until the end of the fighting on the Somme, on November 11, 1916, all four divisions of the Canadian Corps became engaged. The Canadians suffered more than twenty-four thousand killed and wounded in those two months. But not one of the Canadian battalions took as many casualties in as short a time as the Newfoundland Regiment did on July 1. To honour that sacrifice, a 30-hectare memorial park was dedicated, ironically by Haig himself, on June 7, 1925. The centrepiece of the memorial, located near the spot where the Newfoundlanders' advance began, is a large bronze statue of a caribou, defiantly facing the former positions of the German trenches. The caribou is situated on a mound surrounded by rock and shrubs native to Newfoundland. At the base of the mound are three large bronze tablets that contain the names of the 820 members of the Newfoundland Regiment, the Newfoundland Royal Naval Reserve, and the Mercantile Marines who were killed in the First World War but have no known graves.

The Newfoundland Regiment was slowly rebuilt after that first day on the Somme, and returned to action time and time again before the end of the war. Of the 6,241 Newfoundlanders who served in the regiment, 72 percent were killed or wounded, with over 1,500 of them dead. In 1918, after the Battle of Cambrai, the regiment was given the honour of using the prefix "Royal." The Royal Newfoundland Regiment was disbanded in 1919, but a Royal Newfoundland Regiment was reorganized in 1949 after Newfoundland became Canada's tenth province. It perpetuates the First World War regiment and is now a reserve formation in the Canadian army. The virtual destruction of the Newfoundland Regiment on the first day of the battle—July 1, 1916— has been marked by islanders ever since as a memorial day, the same day on which other Canadians celebrate the Confederation of 1867—the official birth of a modern, united Canada.

Chapter Eight

REDEMPTION: THE VAN DOOS AT COURCELETTE AND THE 85TH BATTALION AT VIMY RIDGE

Even if we are going to the slaughter . . . morale is extraordinary. And we are determined to prove that Canadiens are not cowards.

—Lieutenant-Colonel Thomas-Louis-Eugène Tremblay, CO 22nd Battalion, September 15, 1916

SINCE THE BOER WAR AT LEAST, every Canadian army formation at war has been obliged to keep a war diary—a daily summary of events usually compiled by a unit intelligence officer and attested to by the unit commanding officer. The war diary constitutes part of the official record of the unit—what it did, where and who was involved. The war diary of the 22nd Battalion (now the Royal 22e Régiment) of the 5th Canadian Brigade, 2nd Canadian Division, records the following for a day in mid-September, 1916:

15/9/16
At 10.30 a.m. left for trenches 1000 yards S.E. of POZIERES. At 5.00 p.m. order received that Battalion is to advance through 27th Battalion to take COURCELETTE and occupy line North and East of village. At 6.16 p.m. assault launched. Objective gained at 7.00 p.m. Seven counter-attacks beaten off during the night, mainly against quarry and cemetery.

The commanding officer of the 22nd Battalion on the night of September 15–16 was Lieutenant-Colonel Thomas-Louis-Eugène Tremblay, who had been only twenty-eight years old when he was appointed to command the battalion. A graduate of the Royal Military College, a superb athlete and an engineer, he had remained active in the militia until the outbreak of war, when he had volunteered for action overseas. In the words of the official historian of the Royal 22ᵉ Régiment, Serge Bernier, "Tremblay's experience in the artillery and the infantry, his Royal Military College education and his passion for the military made him an ideal candidate [to assume command] despite his relative youth." But Tremblay was something else too—he was a man who could record his deepest feelings while also describing the virtually indescribable death and destruction of battle. The 22nd Battalion's war diary for the night of September 15 may have been laconic, but Tremblay was somewhat more effusive when, the next day, he described the opening night of the Battle of Courcelette in a letter home:

> We were fortunate to enter Courcelette right away with our barrage . . . some Germans were caught off guard in their dugouts . . . and were forced to surrender without resisting. Their dugouts turned out to be . . . traps for them. Two whole companies surrendered to a few of our men . . . but we paid dearly for our success. . . . It is impossible to describe the horrific conditions that we endured from 8 o'clock in the evening of 15 September to 3 o'clock the next morning between the sugar factory and the Courcelette-Martinpuich road. It was like a bad dream: houses on fire south of the village, shells falling by the hundreds, blowing up everything, fighting with grenades, bayonet charges, battles, corpses everywhere and the constant writhing of the wounded. Man's mental and physical endurance is incredible. If hell is as horrible as what I saw there, I wouldn't wish it on my worse enemy.

The attack on Courcelette produced one of the earliest battle honours awarded to the Royal 22ᵉ Régiment, which became known to history as the Van Doos and is now one of the Canadian army's three permanent infantry regiments.

—m—

FRENCH CANADA has had an ambiguous relationship with the Canadian military since at least the late nineteenth century. Even in early 2008, as a Van Doos–led battle group led the fight against the Taliban in the wartorn Kandahar Province of Afghanistan, Quebecers were in large measure opposed to the deployment. In the First World War, when some 600,000 men (and a handful of women) from Canada served in the Canadian army—at the front with the Canadian Corps, in the United Kingdom, or elsewhere—estimates as to the number of French-speaking Canadians who served run at about 35,000, including 15,000 conscripts (conscription was introduced in mid-1917). This ratio is at least 90 percent lower than the number of either British-born Canadians or Canadians born in Canada who served.

Quebecers were, in general, not enthusiastic about British imperialism, and many saw the war as an imperial event being fought for purposes that had little or nothing to do with their daily lives. The German attack on France did not kindle much patriotic fervour in the hearts of Quebecers, who had been taught for generations since the French Revolution that their one-time mother country had been transformed by the revolution into a hotbed of radical republicanism and socialism inimical to their beloved Roman Catholic religion and traditions. In the decades after Confederation, when English-Canadian militia regiments were springing up around the young Dominion, pride in being a part of the British imperial and military tradition had played a key role in the development of regimental traditions. It was hard for many French Canadians to feel a part of that pride. When the small permanent force set down its roots in the 1870s and when the Royal Military College (RMC) opened its doors in 1876, British military traditions were very much part of the founding principles of both institutions, and again, those traditions were inextricably tied to British imperialism. In the case of RMC, only thirty-nine of the thousand or so who had graduated by 1914 were French-speaking.

The decades-long erosion of military tradition in Quebec formed the backdrop for the horrendous failure of Sam Hughes's recruiting efforts among the French-speaking population in that province. Put simply, it would have taken a special effort at recruiting, an effort over and above that which was being made elsewhere in the country, to encourage significant francophone recruitment in Quebec. As Hughes's biographer puts it, "Quebec was going to need special care if recruiting for a foreign war was to succeed in the province." Hughes (and Prime Minister Borden) was not about to make that effort.

Hughes himself was part of the problem. As his biographer writes, he had "always been remarkably insensitive to French-Canadians." He was one of Ontario's leading Protestant politicians and he had never made a secret of his opposition to separate, tax-supported Roman Catholic schools, Quebecers serving in the papal guard, French priests, or a visible French-Canadian presence in military ceremonies. He was a prominent and even militant member of the Loyal Orange Lodge, a vocal Protestant organization that considered Roman Catholics essentially traitors to the Crown and Empire. The order strongly opposed what they viewed as "special rights" for French Canadians. To top it all off, Hughes was a strong imperialist. Very few French Canadians trusted him personally, and as events turned out, they were quite correct not to do so.

No one really knows whether or not Hughes ever gave a thought to how his plan to place volunteers in numbered battalions would hinder French-Canadian enlistment, but it did. There were half a dozen or so French-Canadian militia regiments in Quebec at the outbreak of war, but in no case did any of those regiments have enough men to form a new numbered battalion of its own. That was equally true of many regiments outside Quebec, and where it was true—as was the case with the 10th Battalion, for example—men from different regiments were combined into a single battalion. Hughes, who made all the key decisions at Valcartier, could have done the same with the French-speakers who showed up, because there were certainly enough to form a single French-speaking battalion in the first contingent. Instead they were placed into English-speaking units such as the 12th and 14th battalions. Since a battalion was the basic unit not only for training but also for fighting, it was important, if not crucial, for the members of that unit to be able to understand one another. The simple fact is that Hughes had no intention of allowing a separate French-speaking battalion to form or even use the handful of experienced French-speaking officers he did have at his disposal in key positions in the expeditionary force he was building.

The first contingent of the CEF thus departed without a French-speaking battalion, but some prominent Quebecers were determined that the next contingent would not. When, under pressure from old regimental hands, Hughes decided that some of his numbered battalions would be designated as Irish or Scottish (i.e., Highland) battalions, he left the door open for a French-Canadian unit. Throughout September 1914 prominent French Quebecers came forward to make the case for such a unit. Among them were Sir Wilfrid Laurier, former prime minister and leader of the Opposition in Parliament, Conservative cabinet minister Louis-Philippe Pelletier, and Dr. Arthur Migneault, a physician and pharmaceutical manufacturer who, following the precedent set by Hamilton Gault with the PPCLI, offered $50,000 to help raise a regiment. As Serge Bernier writes, "What can we say of the political maneuvers that were necessary before government consent was obtained to create a French-speaking unit such as the 22nd French Canadian battalion? The situation is all the more striking when compared to the ease with which Hamilton Gault . . . obtained official permission to found an entirely new regiment."

The pressure worked. On October 15, 1914, the government announced that a French-speaking battalion would be raised and would accompany the second contingent (eventually the Second Division) when it sailed for Europe. A huge recruitment rally was held that evening for what was proposed to be called the "Royal Canadien-Français," while Militia Districts 4 (Montreal) and 5 (Quebec City) were ordered to raise three French-speaking battalions, intended to be the 22nd, 23rd, and 24th. In fact, though, only the 22nd was officially declared to be a French-speaking unit.

Officially the 22nd was a numbered battalion like all the rest of the units in the CEF, but from the very beginning it developed a sort of regimental aura. A cap badge was designed very soon after the battalion was formed, consisting of the royal crown on the back of a beaver sitting on a log that bore the provincial motto of Quebec, "Je me souviens." On the left side of the beaver was a ring with the words "Régiment canadien-français" encircling the Quebec coat of arms. The number 22 was superimposed at the bottom of the ring. This is the cap badge of the Royal 22e Régiment to this very day. Like the PPCLI, the 22nd battalion also carried a unique camp colour to Europe, apparently sewn by women from Saint-Jean, Quebec, where the unit spent most of the fall and winter of 1914–15 in training. The battalion's first commanding officer was Colonel Frédéric Mondelet Gaudet, one of RMC's first French-speaking graduates, an artillery officer and an engineer. He was a well-qualified and much respected officer, but he was forty-seven years old and not likely to easily endure the rigours of leading a fighting battalion into action.

The battalion was housed in the former quarters of the Royal Canadian Dragoons at Saint-Jean, south of Montreal; by December 1914 it had reached its full war establishment of more than 1,100 men. It was no doubt encouraging that so many French Quebecers were prepared to enlist for overseas service, but there was a long delay between the weeks when the battalion first mustered in October and its departure, first for Amherst, Nova Scotia, in March 1915 and then to the U.K. in May. The facilities in Saint-Jean were adequate but equipment was in short supply. The official historian of the Van Doos writes: "The weeks of monotonous, repetitive exercises took their toll: dozens of discipline problems cropped up, including many desertions. Montreal was an irresistible magnet for these young men." Nevertheless the battalion more than survived the long winter. In March 1915, just prior to the battalion's departure for Nova Scotia, Gaudet hand-picked Tremblay as his replacement. On May 1, 1915, the 22nd Battalion joined the 25th Battalion on board the transport ship *Saxonia* to begin the journey to war as part of the 5th Brigade of the 2nd Canadian Division.

—⚊—

THE 22ND BATTALION trained in the U.K. for three and a half months along with the rest of the 2nd Canadian Division before leaving for the front in mid-September 1915. Although the 2nd Division saw heavy action at St-Eloi in April 1916, the 5th Brigade did not take part in that disaster. The brigade and especially the 22nd Battalion did see action in a small victory at Mount Sorrel, also at the edge of the Ypres Salient, in the first half of June, but were fortunate enough to miss the opening phases of the Battle of the Somme. The Canadians' turn at the Somme did not come until September, when Haig ordered them to lead yet another phase of his now six-week-old offensive. This was the Battle of Flers-Courcelette.

The Battle of Flers-Courcelette was intended to be a two-army attack to open on September 15 against newly built German defensive positions. Two innovations would be used in the offensive—the newly invented tank and the creeping barrage. The first would have been of no use to the 22nd Battalion in its assigned objective, the village of Courcelette, but the second proved very effective. It was specifically intended to give advancing infantry close cover as they attacked. In effect, artillery behind the front was to "lift" or advance its fire at regular intervals—usually a 5-metre lift every few minutes. By following close behind this moving wall of exploding shells, attacking troops were supposed to be able to advance right up to the enemy's defences. Because communications between the artillery and the attacking forces were usually poor and prone to complete breakdown, there was generally no opportunity for the advancing troops to tell the artillery to speed up or slow down the lift. Thus infantry were trained to "lean into" the barrage—to get as close as possible to advancing explosions and stay close as it moved toward enemy positions.

On September 10 the 22nd Battalion arrived near Albert, where it encamped in brickyards; on September 15 it advanced to near brigade headquarters, south of Pozières. The initial Canadian attacks on the 15th were launched at dawn as the 4th and 6th brigades assaulted German defences at the towns of Courcelette and Martinpuich and a major German trench known as Fabeck Graben. The terrain increased the difficulty of the advance—"a wasteland whose undulating hills made it impossible for a soldier on the ground to see the immediate effects of the attack he was involved in," writes the official historian of the 22nd Battalion. He notes that "the folds of land are sometimes remarkably deep and it is startling to come upon villages down below, even if one has been told about them in advance." Nonetheless, the creeping barrage and the handful of tanks (only seven were assigned to the two attacking brigades and six were rendered useless by mechanical breakdown or shellfire) brought complete success; by 10:00 AM the first objectives had been taken.

Canadian Corps Commander Julian Byng then ordered the 5th Brigade to follow up and capture Courcelette itself. Tremblay asked the brigade commander to let his battalion have the honour of being one of the two assaulting battalions. He got his wish, with his battalion reinforced by two companies of the 26th Battalion to move in behind the Quebecers and mop up any resistance that the 22nd left behind. The attack was set for 6:00 PM but actually began fifteen minutes late. Tremblay saw this fight as the first major test of his battalion's spirit. Bernier's history records that Tremblay wrote, "Even if we are going to the slaughter . . . morale is extraordinary. And we are determined to prove that Canadiens are not cowards." It was essential, he told the troops, that the 22nd's first attack, to be launched exactly one year after the battalion had arrived in France, succeed "for the honour of French Canadians whom we represent in France."

With two companies in the lead and two behind they advanced through a valley south of Pozières. Before the battalion could even get to its start line it was obliged to advance 5 kilometres over open ground. Here the first of many casualties were taken as German artillery began to pound the ground around and in front of them. Then they passed over a ridge and spotted Martinpuich. As one observer later wrote, "the ground although dry, was a perfect confusion of shell holes, and shattered trenches." The battalion then formed three lines or waves, with one man every metre in the first line, as Tremblay led them away from Martinpuich and toward Courcelette. Tremblay saw that his leading men were heading too far to the right, so he "ran along the whole line, redirecting the advance." They moved steadily behind their own barrage, but with each passing moment "men were struck down and killed or blown up and buried." Tremblay suffered at least three very narrow escapes. Still the Quebecers advanced, doubling their pace, even beginning to outrace their own covering barrage. At the edge of Courcelette they paused for a few moments until the barrage lifted, then swept into the village with bayonets fixed, "in an irresistible flood." They hurled grenades into dugouts, then shot any enemy who emerged alive. They fought Germans with bayonets and anything else that might inflict a wound or kill, while close-range machine-gun and rifle fire cut men down on both sides. The 26th Battalion followed, taking hundreds of prisoners—almost three hundred—before the town was secured. But the fight was not over; that night the Germans launched seven counterattacks on Courcelette; all were repulsed. There were more German attacks over the next three days. The battalion held the town. When the 22nd Battalion pulled back into reserve positions on the morning of September 18, they counted 512 killed, wounded, or taken prisoner.

The 22nd Battalion had fifteen days to absorb reinforcements and prepare for the next attack, against a major German position that the Canadians had dubbed Regina Trench. Running southwest to northeast about 1.5 kilometres north of Courcelette, the trench was strongly defended, but if taken would provide good ground to launch further attacks in the direction of Thiepval Ridge. Again the attackers advanced behind a creeping barrage, but this time the results for the 22nd Battalion were very different. The war diary records: "Enemy in great strength. About half way to objective, enemy opened most intense artillery barrage, rifle and M.G. [machine-gun] fire. Only about 50 men succeeded in entering REGINA Trench. After a sharp fight seeing themselves hopelessly outnumbered, they gradually retreated to our original trenches." In this short battle the 22nd lost 339 casualties—dead, wounded, and taken prisoner—to no apparent effect. The Canadian Corps made three more efforts to take Regina Trench, on October 21, October 25, and November 11. The job was finally done by the 4th Canadian Division on November 11, 1916. The campaign to take Regina Trench cost the Canadian Corps more than three thousand casualties.

The 22nd Battalion fought in every major battle from Flers-Courcelette to the end of the war. It was disbanded on May 20, 1919, along with all the other numbered battalions of the CEF. But strong pressure from Quebec leaders, and a growing recognition in the army itself that French-Canadian ties to the military needed to be strengthened, led to almost immediate resurrection of the formation as a new regiment in the Canadian army's permanent force. It was formed as the 22nd Regiment on April 1, 1921, and the unit's distinguished war record (and the awarding of posthumous Victoria Crosses to two of its men) was recognized with the designation "Royal." Later in the decade the Royal 22nd Regiment was officially renamed the Royal 22ᵉ Régiment. In French twenty-two is *vingt-deux,*—thus the regiment's nickname the Van Doos. Close to six thousand men served with the Van Doos in the First World War; two-thirds of them were killed or wounded.

—☙—

THE NOVA SCOTIA HIGHLANDERS of today's Canadian army trace their roots back to April 6, 1871, when three provincial regiments, the Colchester and Hants Provisional Battalion of Infantry, the Cumberland Provisional Battalion of Infantry, and the Cape Breton Highlanders, were founded as part of the expansion of the Canadian militia in the wake of the Fenian threat. All three regiments went through several iterations in the following years and individual volunteers from them served with the Canadian contingent in South Africa during the Boer War. In the four years before the First World War, two more militia regiments were established in the region—the 70th Colchester and Hants Regiment and the 81st Hants Regiment.

The strong attachment of Nova Scotians to Great Britain ensured that the British declaration of war on Germany in August 1914 would bring a torrent of recruits to existing militia regiments and that many of those already in the militia would volunteer for service almost immediately. That was exactly what happened. The 1911 census for Canada showed Nova Scotia with a population of 492,000; just over 29,000 volunteered, or more than 10 percent of the entire male population—one of the highest in the nation for an entire province. Most of those who went overseas with the CEF—a little over 25,000— were recruited through the existing regiments and, like most of the rest of Sam Hughes's army, placed in numbered battalions. The first of the Nova Scotia numbered battalions was the 17th, which fought with the 1st Canadian Division. The 25th was with the 2nd Division. Other battalions were either broken up and their men fed into existing units or they were allotted large numbers of men from outside the province—"not permitted to preserve their regional identity at the front," as one early history of the 85th Battalion records. The 85th was one of the very few later formations that did stay Nova Scotian to the core and that fought as a unit. Their first battle was Canada's most epic of the First World War—Vimy Ridge.

The 85th Battalion, CEF, was authorized on September 14, 1915, under the command of Lieutenant-Colonel A.H. Borden, first cousin to Sir Robert Borden, Canada's prime minister. By this time many of the battalions being raised for overseas service were concentrated, accommodated, and equipped locally—not at Valcartier—where they also received basic military training and drill. The 85th was first mobilized at the local militia camp at Aldershot, Nova Scotia, but transferred to Halifax not long after. They spent the winter there training, filling up their ranks, and fitting themselves out. The battalion was styled as a Highland battalion but did not actually receive kilts until the late spring of 1918. They did adopt an appropriate motto (*Siol na Fear Fearail* in Gaelic, or "The Breed of Manly Men" in English), a distinctive cap badge, and a Balmoral cap with a khaki feather that contained in the centre a small red feather, held in place by the cap badge.

As Borden was overseeing the training and kitting out of his battalion he decided there were still enough potential volunteers in the province to raise an entire Highland brigade. On January 26, 1916, the Nova Scotia Highland Brigade was authorized, with Borden himself in command. Recruiting went very quickly, and by May 1916 the brigade was mobilized at Aldershot. It consisted of the 85th, the 185th, the 193rd, and the 219th battalions. During the summer thousands of men were drilled and trained. They learned how to dig trenches, fire rifles, throw grenades, fight with bayonets. They marched night and day. In the words of one regimental history, they "rapidly developed into a snappy military organization and began to show a consciousness of power and the enthusiasm of confidence in themselves and their ability to take their part in the great world struggle." At the end of September a large presentation ceremony with a drumhead church service was organized; Lady Borden, wife of the prime minister, presented the battalions with their King's and battalion colours—their regimental guidons that would be laid up to await their return from battle. In mid-October the brigade sailed for the U.K. aboard the liner *Olympic,* which had been fitted out as a troopship. They arrived in Liverpool Harbour on the evening of October 18, 1916.

The Nova Scotia Highland Brigade never saw action as a brigade. Like most formed units arriving in the U.K. by the end of 1916, it was broken up. There was no place in the Canadian Corps order of battle for another brigade but there was more than enough room for the thousands of men who had come over with the brigade. The 193rd, 185th, and 219th battalions were stripped away and broken up and their men fed into existing battalions already at the front. The 85th might have suffered the same fate but for two factors: that its commanding officer was the prime minister's cousin, and the need for an entire new battalion at the front. This need had come about because there had been seven full battalions from the Montreal area with the Canadian Corps, virtually all from the English-speaking population of that city. The army and the government saw that many battalions from one place as dangerous overrepresentation (that is, in the event of a military disaster) and it was decided that two of the Montreal battalions would be broken up and their men scattered into other units. The 85th was assigned to replace one of those two battalions, the 73rd of the 4th Division.

When the 85th Battalion arrived to join the 12th Brigade of the 4th Canadian Division, preparations were already under way for the impending Canadian Corps attack on Vimy Ridge. The ridge was an important objective because it was a salient in the Allied lines (the sector had been held by both the French and the British) that provided the Germans with an especially good observation point for many kilometres around. The attack on Vimy Ridge was to be launched by the entire Canadian Corps, attacking together for the first time, in conjunction with a British attack in the Arras sector, immediately to the south of the Vimy position. In preparation for the attack, a number of innovations were employed, some of which 1st Division Commander Arthur Currie had learned from a tour of the Verdun battlefields and close study of lessons that the French had learned there. Others—such as the creeping barrage—were adopted from lessons that the British had learned. Canadian Corps Commander Sir Julian Byng was determined to bring everything together in one crescendo in a "bite-and-hold" operation that would involve intense preparation and rehearsal, tireless efforts to locate and silence German guns prior to the attack, and the digging of eleven huge underground galleries or tunnels in the chalk below and to the west of Vimy Ridge to give cover to his attacking troops. It was all timed to be ready for the morning of April 9, 1917—Easter Monday.

The 85th Battalion was not at first intended to take part in the attack on Vimy Ridge. As a late arrival, it was used primarily as a labour battalion in the intense preparation for the attack. It was assigned to build and fill ammunition dumps, dig deep dugouts and assembly trenches, and carry and string barbed wire. After the attack began, they were to lug ammunition and escort and guard prisoners. The 4th Division was assigned the northernmost part of the attack; it was the newest of the divisions and had the steepest climb up the ridge. As soon as the attack began in the snowy pre-dawn morning of April 9, the division ran into very stiff German resistance, especially at the highest point on the ridge, Hill 145, where the original German defensive trenches (their second line) were virtually intact despite the Canadian bombardment. Two of the leading Canadian battalions—the 102nd and the 87th—were shot to pieces, leaving a significant piece of ground under German control and threatening the entire 4th Division attack. A number of reserve formations were called in, and the 85th was assigned to take Hill 145.

Although the 85th had been kept very busy with its labour duties in the days leading up to the attack, Lieutenant-Colonel Borden had insisted that every spare moment be filled with regular infantry training, and especially the specific preparations the assault battalions were undergoing, including rehearsed attacks over a 1:1 taped model of the ridge that had been prepared well back of the Canadian lines. When the order arrived in the early afternoon on April 9 to prepare two companies of the battalion to enter the battle, Borden selected D and C companies. They drew rifles, Lewis guns, extra ammunition, and plenty of grenades, and with rations, water, and tools went forward to the entrance of one of the tunnels—Tottenham Tunnel. Borden decided that the two companies would approach the ridge through the tunnel, emerge from its left exit, assemble in the new trenches that had been dug by the first attackers, and then, after the usual preliminary barrage, attack at 6:45 PM.

C Company emerged from Tottenham Tunnel on time and the men filed into their designated trench on the left, followed by D Company on the right. Borden directed his men into position. At the very last moment before the expected artillery barrage, a messenger showed up from brigade headquarters with the stunning news that the barrage had been cancelled—the brigade commander considered the 85th Battalion men too close to the German positions to risk it. Borden was too far from his two company commanders to get the word to them on time; he decided it was just too late to even try. The battalion war diary then records what happened:

> [The officer commanding] waited to see whether the Companies would advance without a barrage. A half minute after ZERO "C" Company on the left moved calmly and deliberately out of the trenches, the advance was taken up by "D" Company. In spite of Machine Gun and rifle fire from the enemy, which immediately opened, the attack was pressed home, the Companies providing their own covering fire by Lewis Guns firing from the hip and riflemen firing on the move. Many of the Germans finding themselves unable to stop the advance turned and ran but were soon put out of action by our fire.

Borden thought his men had been completely successful, and throughout the night supervised preparations of defences against an expected counterattack. It snowed that night and turned very cold as the men huddled down in shell holes and open trenches. At morning light they discovered that Borden had been too optimistic; Germans were still entrenched on part of the position, and the grim work of digging out the enemy restarted. This time there was no mistake. The battalion stayed on Vimy Ridge until April 14, when they were finally relieved and withdrawn. This little piece of the famous ridge cost the 85th Battalion 25 percent of the unit's effective strength, with 56 killed outright and 282 wounded, many of whom died of their wounds.

By the late spring of 1917, the Canadian Corps was an experienced, well-led, and innovative fighting unit of the British Expeditionary Force. Under the leadership of Julian Byng and Arthur Currie the Corps began to earn a reputation for finishing the tasks given it in methodical fashion, using artillery, signals, engineering troops, and training techniques in new and innovative ways that produced results. Both corps commanders knew that Canada's small national army—for that is what the Canadian Corps was—could not fight long battles of attrition and sustain heavy casualties. They both emphasized using firepower to dominate the battleground instead of massive waves of men. Casualties were still high—Vimy Ridge cost the Canadian Corps 3,598 killed and 7,004 wounded—but at least those casualties purchased success. A corner had been turned. The confusion and outright failures that had marked Canadian battles in the first year and a half after arriving at the front were a thing of the past. Canada's fighting reputation had been redeemed; victory lay ahead.

CHAPTER NINE

VICTORY: THE 58TH BATTALION AT PASSCHENDAELE
AND THE ROYAL CANADIAN REGIMENT AT CAMBRAI

I saw Pat coming up carrying his gun on his shoulder. I remember saying to myself "Good old Pat, now Fritzie will get it" but . . . as he got into position, a German sniper shot him with a rifle bullet through the forehead.

—Lieutenant Don Cameron, 58th Battalion, CEF, after the Battle of
Passchendaele

THE ROYAL REGIMENT OF CANADA is today one of the oldest and most active regiments in the Canadian Army Reserve. It was formed on March 14, 1862—one of the regiments established to beef up the Canadian militia in the early years of the U.S. Civil War. At the outbreak of war in August 1914, the Royal Regiment contributed to recruitment of the 3rd Battalion of the CEF, which served with the 1st Canadian Division through the war. In May of 1915 it was ordered to recruit another battalion—the 58th—from men in the Toronto area and the rural counties west of the city. The 58th Battalion concentrated at Paradise Camp, Niagara-on-the-Lake, in late June under the command of Lieutenant-Colonel Harry A. Genet, a British-born officer with five years' service in a British territorial (reserve or militia) regiment and more than seventeen years in Canada with the 38th Dufferin Rifles. His experiences were not untypical of his men in that almost 56 percent of them had prior military experience of some sort and a majority were from the United Kingdom. The battalion's historian, Kevin R. Shackleton, attributes the great success of the recruiting campaign in the late spring and summer of 1915 to the news arriving from Ypres of the resistance of the 1st Division to the first German gas attack of the war.

The battalion trained and equipped at Niagara-on-the-Lake until the end of October, when it marched to Toronto, then entrained for Montreal and Halifax. On November 22, 1915, the 58th left Canada aboard the troopship *Saxonia* (formerly a liner). The ship carried twice its designed complement of passengers on the early winter crossing and had to be constantly on the alert for German submarines. For some of the men, the food was as much a menace as the Germans. One man wrote home: "For dinner we had potatoes cooked with the great coats on and boiled meat, which I think came from the steer Noah had in the Ark." As they neared the Irish coast they were ordered to sleep fully dressed and wear their lifebelts for fear of submarine attack, but the passage proved uneventful. They docked at Plymouth on December 1 and spent a cold, wet winter at Bramshott Camp doing physical exercises, route marches, drill, and even some grenading and musketry.

In February 1916 the battalion was notified that it was shortly to move to the front as part of the 9th Brigade of the 3rd Canadian Division. The men arrived in the Ypres Salient just after the Germans began their massive attack on Verdun, but took no part in any major action until the last phases of the Battle of the Somme. Then, in the fall, the battalion participated in fighting around the major German defences near Courcelette, including the initial unsuccessful Canadian attack on Regina Trench. The 58th Battalion formed part of the 3rd Division's reserve in the initial attacks on Vimy Ridge in early April 1917, but did not actually climb the ridge until several days after the attack, when German resistance had been completely crushed. Up to that point the battalion had had a relatively easy war; then came the Battle of Passchendaele.

Passchendaele was the third major battle fought by all four divisions of the Canadian Corps and the second under the command of Lieutenant-General Arthur Currie, who had succeeded Sir Julian Byng in June 1917 as corps commander. General Douglas Haig, the British commander-in-chief on the Western Front, had conceived the Passchendaele campaign with a number of objectives. His most important aim was to drive through from the Ypres Salient to the North Sea around Zeebrugge. There his armies would link up with a Royal Navy landing to destroy German submarine bases and form a firm foundation for an attack eastward, into Germany itself. Even if these ambitious objectives could not be achieved, a major British assault in Flanders would put pressure on the Germans at a time when the French army was in disarray from mutinies in the ranks and Russia was on the verge of collapse.

The battle began in mid-June with a massive push east by the British Fifth Army from positions near Ypres. The immediate objective of the attack was the town of Passchendaele, less than 10 kilometres away. Once it had been taken in the first phase of the offensive, the armies would move on to the ridge beyond in the second. The initial attacks were carried out by the British, aided by Australians and New Zealanders. There was heavy enemy resistance and British and ANZAC casualties mounted. The attackers faced two main difficulties. First, the heavy shelling that preceded and accompanied the attacks destroyed the drainage system in the polders to the east of Ypres and created a sea of mud. Second, the already sodden ground was made even wetter by an unseasonably early beginning to the autumn rains. The fall of 1917 turned out to be one of the wettest on record. To make matters worse, the Germans had developed a new system of "defence in depth." Instead of putting the bulk of their defenders in the front trenches, where many would be killed by improving British artillery techniques and better guns and shells, they laid out defensive belts that were thinly held at the front, more thickly manned to the rear. Each belt consisted mainly of machine guns in bunkers or "pillboxes" with interlocking fields of fire so that each could protect the other and the ones in front could be covered by others to the rear.

For four bloody months Haig pushed his commanders forward, even after the Royal Navy had bowed out of the venture and there was no chance at all that his original aim might be achieved. By mid-September the British lines had been pushed only about half the distance to Passchendaele, which had virtually disappeared from the face of the earth. In early October Haig called on Currie to bring the Canadian Corps into the fight. Currie reluctantly agreed, but under a number of conditions: the Canadian Corps must fight together; it must not fight under the Fifth Army—whose commander Currie thought incompetent—but under the Second Army; he and his staff must have sufficient time to prepare the attack. Haig had little choice but to agree, since Currie was ultimately responsible to Ottawa for the overall welfare of the Canadian Corps, not to him.

Currie's preparations centred on building proper roads to bring up supplies, draining as much of the land as possible prior to the fight, and readying the artillery for massive fire support of the infantry. This last was a typical Currie concern. He believed in expending shells instead of lives. His attack plans usually contained carefully laid out fire-support schemes and massive use of artillery. In most cases the men were called upon to advance behind a creeping barrage, consolidate their positions, and then advance again after the artillery had been brought up. Thus Currie's plan for Passchendaele was a traditional bite-and-hold attack of the sort that had been so successful at Vimy Ridge.

On October 19 the 58th Battalion—as part of the 9th Brigade—began to prepare for its part in the impending Canadian assault. One private wrote home: "We are having a very uncomfortable spell of weather now. . . . The fine days seem to have gone and the rain and cold have come again. The mud has begun to get quite thick and deep again. I don't know, but hope, and have an idea, [the war] may quit about Christmas time." Several days later the battalion was in reserve building "duckboards," wooden slats laid down to enable them to traverse areas of deep mud. One of the officers later wrote: "it was mud-mud-mud; a sea of mud; churned and churned by shellfire; over and over again. I remember going up to what we thought were trenches & all we had to walk on was what we called a bath mat; two strips [of wood] with crosspieces."

The first of Currie's attacks—there were eventually four of them—was scheduled for the early morning hours of October 26, 1917. Under a wet mist that changed to rain later in the day, the battalion assembled at the jumping-off trench and waited for the opening barrage. At 5:40 AM, the barrage began. "The first assaulting waves of the 58th Battalion followed it up as close as possible," the war diary records. But the barrage was uneven; it moved forward more slowly on the right flank than on the left, and some of the men fell victim to their own shells. But in the face of heavy machine-gun fire and a German counter-barrage the men advanced by companies and platoons. They moved quickly from strongpoint to strongpoint, taking out the bunkers one by one with dozens of incredible acts of courage: pin down the machine-gunners inside, approach the bunker from the flank, throw in a grenade or drench it with Lewis-gun fire, secure it, then move on to the next one.

The war diary records one small part of the day's battle: "Our men occupied shell holes in front of [the German] positions and a severe fight ensued for the possession of CONTOUR TRENCH which continued until 2:30 p.m. October 26th when four German officers, of which two were majors, and sixty other ranks—unwounded—surrendered. After this, possession was gained of the German trench on our frontage. . . . Throughout these operations, in which heavy casualties were incurred, conspicuous devotion to duty was shown in the face of heavy fire from the German 'Pill boxes' and trenches."

War diaries are usually spare in their recording of events. A letter written by Lieutenant Don Cameron to the family of a dead fellow officer reveals much more of the trial endured in this fight. Shackleton quotes it in the battalion history:

We got well away but almost immediately encountered heavy machine gun fire from both flanks and our men began to drop quite fast. . . . I knew that both Pat [Edgar "Pat" Patten] and I would have to go for that "Pill box" ourselves. I ran across to Pat and found him encouraging his men as calmly and quietly as if he had been on parade. We both decided we should have to open machine gun fire to finish off the Bosch, but as both our machine gun crews had been killed or wounded, we had to go back, find the gun, dig it out of the mud, carry it up on our back and open fire. Well, we did this but I found my gun much closer to hand than Pat found his and I had fired quite a number of rounds when I saw Pat coming up carrying his gun on his shoulder. I remember saying to myself "Good old Pat, now Fritzie will get it" but . . . as he got into position, a German sniper shot him with a rifle bullet through the forehead.

Edgar Patten was one of the 58th Battalion's 303 casualties out of roughly 500 attackers on October 26, 1917. In all, 2,481 Canadians were killed or wounded in that first phase of Currie's offensive at Passchendaele. In the early hours of October 30, the second assault began. Once again Canadians fell by the hundreds as the Germans put up a furious resistance, and once again scant progress was made. The second phase of the attack cost 1,321 dead or wounded. On November 6 the third attack began; 2,238 were killed or wounded but the town of Passchendaele, or what was left of it, was taken. The last assault, to capture the height of Passchendaele Ridge, began on the morning of November 10; the objective was taken by the end of the day. The Canadian Corps accomplished in two weeks what the British had not been able to do in three months, but at a total cost of 15,654 dead and wounded.

MOMENTOUS EVENTS rocked the Western Front in the months after Passchendaele. The Canadian Corps returned to the Vimy sector while the Germans massed for one last major offensive to end the war before the rapidly building United States Army could tip the balance of the war. The United States had declared war on Germany on April 6, 1917, but it took close to a year for the great bulk of American troops to begin arriving at the Western Front. The new Bolshevik government in Russia had sued the Germans for peace in early 1918, and shortly after, German troop trains raced west to disgorge dozens of rested divisions behind the newly built defences of the Hindenburg Line. The German aim was to use those troops to knock Britain and France out of the war before the weight of American manpower could be brought to bear.

The Germans used the thousands of troops from the east and new tactics such as rapid infiltration and envelopment and reinforcement of success to smash through the Fifth British Army on March 21, 1918. The German commander, Field Marshal Erich Ludendorff, was determined to keep the Allies off balance by attacking in four major phases aimed at different sectors of the front. The initial German attacks drove all before them and virtually eliminated the Fifth Army. The Germans almost reached the gates of Paris but were defeated at the Second Battle of the Marne, which began on July 15, 1918, and did not end until early August. The Canadian Corps as such was not involved in this desperate fighting. In fact, Currie temporarily lost all four of his divisions when they were stripped away to plug holes torn in the British lines. When the Corps reassembled, Currie learned that it and the Australian Corps had been selected by Haig to lead the British portion of a major counter-stroke planned for early August at Amiens.

The Canadian attack on August 8 was preceded by weeks of training for what was called open warfare. Each Canadian platoon was now equipped with at least one Lewis gun and trench mortars and was taught how to assault enemy strong points using the cover of terrain and the fire of their advancing comrades. They learned how to move quickly with tanks and mobile machine guns mounted on cars. They learned how to communicate with their own attacking aircraft to direct them to bomb or machine-gun German defenders. The artillery had practised how to move rapidly forward after firing initial barrages and how to communicate more closely with the infantry to focus on individual targets. The Germans they would face would be deeply entrenched behind their massive Hindenburg Line, which combined thick belts of wire, pillboxes, antitank guns, and pre-sited mortars and artillery. For both sides, the day of trench warfare was over.

The Canadians met with spectacular success in their initial assaults, and when resistance stiffened after several days, Currie directed a shift in the area of the attack and attacked again. All battalions, brigades, and divisions of the Corps took part in these opening stages of what would eventually be called the last hundred days or the pursuit to Mons. One of those brigades was the 7th Brigade of the 3rd Canadian Infantry Division. That brigade now contained Princess Patricia's Canadian Light Infantry, which had shifted to the Canadian Corps in November 1915; the 49th Battalion from the Edmonton Regiment; the 42nd Battalion, representing the Canadian Black Watch of Montreal; and the Royal Canadian Regiment—the RCR.

As Canada's only standing regular-force infantry regiment at the outbreak of the war, the RCR had expected quick mobilization to war strength and a fast trip to the front. That was not to be. The Governor General, the Duke of Connaught, insisted that the RCR be sent to Bermuda to guard the island, thus freeing up a British unit to return to fight with the BEF. Hughes obligingly agreed, no doubt because of his less than benign view of regular soldiers, thus depriving the First Canadian Contingent of its only real source of expertise. Nonetheless, in August 1915 the folly of this move was corrected when the RCR was withdrawn from Bermuda and sent to France to join the 7th Brigade. The regiment stayed with the 7th throughout the war and saw heavy action at the Battle of the Somme, Vimy Ridge, and Passchendaele, as well as in other major encounters with the enemy. The RCR was heavily involved in the opening phases of the last hundred days and in the several key battles, such as Arras, that followed in the weeks after August 8, when the Australians, British, and Canadians made steady progress eastward. But one of the Royals' greatest tests of the war was the attack on the Marcoing Line on September 28, 1918.

The Marcoing Line was a secondary German defence position that ran north–south to the west of the city of Cambrai. It was approximately 7 kilometres east of the Canal du Nord, a transportation and communications waterway that had been empty of water and under construction when war broke out four years earlier. The Germans had heavily fortified the Canal du Nord; it took four divisions, three Canadian and one British, two days to take and cross the canal, with very heavy casualties. But before the Canadians could liberate Cambrai, the Marcoing Line awaited. The RCR moved up to the front on September 26 and encamped in Bourlon Wood, about 3 kilometres from their objective. At 5:30 AM on September 28, after the usual artillery bombardment and supported by three tanks, three RCR companies attacked the Marcoing Line. At first there was little opposition, but soon the morning was rent by heavy German machine-gun fire. The RCR pressed on and crossed a railway embankment, then they passed over the high ground to the west of the Line. The official history records what happened next: "when the assault reached the crest of sloping ground beyond which lay the Marcoing Line, the men realized the grim nature of the task before them. Defended by great belts of wire and by many strong points, each with a garrison of trained machine-gunners and two or more guns, the German position constituted a barrier which, obviously, could be stormed only by an effort of supreme valour and determination." To make matters worse, a heavy German barrage began to rip apart the ground, quickly cutting communications between the forward companies and battalion HQ and forcing the attackers to fight in sections and platoons as they took on the German wire and strong points.

One of the heroes of the afternoon was Lieutenant Milton Gregg, who was leading D Company on the right flank of the RCR attack. Crawling out in front of his men, Gregg spotted a narrow gap in the

German wire and realized that if his men approached that gap from a particular direction, they would have partial cover. He then rejoined his men as fast as he could, explained the situation to them, and led them back to the wire. The official history records that after returning to the gap in the German wire, Gregg "advanced by a series of short sprints and quick tumbles and finally dropped into the Marcoing Line." Most of his men were able to follow despite the German machine-gun fire. Then they began to move up the German trench, shooting and bombing as they went until their grenades began to run short. Gregg then made his way back to collect grenades from the other companies before returning to his men. By the time he had done so he had been wounded twice, but he still led them to resume their grim work in the trenches. The Germans counterattacked several times, but Gregg persisted, killing eleven himself and taking twenty-five prisoners. Gregg was later awarded the Victoria Cross for his leadership in extremely dangerous circumstances.

On the left of the RCR attack, C Company, under the command of Lieutenant W.G. Wurtele, led a charmed life for the first 2 kilometres of their approach to the Marcoing Line. But they too ran into a storm of machine-gun fire as they descended toward the Germans. Wurtele would later recall: "With only about 20 unwounded men available I realized that it would be foolhardy to make a frontal attack and so I decided we would endeavour to render assistance to Lieutenant Gregg by putting in a flanking attack." He too was able to find a spot to lead his men through the wire, though only a single platoon followed him. Eventually he guided them to a place where they were able to set up a machine gun borrowed from a nearby Canadian battalion. They might have dominated the enemy's rear by fire, but the battalion had taken so many casualties by that time (including the CO, who was wounded when a German shell struck the battalion HQ) that Wurtele and his men were forced back. Still, by the end of the day, the Marcoing Line had been taken. The next day, with the battalion reorganized into three companies, the RCR attacked again with the PPCLI and the 42nd Battalion on their right and the 44th

Battalion of the 4th Division on their left. They crossed the road from Cambrai to Douai and reached a spot about 500 metres northwest of the hamlet of Tilloy, on the northern edge of Cambrai. They stayed there until relieved on the morning of October 1.

The RCR paid heavily for their success: 38 killed, 201 wounded, and 32 missing. But this was their last major bloodletting of the war. After Cambrai, the Germans in the Canadian sector went into full retreat; this short period is recorded on the regimental colour as "Pursuit to Mons." On November 10 a concealed German machine gun killed a number of men—the last RCR losses of the war. The next day, November 11, 1918, just before the armistice, an RCR platoon reached the town hall in Mons and signed the mayor's Golden Book. Then, at 11:00 AM, a few last shots crackled before the whole Western Front went quiet for the first time since July 1914. The fighting was over. The RCR suffered 3,113 casualties in the war, with 701 killed in action.

OUT OF 620,000 WHO SERVED, the vast majority of them with the army either at home or overseas, fully 60,000 were killed in action or died on active service and a further 172,000 were wounded in mind or in body. The toll was particularly heavy when compared to the total population of Canada at that time—between six and eight million people. Within nine months most of the volunteers (and the few thousand conscripts who had reached the front) were back in Canada trying to resume normal lives.

The First World War was Canada's costliest. More men were killed and wounded than in all the rest of Canada's wars, and the casualty rate per number of men serving was a shockingly high 33 percent. In Canada, as elsewhere, ordinary people shrank from the prospect of future wars, while some began to question the reason for fighting the war in the first place. A wave of antiwar pacifism swept through many of the formerly belligerent countries. Accusations were made in the U.S. Congress and elsewhere that international munitions makers and war profiteers were behind the conflict. To add to the anti-war backlash, inflation was still rampant in Canada, returned soldiers found it hard to get jobs, and by 1921 a severe postwar recession was affecting almost everybody. The country was in no mood to maintain an efficient and well-trained and -equipped military; the government eagerly cut the defence budget to the bone.

In the spring of 1919 the Department of Militia and Defence struck a committee under retired general Sir William Otter to decide what sort of postwar military the country should have. The Otter Committee envisaged a permanent force of some thirty thousand and a large militia raised through conscription. The proposal was dead on arrival. Instead the government decided to maintain a permanent force (PF) roughly the size of the one that had existed prior to the war, but with three regular-force infantry regiments instead of one. The PPCLI and RCR were kept and so was the 22nd Battalion as an all-French unit. The Cabinet turned down the army's recommendation to maintain an all-French unit five times; only in 1920 was the move approved. The regiment's name was eventually changed to the Royal 22e Régiment. Each of the three regiments was assigned to a different part of the country—the Van Doos in Quebec, the PPCLI in the west, and the RCR in Ontario and the Maritimes. The Strathconas and the Royal Canadian Dragoons were retained as Canada's permanent cavalry, while the gunners were perpetuated in the Royal Canadian Horse Artillery. None of the PF regiments were at anything like full strength.

Re-establishing the PF was the easy part. Sam Hughes's use of numbered battalions as the building blocks of the overseas army, the Canadian Expeditionary Force, and within it, the Canadian Corps, raised significant questions about the postwar militia. The men had fought in numbered battalions; hundreds of thousands had never had any attachment to the prewar militia regiments. It was hard to imagine that those who wished to stay in the militia would fit in easily or have any real allegiance to those regiments. There was a strong feeling among the First World War veterans that the numbered units should somehow be kept. But that raised another question: which ones? And if some of them were kept, what would happen to the existing regiments? In a very real sense the regimental tradition in Canada was in danger of being significantly undermined. In the end it won out—sort of.

Across the country militia regiments were renamed, consolidated, or cut entirely. In Calgary, for example, the 103rd Regiment Calgary Rifles was designated the Calgary Regiment in 1920, but in 1924 that regiment was divided into the King's Own Calgary Regiment and the Calgary Highlanders. In Victoria the 50th Gordon Highlanders and the 88th Victoria Fusiliers formed the backbone of the Canadian Scottish Regiment. Each of the "new" militia regiments was designated as perpetuating one or more of the CEF's numbered battalions. As this was done, the battle honours that would have gone to those numbered battalions were assigned to the new regiments most closely aligned with them. For example, the Royal Regiment of Canada was assigned the battle honours of both the 3rd and 58th battalions of the CEF.

It did not take long for the militia regiments to decline in military effectiveness. Budget cuts, apathy, and antiwar sentiment all took their toll. Once again training deteriorated, leadership aged and stagnated, kit became obsolete. Regiments again became more important for the social life they provided than for their military preparedness. After all, who could imagine that Canada would ever participate in another war as terrible as the past one? As Canada's ambassador to the League of Nations declared at Geneva in 1924, Canadians lived in "a fire-proof house, far from inflammable materials."

Part Three

THE SECOND WORLD WAR

CHAPTER TEN

DISASTER: THE WINNIPEG GRENADIERS AT HONG KONG AND THE FUSILIERS MONT-ROYAL AT DIEPPE

> When we got within sight of Dieppe, just before dawn, we knew we were going to catch hell. . . . Those last 200 yards were bad. The German fire was getting the range of our boats. I had a hot dry feeling in my throat. I wanted to be doing something—not just sitting in that damned boat.
>
> —Dollard "Joe" Ménard, August 19, 1942

IN THE SUMMER OF 1939, Canadians watched with dismay as the crisis in Europe mounted. For months Germany's Adolf Hitler had been demanding that Poland hand over the city of Danzig and the land corridor to the North Sea that had been added to Poland at the end of the First World War. Hitler's previous threats had been successful, the latest only a year earlier, when Britain and France, with the connivance of the United States, had forced Czechoslovakia to hand over the Sudetenland to Germany. This time the British and the French were giving no signs of conceding. It was increasingly clear in Ottawa that if Hitler tried to grab Danzig and the Polish Corridor by force, Britain and France would go to war against Germany. The Germans did invade Poland on September 1, 1939, and Britain and France declared war two days later. Canada's prime minister, William Lyon Mackenzie King, then called a special session of Parliament to seek a separate Canadian declaration of war against Germany. Canada officially declared war on September 10, 1939. However, the Department of National Defence had started sending warnings to Canadian army, navy, and air force units as early as late August.

The Canadian army and its regiments were not ready for the outbreak of war in September 1939. The Canadian defence budget had been drastically cut in the early 1920s. Everyone was sick of war and no one wanted to maintain a large army in Canada. Canadians generally thought that Europe was a continent that could run itself and they had no desire to come to Europe's aid again in the event of a major diplomatic crisis. What need, then, for an army? With the Royal Navy still controlling the seas—or so Canadians thought—an impassable Arctic, and a friendly southern neighbour, Canada had no need of defence, and the military had no real argument it could present to government to persuade it to spend money on the forces. The military was so desperate for cash that at one point it even conjured up the possibility of war breaking out between Canada and the United States, with great Canadian cavalry sweeps despoiling the northern Plains states. No wonder governments did not take the military seriously!

In the very early 1930s, however, a hint of thunder and lightning spilled over the western horizon when Japan attacked China and conquered Manchuria. Suddenly the Royal Canadian Navy was revived with two new British-built destroyers. Slowly, as international crises followed one another from China to the Mediterranean to the Rhineland in parallel with the growth of fascist power in Japan, Italy, and Germany, a few more dollars began to flow to the Canadian army. A handful of new fighting vehicles was purchased in the early 1930s, horses were removed from the order of battle and cavalry regiments were transformed into armoured regiments, and militia training was increased. Plans were made to replace the old Lewis gun—the section light machine guns—with the Bren gun, a Czech-based British design that was as good as any comparable weapon in the world. And there were significant increases in the defence budget in 1938 and 1939, although most of the new cash went to the navy and the air force; when war broke out the army was still largely equipped with First World War uniforms and weapons and led by First World War veterans.

Canada had adopted plans for mobilization of its forces prior to the outbreak of war, just as it had done prior to the outbreak of war in 1914, but this time the plans were followed. The overall plan, known as Defence Scheme No. 3, called for a possible army of six divisions (though each division would be smaller than the divisions of the First World War) grouped into two corps under the overall command of an army headquarters. Each division was intended to have three brigades and each brigade would have two or three infantry battalions, depending on whether or not it was an infantry or armoured brigade (armoured brigades had two battalions, one infantry and the other armoured). The battalions would be drawn from the three regular-force regiments and from selected militia regiments. At the very start of the war, however, only two divisions would be mobilized: the 1st Canadian Infantry Division, with three brigades each consisting of a regular-force battalion and two militia battalions, plus both regular-force and militia armoured, artillery, and machine-gun regiments, and the 2nd Canadian Infantry Division, formed entirely from militia regiments.

There was no thought whatever at the outbreak of the Second World War that Canada would organize its army along the lines of the CEF, with numbered battalions. Hughes's scheme had succeeded in getting a large body of men to the U.K. relatively quickly, but it created major problems in the reinforcement (replacement) system. It had also left a large pool of officers doing essentially nothing—officers who had led reinforcement drafts to the U.K. only to see their men stripped off and sent to the front while they languished in Blighty. That had led to over-bureaucratization of the CEF's supply and logistics system in the U.K., and worse, had impeded the Canadian military medical system. But the two main reasons why no one ever raised the prospect of numbered battalions were that it was probably too reminiscent of Hughes himself—and he had fallen into almost total disrepute by 1939—and that the regimental system was simply too deeply entrenched. Thus the regiments that existed at Canada's declaration of war were destined to fight that war.

The government sent the 1st Canadian Infantry Division overseas almost immediately, toward the end of December 1939; the 2nd Canadian Infantry Division was not sent to the United Kingdom until the summer of 1940, after the surrender of France. Canada was stunned by that setback—as was most of the world—and the government soon realized that Canada had suddenly become Britain's most important ally. There would be no holding back after that. Thus the government also embarked on the creation of two corps and one army headquarters and the three more divisions envisioned by Defence Scheme No. 3. Eventually the Canadian Army Overseas, originally referred to as the Canadian Active Service Force, consisted of the First Canadian Army, the First and Second Canadian Corps, 1st, 2nd, and 3rd Canadian Infantry Divisions, 4th and 5th Canadian Armoured Divisions, and 1st and 2nd Canadian Armoured Brigades, which were both independent brigades, that is, not formally part of any division. This was the equivalent of six full divisions.

Both the regular force and the militia regiments were well under strength when war was declared. Virtually all of the members of the regular-force regiments volunteered to "go active"—to serve overseas—and volunteers were immediately sought to fill the rest of the vacant positions. The battalions all grew to full war establishment (835 men) very quickly. When the 1st Canadian Infantry Division went to the U.K. in 1939 it went with the 1st, 2nd, and 3rd Canadian Infantry Brigades, along with armour, artillery, and engineer troops as well as other non-combat support units. One battalion of each of the three regular-force infantry regiments lay at the core of each brigade—the Royal Canadian Regiment in the 1st Brigade, Princess Patricia's Canadian Light Infantry in the 2nd Brigade, and the Royal 22e Régiment in the 3rd Brigade.

The militia regiments functioned in a different manner. To begin with, they could not simply be mobilized and sent overseas, since

Canadians were obliged by law to volunteer for overseas service. Thus the militia regiments that were selected to participate in the 1st and 2nd Divisions were obliged to form 1st battalions in the Canadian Active Service Force. Regiments in the vicinity that were not activated were told to seek volunteers from within their ranks for those regiments that were. Thus, for example, the Calgary Highlanders—a successor to both the 10th and the 50th battalions of the CEF—formed a 1st Battalion for the Canadian Active Service Force and a 2nd Battalion that stayed in Canada as part of the reserve army at home (not all regiments did this, but many did). Men from regiments such as the 15th Alberta Light Horse (which was itself activated later in the war) joined the 1st Battalion of the Calgary Highlanders, which was part of the 5th Brigade, 2nd Canadian Infantry Division.

The Winnipeg Grenadiers were a successor to the 100th Regiment, formed on April 1, 1908, and redesignated the 100th Winnipeg Grenadiers on May 2, 1910. The regiment contributed to the 11th, 78th, and 100th battalions of the CEF, of which the 11th and 78th served in France and Flanders. The Winnipeg Grenadiers were among the first of the western Canadian militia regiments to be activated in September 1939, but unlike the other B.C. and prairie regiments—Vancouver's Seaforth Highlanders, the Loyal Edmonton Regiment, the Calgary Highlanders, and the South Saskatchewan Regiment (all infantry), and the Saskatoon Light Infantry, a machine-gun battalion—they were not attached to a division.

Originally designated as a machine-gun battalion, the Grenadiers were converted to infantry and sent to Jamaica in late May 1940, to replace a British battalion returning home after the disastrous opening round of the Battle of France. The Grenadiers were well equipped but only partly trained. In Jamaica training took second place to guarding prisoners of war, manning the Kingston harbour defences, and enjoying the many tropical delights—bars, dance halls, women—that this easy-going island had to offer. In June 1941, as they prepared to return to Canada, Lieutenant-Colonel J.L.R. Sutcliffe took command of the battalion. He led the Winnipeggers home just as tensions were mounting in the Pacific between Japan—allied with Nazi Germany—and Britain, the United States, and the Netherlands.

—⁓—

JAPAN'S AGGRESSIVE INTENTIONS TOWARD CHINA had first exploded into war in the 1890s, when it gained important trade and territorial concessions from China after a short war. Japan's ambitions were not abated, however. In 1931 it seized Manchuria, set up a puppet government, and renamed the territory Manchukuo—a virtual Japanese colony. Then, in 1937, Japan attacked again in a full-scale war. By the time Japan attacked Pearl Harbor—and every American, British, and Dutch possession or base within reach—its troops occupied most of Guangzhou (formerly Canton) Province, just to the north of Hong Kong.

Hong Kong had been British territory since the nineteenth century. The colony consisted of the island of Hong Kong itself; on the mainland, a settlement on the Kowloon Peninsula; and, to the north of that, the scrubland of the New Territories up to the border with China. The island is about 16 kilometres across at its widest point and is separated from the mainland by Victoria Harbour and the Lye Mun Passage, which is about 500 metres across. The island and the Kowloon Peninsula are mountainous and the land is dominated by a number of very high peaks. A defensive line had been built along the border with China in the 1930s—it was called the Gin Drinkers Line since its western end lay on the shore of Gin Drinkers Bay. But almost everyone, including Winston Churchill, believed the island was indefensible and that any reinforcements sent there would be lost in the event of a Japanese attack.

When France surrendered to Germany in June 1940, the Japanese took the surrender as a signal to occupy French Indochina (Laos, Cambodia, and Vietnam), and the British began to change their thinking on Hong Kong. Perhaps the territory might serve them well as a forward base for operations against the Japanese in southern China. Some commanders even thought that reinforcing Hong Kong might deter a Japanese attack. One of those men was Major-General Edward Grasset, a Canadian serving in the British army who visited Canada in August 1941. He was on his way back to the U.K. after his assignment as British military commander in Hong Kong had ended. Grasset discussed Hong Kong with H.D.G. "Harry" Crerar, an old classmate from RMC who was then Canada's chief of the general staff. He convinced Crerar, and through Crerar the Canadian government, to agree to offer troops to reinforce Hong Kong if asked by the U.K. In mid-September 1941 that request was made and Canada agreed. A new formation, known as C Force, was authorized to be sent under command of Colonel J.K. Lawson, who was then director of military training. Lawson was promoted to brigadier.

Crerar's choice for the two battalions to form the core of C Force was the Royal Rifles of Canada, from Quebec City—also recently returned from garrison duty (in Newfoundland)—and the Winnipeg Grenadiers. He explained his preferences to the minister of national defence, J.L. Ralston, this way: "These units returned not long ago from duty in Newfoundland and Jamaica. . . . The duties which they there carried out were not in many respects unlike the task which awaits the units to be sent to Hong Kong. The experience they have had will therefore be of no small value to them in their new role. Both units are of proven efficiency." There were other reasons: assigning the two battalions to home defence might hurt unit morale, as the men had volunteered for active service and wanted to go; one unit was from the west and one from Quebec City, with a sizable francophone contingent of about 35 to 40 percent; and neither unit was well trained enough to go immediately to the U.K. to join the newly forming 4th Canadian Infantry Division (which was later converted to armour).

When the Grenadiers arrived back in Canada, many men who were sick of garrison duty and wanted to get to the U.K. as soon as possible applied for and received transfers, but some four hundred men signed up to replace them. No one was told the Grenadiers' exact destination but recruits were informed that it would be a "semi-tropical" environment. Eventually the battalion was brought up to normal establishment of 835 men, with about 150 extra men for reinforcements. They were equipped with tropical clothing and foot-wear and sent by train to Vancouver, where they arrived on October 27, joining the Royal Rifles. Their ship, *Awatea*, left for Hong Kong that night accompanied by the converted liner HMCS *Prince Robert*. Aboard were all 1,937 men of C Force. Although some training was done aboard ship, the men who disembarked on November 16 and marched to the Sham Shui Po barracks in Kowloon were still nowhere near ready for combat. To make matters worse, the vehicles that were supposed to accompany them had arrived late in Vancouver and had been loaded onto a U.S. cargo ship, *Don José*. That ship was still at sea when war broke out on December 7 and was diverted to the Philippines.

The Grenadiers and the rest of C Force spent the first few weeks in Hong Kong settling in, drilling, and training. British Major-General C.M. Maltby, commander of the Hong Kong garrison, ordered most of the Canadians to occupy defensive positions on the southern perimeter of the island. The Grenadiers were allotted the southwest sector, though one company of Grenadiers was sent to help defend the Gin Drinkers Line. The line fell very quickly after the Japanese attacked on December 8 (December 7 in Hawaii) and the defend-ers were forced to withdraw to Kowloon. The Canadians helped to cover the withdrawal and were then pulled back to the island on the night of December 11. They then rejoined the rest of the battalion as part of West Brigade, a scratch formation that had just been pulled together. The brigade consisted of a mixed force of Canadian, British, and Indian troops and Hong Kong volunteers. The rest of the island was defended by East Brigade, another mixed force, commanded by British Brigadier C. Wallis.

On December 18 the Japanese crossed the Lye Mun Passage in small boats pulled by ferries under cover of heavy shellfire. The

Indian colonial troops defending the coast were virtually wiped out. Then the Japanese launched four columns toward the centre of the island; they were supposed to converge at the Wong Ne Chong Gap, where Colonel Lawson's headquarters for West Brigade was located. Like a relentless tide, the Japanese advanced across heavily forested steep hills and deep ravines. The Japanese knew that the Gap was the key to the island's defences. Two important roads passed through it— one that connected Victoria Harbour, on the island's north coast, to Repulse Bay and the town of Stanley on the south coast, and another that linked Aberdeen, in the southwest of the island, to the Ty Tam Tuk Reservoir to the east. If the Gap were to be taken, communications among the island's defenders would be severely disrupted and it would be virtually impossible for either defending brigade to reinforce the other.

Lawson's headquarters were in turmoil as the Japanese closed in. No one had any solid information on how many Japanese had landed on the island, where they had come ashore, or what direction the main body of their troops was heading in. The darkness of night was intensified by smoke from oil fires burning in Victoria, on the northern coast of the island. Japanese sympathizers and fifth columnists were cutting telephone wires to disrupt the defenders' communications. Then it began to rain. When Lawson learned that two Japanese regiments were closing in on the summits of Jardine's Lookout and Mount Butler, just to the east of the Gap, he ordered three platoons to stop the attackers. The platoons consisted of men from the Headquarters Company of the Winnipeg Grenadiers under the command of Lieutenant G.A. Birkett. Birkett found it impossible to climb the high peaks to the east of the Gap in the rain and darkness and decided to wait until dawn. Then, outnumbered by about six to one, Birkett's men advanced but were quickly pushed back, with two platoon commanders killed. Lawson then ordered his only reserve force, A Company of the Winnipeg Grenadiers, to attack.

The men of A Company were last seen climbing up through the rain and fog; most were never seen alive again. Survivors liberated from Japanese prison camps in August 1945 described how part of A Company, under Company Sergeant Major John Robert Osborn, captured the peak of Mount Butler with a bayonet charge.

Osborn, a forty-one-year-old veteran of the First World War, had served in the Hawke Battalion, a unit of the 63rd (Royal Navy) Infantry Division. He had been gassed, the effects of which affected his lungs for several years afterwards. At one point in the war he had also been captured by the Germans, and he was determined never to repeat the experience "under any circumstances." Osborn had moved to Saskatchewan after the First World War; he had farmed for two years before settling in Winnipeg, where he married and had five children while working for the Canadian Pacific Railway. In 1933 he had joined the Winnipeg Grenadiers.

Osborn's men held the peak of Mount Butler for three hours under constant rifle, machine-gun, and mortar fire. Casualties mounted. The Winnipeggers could not hold; they began to withdraw the way they had come, but ran into a Japanese ambush. The attackers closed in on the surrounded Canadians, throwing grenades. Osborn threw several of them back at the Japanese but could not reach one of them in time; he threw himself on it to protect his men and was killed instantly. Almost all the rest of the company were eventually killed also. When the handful of survivors were liberated after the war, they recounted the story of Osborn's bravery and he was posthumously awarded the Victoria Cross—in effect, the first Canadian soldier of the Second World War to be so honoured.

Osborn's futile defence gained but a few hours; by noon on the 19th Lawson's HQ was overrun and he was killed in the fighting. The remains of D Company of the Grenadiers surrendered, but the rest of the battalion fought on under Sutcliffe's command. The resistance put up by the remainder of the two Canadian battalions, the British and Indian troops, and the Hong Kong volunteers was brave, stubborn, and costly to the Japanese, but it was useless. No help was coming to Hong Kong from anywhere and casualties were mounting by the hour among both the defenders and the civilian population. And the

Japanese were unrelenting—they pushed the remainder of the West Brigade back to a line between Victoria in the north and Aberdeen in the south, forced Wallis's East Brigade to withdraw to the vicinity of Stanley Prison, and consolidated their hold on the island's centre. On Christmas morning the Japanese contacted the island's British governor, seeking a surrender. At first he refused, but Japanese attacks resumed on both fronts in the early afternoon and casualties among the defenders continued to mount. Maltby decided that the struggle was over and informed the governor that they must surrender. A white flag was hoisted over Maltby's HQ and a small party was sent to Wallis, still holding out as OC East Brigade, to confirm the order to lay down arms.

All fighting ceased in the early hours of December 26. The killing, however, did not stop. In various parts of the island Japanese soldiers unleashed their wrath on the now helpless defenders, bayoneting and machine-gunning prisoners and slaughtering both wounded and medical staff in hospitals and aid posts. The Canadians were then imprisoned on the island and kept in appalling conditions—starved, deprived of medical supplies, and beaten. Before being shipped off to slave-labour camps in Japan, they were sometimes summarily executed. Of the 1,937 officers and men who left Canada in October 1941, 555 never returned, and many of those who did were so broken in body and spirit that they died prematurely in the years that followed.

The Winnipeg Grenadiers were reborn in Canada on January 10, 1942, and selected to join the 13th Canadian Infantry Brigade Group for the campaign to recapture Kiska Island in the Aleutian chain. It and Attu had been occupied by the Japanese in June 1942 as a diversion during the Battle of Midway. The landings took place on August 16, 1943, but Kiska was deserted—the Japanese had already pulled out. The Grenadiers remained in the Aleutians for four months before returning to Canada, then were sent to the U.K. as a training battalion in late May 1944. After the war the active service battalion was disbanded in 1946 but a reserve formation continued until 1965, when it was placed on the supplemental order of battle. Currently a cadet formation from Minto Barracks in Winnipeg perpetuates this brave but ill-fated regiment.

—⁂—

LIEUTENANT-COLONEL DOLLARD "JOE" MÉNARD was right where he wanted to be at about 6:50 AM on August 19, 1942: his landing craft was headed for the formidable cliffs at the western end of the narrow stone beach in front of the French port town of Dieppe. His was the first of some 26 assault boats loaded with 583 men of the Fusiliers Mont-Royal (FMR), a French-speaking battalion from Montreal. Only minutes before, Ménard and his men had been sent by Major-General J.H. Roberts, in command of the assault force on the command ship *Calpe,* to reinforce the Royal Hamilton Light Infantry (RHLI). The "Rileys," as they were known, had landed in the first wave, made it up from the beach under intense fire, vaulted a seawall at the head of the beach, then charged into the Dieppe casino, right near the beach. They were locked in a desperate fight with the Germans to capture the building. Roberts thought—mistakenly—that the western end of the beach, below a massive cliff and open to intense German fire, had been secured. He also thought—again mistakenly—that if he committed his only reserve battalion, the FMRs, it would tip the balance in the assault.

A motor launch ran in ahead of the FMR assault boats to lay smoke along the beachfront to obscure the landing from German fire. One official historical report describes what happened next:

> When the boats came out of the smoke, the beach was sighted at varying distances between 50 and 200 yards. Very heavy firing was opened on all boats from buildings in front of the beach, machine guns which appeared to be on the boulevard, and from the top of the west cliff further heavy machine gun fire, mor-

tar fire and grenades. The boats were spread out over the entire range of Red and White beaches, and with the exception of three boats who [*sic*] landed their soldiers with very few casualties, all the remainder reported . . . very heavy casualties.

Ménard never forgot those few minutes: "When we got within sight of Dieppe, just before dawn, we knew we were going to catch hell. . . . Those last 200 yards were bad. The German fire was getting the range of our boats. I had a hot, dry feeling in my throat. I wanted to be doing something—not just sitting in that damned boat." Amid the smoke and incoming fire, with his Tommy gun slung loosely under his arm, Ménard appeared staunch and resolute. He urged his men on with shouts of "show 'em what French-Canadian boys can do!"

When Canada declared war, Ménard had been far away in India. He had been serving with a Sikh regiment in Waziristan for two years, guarding the Khyber Pass between India and Afghanistan. The eldest son of a railway engineer from Notre-Dame-du-Lac, Quebec, he was a graduate of the Royal Military College. He had been disgruntled about the lack of excitement in the Canadian army in peacetime and so had volunteered for service in the British army in India. But in September 1939 he resigned his commission and wrote to Ottawa asking to be reinstated in the Canadian army. The Department of National Defence did not want to pay his passage back to Canada; he had gone to India of his own volition, they maintained, and he would have to pay his own way back or stay where he was. Ménard was not deterred. He made his way to Hong Kong via Mumbai, joined the Royal Navy, then waited until he finally found himself in Halifax, where he doffed his navy uniform and headed for Ottawa. When he reached the capital, the general staff welcomed him to Canada, reinstated him, then sent him off to a staff course—experienced French-Canadian officers were not easy to find. Eventually, at a very young twenty-nine years of age, Ménard was placed in command of the Fusiliers Mont-Royal.

The FMR's roots dated back to June 18, 1869, when the Mount Royal Rifles were authorized as one of several regiments created to defend Canada against the Fenians. It was soon redesignated the 65th Battalion, Mount Royal Rifles, and sent to serve with General Strange's column in the Northwest Rebellion in 1885. By then the regiment had acquired a distinctly French character (which was one reason it was relegated to Strange); in acknowledgement of that reality, its name was changed to 65 Régiment Carabiniers Mont-Royal in 1920. It became the Fusiliers Mont-Royal on April 15, 1931.

The regiment mobilized an active service battalion on September 1, 1939. At one point the government may have considered forming a French-speaking brigade, but if so, that notion was never acted on. The political and symbolic importance of including the Van Doos—a permanent-force regiment—in the 1st Division outweighed all other considerations, making it impossible at that stage of the war—or even later as it turned out—to create a brigade of three experienced French-speaking infantry battalions. Only three French-speaking infantry battalions served during the course of the war: the Van Doos, the Régiment de Maisonneuve (R de Mais) from Montreal, and the FMR. The Régiment de la Chaudière, a French-speaking machine-gun battalion, was also raised; French-Canadian units formed part of six other formations, including the Three Rivers Regiment and the Fusiliers de Sherbrooke, both armoured formations.

With the Van Doos already in the U.K. (with the 1st Canadian Division), an all-Quebec (in fact, all-Montreal) brigade was created—the 5th Brigade of the 2nd Canadian Infantry Division, which included the FMR, the R de Mais, and the English-speaking Black Watch (Royal Highland Regiment of Canada), under the command of Brigadier P.E. Leclerc. However, in July the FMR was rushed to Iceland to defend the island nation against possible German attack, and the Calgary Highlanders took its place in the 5th Brigade. When the FMR arrived in the U.K. to rejoin the 2nd Division in October 1940, it was inserted into the 6th Brigade. Ménard was appointed to command the battalion in the spring of 1942, just about when the idea of a major raid on the French port of Dieppe was being hatched in the mind of Vice-Admiral Louis Mountbatten, chief of Combined Operations and therefore responsible for all commando-style raids on the French coast.

———

A NUMBER OF FACTORS COINCIDED to put Joe Ménard and his 583 men—along with some 4,500 others, mostly Canadian but also British and American—in harm's way on the morning of August 19, 1942. British Prime Minister Winston Churchill had been determined since the start of the war to make Germany bleed any way he could, in however minor a fashion, as a way of reminding the foe that the British were in this war for the long haul. In order to pursue this strategy a new office was created in the British Ministry of Defence—Combined Operations—with a mandate to use land, air, and sea forces to mount raids on the French coast. But Churchill was dissatisfied about what he believed was the reticence of Combined Operations commander Admiral Lord Keyes to act aggressively; in October 1941 Admiral Louis Mountbatten replaced Keyes. Churchill urged him to put some life into Combined Ops and Mountbatten responded by increasing the tempo of cross-Channel raiding, with attacks such as the British commando raid on the German submarine facilities at Saint-Nazaire, France, in late March 1942. Dieppe was planned as the biggest raid to date.

There is controversy to this day about exactly why Dieppe was chosen for this very large assault, but there can be no doubt that at least part of the reason was to mount a strong demonstration on the French coast. The aim was to show the Soviet Union that the western Allies were intent on taking some pressure off the eastern front and to satisfy U.S. commanders that the British were serious about a full-scale landing at some point. Dieppe was thought to be a good location because it might also offer lessons on how to attack a defended port, while it was close enough to the British coast to afford fighter cover over the beaches.

At the very time that Mountbatten was beginning to plan the raid, the commander of the First Canadian Army, General A.G.L. McNaughton, was looking for a place where his soldiers could get into the fight. The months were dragging by and the Canadians seemed to do nothing but train. These eager young men had volunteered to fight a war and they were not. Morale was dropping and discipline was declining. In reality McNaughton himself was one of the reasons for this inaction, because he insisted that the Canadian army be committed to action together, not piecemeal. But there was not sufficient sea transport, or even a place in any order of battle, to accommodate the entire Canadian army. When the British asked McNaughton if he might be interested in having Canadian troops take part in the raid, he agreed and volunteered two-thirds of the 2nd Canadian Infantry Division for the task.

The original plan for the raid was highly complex, involving paratroopers, heavy bombers, and capital ships such as cruisers and battleships to accompany the infantry ashore and provide cover. The raid was first scheduled for July but was cancelled partly because of bad weather and partly because of fear that German reconnaissance aircraft had spotted the ships and landing craft assembled in harbour for the raid. When it was remounted for August 19, there were no battleships or cruisers in the plan, no paratroopers, no heavy bombers—just eight small destroyers and a gunboat and six squadrons of fighter bombers. To make matters worse, the raid flotilla accidentally ran into a small German convoy at sea in the early morning hours of August 19; the gunfire warned the defenders ashore that something was up. When the almost five thousand Canadians, a hundred or so Americans, and several hundred British commandos and Royal Marines hit the beaches just before dawn, the Germans were wide awake and waiting.

—ⵊ—

MÉNARD'S IMMEDIATE OBJECTIVE on landing was a pillbox on top of a 2-metre parapet some 100 metres in from the beach. He took two or three steps and was hit by a piece of shrapnel. He later recalled:

> You say a bullet or a piece of shrapnel hits you but the word isn't right. They slam you the way a sledgehammer slams you. There's no sharp pain at first. It jars you so much you're not sure exactly where you've been hit—or what with. This piece of shrapnel hit me in the right shoulder and knocked me down. I felt confused and shaken up, the same feeling you get on the football field after getting tackled from behind. Stunned, surprised, frustrated.

Ménard managed to get to his feet and started to bandage himself up, but he was soon hit again, this time in the cheek. His cheek "felt raw, as though someone had ripped a fish hook through it."

Ménard crouched and kept moving toward the pillbox. A close friend was hit in the gut, right beside him. Ménard gave him some morphine and moved on; there was nothing else to do. Up to that point bravery and adrenalin had kept him going, but then he got angry: "now, with my friend lying there, I was so blind angry that it seemed to push everything else out of my head. All I wanted was to kill, to get even." As he got close to the pillbox, Ménard was hit a third time, this time by a bullet. It went clean through his right arm above the wrist and he fell back on a steel picket, badly hurting his back. He kept on and reached the pillbox, which other FMRs had cleared, then tried to direct his battalion from there by radio. Trying to reach higher ground for a better view, he was hit again by shrapnel, in the right leg. Ménard managed to stay on his feet for a while, but he was bleeding profusely. He fell, tried to get up, then passed out. His men carried him to the beach to await evacuation.

All along the beach and at the two landing sites that flanked the beach Canadian soldiers were being shot down by the score. Landing craft were blown up as they approached the beach, killing or mangling all aboard. The tanks that had been landed to add some firepower had severe difficulty getting any traction on the stones; few made it off the beach. Most were hit by antitank guns, which did little damage to the tanks themselves but destroyed their tracks. Some men made it over the seawall and onto the promenade and the field in front of the town before getting killed. The noise of explosions, gunfire, and screaming men was overwhelming. Hundreds of Canadians died in the water, their bodies floating on the tide, blood staining the stones. But some managed to get into the town, and at least two groups of Fusiliers were among them. One was led by Captain Guy Vandelac, the other by Sergeant Pierre Dubuc.

Dubuc was carrying a Bren light machine gun when he landed near the west end of the casino at about 7:00 AM. He sprinted 150 metres to a shallow depression and took cover along with Private N. Daudelin, who was manning a smoke generator. He and Daudelin stayed for a while, then attacked a nearby pillbox with grenades. Dubuc then made his way back to the beach and got into an empty tank along with another man; they fired the tank's gun at German positions on the cliff until they ran out of ammunition. Dubuc then worked his way over to the cliff and found a group of eleven or so Fusiliers, whom he led into the town via the back alleys of rue Alexandre Dumas. They saw Vandelac and his men engaging German positions, then made their way to the town's boat basin via the public gardens, killing a German machine-gun crew on the way. When they reached the southwest corner of the basin, they ran out of ammunition when about fifteen Germans appeared from different positions.

Dubuc and his men surrendered and were made to doff their uniforms, but they were left in charge of only a single guard. Dubuc asked the man for some water; when he turned away, one Fusilier "picked up a long piece of pipe which lay to hand, and swinging it over his head cut the German's head in half." The Canadians scattered and ran. Dubuc reached the beach and headed toward three stranded tanks, where he found Vandelac and Ménard along with some other Fusiliers. By this time Roberts had grasped the extent of the slaughter unfolding on the beach and had ordered a full evacuation. Ménard refused to leave until all the FMRs on the beach had been taken off. Of the seven major Canadian units taking part in the raid that day, he was the only CO who returned to England. But 119 of Ménard's Fusiliers were killed in action within a four-hour time span, and another 344 were taken prisoner. Only 121 returned of the 584 men who had started out the day before.

Unlike the Winnipeg Grenadiers, the Fusiliers Mont-Royal survived their first encounter with the enemy—just. The unit was rebuilt over the next twenty-three months and entered the Battle of Normandy along with the rest of the 6th Brigade in late July 1944. The FMR compiled a distinguished war record over the next ten months, much of it under the command of Jacques Dextraze, who had enlisted in the Fusiliers as a private in 1940. The regiment would eventually be awarded twenty battle honours; Dieppe was the first.

Chapter Eleven

THE FORGOTTEN CAMPAIGN: THE HASTY PS IN SICILY AND THE LOYAL EDDIES AT ORTONA

> We used the anti-tanks in a unique way. The shells could not penetrate the granite walls, sometimes 4 ft thick. So we just put them through the windows [and fired] and they [the shells] bounced around inside much like they would in an enemy tank doing horrible damage.
>
> —Soldier of the Loyal Edmonton Regiment at Ortona

THE HASTINGS AND PRINCE EDWARD REGIMENT began life on January 16, 1863, as the 15th Battalion Volunteer Militia (Infantry) of Canada, drawing its members from the rural counties of Prince Edward, on the north shore of Lake Ontario, east of Toronto, and Hastings, to the north of it. Men from the two counties had taken up arms in defence of British liberty and their own farms and families as far back as the turn of the nineteenth century. Two other local regiments with roots in the 1860s—the 16th Prince Edward Regiment and the 49th Regiment, Hastings Rifles, were amalgamated with the 15th Battalion before the Second World War, while the 15th Battalion itself went through a number of iterations from its founding until 1939. Volunteers from these formations served in the Northwest Rebellion of 1885, the South African War, and the First World War. In the last case, many joined the 2nd Battalion of the CEF, which saw action right through the war.

The boys from the Hastings and Prince Edward Regiment called themselves the "Plough Jockeys," a disdainful term that in fact reflected great pride in their rock-solid British and Canadian rural roots and values. At the very beginning of the Second World War, the regiment was mobilized as part of the 1st Canadian Infantry Division; it eventually sent some four thousand men to war. Perhaps the most famous of the "Hasty Ps" was Canadian author Farley Mowat, an infantry officer who in the mid-1950s chronicled the battle history of the formation in a book called simply *The Regiment*. In that book Mowat gave his perspective on why the men of the county were so quick to answer the call at the outbreak of war after so many years of neglect of the local militia:

> Why did they come? Not out of the empty patriotism of a bygone age—that much is certain. Perhaps some of them came simply to escape the insecurity of hard times. Perhaps some of them came to escape the consequences of failure. Perhaps some came only to escape from boredom, from ugliness, from misery at home. Yet these were the minority. Most of them came because they could not help the spirit that was in them; because the Regiment itself had meaning for them that few could have expressed in words. They came because it was the hour of their pride, the hour of need.

The Hasty Ps went to the U.K. with the rest of the division before the end of December 1939 and spent the next three and a half years there. They were one of three infantry battalions that made up the 1st Canadian Infantry Brigade. The other two were Toronto's 48th Highlanders and the Royal Canadian Regiment. In the U.K. they trained, went on exercises large and small, guarded parts of the U.K. coast, and joined the rest of the division in the last days of the Battle of France. It was a futile effort to help stem the German tide, and the division pulled back to the U.K. before first contact was even made with the rapidly advancing Germans. The Hasty Ps sat by while two-thirds of the 2nd Division was mangled on the beaches of Dieppe. But finally, in early 1943, rumours swept the ranks that they were bound for Tunis. Suddenly the pace of training picked up. Then the regiment was sent to Scotland to practise assault landings. In late May and early June new equipment began to arrive—shorts, cotton shirts, malaria pills, other tropical gear, and Tommy guns—American Thompson submachine guns that were used in the Mediterranean theatre. On June 28 they joined a large convoy heading south from Greenock, Scotland, through the Strait of Gibraltar to Sicily.

The 1st Canadian Infantry Division, commanded by Major-General Guy Granville Simonds, was going to land on the southwest side of Sicily's Pachino Peninsula. The division had been added to the order of battle for the landing only after the start of the year; it was assigned a flanking role to the immediate west of the main British assault on the southeast coast of the island. The Americans would land farther to the west. The main effort in this campaign was to be undertaken by the British, who were supposed to drive north along the island's east coast past Mount Etna to Messina, at the northeast tip of the island. Once they were there, the German and Italian defenders of Sicily would be trapped. The Canadians were supposed to play a supporting role.

On the morning of July 10, 1943, the 1st Canadian Infantry Division assaulted beaches just to the west of Cape Passero. The landing went almost unopposed; the Italian troops manning the beach defences had little stomach for fighting. That was fortunate, since the landings suffered from the usual confusion of an assault—some landing craft ran aground far from shore, others dropped their bow ramps in places where soldiers advanced straight into water that was over their heads. Units landed in the wrong places or on the wrong beaches, men and vehicles bunched up where they should not have been, exposed to enemy fire. Of course, some Italians could and did shoot, as Mowat recalled: "The first to die was Sgt.-Maj. Nutley, a man who had spent twenty years in the peace-time militia and who had been allowed to accompany the Regiment into action only because he had so tenaciously insisted that his life of service would otherwise become a mockery."

For the most part the division survived the landings almost intact and moved ashore and into the foothills. Then, suddenly, the Canadians were thrust into a major role in the campaign. The British on the island's east coast ran into unexpectedly stiff German resistance near Mount Etna, and British General Bernard Montgomery, in overall command of the British and Canadian forces, changed his plan to have the British army lead the drive to the north, at least until the Germans were bypassed or defeated. He ordered Simonds to make for the centre of the island as rapidly as possible. Simonds obliged.

Sicily is a dry and mountainous island. As the Canadians penetrated into the island along its narrow, twisty roads, the heat, dust, and unrelenting sun of July made life very unpleasant for the soldiers. Sicily was then the poorest part of what was essentially a poverty-stricken country. Almost no one was prepared for the swarms of flies and the stench of rotting garbage and open sewers. The men had been issued cotton shorts and short-sleeved shirts for the campaign—legs and bare arms fried in the sun. To make matters worse, much of the division's motor transport and its artillery had been lost at sea when the transport ship carrying them had been torpedoed. Local mule skinners suddenly found themselves in great demand, their animals the prime means of transporting equipment and supplies over the mountainous countryside.

The Italian soldiers who were defending the coastal plain and the foothills mostly surrendered when confronted; the German armour and infantry lurked higher in the mountains. The Germans' strategy in the Canadian sector was to fight, then retreat to new defensive positions as they made the Canadians pay for every kilometre. It was five days before the Canadians ran into the Germans, on July 15 at Grammichele, but it was a short fight; although two companies of Hasty Ps came under fire, the regiment suffered no casualties. On the road past Grammichele the Canadians climbed as they approached the small villages of the interior—Caltagirone, Piazza Armerina,

Valguarnera. They occasionally ran into German rearguards who set ambushes or blew culverts or bridges before withdrawing further. Still, the Canadian advance was steady—until they confronted the towns of Leonforte and Assoro on July 19.

The twin towns of Leonforte and Assoro were 3 kilometres apart on either end of a long, steep ridge. Simonds ordered Howard Graham's 1st Brigade to take Assoro; the 2nd Brigade would attack Leonforte. Assoro clung to the side of a peak several hundred metres above a valley floor. Like Leonforte and many other Sicilian towns, it was built centuries ago with narrow streets and stone-walled houses. It lay at the end of a long, twisty, narrow road with an approach that could be observed for many kilometres. The Germans on the heights above Assoro, some 6 kilometres away, could spot an attacker's every move.

The 1st Brigade set out after dark to cross the dry riverbed of the Ditaino in front of Assoro Mountain. The 48th Highlanders were able to secure a crossing during the night. The RCR and the tanks of the Three Rivers Regiment followed in the dark. But just before dawn, the Germans bombarded the brigade with well-directed artillery fire. Nine tanks were lost to mines and the infantry were pinned down. Graham then met with Lieutenant-Colonel Bruce Sutcliffe, CO of the Hasty Ps, and Sutcliffe's intelligence officer, "Battle" Cockin, to plan a way up.

Sutcliffe and Cockin set out to get a closer look at the cliff. As they studied it through their binoculars, they inadvertently exposed themselves to a German gun crew somewhere in front of them. A shell was slammed home into the breech of a German "88" antitank gun, then fired. The gun had a very long range and a flat trajectory. There was only the quick shriek of an incoming shell, an explosion, and Sutcliffe lay dead, with Cockin mortally wounded. Farley Mowat recalls the after-effect of the death in his history of the regiment: "The tragedy had a remarkable effect. It irrevocably and utterly destroyed the pale remainder of the illusion that war was only an exciting extension of the battle games of 1941 and 1942. The killing of the C.O. *before* the battle seemed to be an almost obscene act, and when the news came to the men it roused in them an ugly resentment. . . . Hatred of the enemy was born."

—m—

THERE WAS LITTLE TIME TO MOURN—Assoro had to be taken. Command passed to Major Lord John Tweedsmuir, the tall, slender, and intense thirty-one-year-old son of Lord Tweedsmuir, former Governor General of Canada. His real name was John Buchan, but as a hereditary peer he was entitled to call himself Lord. The men called him "Long John" or "Tweedie" (he liked to be known as John Tweedsmuir). Tweedsmuir and his company commanders looked over the terrain; Tweedsmuir knew that a direct assault up the road to Assoro was a "physical impossibility," in the words of *The Official History of the Canadian Army in the Italian Campaign.* Instead he decided on a cross-country night march to the foot of Assoro Mountain, then a climb straight up the steep eastern face of the peak using whatever goat tracks could be found to reach the top. The assault force would have to reach the top of the mountain by dawn. The rest of the Hasty Ps would follow. While they were climbing, artillery and Bren-gun fire on the western slope might divert German attention long enough to allow them to pull it off. Once the mountaintop and the ruins of a twelfth-century Norman castle had been secured, the Canadians would dominate the town of Assoro and could call down artillery fire on the German defenders.

A small assault team was chosen from each of the rifle companies and armed with automatic weapons. Leaving all unessential equipment behind, and with each man bearing a heavy burden of ammunition, mortar or Bren-gun parts, or a heavy radio, they climbed through the dark. They made their way over boulder-strewn watercourses and they scrabbled over knife-edged ridges, bright moonlight guiding them. They kept absolutely silent. They knew they must be in position when the first light of dawn revealed the peaks or they would be exposed to enemy fire and die on the rocks. Mowat writes: "Each man who made that climb performed his own private miracle. From ledge to ledge the dark figures made their way, hauling each other up, passing along their weapons and ammunition from hand to hand. A signaler made that climb with a heavy wireless set strapped to his back—a thing that in daylight was seen to be impossible. Yet no man slipped, no man dropped as much as a clip of ammunition."

Just before dawn the first two Hasty Ps dragged themselves over a stone wall and onto the crest. Three surprised, sleepy Germans were quickly subdued. The Hasty Ps took the peak, then, when the rest of the regiment was in place, opened fire on the Germans below. Heavy fighting followed. The Germans assaulted the crest and pounded it with shellfire, mortars, machine guns, and "moaning minnies"—six-barrelled rocket projectors. The Hasty Ps held on, then advanced to take the town. The Germans counterattacked. The Hasty Ps still held on, but were quickly using up the precious food, water, and ammunition they had lugged with them. It was thirty-six hours before a trickle of supplies reached them, courtesy of the Royal Canadian Regiment. As darkness fell on July 22, the Germans began to pull back. Late the next day the Hasty Ps were relieved.

Assoro was the first battle honour the Hastings and Prince Edward Regiment earned in the Second World War, and it was a signal honour. When the division took the twin towns, it broke open the main German line of resistance in the centre of the island. The German defences began to unhinge as the Canadians turned east; the British near Etna recommenced their advance. At the same time the Americans, farther west, turned the corner of the island at Palermo and drove east along the north coast. The 1st Canadian Infantry Division was taken out of the line in Sicily on August 7, 1943—"pinched out" as the battle front grew narrower. The German and Italian forces withdrew to Messina and then across the strait to the Italian mainland. The battle for Sicily ended on August 17, when British and American forces finally marched into Messina.

—⁓—

THE LOYAL EDMONTON REGIMENT dates back to April 1, 1908, when the 101st Regiment was established in the city that had been selected as capital of the three-year-old province of Alberta. In 1909 it was redesignated the 101st Regiment (Edmonton Fusiliers). In the First World War the regiment sent a large number of troops to the 9th and 49th battalions of the CEF. In 1920 it became known as the Edmonton Regiment, but it was reorganized in 1924 into two regiments, the Edmonton Regiment and the Edmonton Fusiliers, which were subsequently renamed the 19th Alberta Dragoons. The Edmonton Regiment was mobilized on September 1, 1939, and began immediate recruitment in the province from Red Deer to Peace River. The battalion reached full war strength of 835 men by the beginning of October and trained at the Prince of Wales Armoury before embarking for the United Kingdom as part of the 2nd Brigade of the 1st Canadian Infantry Division, alongside the PPCLI and the Seaforth Highlanders from Vancouver. Just a few days before the landings in Sicily, the regiment was designated the Loyal Edmonton Regiment— the "Loyal Eddies."

Some German and Italian troops were captured when Sicily fell, but the great majority got across the Strait of Messina and onto the toe of the Italian boot with virtually all their heavy equipment. The Allies prepared to go after them. On September 3, 1943, the Canadians crossed the Strait of Messina as part of the 13th British Corps under the command of Lieutenant-General Miles Dempsey. There was almost no opposition to the crossing, and the British and Canadians moved quickly inland. Within one week the Canadians had reached Catanzaro, about 120 kilometres from the crossing point.

The crossing of the strait coincided with a major British and American landing at Salerno, on Italy's west coast. The idea was to drive inland and trap the Germans or at least pull them away from the south so that Dempsey's corps would have an easier time of it. The Germans resisted strongly. Their commander, General Albrecht

"Smiling Al" Kesselring, was well aware that the Bay of Salerno was the northernmost suitable landing place available to the Allies that was within fighter cover of Sicily. When the Italian government suddenly surrendered to the Allies on the night of September 8, Kesselring knew the invasion would take place within hours. He was right; the Allied troops came ashore the morning of September 9 and ran into a maelstrom. It took more than five days of heavy fighting and some thirteen thousand Allied casualties before the British and Americans broke out of the beachhead and headed for Naples, which they entered October 1.

Kesselring's basic strategy after the fall of Naples was to withdraw gradually to the north, killing as many Allied soldiers and causing as many delays as possible while building a number of strong defensive lines across the peninsula in the mountains south of Rome. Thus the Canadian and British troops who had crossed into Italy at Messina had a relatively easy time of it—for a while. Simonds's 1st Canadian Division dashed to Potenza, reaching it on September 19. The town fell almost immediately and the Canadians drove on. By the end of the month, the hot and dusty Italian summer was giving way to fall, with cold nights, rain, and mud. The Canadians struggled upward into the mountains along narrow roads and mountain paths. The advance began to slow considerably. A pattern was repeated over and over again, as it had been in Sicily. The Germans held fast as long as they could, forcing the Canadians to stop and fight. Then they'd pull out, leaving blown bridges, mined roads, caved-in culverts, and sometimes a small rearguard to harass the Canadians as they recommenced their advance.

The rainy weather and bad roads made a mess of logistics; the 1st Canadian Division had to move slowly in order not to outrun its supplies. They crossed the Fortore River against stiffening German opposition, then pushed on to Gambatesa on the important Highway No. 17, which led west to Campobasso. Finally, on October 14, the Royal Canadian Regiment entered Campobasso, high in the mountains. The Canadians quickly dubbed this small city of some seventeen thousand people "Maple Leaf City." The division rested there until the end of November, then broke camp and headed for the Adriatic coast and the Moro River. Their task would be to cross the Moro and, accompanied by the 1st Canadian Armoured Brigade, capture the small coastal town of Ortona, about 3 kilometres farther on. By December 4 the Canadians were in their new positions on a ridge overlooking the south bank of the Moro. One of the hardest-fought Canadian battles of the war was about to begin, with the Loyal Edmonton Regiment in the thick of it. And when the battle began, the regiment was already significantly undermanned.

—⁓—

ORTONA IS A PRE-ROMAN TOWN dominated by a fortress. It stands on a promontory alongside the small harbour and was dominated by a cathedral and two massive defensive towers. The streets are narrow, the buildings stone or brick, with many sharing common walls. At the time of the Second World War there were three large squares in Ortona. The Germans demolished buildings and blocked streets to force the Canadians into the squares, where every metre was covered by heavy concentrations of automatic weapons, mortars, and even flame-throwers. They dug tanks into the rubble of blasted buildings. Houses were fortified and windows covered with chicken wire to prevent grenades from being lobbed in. The few open avenues leading to the squares were killing zones completely covered by German snipers, machine-gunners, and grenadiers.

Ortona and the ground around it were defended by tough German paratroopers who were dug in in virtually every square metre from the north bank of the Moro River to the southwestern approaches to the town. To reach Ortona, the Canadians would have to cross the Moro, work their way up the bluffs on the north side of the river, then cross a deep but narrow gully before gaining the main highway into the town. The heavily overgrown gully was well defended, with the

Germans dug in on the reverse slope and multiple bands of barbed wire strung through the brush. The battle opened on the night of December 5 with a 1st Brigade attack across the Moro; for the next thirteen days every battalion of the 1st Canadian Infantry Division was heavily engaged in fighting across the 3 short kilometres to the town. This was the Somme or Passchendaele all over again. Casualties were very heavy, especially in the fight to take the gully. But finally, on the morning of December 19, a key crossroads leading to Ortona fell to the Van Doos. The road into Ortona was open.

The next day the Loyal Eddies advanced toward Ortona from the crossroads. By nightfall they and the Seaforths, who covered their right flank, were into the western edge of the town. The fighting was hard, vicious, and close. Platoons, sections, even half-sections of three or four men would ease their way up to a door, covered by a Bren-gunner, kick the door in, throw in grenades, then rush in immediately after the explosion, guns blazing. The streets were so deadly, however, that Loyal Eddy Captain Bill Longhurst came up with an alternative solution—blast through the wall of the house right into the adjacent building. In one row house he asked the engineers to bring a large "beehive"—a cone-shaped charge made up of plastic explosive—to the top floor. To get the right height, the charge was placed on a chair leaning against the wall. The room was cleared and the charge exploded, but when everyone rushed back in, they found that there was a double wall between the two buildings. A second charge was set and exploded, and this produced the desired result. They rushed into the adjoining building and with guns blazing cleared it from the top down.

Word of Longhurst's successful experiment spread quickly. The Canadians dubbed this technique "mouseholing"; it is still used today by armies engaged in close fighting in urban areas where houses abut one another. The Loyal Eddies also found a new use for the 6-pounder antitank guns attached to every Canadian infantry battalion. One soldier later recalled: "We used the anti-tanks in a unique way. The shells could not penetrate the granite walls, sometimes 4 ft thick. So we just put them through the windows [and fired] and they (i.e., the shells) bounced around inside much like they would in an enemy tank doing horrible damage."

The advance was slow and very painful. The Eddies were effectively led by company commander Major Jim Stone because the battalion CO, Lieutenant-Colonel Jim Jefferson, had established his headquarters on the outskirts of Ortona and was therefore not in close touch with the fighting in the town. Stone was the senior commander on the spot. According to historian Mark Zuehlke, Stone was "resourceful, independent-minded, determined, brave to the point of near recklessness, and, because he had come up through the ranks, well-versed in small unit tactics." Stone would later go on to become the battalion commander.

As the fighting raged, casualties mounted to the point where both battalions in the town were reduced almost to the size of infantry companies. But still they fought on. The battle for Ortona was well covered by Canadian war correspondents, including the CBC's Matthew Halton with one of the corporation's innovative sound-recording trucks. Soon Halton's voice was being heard in every kitchen and living room across Canada as his reports from literally metres away from the fighting front grabbed the nation's attention. With the noises of gunfire and explosions in the background, Halton's precise and unhurried reports followed the slow progress of the Canadian soldiers battling for the town. Canadians were told—with more than a little exaggeration—that Ortona was becoming the Stalingrad of the Italian front. In fact the battle for Stalingrad, fought some twelve months before on the Eastern Front, dwarfed the fight for Ortona. Still, it was very costly for Canada's small army.

On Christmas Day 1943 the Loyal Edmonton Regiment was in the thick of the fight alongside the Seaforth Highlanders of Vancouver in a vicious metre-by-metre struggle for control of the town. The official history of the Canadian army in Italy describes the melancholy of that day: "Nothing could be less Christmas-like than the acrid smell of cordite overhanging Ortona's rubble barricades, the thunder of collapsing walls and the blinding dust and smoke which darkened the alleys in which Canadians and Germans were locked in grim hand-to-hand struggle." One German account of the day reflected the hard fighting from the enemy's perspective: "In Ortona the enemy attacked all day long with about one brigade supported by ten tanks. In very hard house-to-house fighting and at the cost of heavy casualties to his own troops [he] advanced to the market square in the south part of the town. The battle there is especially violent. Our own troops are using flamethrowers, hand grenades and [anti-tank rocket launchers]."

But it was Christmas. The Seaforths managed to arrange a dinner in the abandoned church of Santa Maria di Constantinopoli, just blocks from the fighting, where places were set at long rows of tables with white tablecloths, a bottle of beer per man, candies, nuts, chocolates, cigarettes, and apples. The Seaforth riflemen came in from the fighting company by company and sat down to organ music and a meal of soup, pork with applesauce, cauliflower, mixed vegetables, mashed potatoes, gravy, Christmas pudding, and mince pie. All the while the *crump* of explosions and the constant sounds of machine-gun and rifle fire accompanied the music, reminding the men of what they were about to face once they left that small island of relative tranquility. The Seaforth war diarist recorded: "The expression on the faces of the dirty bearded men as they entered the building was a reward that those responsible are never likely to forget."

But the Loyal Eddies were less fortunate—they dined where they could. Some were able to make their way in small groups back to a position near the fighting to grab a quick meal. One Eddie later recalled: "We were just down from St. Tommaso Square. We rotated back to the dinner. We were out for about half-an-hour and then it was back to the fight . . . a soldier has very little appetite when in the midst of battle." Jim Stone, then a company commander, ate his Christmas dinner in the midst of the fighting: "On Christmas Day 1943, I was on the main street of Ortona, directing a local attack ordered by my C.O. Three of my men were killed on the street before

0900 hrs. My Christmas dinner was a cold pork chop brought forward on a 'Bren' carrier. A most unhappy day."

Two days before Christmas, Major-General Chris Vokes, commander of 1st Canadian Infantry Division, had ordered his 1st Brigade to cut off the German escape and supply routes to the west of the town. The Hastings and Prince Edward Regiment and the 48th Highlanders broke through to the high ground west of Ortona, but were then cut off themselves. On the night of December 25 a party of Saskatoon Light Infantry reached them with supplies and ammunition, and the next day tanks from the Ontario Regiment broke through. The German position in Ortona was now untenable; they too had suffered heavy casualties and all their escape routes were about to be cut off. On the 27th they began to pull out of Ortona; they were gone by the 28th, their unburied dead rotting in the streets.

The battle for Ortona took eight days of hard fighting; the Loyal Edmonton Regiment lost 63 killed and 109 wounded or taken prisoner in those eight days, while the Seaforths suffered 41 killed and 62 wounded. For both regiments, as well as for the rest of the 1st Canadian Infantry Division, the month of December 1943 was one of the costliest periods of the entire war. In just 24 days—from the assault crossing of the Moro River that began on the evening of December 5, 1943, to the end of the fight for Ortona on December 29—the 1st Canadian Infantry Division lost 2,339 men killed and wounded, with another 1,617 men taken out of the line by illness, many afflicted with battle exhaustion. That was almost 20 percent of the division's strength.

The Loyal Edmonton Regiment's 1st Battalion fought with great distinction for the rest of the war, then came home to Canada and was disbanded in October 1945. The Loyal Edmonton Regiment continued to exist as an active regiment in Canada's reserve army. Today the regiment is also the fourth (reserve) battalion of Princess Patricia's Canadian Light Infantry.

CHAPTER TWELVE

BLOODY FIGHTING: THE GEE-GEES IN THE LIRI VALLEY AND THE SHERBROOKES IN NORMANDY

> In those few miles between the hills, a thousand guns suddenly let go as one, and then they kept on firing. We'd never seen or heard or imagined anything quite like this.
>
> —A Canadian officer at the opening of the battle for Rome, May 11, 1944

IN THE THIRD WEEK OF MAY 1944, a huge force of fighting men and equipment milled about in the southern and beachside towns of England, waiting for the word to go—to launch the largest invasion in history. D-Day—the invasion of Normandy—was fast approaching; the tightly wound coil of seven Allied airborne and assault divisions, and the thousands of ships and aircraft that would fling them into the teeth of the German-built Atlantic Wall along the coast of France, was ready to be released. Everyone knew that the long-awaited invasion of France was mere days away and that the outcome of the battle would weigh heavily on the course of the war.

But while those assault troops readied themselves for their moment of truth, the war in Italy dragged on. The Canadians fighting as part of the British Eighth Army, with its agglomeration of British, Indian, Polish, Free French, New Zealand, Canadian, and other troops, continued to batter their way up the east side of the Italian peninsula, with the American Fifth Army pushing forward up the west side. In between lay the rugged spine of Italy's high Apennine Mountains. In front was "Smiling Al" Kesselring with his very determined German troops forcing the Allies to fight for every pass, every mountaintop, every village, every possible means of approach to the Italian capital—the Eternal City of Rome.

By January 1944 the U.S. Fifth Army had reached the Gustav Line, at the entrance to the Liri Valley. The line had been built by the Germans after the invasion of Italy was launched in early September and the Italian government had sued for peace with the Allies. The Gustav Line was not a continuous defensive position as might have been constructed on the Western Front in the First World War. Rather it was a string of mutually reinforcing fortified positions built using the heavily wooded and hilly terrain to best advantage and backed by well-entrenched antitank guns and machine guns, with anti-personnel and antitank mines strewn liberally through thick belts of barbed wire to create kill zones. The line was backed by thousands of German infantry and dozens of armoured formations. What made it so particularly difficult to assault was that many of the German defensive positions lay behind rivers and streams that flowed at cross angles to the Allied line of approach.

In the country south of Rome, the Gustav Line was dominated by the high peaks to the immediate east of the valley of the Liri and Rapido rivers, especially Monte Cassino, with its famous old abbey, which loomed above the town of Cassino at the entrance to the Liri Valley. On the night of January 20, 1944, the U.S. 36th Division tried to force a crossing of the Rapido River and experienced "one of the bloodiest failures of the war." Clearly the Allies had to try something else. That something else was Operation Shingle—a landing at Anzio, on the Italian coast just southwest of Rome. It might outflank the German defences; it might even cause Kesselring to pull troops from the Gustav Line to shore up the Anzio defences. But that did not happen; fifty thousand troops went ashore at the small port of Anzio on January 22, but hesitation and caution on the part of the commanding officer allowed the Germans to rush defenders to the area from Rome itself. The Allies were trapped in full view of the Germans in the surrounding hills, and they would stay trapped for months. Instead of the Germans weakening the Gustav Line by stripping troops from it to send to the Anzio front, the Allies began to ponder stripping troops from the main U.S. Fifth and British Eighth armies to shore up their position at Anzio. Once again there was but one way to Rome—from the south, passing by Monte Cassino and up the Liri Valley.

—⁂—

TOWARD THE END OF 1943 the Canadian contingent in Italy was strengthened by the arrival of the 5th Canadian Armoured Division, a new formation sent to shore up the Canadian presence there. One of the formations of the new division was the 3rd Armoured Reconnaissance Regiment of the Canadian Armoured Corps—also known as the Governor General's Horse Guards. With roots dating back to a number of colonial cavalry units organized in the early 1800s, the Governor General's Body Guard for Upper Canada emerged as a full-fledged cavalry troop in April 1866. The unit was sent into the field during the Fenian invasion of the Niagara Peninsula in June 1866, but did not actually engage the enemy at Ridgeway. On July 1, 1867, the unit became the Governor General's Body Guard for Ontario. John Marteinson, author of the regiment's official history, calls its commander during those years, Colonel George Taylor Denison III, "the first Canadian military intellectual." He wrote two books, *Modern Cavalry* and *A History of Cavalry,* and received wide acclaim for his ideas about how cavalry ought to be used, particularly his suggestion that they fight as mounted riflemen.

The Governor General's Body Guard for Ontario saw action in the Northwest Rebellion of 1885, where it earned its first battle honour. On May 17, 1889, it was authorized as a full cavalry regiment in the Canadian militia; it was designated the Governor General's Body Guard on July 13, 1895. The regiment committed forty-three men to the Canadian contingent serving in the Boer War, where Captain H.Z.C. Cockburn was awarded the regiment's first Victoria Cross. The regiment contributed volunteers to both the 3rd Battalion of the Canadian Expeditionary Force and the 4th Canadian Mounted Rifles in the First World War. In 1936 the regiment was joined with the Mississauga Horse to become the Governor General's Horse Guards, nicknamed the "Gee-Gees." Like the rest of the Canadian cavalry, the unit had been converted to an armoured role by the outbreak of the Second World War.

Coming from Toronto and with its distinguished early leadership, the Horse Guards considered themselves an elite unit. The regimental history asserts: "By the time of the North-West Rebellion in 1885, the Body Guard [Horse Guards] had earned a reputation as being the finest cavalry in the country." Notwithstanding what other cavalry regiments might have thought of the Body Guard or of themselves, the assertion reflects the regiment's ongoing sentiment that it was special. Certainly the leading citizens of Toronto must have thought so. On November 23, 1938, the Governor General of Canada, Lord Tweedsmuir, honorary colonel of the Horse Guards, presented the newly amalgamated regiment's first regimental standard to a packed audience at a dismounted parade in Toronto's University Avenue Armouries. The *Toronto Telegram* reported that "thousands thronged the galleries" for the ceremony, which was carried out with due honour and ceremony by the Governor General, who presented the standard in the King's name to the commanding officer of the regiment, Lieutenant-Colonel A.E. Nash, a decorated veteran of the First World War. The Anglican archbishop of Toronto himself consecrated the standard. After the ceremony the Governor General took the regimental salute as the whole unit marched past him to the tune of "Men of Harlech," the regimental march. Afterwards drinks and food were served at the officers' mess and an all-ranks dance was held on the floor of the armoury.

The Horse Guards were not authorized for overseas service in the Second World War until February of 1941, when they became the 3rd Armoured Regiment (The Governor General's Horse Guards). This form of designation was used for all of Canada's armoured and armoured reconnaissance regiments. For example, Lord Strathcona's Horse, which was slotted into the 5th Canadian Armoured Brigade of the 5th Canadian Armoured Division, was designated the 2nd Armoured Regiment (Lord Strathcona's Horse [Royal Canadians]). Even the venerable Royal Canadian Dragoons became the 1st Armoured Car Regiment (Royal Canadian Dragoons).

When the 5th Canadian Armoured Division was formed, the Gee-Gees were converted into an armoured reconnaissance regiment under the direct command of divisional headquarters—it was not part of an armoured brigade. John Marteinson, the official historian of the Royal Canadian Armoured Corps, explains: "The main task of the divisional reconnaissance units was to collect information for the divisional commander about enemy locations, movement and strength as well as ground conditions that could affect operations." In other words, the regiment was to be the ground-based eyes and ears of the division, normally ranging ahead of its fighting formations to find the enemy and evaluate his strength. For that reason, units such as the Gee-Gees were equipped with only a minimal number of tanks along with scout cars, armoured cars, and Bren-gun carriers. They were not intended to slug it out with the enemy, but to move fast and to back up the regular fighting formations only when necessary, when ordered to do so, and usually when reconnaissance duties had been completed. On the morning of May 24, 1944, the Gee-Gees were ordered to support a major thrust by the 5th Canadian Armoured Division from the small San Martino River, about 2 kilometres north of the town of Pontecorvo in the Liri Valley, across the Melfa River—about 8 kilometres to the northwest—in a massive effort to break through German defences south of Rome.

—⁓—

CONTINUING BRITISH AND AMERICAN FAILURES to reach Rome over the winter of 1943–44 gave way to a new plan, one drawn up by British Lieutenant-General Sir John Harding. It was called Operation Diadem. Harding's plan envisaged bringing the U.S. Fifth Army from Italy's west coast and the British Eighth Army from the east coast for a joint attack through the Liri Valley. The Liri River is one of the very few rivers south of Rome that flow in a general east–west direction. The river valley has long been used as an invasion route to Rome, and the Germans, in full knowledge of the history and geography of the region, had strongly fortified the eastern end of the valley. If the Allies could reduce or bypass those defences, they would penetrate the Gustav Line and a secondary defence position behind it known as the Hitler Line and turn the flank of Kesselring's Tenth Army. British General Sir Oliver Leese, commanding the Eighth Army, would thus have three corps under his command—the 13th British, the 2nd Polish, and the 1st Canadian; the Americans would protect Leese's left flank.

The attack began an hour before midnight on May 11 with a massive artillery barrage. One Canadian officer described it this way: "In those few miles between the hills, a thousand guns suddenly let go as one, and then they kept on firing. We'd never seen or heard or imagined anything quite like this. You could see the flashes of nearby guns and you could hear the thunder of dozens and hundreds more on every side and you could only imagine what sort of Hell was falling on the German lines. It damn near deafened you."

Despite vigorous German resistance that caused heavy Allied casualties, Indian infantry, assisted by Canadian armour, penetrated through the initial Gustav Line defences by the late afternoon of May 13 and were able to establish a number of bridgeheads across the Gari River. Then British and Free French troops began to advance toward the next of Kesselring's defensive positions—the Hitler Line, some 13 kilometres west of the Gari River, which was weaker than the Gustav Line but still fraught with danger. Leese called upon Lieutenant-General E.L.M. Burns and the troops of the First Canadian Corps to punch through the Hitler Line and continue the drive to Rome. Burns ordered the 1st Canadian Infantry Division to lead the attack, followed by the 5th Armoured under the command of Major-General Bert Hoffmeister, a former militia officer from Vancouver.

The attack began in the early morning hours of May 17, part of an Allied offensive designed to close up the Hitler Line along its length. Surprisingly, the Germans melted away at nightfall, allowing both Canadian brigades to advance quickly to the vicinity of the Hitler Line defences. It was a different story when they actually reached the line two days later; the Ontario Tank Regiment lost thirteen tanks destroyed and many others damaged on May 19 while supporting an attack on the line by the British 78th Division. The Van Doos suffered particularly heavy casualties in a direct assault on the line's barbed wire. The attack ran out of steam by nightfall.

It took Burns three days to prepare another push, which began on the morning of May 23. It started with a bombardment over a front of some 2,000 metres, followed by an advance by two brigades from 1st Division, with the 2nd Brigade on the right and the 3rd Brigade on the left. Burns's plan was to fight the 1st Division through the Hitler Line, then send the 5th Armoured Division through the hole, across the Melfa River, and up to Rome on Highway No. 6. Although the 2nd Brigade ran into murderous opposition on the right of the attack, the 3rd Brigade broke through on the left, where the Canadian infantry moved quickly through the German defences and on to the all-important Pontecorvo-Aquino road. Major-General Chris Vokes, commander of the 1st Canadian Division, quickly decided to reinforce the breakthrough success and threw his divisional reserve into the battle. The renewed advance started late in the afternoon in a heavy rain. The Germans were caught in the open preparing to counterattack; the Canadians killed many of them and widened the breach. To their left the 4th Reconnaissance Regiment (Princess Louise Dragoon Guards) and the Royal Canadian Regiment cleared the town of Pontecorvo.

When Hoffmeister realized that the Hitler Line had been breached, he called Burns and told him that the 5th Armoured Division was going to attack. Heavy rains and the return of British tanks to the lines to refuel and rearm delayed the advance until morning. Hoffmeister selected his 5th Armoured Brigade to carry out the attack but divided the attacking troops into two ad hoc battle groups. One was "Vokes Force," led by Divisional Commander Chris Vokes's younger brother, Fred, who was commander of the British Columbia Dragoons, an armoured regiment. The Irish Regiment, an infantry battalion based in Toronto, made up the balance of his force. The other was "Griffin Force," led by P.G. "Paddy" Griffin's Lord Strathcona's Horse and the motorized infantry of the Westminster Regiment from New Westminster, B.C. The Governor General's Horse Guards were assigned to cover the flank of the attack.

The advance began at about 6:00 AM on May 24, a cold, misty morning. It was hard to see and much of the ground on the east bank of the San Martino River had been churned up into impassable mud. Engineers were supposed to have thrown a Bailey bridge across the river in the night but had been prevented from doing so by heavy enemy shellfire. The Bailey bridge was a prefabricated structure designed by British engineer Donald Bailey that could span gaps of up to 60 metres. It could support tanks and could be constructed without welding, riveting, or heavy construction equipment.

An easier crossing had to be found; until it was the attack was delayed for two hours. Finally, at about 8:00 AM, Vokes Force went across, followed by Griffin Force. The Gee-Gees crossed the San Martino about an hour and a half later. B Squadron of the Gee-Gees, led by Major Tim Hugman, crossed first to cover the left flank of the attack. Their immediate task was to advance northeast toward the Melfa River about 1 kilometre to the left of Vokes's and Griffin's column. C Squadron of the Gee-Gees, commanded by Major Allan Burton, followed, but swung north along the rear of the Hitler Line to protect the right flank of the attack. A Squadron remained in reserve near Pontecorvo.

B Squadron's main job was to advance parallel to the lead tank of the 5th Armoured Brigade to detect and attempt to clear major concentrations of infantry equipped with antitank guns or German armour that might ambush the 5th Brigade column. As the squadron crossed the San Martino it came under immediate fire from German artillery and the multi-barrelled rocket projectors known in German as *Nebelwerfer*s, which the Allied soldiers called "moaning minnies." The crossing itself took almost two hours because of the terrible condition of the riverbank. This was the first time the squadron had been in a battle, and many of the crew commanders were both nervous and cautious. The move through olive groves and vineyards was slow going, with guy wires and low branches restricting the view from the armoured drivers' observation slits. On top of that the maps were less than accurate. One troop was "hopelessly lost for the greater part of the day," according to the unit war diary.

It wasn't long before B Squadron ran into direct enemy fire. One troop leader, Lieutenant Doug Chant, destroyed an enemy machine-gun post and took twelve prisoners before turning to clear out a house the Germans had been using to harass the Canadian infantry. The squadron suffered its first fatal casualty later in the afternoon, as the official history records: "A Sherman commanded by Corporal Dave Bradshaw took a direct hit from an 88mm anti-tank gun and quickly brewed up (began to smoke). With Corporal Bradshaw's help, all of the crew got out except trooper Howard Conn, the driver. Conn had been injured or knocked out by the explosion, and despite desperate efforts by the others, the driver's hatch could not be opened from the outside before the tank was engulfed in flame."

C Squadron crossed the San Martino shortly after B Squadron. They too ran into immediate problems with moving cross-country through tangled vineyards and along sunken farmers' tracks that were not on their maps. Mortars and artillery dogged them as they slowly advanced about 2,000 metres along the backside of the Hitler Line fortifications, which were still manned by surviving German defenders. Major Burton later wrote: "I ordered the advance to proceed slowly, keeping in visual contact and together as a unit. We saw the heavy tank-tracks of vehicles recently departed when we came to our first clearing, an inviting open space with a house about two hundred yards away. . . . I ordered every tank available to open fire on it simultaneously with machine guns and high explosives." It was a good guess; more than seventy Germans had taken refuge in the house, and both a 75mm antitank gun and a self-propelled 88mm antitank gun were destroyed in the barrage. Burton's men also found a German radio code book in the wreckage.

The squadron cleared the area immediately west of the small village of Aquino and advanced toward Highway No. 6 and a rail line north of the town. They were challenged often by German defenders. The unit war diary records one such encounter: "One of Mr. Murphy's tanks had been ditched . . . and . . . he could not get it out without the aid of a recovery vehicle. . . . As Mr. Murphy was standing on the back of his tank, cheerfully reporting to the Sq[uadro]n Com[mande]r that there were no enemy in sight, he was fired on by two very real and hostile machine guns. Mr. Murphy hastily went to ground and the troop opened fire with their main guns and the coax (machine guns)."

One of the troopers broke cover and ran toward an unmanned machine gun that he used to pour fire on some German paratroopers, allowing the Canadians to reorganize and beat off the attack. For his bravery, Trooper Thomas Edwin Dickenson was awarded the Military Medal—the first member of the Gee-Gees to be cited for bravery in action in the Second World War. Burton's squadron captured a hundred prisoners that day at very little cost to themselves. For a first day in battle it was a remarkable achievement, and Burton was awarded the Distinguished Service Order (DSO) as recognition of his unit's feat.

By nightfall Hoffmeister's division had forced a crossing of the Melfa. They held the bridgehead the next day while the 11th Infantry Brigade crossed and began to probe to the west; by midday on May 25, the division was across the Melfa on a two-battalion front. But then problems arose. The rear area of the division was a confused and tangled mass of vehicles and men; supplies, ammunition, and bridging equipment could not be brought up quickly and the infantry of 11th Brigade were forced to curtail their advance toward the Liri. They did not cross that river until May 26 and it was not until May 27 that they were able to occupy the town of Ceprano, on the road to Rome. The delay prompted General Leese to assign the final drive to Rome to the Americans. The only Canadians who entered the Italian capital on June 4 were the men of the 1st Special Service Force—the Devil's Brigade—a combined Canadian and American commando unit.

But while Mark Clark's Fifth Army seized Rome, he allowed the bulk of the Tenth German Army to slip away to the north. It was a major error that gave Kesselring ample troops and weapons to man other strong defensive positions farther north, such as the Gothic Line, which ran from north of Pisa on the west coast of Italy to south of Rimini on the east coast (this is sometimes referred to as the Pisa-Rimini Line). Thus the Allies would continue to slog north for the next ten months. The Canadians, however, left Italy at the end of the year and rejoined the rest of the First Canadian Army in Holland for the final push of the war, to liberate Amsterdam and the western Netherlands.

The Liri Valley campaign was the first battle honour earned by the Governor General's Horse Guards in the Second World War. The Gee-Gees continued with the push through the Gothic Line and the liberation of the Netherlands. They returned to Canada and were disbanded as an active service regiment in 1946. The regiment continued on in both reconnaissance and armoured reconnaissance roles and is today an armoured unit in the 32nd Canadian Brigade Group, Land Forces Central Area, Canadian Army Reserves.

—m—

WHETHER IT IS CALLED D-DAY, the Longest Day, or simply the sixth of June, the invasion of Normandy on June 6, 1944, is one of history's truly memorable days. In the final minutes of June 5, paratroopers from one British and two American airborne divisions (including the 1st Canadian Parachute Battalion) began to land on the flanks of the five beaches designated as invasion objectives. Several hours later 100,000 Allied troops forced their way ashore against determined German resistance. The two American beaches on the far right (western) flank were code-named Utah and Omaha. To the left of Omaha were Gold, a British objective; Juno, the Canadian beach; and Sword beach, just west of where the Canal de Caen and the Orne River flow into the Baie de la Seine, near the seaside town of Ouistreham.

Juno Beach was the objective of the 3rd Canadian Infantry Division, whose two attacking brigades, the 7th Canadian Infantry Brigade and the 8th Canadian Infantry Brigade, were accompanied respectively by the 6th Armoured Regiment (1st Hussars) from London, Ontario, and the 10th Armoured Regiment (Fort Garry Horse) from Winnipeg. For these assaulting formations June 6 was no doubt one of the toughest days of the war; for the 3rd Division's reserve brigade—the 9th Canadian Infantry Brigade accompanied by the 27th Armoured Regiment (Sherbrooke Fusiliers)—the next day, June 7, was a day no man would ever forget.

Vincent Owen "Bud" Walsh first joined the army cadets when he attended high school at Montreal's Loyola College in the late 1930s. In August 1940 he heard that Colonel E.L.M. Burns (commander of First Canadian Corps at the Battle of the Liri Valley) was forming an armoured division, and he went active. He was trained in Canada as a driver/gunner and radio operator in tanks, then, in January 1941, he was sent to join the Sherbrookes, who had just returned from garrison duty in Newfoundland and were about to be transformed into an armoured regiment. By D-Day he was one of the regiment's longest-serving officers and commander of C Squadron. He would later recall that his landing in the second wave on D-Day was "completely uneventful and in the best Exercise tradition. The LCT [landing craft—tank] landed us approximately at the point planned and the move up from the beach was hindered by the usual conglomeration of vehicles and MPs [Military Police]. One difference which made this affair more realistic was the presence of a few bundles of grey bags which had been men. The sight of these came something as a shock to most of us."

In conjunction with the North Nova Scotias, an infantry battalion, the Sherbrookes had moved well inland by nightfall, with only a few brushes with the enemy. Walsh recalls that at night "we had not yet learned to be afraid." But that would change very quickly and dramatically the next afternoon, when the column resumed its advance south of the beach. Suddenly the voice of the Sherbrookes' CO, Lieutenant-Colonel Mel Gordon, crackled over Walsh's tank radio: "Trouble on the left. Send me some troops to the left," then, "Send me some troops to the right." Gordon's call for tank troops (four tanks to a troop) was Walsh's first sign that the unblooded Sherbrooke Fusiliers had run smack into a brigade-size force of the 12th SS Panzer Division, one of the toughest and most vicious adversaries the Canadians would meet from the day after D-Day to the very end of the war.

The Sherbrooke Regiment traces its direct history to the Sherbrooke Battalion of Infantry, formed on September 21, 1866, in response to the continuing Fenian threat from northern New York State and Vermont. Most of the regiment's members were farmers or lumber workers from the then predominantly English-speaking Eastern Townships, southeast of Montreal. In 1867 the regiment became the 53rd Sherbrooke Battalion of Infantry, with a drill hall at the corner of Montreal and William streets and a 4-acre (1.6 hectares) drilling field not far away. Some members of the regiment volunteered for service in both the Northwest Rebellion and the South African War, and the regiment (redesignated the 53rd Sherbrooke Regiment in 1900) recruited for the 12th and 117th battalions of the CEF, though only the 12th fought as a unit. On April 1, 1920, the regiment's name was changed again, this time to the Sherbrooke Regiment. The unit became a machine-gun battalion in 1936 and was thus referred to as the Sherbrooke Regiment (M.G.).

No Eastern Townships combat regiments were mobilized at the outbreak of the Second World War. As a result, the 117th Eastern

Townships Battalion Association along with members of the Sherbrooke Regiment (M.G.) urged the government to establish a unit for active service overseas. The government responded by amalgamating the Fusiliers de Sherbrooke and the Sherbrooke Regiment (M.G.) into the Sherbrooke Fusiliers Regiment, a unit that would encompass both English- and French-speakers from the surrounding region. In 1942 the unit was converted into an armoured regiment and became the 27th Armoured Regiment (The Sherbrooke Fusilier Regiment). Originally destined to become part of the 4th Canadian Armoured Brigade of the 4th Canadian Armoured Division, it was eventually attached to the 9th Brigade of the 3rd Division.

At the heart of a Canadian armoured regiment in mid-1944 were three squadrons of tanks and other vehicles, each squadron consisting of a headquarters troop and four tank troops. The three tanks of the HQ troop were specially equipped with more and larger radios so as to direct the fighting troops. Each fighting troop consisted of four tanks, all U.S.-designed Sherman medium tanks. Three of the four Shermans were equipped with low-velocity 75mm guns, which were virtually ineffective against the newer German Panther and Tiger tanks but a veritable match for the older German Mark IV tanks. The troop leader drove a "Firefly"—a Sherman with a specially modified turret equipped with a British high-velocity 17-pounder antitank gun. The Firefly gun could penetrate the armour of both the Tiger and Panther tanks, but the armour on the Sherman was no match for the 75mm gun on the Panther tank or the 88mm gun on the Tiger. Besides, the Firefly's seventeen-pounder was much longer than the normal Sherman tank gun, and thus they were easily identified by the enemy as choice targets to be picked off first whenever possible.

The 9th Brigade's major objective for the evening of June 6, 1944, was the small town of Carpiquet, east of the city of Caen and site of the Caen airport. The brigade was to pass through the beachhead seized by one of the assault brigades and move inland toward the high ground near the villages of Authie and Buron, establish a base for further operations, then cross the Caen-Bayeux highway and advance to

Carpiquet. Taking Carpiquet would secure the western approaches to Caen, which was the immediate objective of the British and Canadian invading forces. Caen was not only the historic and administrative capital of Normandy, it was also a key rail, road, and canal junction, a good place to cross the Orne River and the terminus of a long, straight highway that led southeast to Falaise, on the way to Paris. The commander in charge of the British, Canadian, and American landing forces, British General Bernard C. Montgomery, hoped to take Caen in the first or second day of the Normandy campaign.

Because of congestion on the beach, it took the Sherbrookes and the North Novas several hours to assemble outside the small town of Beny-sur-Mer, about 4 kilometres south of the beach. A combined column of tanks and infantry finally began to worm its way south at about 6:00 PM. The Sherbrooke Fusiliers' reconnaissance troop, made up of eleven U.S.-built Stuart light tanks armed only with 37mm guns, led the way. Being lightly armed, the Stuart's only advantage over the Sherman was its faster speed. Next came eighteen North Nova half-tracks carrying C Company, followed by a platoon of the Cameron Highlanders of Canada—the brigade's machine-gun regiment—mounted on Bren carriers. Then came a contingent of M10 tank destroyers; the North Novas' pioneer platoon and the mortar platoon—both on Bren carriers; the 6-pounder antitank guns towed by carriers; and then the remaining Shermans of the Fusiliers, carrying the rest of the North Nova infantry on their backs. The North Novas and the Sherbrookes had been training together for months. With the support of a field artillery regiment following behind, Allied fighter bombers, and the huge naval guns just offshore, the men felt as confident as they could be under the circumstances. Mark Zuehlke's history of D-Day sums the moment up well:

> "Everyone was keen," the North Novas' regimental historian wrote, as the powerful battle group broke out into the open past Colomby [-sur-Thaon, about 3 kilometres south of Beny-sur-Mer]. It was "as if they were on a new sort of scheme that played

for keeps, but was exciting and not too dangerous. They knew the main objective was Carpiquet Airport and did not think they would have much trouble getting there."

At the hamlet of Villons-les-Buissons the battle group dug in at dusk and nervously awaited a counterattack. Minor clashes burst out in the dark as small groups of German stragglers tried to infiltrate their positions, but the night passed without a major confrontation.

At 7:45 AM, the North Novas and the Sherbrookes resumed their advance. Their main objectives were to capture the towns of Buron and Authie, cross the Caen-Bayeux highway, and get on to Carpiquet airport. For the first few kilometres the Canadians encountered only minor resistance, but as the lead tanks from the reconnaissance squadron approached Buron, incoming fire increased from the village ahead and from both flanks of the road. Mortars and artillery began to explode in the fields to the left. After a minor skirmish with a German antitank gun, the column secured Buron and pushed off to Authie, about 1 kilometre farther south. Despite increased resistance from the Germans, Authie was taken and the Sherbrooke reconnaissance squadron pushed through the town toward Franqueville and Carpiquet. The lead tanks could see the airport clearly ahead of them, just across the Caen-Bayeux highway.

Looming above the Buron-Authie road just a few kilometres to the south was the old and abandoned Abbaye d'Ardenne, a twelfth-century monastery used by local farmers to store hay and stable horses. But on this day the Abbaye was much busier and more crowded than usual. In its courtyard were parked vehicles belonging to the 25th SS Panzergrenadier Regiment of the 12th SS Panzer Division (Hitler Jugend). This division had been formed in Belgium in 1943, with a combination of officers and non-commissioned officers who had ample battle experience in the hard fighting on the eastern front and fanatical seventeen-year-old troopers from the Hitler Youth. This was a "heavy" division, with more tanks and other vehicles and more men than a normal German *panzer* (armoured) division.

The Canadians were completely unaware of the presence of this formation, which had arrived in the night. In the northernmost tower of the Abbaye, SS Colonel Kurt Meyer watched the advancing Canadians through his binoculars. He couldn't believe his eyes; the Canadians were moving in a column with open flanks not 3 kilometres below. "Did I see right?" he would write in his memoirs. "An enemy tank pushed through the orchards of St. Contest. Suddenly it stops. The commander opens the hatch and scours the countryside before him. Is the fellow blind? Has he not noticed that he stands barely 200 yards from the grenadiers of my 2nd Battalion, and that the barrels of their anti-tank guns are pointed at him?" Meyer decided to wait until the column was completely drawn out, then attack with two battalions of infantry and about fifty tanks.

Just after 2:00 PM, Meyer ordered the attack; a company of SS Mark IV tanks hit the Sherbrookes' A Squadron near Franqueville, while another two tank companies and a battalion of infantry attacked the Canadian column strung out between Authie and Buron. The Sherbrooke tanks to the west of Authie began to withdraw after losing three of six Shermans. On the east side of Authie another eleven Shermans fought a close-range battle with one or two companies of German Mark IV tanks. Lieutenant Norman Davies later wrote of that encounter:

> I spotted seven or eight enemy tanks at 1,000 yards on my left. I halted, stopped two of them with the 17 [17-pounder—he was commanding a Firefly], advanced, halted, and fired again scoring another hit, then all hell seemed to break loose. There were tanks coming up at full speed to my rear (our own), tanks to my left firing at us, anti-tank guns blazing away from our left and rear, and tracer and 75mm gun flashes all over the place. . . . Tanks were hit and burning all around us by then and it was impossible to know who was who. One was hit directly in front of me, one right beside me . . . so I decided to withdraw with what was left of 2nd and 3rd troops.

Later, after the clash, Davies "counted noses and found we had 5 tanks left out of 20 which had gone in." Sidney Radley-Walters was second-in-command of C Squadron. He later wrote: "as a youngster going into action for the first time, the thing that hits us all apparently, was that tremendous surprise. All of a sudden there's a rain of fire came [*sic*] down, tanks started getting knocked out, and communications and the command and control started to break down. And in your first battle, you make all the mistakes."

From early afternoon to nightfall on June 7 the North Novas and the Sherbrookes were locked in a vicious death struggle for a few square kilometres of vital ground northwest of Caen. The SS launched three distinct attacks, driving the Canadians back out of Authie and then out of Buron. The lead elements of the Sherbrookes that had reached or crossed the Caen-Bayeux highway in their Stuart light tanks simply disappeared, no doubt wiped out by the German Mark IV tanks. Buron was retaken by the North Novas with the support of the Sherbrookes, but then abandoned when the commander of the 9th Canadian Infantry Brigade, D.G. Cunningham, ordered his brigade to regroup north of Authie to form a brigade defensive position. One company of the North Novas was dug in near Buron and needed cover fire from the tanks in order to withdraw. Radley-Walters was in temporary command of C squadron:

> The job fell to me to try to do it. It was about dark, 8 or 9 p.m. and I went out across the wheat fields to Buron. I had 7 out of 19 tanks left. I could see all the dead and the dying where the Germans had come right across them. We pushed them back, but the enemy came back in another attack. One Canadian sergeant in the North Nova Scotia group was in a trench. I waved to him as I passed and he pointed to a dead German hanging over the side of the trench with a bloody knife in his back from a close fight. Most of that company got back. We saved most of them.

The Sherbrookes and the North Novas paid a high price that day, with 110 killed, 64 wounded, and 128 taken prisoner; 26 of the dead were Sherbrooke Fusiliers and 34 of the wounded. The regiment lost twenty-one tanks, with another seven damaged. The drive to Carpiquet was completely halted; the Canadians would not even see the airport again until the end of the month as German resistance stiffened north of Caen and on both of its flanks. One analysis of this key clash is that of Roman Jarymowycz, one of the leading Canadian experts on the Normandy fighting: "There can be little fault found in the conduct of the Sherbrooke Fusiliers. They and the Novas were victims of a doctrine out of place in Normandy."

That may well be so, but the judgment cannot be applied to the courage and fighting spirit of either of the two Canadian regiments that slammed into Kurt Meyer's wall of SS men on the afternoon of June 7. Green farm boys, miners, lumber workers, and fishermen led by eager but equally green officers had been ambushed by a powerful force of highly motivated and very well-equipped SS troops and had held their own in what was often hand-to-hand and tank-to-tank fighting. No one will ever really know whether it was regimental spirit that fortified those young and untried Canadians or simple individual self-preservation. But in either case the result was the same. The Canadians discovered that the Germans were not supermen, not even the SS, and that boded well for the rest of the Normandy campaign and, indeed, the rest of the war.

The Sherbrooke Fusiliers fought with the 3rd Canadian Infantry Division for the balance of the war, then returned to Canada under Radley-Walters's command. From D-Day to VE Day the regiment suffered 128 dead and 262 wounded, earning 22 battle honours. The Sherbrooke Regiment underwent a number of changes to its official name until February 1965, when it was joined with the 7/XI Hussars to form the Sherbrooke Hussars. It is today an armoured regiment in the 34th Canadian Brigade Group, Land Forces Quebec Area, Canadian Army Reserve.

Soldiers of the PPCLI in front of a 17-pound antitank gun in the field in Korea.
—Reproduced with permission from the PPCLI Regimental Museum and Archives/p110 (56.8).

Lieutenant "Smokey" Leblanc briefs the 2nd Battalion of the Royal 22ᵉ Régiment before a patrol on Hill 201 in Korea, December 12, 1951.
—Musée du Royal 22ᵉ Régiment, Fonds Première Guerre Mondiale, Ph5/172/349.
National defence photograph.

The Second Regiment RCHA, in support of 2nd RCR, patrols towards Hill 730, June 21, 1953.
—Reproduced with the permission of the Minister of Public Works and Government Services, 2008/(SF 2019).

Lord Strathcona's Horse (Royal Canadian) patrolling in Korea.
—Reproduced with the permission of the Minister of Public Works and Government Services, 2008/(SF 1963).

The Black Watch parade in Hanover, Germany, May 1952.

—Reproduced with permission from the Black Watch (RHR) Regimental Museum and Archives.

A light armoured vehicle (LAV) from the 1st Battalion PPCLI, part of NATO's stabilization force in Bosnia-Herzegovina, finds itself in local traffic, November 5, 2002.

—Department of National Defence/IS2002-6672a.jpg. Reproduced with the permission of the Minister of Public Works and Government Services Canada, 2008.

Members of the Royal Canadian Dragoon battle group, part of NATO's stabilization force in Bosnia-Herzegovina, in their Coyote armoured vehicle on the streets
of Velika Kladuša, November 26, 2003.

Members of 4 Engineer Support Regiment, part of Canada's contribution to the United Nations Operation ECLIPSE in Ethiopia and Eritrea. The 540-strong Canadian contingent built base camps, assembled power grids, established watering sites, and cleared mines from main roads.
—Department of National Defence/ISD01-0062a.jpg. Reproduced with the permission of the Minister of Public Works and Government Services Canada, 2008.

Hotel Company of the 2nd Battalion of the Royal Canadian Regiment prepares to leave Camp Moncton in Gonaïves, Haiti, on July 22, 2004. The RCR contributed to Canada's Operation HALO, the UN mission to stabilize Haiti.
—Department of National Defence/HS048103d03.jpg. Reproduced with the permission of the Minister of Public Works and Government Services Canada, 2008.

In the mountains of Paktia Province, east of Gardez, Afghanistan, members of an anti-tank team from the 3rd Battalion, PPCLI battle group, take a much-needed rest on the trail on March 15, 2002.

—Department of National Defence/APD02_5000-210. Reproduced with the permission of the Minister of Public Works and Government Services Canada, 2008.

Turned out in full battle order, soldiers of the 3rd Battalion, PPCLI battle group, wait to board U.S. army Chinook helicopters for Operation HARPOON, the Canadian army's first non-defensive combat mission since the Korean War, on March 14, 2002.

—Department of National Defence/PD02_5000-195e. Reproduced with the permission of the Minister of Public Works and Government Services Canada, 2008.

Corporal Robert Giguère of B Company (3rd Battalion, Royal 22e Régiment battle group) on a foot patrol in Kabul, near Camp Julien, March 29, 2004.

—Department of National Defence/KA2004-R101-294d. Reproduced with the permission of the Minister of Public Works and Government Services Canada, 2008.

Master Corporal Mark Dennis (3rd Battalion PPCLI) gestures to curious local Afghan children while watching the perimeter in a Kandahar neighborhood, November 21, 2005.

—Department of National Defence/IS2005-0451. Reproduced with the permission of the Minister of Public Works and Government Services Canada, 2008.

For the first time since the end of the Korean War, Canadians relieve Americans in a combat zone. Soldiers of 5 Platoon of Bravo Company, 3rd Battalion PPCLI, move into positions on the defensive perimeter of Kandahar International Airport on February 12, 2002, as soldiers of Charles Company, 101st Airborne Division, U.S. Army, are withdrawn.

Soldiers from 1st Battalion, the Royal Canadian Regiment battle group, assemble in the light armoured vehicles of A Company at Forward Operating Base, Masum Ghar, December 19, 2006.

CHAPTER THIRTEEN

HARD VICTORY: THE BLACK WATCH AT VERRIÈRES RIDGE AND THE ESSEX SCOTTISH IN THE RHINELAND

[We] started off across country at 0900 hrs to attack it. By then the Jerries were thoroughly awake as to what was going on, and from the start we had trouble from very heavy machine-gunning from the flanks, mortars and arty [artillery] fire.

—Captain John Taylor, Verrières Ridge, July 25, 1944

MONTREAL'S BLACK WATCH, officially known as the Black Watch (Royal Highland Regiment) of Canada, is one of the nation's oldest continuing military units and the oldest Highland regiment in Canada. Founded in Montreal on January 31, 1862, it easily attracted the young men of the city's large Scottish community. As Terry Copp has written, "it became part of the fabric of Montreal society. The armoury on Bleury street near the centre of the city had been built in 1905." Adopting the dress uniform, tartan, headdress with red hackle, and other accoutrements and traditions of the Black Watch (Royal Highland Regiment) of the United Kingdom, after which it was fashioned, the Canadian regiment was virtually indistinguishable from the British for a time. In the First World War the Canadian Black Watch raised three battalions, the 13th, 42nd, and 73rd, which all saw action on the Western Front. Black Watch officers played a leading role in the higher ranks of the Canadian Corps.

Things were much the same in the interwar period, as Copp records: "the regiment . . . continued its central role in the Quebec militia. With Sir H.M. Allan [the shipping millionaire] as Honorary Colonel and a good number of the sons of Montreal's most influential families among its officers, the Black Watch could afford to maintain activities that kept it up to 'good strength' and in an 'excellent state of efficiency.'" The regiment volunteered en masse for active service when the 1st Battalion of the Black Watch (Royal Highland Regiment) of Canada was mobilized on September 1, 1939. Eventually the regiment was placed in the 5th Brigade of the 2nd Canadian Infantry Division along with the Calgary Highlanders and Montreal's Régiment de Maisonneuve. The 5th Brigade was left out of the order of battle for the Dieppe raid, but much of the rest of the 2nd Division was devastated. The 2nd Division was, therefore, left out of the Normandy landing on June 6, 1944, and did not enter the Battle of Normandy until early July.

When the Black Watch landed in Normandy on July 6, 1944, the battle for Caen was in its fifth week. The Canadians had failed to outflank the city after Meyer's 12th SS Panzer Division entered the battle on June 7, and a subsequent British effort by the 7th Armoured Division also failed. The Battle of Normandy degenerated into a war of attrition; the Germans fought desperately to keep the Allies bottled up near the beaches while the Allies tried to push inland to make room for the dozens of additional divisions and the thousands more tanks and other fighting vehicles still sitting in the U.K. In the weeks following the invasion, three more German armoured divisions were moved to the Caen front. The armour stiffened German defences, and the ponderous tactics of the Allies, including the piecemeal insertion of new units into battle, left the front virtually unchanged. The Germans could not hope to throw the Allies into the Channel, but they just might be able to bottle them up indefinitely.

Virtually all of the units of the 3rd Canadian Infantry Division, commanded by Major-General Rod Keller, spent the last half of June in reserve, but on July 4 Keller's troops joined Operation

Charnwood—a British-led attack to take Caen. The Canadian aim, ironically, was to finally capture the Carpiquet airport—their original objective on June 7. The Black Watch came ashore and moved to their brigade assembly area near the beach; the constant sound of heavy guns and, at night, light flashes on the horizon marked the closing stages of the fight for Carpiquet. The airport was partially taken with very heavy casualties, but the fight for Caen itself raged on for five more days. The city was secured by the night of July 9; 1,194 Canadians had become casualties in taking the city, 334 of them killed or fatally wounded. But the suburbs of Colombelles, northeast of Caen, and Vaucelles, across the Caen canal to the south of the city, remained in German hands, as did the key Verrières and Bourguébus ridges, which lay about 6 kilometres to the south of Vaucelles. Those were to be Montgomery's next objectives. The Orne River had to be crossed on the west side of Vaucelles while Colombelles had to be secured; that would leave the Germans outflanked and force their withdrawal farther south. Once that happened, the Canadians and British could continue their push toward Falaise, southwest of Caen, preferably along Route Nationale 158, which ran straight as an arrow from Caen to Falaise. Montgomery dubbed the attack to secure the southern reaches of Caen and its suburbs Operation Atlantic.

The attack on the Canadian front was launched on July 18 by the 3rd Division's 8th Brigade and the 2nd Division's 4th Brigade—the first time the division had gone into action since Dieppe. At 10:15 PM on the 18th the Black Watch led the 5th Brigade across the Orne River into the southern suburbs of Caen. Once the river was crossed, the 5th Brigade's three infantry battalions began to leapfrog one another, moving in concert with the 6th Brigade almost due south toward Verrières Ridge, about 12 kilometres south of Caen. Some 6th Brigade soldiers managed to reach the ridge in a heavy rainfall, but were driven back by the defenders, who were well entrenched and supported by armour, antitank guns, moaning minnies, and artillery. The ridge remained in German hands despite very heavy Canadian casualties. The commander of Second Canadian Corps, Lieutenant-General

Guy Simonds, had to try again, soon, if momentum was to be restored on the Canadian front. Thus, on July 25, he launched Operation Spring, a two-division attack to capture Verrières Ridge and clear the way for a Canadian and British breakout to the south.

Spring was to be fought in four phases; the first and most important was to begin at 3:30 AM on the morning of July 25 and be completed within two hours. Within those two hours troops of the two Canadian infantry divisions were to secure May-sur-Orne, at the bottom of the western slope of Verrières Ridge; Verrières village, on the crest of the ridge; and Tilly-la-Campagne, about 1.5 kilometres east of Verrières village. Once they were secured, two British armoured divisions, the 7th Armoured and the Guards Armoured, accompanied by the 3rd Canadian Infantry Division, would cut through the remaining German defenders and head for Falaise.

The attack did not go well, especially on the 5th Brigade front— the start line was not secured on time. The objective of the two leading companies of the Calgary Highlanders was the small village of May-sur-Orne. Once they had occupied it, they were supposed to cover the right flank of the Black Watch as it ascended the ridge. The Highlanders reached the vicinity of May-sur-Orne after a confused and disorganized night approach, but they were quickly driven out of the town and several kilometres back by German armour and self-propelled guns. The Black Watch did not know it, but as they prepared for their advance up the ridge, dozens of German tanks and antitank guns and hundreds of German infantry lay in wait for them.

The advance up Verrières Ridge should have started at 5:30 AM, by which time May-sur-Orne was supposed to have been secured. But the Black Watch had to fight their way to their start line; in that fighting the CO, Lieutenant-Colonel Stuart Cantlie, was killed and the senior company commander, Major Eric Motzfeldt, was mortally wounded. The burden of command fell on Major Philip Griffin, described by Terry Copp as "a tall, slim, twenty-four year-old." Another Black Watch officer, Major Edwin Bennett, later described Griffin and his smooth takeover of the battalion: "Major Griffin is a brilliant officer of absolutely outstanding courage and ability. His takeover in this strained and ticklish situation was superb. There was no uncertainty whatever in his actions. He foresaw only a delay, which would at the outside be two hours, while he rearranged timings and obtained essential information." But the tanks that were supposed to support the infantry advance were late, and the Black Watch were forced to move off without them in order to take advantage of a rolling artillery barrage that Griffin had just arranged. Because of conflicting and confusing reports on the status of the Highlanders' positions, Griffin was unsure whether or not May-sur-Orne had been secured. At one point Brigadier W.J. Megill, the commander of 5th Brigade, suggested that Griffin might want to secure May-sur-Orne himself before advancing up the ridge, but Griffin was focusing on the ridge, almost as if the problem on his left flank would somehow resolve itself.

At about 9:30 AM, Griffin led his men toward the start line at the foot of the ridge. They immediately ran into heavy German mortar and machine-gun fire. They reached the start line too late to follow the artillery barrage, which advanced up the ridge without them. As the sun rose higher in the Norman sky, the heat became oppressive, but still Griffin led his men on. Captain John Taylor later described what came next: "[We] started off across country at 0900hrs to attack it. By then the Jerries were thoroughly awake as to what was going on, and from the start we had trouble from very heavy machine-gunning from the flanks, mortars and arty [artillery] fire. The troops were steady as a rock and we kept going. I was the left forward Company and on my right was B Company then commanded by Sgt. Foam, all the officers having been knocked out. We over-ran two strong points, then got hit."

As Taylor lay in the tall wheat, the remainder of the battalion pushed on. Griffin led about sixty men from the original three hundred over the crest of the ridge. Captain John Kemp, commanding D Company, urged Griffin to abandon the advance, but Griffin was reported to have replied "that the orders were to attack and that the battalion would therefore carry on." For Griffin, the pride and reputation of the famous

Black Watch were at stake. There would be no turning back. But then the survivors encountered a "strong and exceptionally well camouflaged enemy position" with tanks and self-propelled guns concealed in haystacks. The intense fire forced the Black Watch to ground. Griffin, mortally wounded, ordered every man to make his way back as best he could, and then died. His body was found when the ridge was finally taken in early August.

July 25, 1944, will always be marked by the Black Watch as the worst day of the Second World War. In a little less than two hours the regiment suffered 123 killed, 101 wounded, and 83 taken prisoner. Save for the total disasters of Hong Kong and Dieppe, that day was the worst for any battalion in the Canadian army in the Second World War. Not only was half of the Black Watch's fighting strength wiped out, but many experienced and stalwart officers were now dead. The battalion had to be rebuilt with reinforcements and new officers and trained back to a point where it could be counted on to share its burden of fighting. That took almost two months, during which the Black Watch was forced to play mostly a secondary role in the 5th Brigade through the rest of the Normandy campaign and the first weeks of the Battle of the Scheldt Estuary. Then disaster struck the Black Watch a second time.

—∞—

ON OCTOBER 13, 1944, the 2nd Canadian Infantry Division was in the thick of a fight to take the eastern end of the South Beveland peninsula, which is in the Netherlands near the Belgian border. The Germans held both banks of the Scheldt estuary and had mined it to prevent Allied shipping from using the Belgian port of Antwerp for bringing in much-needed supplies. Montgomery had given the First Canadian Army the job of clearing the estuary, a large task for a small and increasingly undermanned army. Guy Simonds had temporarily taken command as acting army commander (Crerar was sick with gastroenteritis) and planned a three-phase campaign. First, the Canadians would clear the south bank of the estuary around Breskens. Second, they would capture the neck of land connecting South Beveland to the mainland and advance west to the tip of the peninsula. Finally they would capture Walcheren Island, which lay just a kilometre or so from the western tip of South Beveland, across a shallow tidal flat crossed by the narrow Walcheren Causeway.

The Black Watch's task on October 13 was to move through the recently captured town of Woensdrecht, then push beyond it to secure a railway embankment that lay almost within a stone's throw of the shore of the East Scheldt. The track atop the embankment, which also acted as a dike, carried the main rail line from Bergen op Zoom to Walcheren. At 6:45 AM that morning, C Company of the Black Watch passed through positions of the Royal Regiment of Canada and began to advance toward the railway embankment. The plan was to shoot two companies onto the position with the aid of tank, mortar, and artillery fire, but the attack ran into difficulty almost from the start. C Company began to take heavy casualties from small-arms fire not long after leaving its jumping-off point. B Company, assigned to pass through C Company, was heavily mortared at its start line. Under cover of smoke, these two companies were eventually able to advance to the embankment but were then pinned down, taking more casualties. Both company commanders were wounded. Later, under cover of artillery fire and air strikes and accompanied by Wasp flame-throwers, the other two Black Watch rifle companies tried to complete the battalion's assigned task. But their artillery spotters found it difficult to pinpoint targets in the almost featureless landscape, while the RAF fighter bombers could not attack the far side of the curving railway embankment without gravely endangering the Canadian troops. By nightfall the offensive had been called off. It was a complete failure; fifty-six Black Watch were killed or died of their wounds, sixty-two were wounded, and twenty-seven were taken prisoner. Most of the Black Watch dead lay exposed and unburied along the railway embankment until October 24, when the Calgary

Highlanders finally took and held this small piece of contested and bloody ground.

This proud regiment did not take the most casualties of the three battalions in the 5th Brigade—that dubious honour went to the Black Watch's sister battalion the Calgary Highlanders—but the casualties were bad enough. In the course of the fighting between Normandy and victory, the Black Watch suffered 470 killed in action or dead on active service, 1,118 wounded, and 230 taken prisoner. The regiment was awarded nineteen battle honours. The 1st Battalion was disbanded in November 1945 and the Black Watch continued as a militia regiment until the end of the Korean War, when it was revived as a regular-force regiment with two active service battalions. Those battalions saw service in Korea (after the war ended), Germany (with NATO), and in various U.N. peacekeeping assignments. The Black Watch was removed from the order of battle of the active army in 1970 and reverted to reserve status. It is now an infantry regiment in the 34th Canadian Brigade Group, Land Forces Quebec Area, Canadian Army Reserve.

—⁂—

THE BATTLE OF THE SCHELDT ESTUARY ended in early November with a decisive victory after Montgomery sent British and American forces to help out the Canadians. The Canadian army then went into winter quarters in the southeastern Dutch town of Nijmegen through December and January as a massive battle raged to the south on the American front. The Battle of the Bulge, Hitler's last big gamble in the west, opened with a surprise attack on a thinly held portion of the American front in the Ardennes forest on December 16, 1944, and raged until January 25, 1945. It was the costliest battle of the war in Europe for the United States, which suffered more than twenty thousand casualties. But when it was over, Germany's last hope of forcing a stalemate in the west was gone.

Two weeks after the end of the fighting in the Ardennes, Montgomery launched Operation Veritable on February 8, 1945, to clear the Rhineland (the part of Germany lying to the west of the Rhine River) in preparation for a Rhine crossing and a final drive into the heart of Germany. The first stages of Veritable aimed to secure the ground between the Dutch–German border and the Hochwald, a forest reserve that guarded the approaches to the cross-roads town of Xanten, the key to the Rhine bridges at Wesel. After the Hochwald had been reached, the attacking forces were to halt for regrouping and redeployment. The artillery would be brought forward in classic set-piece fashion. Then stage two of the offensive would begin. Operation Veritable was carried out by General H.D. Crerar's First Canadian Army bolstered by the British 30th Corps and an American division. In sheer manpower it was the largest agglomeration of troops ever commanded by Crerar's HQ—more than 500,000 men in 13 divisions.

The Canadian divisions played a small but vital role in the first phase of the operation. On the northern or left flank, the 3rd Division—aptly nicknamed the "Water Rats" because of the polder fighting they had done during the Scheldt campaign—advanced in amphibious vehicles across flooded fields to take possession (if one could take possession of flooded land) of the area between the Waal River and the Nijmegen-Cleve-Calcar road, which was one of the main axes of attack. The task of the 2nd Division (especially the 5th Brigade) was to secure the left flank of the 15th (Scottish) Division by taking the fortified towns of Wyler and den Heuvel. The Calgary Highlanders and the Maisonneuves did that in one day, though the Highlanders suffered heavy casualties when one of their assault companies ran into a well-prepared killing zone sown with mines and covered by German mortars and machine guns.

At first the Veritable offensive went well. The Germans were surprised; they had not expected Montgomery's main effort to come from the Canadian sector. Lavish use of air power and artillery gave the British and Canadians a good jump-off. Within forty-eight hours the 30th Corps had captured "virtually all its objectives for Phase One of 'Veritable.'" But no battle ever runs smoothly, and major problems began to beset Montgomery's armies on the third day of the attack. An attack from the south by the U.S. Ninth Army, scheduled to coincide with Veritable, was postponed when the Germans blew up the Roer River dams, inundating the land over which the American attack was to be launched. All over the front, Germans destroyed dikes and canal locks, flooding as much country as they could so as to force the Allies to use the few roads that ran above the rising waters. The Allied bombing rendered towns such as Cleve virtually impassable and an early thaw turned the hard-frozen ground into mud, hindering the movement of both men and vehicles. Not many crack German troops were left, and most of their armour had been destroyed in the Battle of the Bulge, but now they were defending the soil of Germany itself, and they fought desperately to hold the Allies back.

On the night of February 19–20, the Royal Hamilton Light Infantry and the Essex Scottish of the 4th Brigade were hit hard in their positions on the Goch-Calcar road by a German battle group scrounged from elements of the 116th Panzer Division. It took almost twenty-four hours of continuous fighting before the German counterattack was thwarted, and the cost was very high. The brigade, and the Queen's Own Cameron Highlanders from the 6th Brigade, suffered some 400 casualties in that twenty-four-hour period. The Essex Scottish alone lost 204 killed, wounded, or missing.

—⁓—

THE ESSEX SCOTTISH had been authorized as the 21st "Essex" Battalion of Infantry on June 12, 1885, as the fighting in the Northwest Rebellion had tapered off. The men of the Ontario border area had long rallied to the colours whenever homes and livelihoods were threatened, especially in the War of 1812. Even after that war, when peaceful relations took hold between the border communities of Windsor and Detroit, an active local militia continued to drill and hold social events. When the 21st "Essex" Battalion of Infantry was created in 1885, it combined five militia infantry companies already in the area. The regiment became the 21st Battalion "Essex Fusiliers" in 1887 and the 21st Regiment "Essex Fusiliers" in 1900. During the First World War the Essex regiment recruited for the 1st and 18th battalions of the CEF and for two recruiting battalions that never saw action.

The regiment became the Essex Fusiliers in 1920, but seven years later converted to a Highland unit in the hope that the legacy of Highlanders as hard-fighting men would attract more recruits. Thus on July 19, 1927, the Essex Scottish was born. A 1st battalion was activated as the Essex Scottish Regiment, Canadian Active Service Force, on September 1, 1939, and attached to the 4th Brigade of the 2nd Division. The Essex Scottish took part in the Dieppe raid of August 19, 1942, suffering 530 casualties out of the 553 men who had left England; 114 were killed in action or died of their wounds. Like the rest of the 2nd Division, the Essex Scottish was subsequently in the thick of the action in both the Battle of Normandy and the Battle of the Scheldt Estuary. Eventually the regiment would suffer 550 dead and more than 2,500 wounded, the highest for any Canadian unit in northwest Europe.

When the U.S. Ninth Army finally launched its long-delayed attack on February 23, the Germans battled them every metre of the way. This forced a change in Canadian plans; Crerar's forces would have to shift their axis of attack to the southeast to take pressure off the Americans. This meant capturing the Hochwald forest, a state reserve that guarded the eastern approaches to the key road and rail junction of Xanten, which was close to the Rhine and was the last major town before Wesel. This second stage of the attack was dubbed Blockbuster.

The attack was launched on February 26, but progress was slow and casualties high because of the terrain, the thickly wooded forest, and a stiff German defence. The Hochwald is on a plateau that slopes up from west to east. In front of the forest was the Schlieffen Position, a belt of strong defences backed up by nine German infantry divisions. It stretched from Rees, on the opposite bank of the Rhine, to Geldern. The Hochwald is L-shaped, with a gap roughly where the north–south part of the forest meets the east–west part; a rail line ran through the gap. Blockbuster began on schedule with the 4th Canadian Armoured Division pushing toward the gap while the 2nd Division's 5th and 6th brigades hit the northern edge of the forest.

The 4th Brigade entered the battle on the left flank of the 5th Brigade in the early morning hours of March 1, led by the Essex Scottish. Two companies of the Essex, A and B, approached the forest and ran up against apparently impregnable defences. The Essex regimental historians write that one patrol from B Company went out at 2:40 AM and "came under heavy fire and was forced to withdraw. It reported that the enemy positions consisted of barbed wire and trenches with medium machine guns and mortars sited to cover the approaches to the forest. A Company sent out a similar patrol and reported the enemy in strength only 200 metres ahead." The battalion commander decided to commit his other two companies to pass through A and B Companies, supported by a squadron of Sherman tanks from the Sherbrooke Fusiliers.

At 7:45 AM Acting Major Fred Tilston led C Company's attack behind a creeping barrage. Tilston was thirty-four years old and had never been in action before. He was a graduate of the University of Toronto and the Ontario College of Pharmacy. His men thought of him as mild-mannered, even affable, no firebrand, and certainly too old for combat. But Tilston had been very determined to get to where he now found himself. A pharmaceutical sales manager at the start of the war, he had had to falsify his birth records to show himself younger than he was in order to enlist. He was wounded in training in England and his Jeep ran over a mine during the fighting at Falaise in August. But he kept coming back to the Essex, first as the adjutant, an administrative position, then as acting company commander.

The ground ahead of Tilston was sodden and muddy from rain and snow. It was about 500 metres from where Tilston's men started off to the German trenches at the edge of the forest. The ground was littered with mines and tripwires. As the men moved up, Tilston kept them as close to the advancing barrage as he dared. They began to take casualties, but Tilston forged ahead. Then he was wounded in the head by shell fragments. He kept on, through a 3-metre belt of barbed wire, to the enemy trenches, firing his Sten submachine gun and throwing grenades. He destroyed one German machine-gun position with a grenade, then led his men to a second defence line. He was hit again, in the hip, and fell to the ground, but struggled back to his feet and pressed forward. At the German positions, the Essex and the Germans killed one another with rifle butts, bayonets, knives, and guns; some of the enemy were captured and some managed to flee. Tilston then organized his men for the inevitable German counter-attack. His company was now down to about forty men, 25 percent of its fighting strength, but Tilston kept going, carrying ammunition and grenades to the company on his right.

Fred Tilston was awarded the Victoria Cross for his courage and leadership. The citation read: "On his last trip he was wounded for the third time, this time in the leg. He was found in a shell crater beside the road. Although very seriously wounded and barely conscious, he would not submit to medical attention until he had given complete instructions as to the defence plan, had emphasized the absolute necessity of holding the position, and had ordered his one remaining officer to take over." His men held the position, and later in the day the remaining Essex companies passed through and took the battalion's objective for the day. The battalion suffered 139 casualties but killed a large number of Germans, took 100 prisoners, and captured three 88mm guns, a medium mortar, and many machine guns. Better yet, it was the beginning of the end for the defenders of the Hochwald.

By March 3 the forest had been cleared of Germans as the troops of the 30th Corps joined the Americans driving up from the south. In subsequent heavy fighting Xanten and Wesel were taken but the Germans destroyed the Wesel bridges and withdrew to the east bank of the Rhine. On March 7 came the electrifying news that the U.S. First Army had captured a railway bridge across the Rhine at Remagen, between Bonn and Koblenz, and were pushing straight across the river. By the night of March 10, all German resistance west of the Rhine had ended. The Battle of the Rhineland was over.

—m—

BY THE END OF MARCH 1945, British, Canadian, and American troops had pushed across the Rhine in several places and poured into Germany from the south and west. In the east, Soviet troops soon completed the encirclement of Berlin and began the block-by-block fight for the capital itself. The First Canadian Army, now united with the arrival of the First Corps from Italy, drove north to the North Sea, then turned west to liberate the last parts of Holland still in German hands. Hitler killed himself in his bunker deep below Berlin's Tiergarten on his birthday, April 30, 1945, and his successor, Admiral Karl Doenitz, sued for peace almost immediately. Fighting ceased on May 7, and May 8, 1945, was celebrated throughout western Europe, the United States, and the British Commonwealth as VE (Victory in Europe) Day. More than 1.1 million Canadians had served in uniform, an astonishing 10 percent of the entire population; more than 42,000 were killed on land, at sea, and in the air, and more than 54,400 were wounded. After a brief period of occupation duty in Holland and northwestern Germany, the Canadian army came home. From Hong Kong to Holland, Canada's regiments had acquitted themselves with great fortitude and courage, and the Canadian regimental system emerged from the Second World War stronger than ever. But after so much spilled blood and so many battle honours, no thought whatever was given to the future of the regiment in the Canadian army.

Part Four

FROM KOREA TO AFGHANISTAN

Chapter Fourteen

KAP'YONG: THE PATRICIAS IN KOREA

The first wave throws its grenades, fires its weapons and goes to the ground. It is followed by a second which does the same, and then a third comes up. They just keep coming.

—A Canadian sergeant in Korea

THE POSTWAR YEARS marked a new beginning for Canadians. Veterans returned by the hundreds of thousands and restarted their lives. Government programs put money in their pockets, paid their way through colleges and universities, and provided them with mortgage money for new homes. Pent-up consumer demand gave way to a surge of buying—cars, houses, consumer goods of all kinds. The country was booming. Suburbs sprung up around Canada's biggest cities. Boomer babies were born in the thousands across the nation and tens of thousands of immigrants arrived from a still war-ravaged Europe. It was the best of times for Canada and Canadians, with the Depression now a distant memory and the war safely tucked into the recent past.

Canada did not have much of an army in the summer of 1950. As soon as the Second World War ended, the government chopped the Canadian army, navy, and air force to the bone. After all, peace was at hand, there was no enemy in sight, and the bills for the war had to be paid. By the end of the fighting the Canadian government had chalked up the largest deficit and the biggest debt in its history. Borrowed money had paid for the men and women in uniform. It had paid for their very uniforms, and for the food, weapons, vehicles, planes, and everything else that had been needed to defeat the Axis. Now it had to be paid back—mostly to the Canadians who had loaned it to the government in the form of war bonds, while new social programs such as family allowances had to be paid for.

The Canadian army was reduced to three infantry battalions, one from each of the prewar permanent-force regiments: the Patricias, the Van Doos, and the Royal Canadian Regiment. Two armoured regiments were kept—the Royal Canadian Dragoons (1st Armoured Regiment) and Lord Strathcona's Horse (2nd Armoured Regiment)— and one regiment of artillery. This force was formed into a single brigade for the defence of Canada. In the late 1940s it was decided that all three battalions would be converted into parachute units, the whole to constitute the Mobile Striking Force. The Force was intended to defend the Canadian North in the event of a Soviet lodgement and hold it until Canada's reserves could be mobilized. Those reserves would come, once again, from the militia regiments that had been mobilized in the Second World War. But the postwar reserves, all thirty-four thousand of them, were allowed to languish. No one thought they would be of much use, any more than the permanent or active force.

But on June 25, 1950, halfway around the world, North Korea attacked South Korea. Most Canadians probably didn't have a clue where the Korean peninsula was, nor the 38th parallel that divided Communist North Korea from non-Communist South Korea. But within six short weeks, Canada's army was on its way to war again.

Almost as soon as news of the Communist invasion of South Korea reached Western capitals and the United Nations in New York, the U.S.—supported by Britain—determined that the invasion could not be left unchallenged. U.S. President Harry Truman and British Prime Minister Clement Attlee, with the strong support of U.N.

Secretary-General Trygve Lie, saw the invasion as a direct challenge to the West. Truman and other leaders of the newly formed North Atlantic Treaty Organization (NATO)—founded in July 1949 by the Treaty of Washington—believed that if the North Koreans succeeded in annexing South Korea by force, western Europe might be next. The U.S. committed itself to the defence of South Korea, sent troops from its occupation forces in Japan, and ordered U.S. warplanes based in Japan to attack the Communist invaders.

The Americans also approached the U.N. to become involved. At that very moment, the Soviet delegate to the U.N. Security Council was boycotting Council deliberations in a dispute over whether or not the sitting Chinese delegation to the U.N. should be replaced by representatives of China's new Communist government. According to the U.N. Charter, any major decision made by the Security Council needed the affirmation of all five permanent members of the Council—Britain, France, the U.S., the USSR, and China. The boycott was a major diplomatic blunder; with the USSR absent from the table, the Security Council issued a call for all member nations to help South Korea resist the invasion by all necessary means.

Canada was not only a charter member of NATO but also a strong supporter of the United Nations. Canadian Prime Minister Louis St. Laurent decided almost immediately to send military assistance. On June 30 he announced that three destroyers would be sent from the naval base at Esquimalt to operate in Korean waters under U.N. command. That was followed on July 19 by the dispatch of an RCAF transport squadron flying new four-engine North Star aircraft to aid the U.S. in flying supplies and equipment from the west coast of the United States to Japan to support the war in nearby Korea. Finally, on August 7—under intense pressure from most English-speaking Canadians, the United States, Britain, and the United Nations—St. Laurent announced that Canada would send a brigade group of roughly eight thousand soldiers to fight the Communist invasion under U.N. command. The formation would consist of three infantry battalions, an armoured regiment, an artillery regiment, and supporting troops such as combat engineers, logistics troops, and a brigade headquarters.

But where were these troops to come from? Canada could not send its sole active service brigade to Korea because that would leave the country denuded of defences. At the very same time NATO was also seeking a brigade from Canada. The solution arrived at in Ottawa was to launch a new recruiting drive, aimed at Second World War veterans, for a Canadian Army Special Force designated for Korea but also available for service with NATO in Europe. The Special Force would use Second World War British/Canadian-pattern equipment as much as possible, thus cutting down on training time, and—if sent to Korea as was intended—might even combine with British and other Commonwealth forces in a Commonwealth division. Each of the standing regiments would create second (and, if necessary, even third) battalions for Korean service. The standing regiments would thus become the first battalions and would be responsible for training the second battalions.

For the first time in modern Canadian history, Canadian Permanent Force regiments would have multiple formations, as in 1st, 2nd, and 3rd battalions of the Princess Patricia's Canadian Light Infantry, the Royal Canadian Regiment, the Royal 22e Régiment, and so on. It was intended that recently retired Second World War officers with extensive combat experience would be tapped to command the second battalions. The first commander of the Canadian brigade would be retired brigadier-general John Meredith Rockingham, who had commanded the 9th Canadian Infantry Brigade at the end of the Second World War. He and the chief of the chiefs of staff, General Charles Foulkes, and the chief of staff of the army, General Guy Simonds, selected the battalion commanders, all of whom were approved by the minister of national defence, Brooke Claxton. Since no base in Canada—at least not one close to the West Coast—was prepared to suddenly receive some eight thousand Canadian troops for concentration and training, the government arranged for the Special Force to use Fort Lewis, in the state of Washington.

Recruiting began immediately; when the recruiting depots opened the morning after St. Laurent's speech, hundreds of men were already waiting. Many were indeed Second World War veterans, while others had missed the war and wanted to get in on the action. Still others were genuinely motivated by the cause of fighting Communism. Claxton chafed at the slow pace of processing the volunteers and insisted that the usual procedure of examining each man's background for physical and emotional suitability before attestation be omitted. That did speed things up but also allowed a number of men who were unsuitable to be taken in—the weeding-out process continued even after the Canadians went into action in February 1951. Time was of the essence because the South Koreans, along with the Americans, who had shown up very quickly, were in headlong retreat.

By the end of August, when the Canadian volunteers were only starting to be formed into battalions and arrangements were being finalized to transport them to Fort Lewis, the Communist forces had taken almost all of South Korea. A small perimeter of unconquered land remained around the southern port of Pusan. If the United Nations forces lost the fight to save the territorial integrity—indeed, the very existence—of the Republic of Korea (South Korea), the U.N. itself was doomed. The concept of collective security that had evolved out of the Second World War would have been proven a failure. That fact was bad enough, but even worse was the example it would have set—a Communist country would have more than doubled in size and resources by means of a blatant act of aggression. In effect, the rule of international law, which appeared to have been restored with the defeat of the Axis in 1945, would have been proven completely ineffective in the face of unprovoked use of force. Defeat appeared imminent.

Then, on September 15, 1950, the picture in Korea brightened considerably. The U.N. commander in Korea, U.S. General Douglas MacArthur, carried off a stroke of military genius with a landing at Inchon, a small port on the west coast of Korea not far from the overrun South Korean capital of Seoul. By driving in behind the main body of North Korean troops, the landing threatened to cut off the invaders, and they were forced into retreat. At the same time U.S. Marines and British, Australian, and other national contingents arrived to bolster the U.N. force. Within weeks the North Koreans had been driven out of the south and U.N. forces were advancing across the 38th parallel and north toward the North Korean border with China. The usual hope of "home by Christmas" began to permeate the ranks of the U.N. troops.

Ottawa was not sure what to make of events after the Inchon landing. Each day seemed to draw U.N. victory closer. Was there any point in sending the Special Force to Korea now? After all, NATO was demanding that Canada also send a brigade to Europe, and although the men who had volunteered for the Special Force had signed up primarily to serve in Korea, they had been told there was a chance they might be sent to Europe instead. The government tried to convince the Americans that the Canadian brigade group would not now be needed in Korea and that Canada should instead send it to Europe after it was trained up at Fort Lewis. But Washington insisted that at least one of the Canadian battalions go to Korea anyway, even if only to help with the occupation of North Korea. Ottawa reluctantly agreed and Rockingham selected the 2nd Battalion of the PPCLI to represent Canada. The sole reason for his decision was that 2 PPCLI was already near the West Coast and its training was at least as advanced as the other battalions.'

The man selected to lead 2 PPCLI was forty-one-year-old James Reilly "Big Jim" Stone. Stone was almost bald and had a thick brush moustache and muscular arms. Born in England, he had migrated to Canada in 1927 and lived as a farmer and forest ranger in Alberta's Peace River country. When war broke out in 1939, Stone enlisted as a private in the Loyal Edmonton Regiment, one of the first militia battalions activated. After the Loyal Eddies landed in Sicily, Stone became a company commander, then commanding officer of the battalion. He was awarded the Distinguished Service Order (DSO) for his outstanding record as battalion CO.

The Patricias departed from the port of Seattle at the beginning of December 1950 aboard the U.S. Navy transport ship *Joseph P. Martinez* and arrived in Pusan on December 18. By the time they arrived, the direction of the war had taken a sharp turn for the worse for the U.N. As MacArthur's troops neared the Yalu River—North Korea's border with China—the Communist government in Beijing had decided to intervene by sending "volunteers" to fight against the U.S.-led force. In late October tens of thousands of these volunteers had started to infiltrate across the frozen Yalu. Unseen by U.N. reconnaissance aircraft, they gathered in the thickly forested and snow-covered mountains just to the north of the U.N. troops. On October 25 they launched the first of a series of counterattacks that caught MacArthur by complete surprise; by the end of November they had sent his forces in headlong retreat back down the peninsula. The Patricias had been sent to Korea in a partially trained state, expecting to take part in occupation duties; they arrived to a newly flared-up shooting war—and they were on the losing side.

Stone strongly resisted American attempts to throw his battalion into the line to help stop the Chinese. He insisted that the Canadians get sufficient time to prepare for the fighting with a rigorous program of training and replacement of some of their obsolete equipment with American-pattern kit. The Americans agreed and the battalion proceeded to Miryang, about 50 kilometres north of Pusan, on December 27. For the next six weeks they undertook extensive training for mountain warfare while Stone weeded out men he judged inadequate for combat. On February 15, 1951, the 2nd Battalion of the PPCLI departed Miryang for the front. They were assigned to the 27th British Commonwealth Infantry Brigade (27 BCIB), which was attached to the IX Corps of the U.S. Eighth Army. The 27 BCIB was attached to the 2nd U.S. Infantry Division, part of the 9th U.S. Corps of Matthew Ridgway's Eighth U.S. Army. The British troops who formed the core of the brigade had been hurriedly dispatched to Korea from garrison duty in Hong Kong the previous fall, then augmented by Commonwealth troops: the 3rd Battalion of the Royal

Australian Regiment (3 RAR), the 16th New Zealand Field Artillery Regiment, and the 60th Indian Field Ambulance. The British troops consisted of the 1st Battalion of the Middlesex Regiment (1 MX) and the 1st Battalion of the Argyle and Sutherland Highlanders (1 A&SH). The PPCLI would stay with the Commonwealth Brigade until the rest of the Canadian Brigade—now renamed the 25th Canadian Infantry Brigade—arrived.

—⁂—

AT FIRST LIGHT ON FEBRUARY 15, 1951, the close to nine hundred men of 2 PPCLI set off for the front, some 240 kilometres to the north. The heavy canvas of their trucks offered virtually no protection against the cold as the convoy carefully negotiated the hairpin switchbacks on the icy mountain roads. This was the central Korean winter in all its glory, threatening men with frostbite, numbing their dog-tired brains, and freezing the gun oil and lubricants on their weapons. They were already learning that the Korean winter was as implacable and dangerous a foe as the Communist troops. It took more than forty-eight hours to negotiate the route from Miryang to the Commonwealth Brigade concentration area at Changhowon-ni. The battalion arrived at 3:00 PM on February 17.

A heavy blizzard dumped about a metre of snow across the brigade positions on the morning of February 18 as the PPCLI set out from the hamlet of Chuam-ni, at the centre of the brigade front. The Canadians were flanked by 1 MX to the left and 1 A&SH to the right as they advanced through deep snow across a broad valley and up the steep eastern slope of Hill 404. Jim Stone knew that troops who were moving down valleys were troops in grave danger, and insisted that his soldiers use the ridgelines to advance, even though the footing was tricky and the icy cold winds made life distinctly uncomfortable. As far as Stone was concerned, he who dominated the heights had the best chance of dominating the battle. The Patricias encountered no opposition at all as they trudged up the ridgeline toward Hill 404, but atop the hill they came upon the stiffened corpses of more than sixty American soldiers laid out for a graves registration party. Their sentries apparently asleep or surprised, the Americans had been caught out in the middle of the night and machine-gunned in their sleeping bags. Stone later remembered: "This was the greatest lesson my troops ever had. . . . They saw the bodies and the sight sure made an impression. After that you couldn't get one of my men into a sleeping bag at the front."

Corporal Kerry Dunphy was in charge of a nine-man section advancing slowly through fresh snow on a nearby slope when he and his men came under Chinese automatic fire. Bullets buzzed above them, shaking the pine needles, cracking the air as they went by. Most of the men reacted as they had been trained, going to ground, or on one knee, searching for the source of the enemy fire. Dunphy carefully exposed himself for a few seconds to get an idea of where the fire was coming from, urged his men forward, slowly, reminding them not to bunch up. Suddenly one of Dunphy's men spotted the Chinese gunner, got down on his knee, and, as he had been trained, squeezed off three shots, killing him. In sharp contrast another of Dunphy's men stood up, a strange look on his face, and began to run through the trees, shouting "I'm in no shape for this! I got to see somebody." He was soon sent home on a medical discharge.

—⚋—

IN MID-MARCH THE CHINESE ARMIES WITHDREW from the front; they were regrouping for a major new attack aimed at retaking Seoul and encircling and destroying the Eighth U.S. Army. The Americans estimated that about seventy Communist divisions were facing them, mostly Chinese, the balance North Koreans, with about half—more than 300,000 troops—on a 65-kilometre front between the Imjin River and the Hwachon Reservoir. The main Chinese offensive opened on the night of April 21–22; 27 BCIB was encamped near the hamlet of Kap'yong, squarely in the path of the Chinese attack.

Kap'yong is about 25 kilometres south of the 38th parallel and some 40 kilometres northeast of Seoul. It not only controls the north–south road through the Kap'yong Valley but also lies astride what was at the time a main east–west lateral road south of the front. The village lies about 1,000 metres northwest of the junction between the Kap'yong River, which is not much larger than a stream, and the Pukhan River. The commander of 27 BCIB, Colonel B.A. Burke, had established his brigade HQ about a kilometre north of the village at the southern end of a Y-shaped depression formed by the Kap'yong River and a small stream known as the Somoktong. From the valley floor to the highest peak to the west the elevation increased by some 800 metres over 3 kilometres; to the east of the Y-shaped valley the hills were somewhat lower, with the tallest reaching just over 500 metres. The terrain and the direction from which the onrushing enemy was coming dictated Burke's battle plan.

Burke knew that the main Chinese advance must come from either or both arms of the Y. He also knew that if the Chinese could be denied the heights along both the Somoktong and the Kap'yong, they could not push through the valley below. To that end he ordered 3 RAR, backed by a company of the U.S. 72nd Tank Battalion, to dig in on the peak and forward slopes of Hill 504, the highest position to the east of the Y. He positioned Stone's Patricias on Hill 677, to the west of the Y, about 5 kilometres across the Kap'yong from the Australians. Burke also assigned a company each of the U.S. 2nd Chemical Heavy Mortar Battalion, with twelve 4.2-inch mortars, to the Australians and Stone's Patricias. In addition Burke had at his disposal one battery of U.S. 105mm self-propelled guns and a battery of the 213th Medium Artillery Regiment firing U.S. 155mm "Long Toms."

When Jim Stone received Burke's order to concentrate his battalion on Hill 677, he organized a complete reconnaissance of possible Chinese attack approaches. Stone, his intelligence officer, his company commanders, and the commanders of his support and communications units went to the north side of 677 and the intelligence officer examined the terrain to the southeast. Stone then assigned defensive positions to his company commanders in a rough semi-circle, with A Company on the lower slopes of the hill facing the Australians, C Company on the north side of the hill, B Company just to the west of C Company, and D Company south of B Company. During the afternoon and evening of April 23 the Patricias prepared their positions. A, B, and D Companies were allotted two Vickers machine guns each.

The rugged terrain of the hill made it virtually impossible for the companies to be mutually supportive, so the plan amounted to each company's defending its own locale—siting its platoons most effectively to support each other—with the artillery, mortars, and machine guns given specific fire tasks of raking the areas between the companies should the Chinese infiltrate the battalion locale. The mortar platoon, with its half-tracks mounting Browning .30 and .50 machine guns, and Stone's tactical HQ were placed about halfway between D and B Companies. It was warm and dry as the Patricias dug their gun pits, laid their wire, and sited their weapons, the best weather they had had for weeks; on the road below them the remnants of two regiments from a Republic of Korea (ROK) division, destroyed by the Chinese, and thousands of Korean refugees went streaming past to the rear.

Just after midnight on April 24 the Chinese hit the Australians. Blowing whistles and bugles, the Chinese infantry rose out of the dark and rushed the RAR slit trenches behind a shower of mortar rounds. Close behind the first line of attackers came a second, hurling hundreds of grenades and carrying explosives to breach the Australian wire. The Australian CO called for defensive fire before losing radio contact with the brigade. As they hit the RAR positions, the Chinese swarmed into the New Zealanders' gun lines a bit to the south of the Aussies, forcing Burke to pull the regiment back to near his HQ.

At brigade HQ and in the Patricias' positions to the west, the loss of contact with the Australian battalion caused confusion and anxious moments. A cacophony of automatic weapons fire and exploding mortar and artillery shells could be heard from Hill 504 as the Patricias saw the sky lit by tracer fire and explosions. After close to two hours of radio silence, the Australians re-established contact through 1 MX. They reported a pitched battle around their battalion HQ and in front of Hill 504. The Chinese had penetrated to the centre of the Australian positions, were swarming around the slit trenches of the forward platoons, and were climbing onto the American tanks helping to defend the north side of the hill. Tanks were being hit, Australian and Chinese infantrymen were firing at one another at point-blank range, and Chinese mortar and machine-gun fire was raking the slopes. Retreating ROK soldiers were still trying to move through the area and the Australians could often not tell who were ROK and who were Chinese Reds. Daylight brought no respite for the Australian defenders. By mid-afternoon it was clear to Burke that they could not hold out another night, and he ordered them to withdraw. At 5:30 PM the Australians, accompanied by the American tanks, began to pull back. They had suffered thirty-one killed and fifty-eight wounded and had lost three men as prisoners. Now it was the Patricias' turn.

Stone had closely observed the battle across the valley and by morning had decided that an attack on his position would most likely come against his eastern slope. He ordered B company to move from its position and prepare new defences south of A company, from where it could protect the "back door" to the battalion area. As B company dug in, it reported seeing large numbers of Chinese infantry moving in and around the hamlet of Naechon, about 300 metres below its positions. At 8:30 PM, just as the Australian withdrawal was being completed, about four hundred Chinese infantry were observed forming up in a valley near B company. Company commander Major C.V. Lilley called for artillery and mortar concentrations but the Chinese attacked en masse. The forward Patricia platoon commanded by Lieutenant H. Ross battled them off as long as it could, but was soon partially overrun and forced to pull back into the B company area. The other platoons of B company were less beleaguered and held their ground. The fighting at close quarters was deadly. One sergeant later told Canadian war correspondent Bill Boss: "They're good. They were on top of our positions before we knew it. . . . They're quiet as mice with those rubber shoes of theirs and then there's a whistle. They get up with a shout about 10 feet from our positions and come in. . . . The first wave throws its grenades, fires its weapons and goes to the ground. It is followed by a second which does the same, and then a third comes up. They just keep coming." The sergeant threw his bayoneted rifle at the attackers like a spear when his ammunition ran out.

In one of the Patricia Bren-gun pits, the situation was desperate almost from the first moment of battle. One soldier later recalled:

> We sat there and held them off as long as we could until we pulled back and Wayne [Mitchell] and I got separated. I don't know how long we were there before Lt. Ross gave us the order to move out. Just as we jumped up Ross added that anyone with any ammo left should cover the retreat of the wounded. I had three shells left so I dropped back down and fired them off. Just as I jumped up again I fell over a Chinaman who was running up the side of the hill. He let fly and got me in the neck then ran into the end of my bayonet.

As B company was being attacked, a small group of Chinese tried to get inside the battalion area by infiltrating up the valley behind Stone's tactical headquarters. The Chinese were silhouetted against the Kap'yong River as they approached. Stone later described what happened: "The mortar platoon, located with HQ, was mounted for travelling on twelve half tracks. Each vehicle was equipped with one .50 and one .30 calibre machine gun. . . . Fire was held until the Chinese had broken through the trees about two hundred metres away. Twenty-four machine guns cut loose together. Only those who have experienced being under the fire of a heavy concentration of tracer bullets can appreciate the terror induced by that kind and volume of fire."

As the night wore on, the Patricias held to their positions, but their situation became increasingly desperate. Heavy fighting continued to swirl around B Company. At 1:30 AM D Company's 10 Platoon, on the western tip of the hill, became the focal point for another heavy Chinese attack. Despite the artillery and mortar fire pouring down around their positions to keep the Canadians safe, about two hundred Chinese came at them from the west. Platoon commander Lieutenant M.G. Levy reported to acting company commander Captain J.G.W. Mills that his men were engaged on three sides. Levy called for close-in fire support from the mortars and the field artillery while making sure his own men were below ground in their slit trenches and gun pits. The shrapnel bursts, set to explode just below treetop height, sent clouds of hot, jagged, twisted metal into the Chinese ranks; below ground, the Canadians were protected. That broke the back of the Chinese attack.

At dawn Stone radioed for an air drop to resupply his exhausted men; six hours later a flight of United States Air Force C-119 "Flying Boxcars" swung over the Canadian positions as loadmasters kicked their payloads out the rear. Food, ammunition, and water floated down onto the slopes of Hill 677—virtually all the supplies fell within the Canadian position. The battle for Hill 677 was over; on April 26 the Patricias were relieved by a battalion of the 1st U.S. Cavalry Division and went into reserve. Ten Canadians had been killed and twenty-three wounded, and several, including Mills, were decorated for bravery.

In the words of one American chronicler of the Korean War, "The holding action of the Commonwealth Brigade at Kapyong had been decisive. It plugged the hole left by the ROK 6th Division and blocked the [Chinese] long enough for the 24th [U.S. Infantry] Division to withdraw." The respite gave the Eighth Army Commander, James Van Fleet, time to set up a new defensive line running just to the north of Seoul, withdraw his units to that line in good order, save the capital, and prepare for a massive counterattack back to the 38th parallel.

The Patricias had held off a Chinese force at least three times its size because of both good luck and good preparation. The luck came from the Chinese decision to hit the Australians first. The good preparation was the result of the presence of tried veterans of the Second

World War—Stone and his officers. He and some of the others had fought in the mountains of Sicily and Italy and knew how to defend a hill. Stone knew that if well-led men were provided with a good defence, lots of ammunition, and no way out, they'd fight and die where they stood rather than break. He had faith in his regiment. For his solid leadership and imaginative planning, Stone received a bar to his DSO. For the crucial forty-eight hours they bought the U.N. at Kap'yong, 2 PPCLI, 3 RAR, and the U.S. 72nd Tank Battalion were awarded a U.S. Presidential Unit Citation. The PPCLI was the first regiment in Canadian history to be so honoured.

CHAPTER FIFTEEN

STALEMATE: THE VAN DOOS AND THE RCR
ON THE JAMESTOWN LINE

> There were Chinese in the trench with me and more on the parapet. There
> were more up top and in the center of the position throwing grenades into
> the trenches while a party worked towards me throwing grenades into the
> weapons pits.
>
> —Lieutenant Laurie Coté, Hill 187, May 2, 1953

WHEN THE FINAL CHINESE OFFENSIVE OF THE WAR petered out after
Kap'yong, the U.N. offensive resumed. In May 1951 the rest of the
Canadian brigade arrived, and in July 1951 it joined with other British
and Commonwealth units to form the 1st (Commonwealth) Division
under the command of British Major-General A.J.H. Cassels. The
division was one of five in I Corps of the Eighth U.S. Army. In the
summer of 1951, tentative ceasefire talks opened between the U.N.
and the North Koreans at Kaesong, near the 38th parallel. While
those talks proceeded, the U.N. offensive was halted. On August 23
the talks were suspended because of disagreements over a number
of issues, and the U.N. push was resumed, continuing until negotiations started up again at Panmunjom on October 25, 1951. The
U.N. then halted its offensive on a position dubbed the Jamestown
Line, which was north of the 38th parallel on the eastern coast of

Korea. From then until the end of the Korean War in July 1953, the war was fought almost entirely on this line, with both sides attacking and counterattacking hilltop strong points for essentially political reasons. Each side wanted to gain some local advantage while the ceasefire negotiations dragged on but neither side was prepared any longer to fight for an all-out victory.

The Canadian commitment remained firm. In the summer of 1951 Ottawa decided that instead of keeping the three battalions in Korea until the end of hostilities, each battalion (and each armoured and artillery regiment) would return to Canada after one year of service. They would be replaced by the first battalions (or armoured or artillery regiments) of the same regiments. Thus 2 PPCLI would be replaced by 1 PPCLI, and so on. Over the course of the Korean War there were two rotations, the first beginning in February 1952 with 2 PPCLI (the rest of the brigade began to rotate out of Korea in the spring of 1952) and the last a year later. With each rotation a new brigade commander was appointed.

In November 1951 the Commonwealth Division held some 12,000 metres of front between the 1st U.S. Cavalry Division to the right and the 1st Republic of Korea Division to the left. The three Canadian infantry battalions in the line were the 2nd battalions of the Royal Canadian Regiment (RCR) and the Royal 22e Régiment, (R22^{e}R), not yet rotated home, and three companies of both the 1st and 2nd battalions of Princess Patricia's Canadian Light Infantry, which was in the midst of its first rotation. They were directly supported by the 25-pounder gun/howitzers of the 2nd Battalion, Royal Canadian Horse Artillery, and the Sherman tanks of C Squadron, Lord Strathcona's Horse (Royal Canadians). They held about 9,000 metres of north–south front roughly along a 100-metre contour line. The land in front of their positions dropped suddenly some 75 metres to a small stream. The dominant peak in the region was Hill 355, or "Little Gibraltar." It and Hill 227, 1,500 metres due west, were held by the 1st Battalion, King's Shropshire Light Infantry (1 KSLI), of the 28th British Infantry Brigade.

When the U.N. forces along the Jamestown Line were ordered to defend the line indefinitely, they should also have been ordered to prepare effective defences in depth and to aggressively patrol the no man's land between them and the Chinese. For the most part that did not happen on the Commonwealth Division front. To make matters worse for the front-line troops, aggressive attacks on the Chinese positions across the valley were strongly discouraged for two reasons: to avoid casualties and to not risk derailing the ceasefire talks at Panmunjom. But the net result was that the Chinese, who had no worries about casualties or public opinion at home, simply attacked whenever they wished. When they did attack, they had all the time in the world to prepare and could attack at times and in places where the U.N.'s superiority in artillery and airpower was nullified.

On the U.N. line, each different contingent seemed to prepare its defences according to its own national doctrines, so the defences were uneven at best. On the Commonwealth Division front the rifle companies were positioned on hilltops in positions encircled by a minefield, a single row of concertina wire, and a single circular main trench with fire trenches radiating outwards from it. The valleys between the hilltop positions were strung with wire and mines were planted there. On the high ground to the rear, powerful searchlights were placed to illuminate enemy troops trying to infiltrate between defensive localities. There was much dead ground on the lower slopes, however, while the minefields surrounding the hilltops had only one gap to allow access for patrolling. Given the roughness and hilly nature of the terrain, the platoons were usually dug in in a manner that made it very difficult to provide defensive or cover fire for other platoons. Manning a single line of defensive hilltops thinned the defences, while the defensive localities were themselves poorly laid out with a single encircling trench that, when under intense fire, offered the defenders little protection. What all this amounted to was that the Chinese were able to seize the initiative, select the time and place for their attacks, make up for whatever firepower deficiencies they had by using the cover of darkness, and attack virtually at will.

When they did attack, they were often through the wire and into the fire trenches as soon as their shelling had lifted. Then the Canadian infantry, with their outmoded bolt-action rifles, were forced to deal at close quarters with Chinese in the trenches firing automatic weapons, or on the open ground with the enemy throwing volleys of grenades down into the trenches.

On November 17 the Chinese pushed the 1st Battalion of the King's Shropshire Light Infantry off Hill 227. In the words of the 25th Brigade war diarist, "this was a serious turn of events as it exposed [a] good deal of the Patricia's right flank previously dominated by the two platoons and company headquarters of A coy [of 1 KSLI] on top of the feature." For three days the hill kept changing hands as British counterattacked and Chinese responded; on November 20, it was permanently lost to the Reds. The loss prompted Cassels, the Commonwealth Division commander, to reposition his forces—the Canadian brigade was placed so as to occupy the saddle formed by the west slope of Hill 355 and the foot of Hill 227. All three Canadian battalions were in the line with all four of their rifle companies—the RCR on the left, the PPCLI in the centre, and the R22ᵉR on the right. The Van Doos held a section of line formerly occupied by most of a brigade.

The Van Doos were commanded by Jacques Dextraze, the much-decorated veteran of the Second World War and former commander of the Fusiliers Mont-Royal, who had volunteered for service in Korea while holding a civilian job with the Singer Sewing Machine Company in Quebec. In his own words, Dextraze was a "meddler" who took a "hands-on" approach to battalion command, even in battle. He began to prepare his battalion for the move onto the saddle at a meeting with his company commanders on November 19. He told them that he would retain control of and assign fire tasks to the 60mm mortars, the 75mm recoilless rifles, and the heavy machine guns. He urged a thorough check of all equipment, even to the state of the Bren-gun magazines. He demanded a tightening up of discipline, with daily inspections, tests of elementary training, and range practice. He insisted on strict five-yard (4.5-metre) intervals between men in the line, no one on forward slopes, and continuous observation of enemy positions. Above all, in the event of attack there was to be "NO withdrawal, NO platoons overrun and NO panic. All would be expected to perform their duty in a typical 'VAN DOOS' manner."

The Van Doos began to move into their new positions on the night of November 21 after a hot Thanksgiving dinner of turkey and all the trimmings, courtesy of the U.S. Army. The battalion took over a triangular defensive position formerly occupied by 1 KSLI. Dextraze placed D Company on a spur that ran north–south across the saddle at the front of the triangle. A Company was sited about 500 metres to the south at the end of the spur, in the middle of the triangle. B Company took the bottom-left corner of the triangle, about 1,200 metres and across a ravine from A Company. C Company was positioned about 1,100 metres to the east of B Company, with the same ravine between it and A Company.

The battalion was in place by 6:30 AM on November 22 and quickly got to work improving the defences. Dextraze himself supervised the laying of additional wire and mines and the siting of the heavy .50 Browning machine guns, the lighter .30 Brownings, and even the .303 Brens. By mid-afternoon his HQ was functioning, with radio and land-line communication to the rifle companies and to Brigade HQ to the rear. Not long after, Chinese shells began to rumble in from across the valley. The shelling grew more intense by the minute, then heavy-calibre rockets began to explode in the Van Doos positions. The Chinese concentrated on D Company and on the American positions atop Hill 355. One Van Doos private was blown to bits when a shell exploded in his slit trench. Others were wounded by flying shards of steel or by the dirt, rocks, and pieces of smashed bunker that rained down on them. The concertina wire in front of the company positions was shredded, telephone lines were cut, the minefield was pulverized. As night fell the shelling continued. It started to snow heavily, the first real snow of the winter, but the Chinese did not come, and when morning dawned on November 23, the shelling slackened.

The men of D Company used the hiatus to repair damage and lay new telephone lines. At mid-morning a Chinese scout was captured near the pioneer platoon wire; minutes later shells began to fall once again, this time on D Company's left flank. The shelling forced the men to ground. At 1:50 PM an observation plane reported at least a company of Chinese infantry advancing from the northwest, about a kilometre away, and called down an artillery concentration. In response the Canadian and New Zealand batteries plastered the paddy land in a valley to the left and front of D Company.

At 4:20 PM Chinese rocket and shellfire began to strike the summit of Hill 355; less than ten minutes later, approximately two companies of Chinese infantry hit the D Company wire. The fighting was close, intense, and desperate. The Canadian infantry threw grenades, worked the bolts of their Lee-Enfield rifles, and fired clip after clip of Bren-gun and belt after belt of Browning machine-gun ammunition at the onrushing Chinese. One Van Doos section broke, but the platoon commander led them back into position. On Hill 355, Easy, Fox, and George companies of the U.S. 7th Infantry were under attack from an entire Chinese battalion. At 5:35 PM word reached Dextraze that American soldiers from 355 were arriving in the A Company area; they had been forced off the hill. This was a "very grave and serious situation," according to the 25th Brigade war diarist. Hill 355 was not only the highest position in the line but it also dominated the lateral road running through the American sector. The Canadian right flank was now completely open; the Chinese could look down into the Van Doos' positions from their U.S.-dug trenches and bunkers.

The Chinese attacked the Van Doos with renewed fury. At one point a single Canadian platoon of some thirty men was almost completely surrounded by an estimated four hundred Chinese soldiers. At Brigade HQ, the Canadian tanks were ordered forward to support the Canadian infantry. At his own HQ, Dextraze worked the radio, ordering his company commanders to hold fast and directing mortar, tank, and artillery fire, sometimes bringing it down virtually on the D Company wire. Four Chinese attacks had been beaten off by morning as the Canadians stubbornly defended their ridge. Just before dawn, a U.S. counterattack retook most of Hill 355, taking considerable pressure off the Van Doos.

The Chinese attackers melted away at first light on the 24th, but intermittent shelling continued. Dextraze ordered a platoon counterattack toward Hill 227. The advancing unit met little resistance and gained the summit of the hill, which it held until withdrawn in the face of another massing of Chinese infantry at about 5:00 PM. Brigade and divisional artillery rained down on the Chinese as they were forming up positions but failed to stop a renewed assault on the Van Doos' D Company. The Chinese came from all directions despite a hail of tank, mortar, and artillery fire. D Company's left forward platoon collapsed back into the main company positions but the company itself held fast. Just before midnight, the Van Doos' scout platoon edged forward to retake the lost platoon position. They succeeded, but were then strongly attacked by at least two Chinese companies and were forced to pull back to take cover in several shell holes. Dextraze then called down heavy mortar fire on the Chinese attackers. At about the same time, a second withdrawal of U.S. troops on the western slope of 355 again exposed the Van Doos' left flank, but once again the Americans retook the hill before first light on November 25.

The Van Doos' D Company fended off one small Chinese probe on the night of November 25, but that was the end of their five-day ordeal. Just before dawn the next day Dextraze ordered D Company relieved by B Company. In the words of the brigade war diarist, "the troops of D Coy . . . had reached the limits of their endurance. They had been exposed to the snow, the cold of the day, the freezing nights, and had had no sleep since the evening of the 21st." They had also received only minimal help from the other three companies of the battalion because the terrain, the poor siting of their positions by the British battalion that had previously held it, and lack of time for correction of the situation had not allowed it.

In the four days between November 22 and 26, the Van Doos lost sixteen men killed—nine from D Company alone—forty-four wounded, and three missing and presumed dead after a direct hit by a Chinese shell on a bunker. Division HQ estimated 2,000 Chinese dead in the operations around Hills 227 and 355, but only 742 enemy dead were actually counted. This small and obscure fight for a lonely hill in faraway Korea, hardly noticed back in Canada, was surely one of the Royal 22ᵉ Régiment's finest hours.

—m—

"THIS IS A WEARING, WEARYING WAR," Canadian war correspondent Bill Boss broadcast on the CBC Radio network on the night of February 10, 1953. "It's harder on the nerves to sit and take it than to be up and at them. There's no change of scenery or even of conversation." It was now two years since 2 PPCLI had joined the 27th British Commonwealth Infantry Brigade in the line of fire. The ceasefire talks at Panmunjom had dragged on until October 1952. By then both sides had agreed they were seeking a ceasefire, but there was no agreement on what to do with prisoners after the fighting ended. The U.N. held tens of thousands of Communist prisoners and had sought to allow them to choose their fate after a ceasefire. They knew the great majority would opt not to return to live under Communism. The Communists had pressed for forced repatriation. After repeated failure to make any headway on this issue the U.N. representatives announced that they had had enough of useless bickering and would return to the table only when the Communists signalled that they wanted to make a serious effort to end the fighting. The U.N. did not resume the offensive—at that point no one had the stomach for dialing up the war once again—but a war of small-scale attrition, of raids, patrols, and artillery concentrations, continued along the Jamestown Line.

All across the U.N. front, men grew bored, complacent, and tired of the daily grind. Each day was like the day before, with little prospect for change tomorrow. During daylight hours they slept, ate, cleaned weapons, wrote letters home, worked on their positions. After dark some waited and watched, weapons charged, senses trying to detect enemy movement in front of them, while others blackened their faces, tied down loose kit, borrowed automatic weapons if they did not have them, and went out to patrol. The casualties occurred in ones and twos, but they formed a steady trickle. Lieutenant-Colonel J.G. Poulin, commanding 3 R22ᵉR, observed at the end of May 1953: "Our tactics have a stereotyped quality that deprives us of initiative and forewarns the enemy. We rarely try to trick the Chinaman. We do not use deception and have lost our aggressive spirit. Commanders and men are dug-out minded. The fear of receiving casualties deadens our reactions and lessens our effort. We are thoroughly defensive minded and yet not thorough in our defence."

ON APRIL 26, 1953, armistice talks resumed at Panmunjom after the Communists suddenly accepted an invitation from General Mark Clark, the U.N. commander, to begin discussions that might lead to an exchange of sick and wounded prisoners, on the very basis of freedom of choice that the U.N. had been proposing for almost two years. By the end of March the Communists had agreed to the exchange, dubbed Operation Little Switch. Historian David Rees believes that Moscow and Beijing had decided in March 1953 to "write off the war." Three factors were behind this reversal: the ruination of the Chinese economy by the continued fighting, the election of Dwight David Eisenhower as U.S. president the previous November, and the death of Soviet leader Joseph Stalin on March 5. Eisenhower's election brought to office in the White House an experienced soldier determined to end the war, by using nuclear weapons against the Chinese mainland if necessary. And Stalin's death removed the chief benefactor of the Chinese and North Koreans.

In mid-April, no doubt in anticipation of the looming armistice, the Chinese began to increase the pressure along the front lines. They renewed efforts initiated in November 1952 to capture the Pork Chop Hill/Old Baldy complex held by the Americans in central Korea. In one intense battle the Americans eventually beat the Chinese back, but not before expending close to seventy-eight thousand artillery rounds over the course of the two days. After their failure to take Pork Chop and Old Baldy, the Communists turned to Hill 187.

On April 21, 1953, Brigadier Jean Victor Allard took command of the Canadian Brigade. Born in Nicolet, Quebec, Allard had received a *collège classique* education and had been a militia officer at the outbreak of the Second World War. In December 1943, while temporarily in command of the Royal 22ᵉ Régiment, he was awarded the DSO for his part in the Battle of the Arielli River in Italy. Though wounded shortly after, he was given command of the Van Doos in January 1944. In March 1945 he was promoted to command the 6th Canadian Infantry Brigade of the 2nd Canadian Infantry Division. He remained in the army after the war as a regular-force officer. In his memoirs, Allard notes the special difficulties he and his troops faced at that juncture of the Korean War: "Our orders were to wage a strictly defensive war. . . . A brigade commander could not, on his own initiative, mount an offensive that would involve more than a platoon. . . . I was unable to test either the defensive capability of my opponents or the offensive capability of my own troops. . . . If our enemy happened to dominate our positions, we had to let him snipe at us, with the ensuing loss of life that might have been avoided by capturing certain peaks from our adversary."

In late April 1953 the Canadian Brigade held several hilltops near Hill 187, halfway between a position known as the Hook and Little Gibraltar. Atop Hill 187, the officer commanding 3 RCR, Lieutenant-Colonel K.L. Campbell, placed his four rifle companies at the corners of a rough square. The position closest to the Chinese was held by C Company; its three platoons—7, 8, and 9—ran east–west along a ridgeline. The position was in deplorable shape. The wiring was insufficient. The main trenches were not deep enough. There were gaps in the communication trenches. The fire bays had been poorly laid out, with inadequate overhead cover. The bunkers were too high and too lightly timbered and had too little overhead cover; they were also too far removed from the fighting positions. There ought to have been ten solidly built bunkers, but by the end of April only two had been constructed. None of the roughly 150 metres of trench within the platoon area or leading to the next platoon had been properly protected with barbed wire.

Chinese patrols, usually covered by shellfire, probed unceasingly forward toward the Canadian positions. They learned much about their opposition—Canadian patrol patterns, patrol routes, defences, the rawness of the new Canadian units. No doubt they also knew the brigade was under new command. Campbell and a British counter-battery officer seconded to Allard's staff were both certain that the Chinese were not simply harassing the Canadians but were also regis-tering targets in the C Company area. The signs of impending attack grew by the day.

Late on the afternoon of May 2, Allard flew to Seoul to accept an invitation to dinner and an overnight stay with U.S. General Maxwell Taylor, now commanding the Eighth U.S. Army. He arrived at Taylor's HQ just in time for cocktails and settled in for an evening with the brass. The Chinese had other plans. Allard later told a news-paper reporter: "I got hot feet about 10:30 [PM]. I had an uneasy feel-ing and cut the evening short." Taylor tried to reassure him that the Chinese rarely attacked this late in the war, but Allard left anyway and was driven back to the front. On the way he heard radio reports that the sporadic pattern of shellfire the Chinese had been throwing at Hill 187 for many days had suddenly changed and intensified. Allard feared the storm was about to break.

ON MAY 2, 1953, at 10:20 PM, in the valley between the Canadians and the Chinese, a sixteen-man fighting patrol from A Company, 3 RCR, lay prone, watching and listening. They had moved out of their lines hours earlier to set up an ambush. Now they waited anxiously along the low wall of a rice paddy as a group of some sixty Chinese infantry moved cautiously toward the Canadian positions on Hill 187. Lieutenant J.G. Maynell waited until he thought the Chinese were past, then whispered into his radio to ask for a flare. As the flare popped into brilliance, the Canadians poked their heads and weapons above the low paddy wall and opened fire, throwing grenades. The Chinese dove for cover and returned fire. Maynell was shot in the head.

Corporal Joseph McNeil, second-in-command of the ambush party, radioed for help, then began to move the remainder of the A Company patrol back toward the Canadian lines. The wounded were dragged and carried; those still capable of shooting or throwing grenades formed a rearguard. McNeil's men broke contact as they approached their own minefield, but were ambushed by a second group of Chinese. The surprise of the ambush and the intensity of fire broke up the little group of Canadians, who now made their way individually back to the A Company positions.

At 10:50 PM, as they approached the top of the hill, the survivors of the A Company patrol met a patrol led by Lieutenant Doug Banton, commander of No. 8 Platoon, C Company, who had been sent to help Maynell's beleaguered men. Hushed greetings were exchanged, then the second group of men disappeared down the hill. Within moments, McNeil and his men heard a heavy volley of small-arms fire. Private W. Hummer was in Banton's patrol: "Banton dropped off Boyce and myself, I had the Bren gun, to cover the section when it withdrew. Shortly after I saw the flash of weapons as Banton's party and the Chinks opened fire on each other." Banton was hit by a grenade or mortar. One of his men hefted him onto his back and tried to carry him back but another grenade blew Banton off. He was dead. The Chinese fire was too intense to recover his body.

The men in the valley were struggling to survive when the Chinese barrage on C Company intensified at midnight. Then Chinese heavy machine guns opened up on the 7 Platoon position, and B Company reported that it too was under heavy shell- and mortar fire. The fire on C Company suddenly lifted toward the rear of the RCR positions and the Chinese infantry swarmed over what was left of the wire into the 7 Platoon positions. Moments later they hit neighbouring 8 Platoon. Despite a growing volume of Canadian defensive fire on the position, the Chinese surged forward, throwing concussion grenades as they moved along the trenches and pulling out dazed Canadian soldiers to take as prisoners. Hummer and his comrades fought back: "We fired at them and they fired at us. . . . We saw six Chinks walking along the top of the crawl trench where we were crouched. Greenaway got three of them with his Sten gun but the others crawled around behind us and dropped grenades into our crawl trench." Hummer and the others were wounded.

Lieutenant Laurie Coté was not far away. He later described the scene to correspondent Bill Boss:

> In the communications trench between two bren-gun pits we saw them. There were Chinese in the trench with me and more on the parapet. There were more up top and in the center of the position throwing grenades into the trenches while a party worked towards me throwing grenades into the weapons pits. Then the [Canadian] bombardment started and forced me to lie in the trench. . . . The Chinese also took shelter though some crawled along the parapet. . . . One was killed and fell on top of me, affording that much more cover.

The Canadian shellfire was directed by Lieutenant Edgar H. Hollyer, who had hunkered down in his bunker when the Chinese poured over the wire. He tried twice to get above ground to size up the situation but failed both times. Miraculously, his radio was still working, so he got on the air to call for proximity fire on his own position. Within minutes the field gunners were slamming breeches shut and pulling lanyards; some four thousand shells rumbled toward the hilltop or toward the Chinese approach routes. Scores of Chinese standing in the open were blown to pieces. Hollyer and signals officer Lieutenant J.G. Coté radioed company HQ for permission to withdraw to the 8 Platoon locality, a few hundred metres to the east. When this was given, they moved out.

Back at Battalion HQ, Allard refused to allow Campbell to stage a company-sized counterattack against the Chinese, because Campbell had no reserve. Allard and Campbell then agreed to order up a company of 3 R22ᵉR, which could fill in for 3 RCR's D Company if Campbell sent it forward to recapture the lost ground. Just at this point, however, Hollyer reached his company command post and told the CO over the radio that he thought the main body of Chinese was pulling back, and a patrol might be enough to reoccupy the lost position. Campbell then sent one group of ten men under Hollyer to take back the position and another group of ten to recover casualties. Supported by tank-fire, Hollyer led this group back into the 7 Platoon position, but when they clambered into what was left of it, they came under concentrated Chinese mortar fire. They were pinned down until first light, when the Chinese pulled out.

At 4:00 AM the Van Doos company arrived to relieve D Company of 3 RCR, which then moved out toward the C Company positions. As the men crept cautiously toward the sound of firing, Chinese smoke shells began to blossom around C Company, while mortar fire intensified on the 7 and 8 Platoon positions. The Chinese appeared to be breaking contact, using the smoke and mortar barrages to cover the pullback.

Just under three hours later, the sound of helicopter blades cutting the air resounded through the early morning as one chopper after another weaved its way around the peaks and up the valleys, landed, and carried the wounded away. No one was really sure what the Chinese had meant to accomplish, although speculation centred on seizing prisoners and providing a diversion for an even larger attack on British positions on nearby Hill 159. The short, sharp battle proved to be the costliest single encounter of the war for Canada: twenty-six soldiers were dead, twenty-seven had been wounded, and eight had been taken prisoner. Korean soldiers attached to the Canadian units for training purposes ("Katcoms") were also among the casualties: four had been killed and fourteen wounded, and four were missing.

One of the Canadian prisoners, Private John Junkins of Ottawa, was released by the Chinese shortly after the battle. A member of Maynell's first patrol, he had been left behind after the initial fire-fight when McNeil led the survivors back toward the RCR positions. Junkins then took refuge in an unoccupied bunker: "I lost the main party. Shells and mortars were bursting all around and I was pinned down. I crawled into a bunker and after a time I heard Chinese voices outside. I . . . flattened myself against the wall. . . . Someone suddenly ripped away the poncho waterproof cape covering the doorway and sprayed the back of the bunker with a burp gun. I lay there for 15 minutes. Two Chinese eventually came into the bunker, pulled me out and told me I was a prisoner." After searching him, the Chinese brought up three more prisoners, then began to move them off toward their lines. For some unexplained reason a Chinese medical orderly gave Junkins a drink of water, stuffed some papers into his uniform—probably propaganda leaflets—and departed with the rest of the Chinese patrol. Junkins crawled back into the bunker and waited for the Canadians to reoccupy the position.

—m—

THE BATTLE FOR HILL 187 was the last major engagement between Canadian troops and their Chinese adversaries, though eighteen other Canadians would die at the front between May 3, 1953, and the armistice. On June 7 agreement was reached at Panmunjom on the general prisoner exchange issue. On July 27 the armistice agreement was finally signed. It provided for a complete ceasefire twelve hours later, followed by withdrawal of all troops from the newly designated demilitarized zone within seventy-two hours. The armistice would be supervised by a Military Armistice Commission composed of five representatives from each side.

On the night of July 27, 1953, the active phase of the Korean War ended. Canada had sent 21,940 of its soldiers to what U.S. President Harry S. Truman had once called a "police action." The official history of the Canadian army in the Korean War lists 1,543 army casualties—309 killed in action, died of wounds, or missing and officially presumed dead, 1,202 wounded, 32 prisoners of war, and 93 soldiers and sailors dead from non-battle causes.

Though many of the Canadians who fought in Korea were veterans of the Second World War, they were nevertheless the first of a new generation of postwar soldiers. They fought a faraway war for a principle and a concept, not because the fate of their nation was at stake. Those Canadians (and the many more soldiers from the U.S., the Republic of Korea, the rest of the Commonwealth, and indeed the entire U.N. Command) were the thin red line of their day—and they held. When they returned to Canada, however, another challenge awaited them almost immediately. The NATO countries believed that Korea had been a test of their willingness and their ability to resist a Soviet effort to either invade or intimidate western Europe. NATO's immediate post–Korean War challenge was to build up sufficient military force in Europe to deter Soviet aggression, and Canada would have to contribute its share. The day of a small standing Canadian army was over—for good.

Chapter Sixteen

SOLDIERS AND PEACEKEEPERS: THE COLD WAR

I deployed our TOW system [anti-armour rockets] mortars, and our own snipers and told him that if we were fired at, we would fire back.

—Colonel Michel Jones, Bosnia, 1992

DURING THE KOREAN WAR most NATO countries laid plans for a rapid expansion of their defence budgets and a buildup of their forces in Europe. Canada had started 1950 with but a single brigade of the active or permanent army and a largely moribund army reserve. In order to meet its international obligations in Korea and Europe, the Canadian army would literally have to triple in size within a very short time. In 1952 the government decided to form yet another brigade, for service in NATO, while expanding the Cold War army, navy, and air force. There would be roughly four times the number of Canadians in uniform at the end of the 1950s as there had been at the start. This was the largest peacetime mobilization in Canadian history.

This brigade for NATO was designated as the 27th Canadian Infantry Brigade. It would be permanently stationed in Germany alongside the British army of the Rhine. This too was a precedent, because never before in Canadian history had a substantial Canadian military force headed overseas to take up a permanent base during peacetime. The army planned to deploy this brigade to Europe in the fall of 1951. The infantry component was made up entirely of volunteers from militia regiments across Canada. These volunteers were formed into six entirely new infantry battalions, designated the 1st and 2nd Canadian Infantry Battalions, the 1st and 2nd Canadian Rifle Battalions, and the 1st and 2nd Canadian Highland Battalions. Numbers were used to designate these formations as a means of rapidly integrating individual militia volunteers from the many different regiments—rifle, Highland (kilted), and infantry—across the nation. It was thought they would fit together better if their overseas battalions were as generic as possible. The experiment was an instant failure. Almost as soon as the 27th Brigade deployed to Germany, significant morale and disciplinary problems surfaced, and although there were many reasons why these issues arose, the lack of a strong regimental tradition in the NATO battalions was thought to be a major hindrance to unit cohesion.

In 1951 Lieutenant-General Guy Simonds became chief of staff of the Canadian army. Simonds was a gunner—an artilleryman—who had had a brilliant career as a divisional and corps commander during the war. A protégé of Field-Marshal Montgomery, he was considered by "Monty" and other Allied generals to be the best commander Canada had produced in the war. Simonds was a strong anglophile and a confirmed believer in the regimental system. In 1953 he reorganized the structure of the army's permanent or regular-force regiments, with the greatest changes taking place in the Canadian Infantry Corps— the overall home of all Canada's infantry regiments, both permanent and militia. He organized the Corps into six permanent-force infantry regiments, adding three new permanent regiments to the three standing ones—the PPCLI, RCR, and R22ᵉR—that had survived the army's retrenchment after the Second World War. Thus the 1st and 2nd Canadian Rifle Battalions of the 27th Brigade were re-badged as the 1st and 2nd battalions of the Queen's Own Rifles of Canada. The Queen's Own was one of Canada's oldest regiments and had deployed a battalion for overseas service in the Second World War. But it had reverted to militia status when the war ended. Now, for the first time in its history, it would become a regiment in Canada's standing army. The 1st and 2nd Canadian Highland Battalions of the 27th Brigade were re-badged as the 1st and 2nd battalions of the Black Watch (Royal Highland Regiment) of Canada. Like the Queen's Own, it had a long and honourable tradition as a militia regiment and had mobilized a battalion for overseas service in the Second World War before reverting to militia status after 1945. Now it too was being transformed into a regiment of Canada's standing army. As for the 1st and 2nd Canadian Infantry Battalions of the 27th Brigade, they became the 3rd and 4th battalions of an entirely new regiment—the Regiment of Canadian Guards, better known as the Canadian Guards. On their return from Korea, the 3rd Battalions of the RCR and the PPCLI became the 1st and 2nd battalions of the Guards.

Simonds's conjuring up of the Regiment of Canadian Guards broke all regimental precedent in Canada. The Guards was not only an instant regiment, it was charged with creating an instant regimental tradition. In a truly astonishing move, Simonds decided that the Canadian Guards would immediately take precedence as the most senior of Canadian regiments—even though it was obviously the youngest—and would recruit from a national base, unlike the other regiments, which were regional. Two Guards battalions were to be based in Camp Petawawa, northwest of Ottawa, and two at Camp Valcartier, in Quebec. One of the Quebec-based battalions was to be bilingual. Simonds's rationale for making the Guards the senior regiment—news that was "not received with joy by the older Regular Force regiments," in the words of the Guards' official history—was that it was going to be a truly national regiment, less "parochial" than the others, and that it would set the highest standards for Canadian infantry. His inspiration was the three-hundred-year-old tradition of the British Brigade of Guards, who were "well trained and disciplined soldiers . . . colourful in peacetime and a credit to the nation in war," in his view. These additional regiments were stood up on October 16, 1953.

What motivated Simonds to resort to such a radical change? Perhaps the better question is what allowed him—a man steeped in regimental tradition—to do it. Guy Simonds was a gunner, and although the gunners, like the engineers, have an honourable regimental tradition of their own, it is different from the regimental traditions of the armour and the infantry. Gunners and engineers are "everywhere" in battle and they take part in virtually all battles. Their motto—*Ubique* (ubiquitous)—reflects this reality. They have no specific battle honours because they draw their regimental pride from having been in every battle. Perhaps this gunner's perspective prompted—or allowed—Simonds to create the Canadian Guards in the way that he did.

The militia regiments also underwent significant changes in the Cold War years beginning in the mid-1950s. For the first time in Canadian history the roles of the reserves and the regular force were reversed. Ever since the founding of the permanent or regular force in the 1870s and 1880s, Canada's permanent soldiers had been intended to form a small professional core for a Canadian military that was made up largely of militia (reservists). The professionals' job was to train the reserves and provide a foundation for reserve mobilization in the event of war. Now, in the atomic age, Western military leaders believed that World War III would likely begin with intercontinental air attacks using nuclear weapons against major cities. There would be no time to mobilize reserves, let alone train them, and any actual fighting that took place on the ground would be conducted by forces "in being"—ready and in place. Most of these forces would obviously be the standing professional army; only a small number of reservists would be required, and most of them would be needed at home to help the civilian population survive after a nuclear attack. Reserve units were consolidated across the country, reserve equipment and training were allowed to deteriorate, reserve numbers dwindled. On December 5, 1963, the government formally announced that the militia would be cut from fifty-one thousand to thirty-two thousand. For example, the Essex Scottish Regiment and the Kent Regiment in Ontario were amalgamated into the Essex and Kent Scottish. The militia was to take on a new role—rescue and recovery, or "snakes and ladders," as reservists derisively called it.

While Canada's reserve regiments busied themselves in the early 1950s with practising disaster relief, the army's regular regiments became more involved with United Nations peacekeeping operations. The U.N. had assigned unarmed military personnel from member countries to monitor truces since the late 1940s. But in 1956 Israel, France, and the U.K. attacked Egypt and created a major diplomatic crisis. France and the U.K. acted to seize the Suez Canal Zone, while Israel occupied the Gaza Strip and the Sinai Peninsula. The Russians and the Americans were deeply upset by these military adventures and demanded withdrawal of the occupying forces. Canada's minister of foreign affairs, Lester B. Pearson, engineered a resolution adopted by the General Assembly to establish a U.N.-commanded force to be known as UNEF—the United Nations Emergency Force—to replace the British, French, and Israeli forces as they withdrew. From then on the force was to act as a buffer between Israel and Egypt along the Sinai and Gaza border and at the tip of the Sinai Peninsula. Since Pearson was Canadian and Canada feared an open split between Washington and London, the Queen's Own Rifles were sent to join UNEF. From then until the mid 1990s, almost every peacekeeping operation mounted under U.N. auspices contained a Canadian contingent.

Peacekeeping was something different for the Canadian army. Peacekeepers, as they became known, wore blue U.N. berets or blue-painted helmets. They painted their vehicles and aircraft white, with the letters "UN" emblazoned in black. They were lightly armed for self-defence. And they were ultimately commanded by U.N. headquarters in New York, no matter what their country of origin. Their ultimate purpose was to move into a disputed area after fighting had stopped and the protagonists had requested U.N. troops to fill a buffer zone between them. The idea was that the lightly armed U.N. troops would essentially become a tripwire that neither side would want to cross. The hope was that the presence of peacekeepers would create an opportunity for the parties in the conflict to end the shooting and begin the talking. Some of the peacekeeping missions that Canadian troops undertook included UNOC in the Congo in 1960, UNFICYP in Cyprus in

1964, UNEF from 1957 to 1967, and UNEF II from 1967 to 1973. Ultimately more than 100,000 Canadians served on these "blue-beret" or "blue-helmet" operations, and more than a hundred of them were killed, almost all of them in accidents related to their missions.

—⁂—

THE MASSIVE CUTBACKS in reserve spending and infrastructure in the early 1960s was a portent for the immediate future of the whole Canadian military. In 1964 a Department of National Defence White Paper was issued by the new government of Lester Pearson that laid out the first steps of a process of unification of the army, navy, and air force into a single service to become known as the Canadian Armed Forces. The minister of national defence at the time, Paul Hellyer, strongly believed that a single service would not only eliminate much waste and duplication among the three services but also increase their fighting effectiveness as, for example, in the cooperation of the air force with both the navy and army in sea or land campaigns. Henceforth there would be a single chief of the defence staff (CDS). The army would be known as Mobile Command, with headquarters at St. Hubert, Quebec; the navy would be Maritime Command, with headquarters at Halifax; and the air force would become Air Command, stationed at Winnipeg. All Canadian service personnel would wear the same green uniform, and army ranks would be used in all cases. There was resistance to unification throughout the military, but it was strongest in the navy, where a number of senior officers resigned in protest. Unification was officially enacted on February 1, 1968.

At first it appeared as if the army and the regimental tradition would escape unscathed—the greatest impact seemed to be on the navy and air force. But unification also ushered in a new era of cuts as the governments of both Lester Pearson and Pierre Trudeau shifted spending to social programs and away from defence. The regular military shrank from 121,000 in 1963—already well down from the more than 140,000 in 1958—to 110,000. In a move to create more fran-cophone units to accommodate the new policy of official bilingual-ism, new French-speaking armoured and artillery units were created as part of a French-speaking brigade headquartered at Valcartier. Both of these units were drawn from Quebec-based militia regiments that had fought in the Second World War. The 12ᵉ Régiment blindé du Canada was a new iteration of the Régiment de Trois-Rivières, while the 5ᵉ Régiment d'artillerie légère du Canada continued the 5th Field Artillery Regiment.

To make room for these new units while also accommodating the required cuts in the army budget, the 1st Battalion of the Queen's Own Rifles was re-badged to become the 3rd Battalion of the PPCLI, while the 2nd Battalion of the Queen's Own Rifles was reduced to nil strength, which effectively meant that the QOR was once more a militia regiment. Similar action was taken with the Black Watch; the 1st and 2nd battalions were amalgamated to become the 3rd Battalion of the Royal Canadian Regiment. The 1st Battalion of the Canadian Guards was disbanded entirely, while the 2nd Battalion became the 3rd Battalion of the RCR. The Fort Garry Horse, which had been reactivated as a regular-force armoured regiment in the early 1950s, reverted to the militia. Thus an entire regiment—the Canadian Guards—disappeared.

—⁓—

IN APRIL 1966 Lieutenant-General Jean Victor Allard, commander of the Mobile Command in the soon to be united Canadian Armed Forces, met with Colonel Don Rochester, commander of the army engineer training base at Chilliwack, British Columbia. Rochester was a Second World War veteran, an army engineer, and a dedicated parachutist who loved to skydive. Allard wanted Rochester to command an entirely new and highly mobile formation, consisting of soldiers who would volunteer from existing infantry regiments to serve two years with the new formation, then return to their home units. The new formation—the Canadian Airborne Regiment—would specialize in training for and fighting insurgencies and guerrilla wars such as the one then raging in Vietnam. Allard was convinced that the NATO countries were ignoring the spread of Communist guerrilla insurgencies in Asia, Latin America, and Africa at their peril; he wanted the Canadian army to prepare its soldiers for this type of warfare. His idea was to have the most capable soldiers, both officers and other ranks, rotate through the Airborne, then return to their units to share the training and experiences they had acquired. The Airborne would be larger than a battalion but smaller than a brigade and would be commanded by a full colonel. Its core would be two "commandos"—larger than companies but smaller than battalions—each commanded by a lieutenant-colonel. One would be English-speaking, the other French.

The men of this new regiment would all be qualified jumpers but would also become a highly mobile, fast-moving force with training in environments as diverse as the arctic tundra in winter, the rainforests of Central America, and the hot deserts of the southwestern United States in summer. The Airborne infantry would be accompanied on its missions by engineers, medical personnel, and other combat arms–related soldiers, and absolutely everyone would be a jumper. Their basic mission in war would be to envelop their objective from the air, then hold it until relieved by heavier infantry forces. The Airborne would also train to leap to the defence of Canada in the Far North or anywhere else required. They would build on the legacy of Canada's two wartime jump formations, the 1st Special Service Force and the 1st Canadian Parachute Battalion, and on the postwar Mobile Striking Force, which was intended to be an airborne brigade made up of Canada's original three regular infantry regiments. Allard was insistent that the Airborne not become a permanent regiment— that its composition should be constantly changing—so as not to compete with existing regiments or to build a strong regimental loyalty of its own. It was to spread its élan throughout the Canadian army—in effect it was to be an operational training unit. Rochester accepted the assignment and selected Edmonton, where there was an airfield and a detachment of Air Force Hercules transport aircraft, as the base for the Airborne.

The Canadian Airborne Regiment was formally stood up on April 8, 1968. Despite Allard's hopes, it quickly developed a life of its own, with all the accoutrements and trappings of a regular-force regiment—its own badges, regimental colour, and traditions. Like airborne units around the world—and largely following British tradition—members of the regiment wore the maroon beret, an almost universal symbol of airborne forces, and special jumper wings with a white maple leaf. The Airborne colour was also based on British airborne tradition, with a blue Pegasus, the winged horse, on a maroon background. It wasn't long before regiment members—particularly senior non-commissioned officers—began to stay with the Airborne instead of passing through it. They and other Airborne members took pride in the rugged training the unit undertook and in their constant jump exercises. Paratroopers around the world consider themselves—and are sometimes considered by their comrades-in-arms—as elite soldiers, the best of the best in physical conditioning, mental preparedness, and the act of jumping itself, which is an inherently dangerous business that simply cannot be simulated. Unlike other military training, jumping out of an aircraft is as real as it gets and a challenge to a soldier's courage every time he (or she) steps out the aircraft door and into the slipstream. It wasn't long before service in the Airborne was virtually *de rigueur* for advancement into the higher ranks of the army.

The Airborne was rushed to Quebec in October 1970 during the FLQ crisis, but its first overseas deployment was in Cyprus in 1974. The members of the regiment soon discovered that this was not going to be an ordinary peacekeeping tour, despite their blue U.N. helmets, when Turkish forces invaded the island on July 20. One Airborne officer later recalled watching Turkish army paratroopers descending north of Nicosia, the capital: "It was a beautiful, still, cloudless morning, and watching the sky fill with parachutes was an awesome sight, especially to our Canadian Airborne Regiment members."

For the next five months constant clashes between Greek Cypriot, Turkish, and Turkish Cypriot forces broke out along the ceasefire line that divided the island's two ethnic communities. Two Airborne paratroopers were killed by sniper fire. Paratrooper Ron Irwin later recalled that after the second man died—Trooper Claude Berger, on September 19—"you could hear a pin drop in the mess hall the next day. The attitude was 'the fuckers killed one of ours.' You realize that you can really get killed."

In 1977 the Airborne was transferred from Edmonton to Petawawa; two years later it was reorganized into three infantry commandos with each drawing on one of the three regular-force regiments. But for all the regiment's intensive and challenging training, it was not deployed overseas until it was designated as Canada's contribution to peace-support operations in Somalia in late 1992. By then much of Allard's and Rochester's early vision had been transformed into something else, something not so desirable. The Airborne had increasing disciplinary problems, caused especially by some troopers who wrongly equated "Airborne" with biker gang–style behaviour. The root of the disciplinary problem lay in the ongoing failure of the regiment's later officers to set true soldierly standards of behaviour and to enforce the strict discipline that is often necessary to keep elite troops focused on their role and their mission. The Airborne did a lot of good work in the area of Somalia assigned to it, but a handful of its members crossed the line on a number of occasions, shooting Somali civilians who posed no threat to them and—in the most infamous episode of all—beating to death a Somali teenager whose sole crime was trespassing on the Canadian base, probably to steal something.

The killing of the teenager—Shidane Arone—on the Canadian base near Belet Huen in March 1993 focused public attention on the Airborne and on some of the bizarre behaviour, especially initiation rituals, of its members. The public was shocked by what it saw—racism, brutality, rogue soldiers, failures of leadership both within the Airborne and without. The "Somalia Affair"—the killing and the subsequent bungling, cover-ups, and Keystone Cops behaviour of some of the military's chain of command—cast a pall over the Canadian Forces that lasted for years. Eventually the government established the Commission of Inquiry into the Deployment of Canadian Forces to Somalia to find out what had happened in Somalia and why it happened, and to make recommendations as to how such incidents could be avoided in future.

The commission was disbanded in the fall of 1996 before completing its inquiry, but it still made sweeping recommendations for change in almost every aspect of force selection, training, and deployment, as well as military justice. Most of those recommendations were subsequently put into operation. As for the Airborne, the government ordered it disbanded on March 5, 1995, despite the objections of Canada's Chief of the Defence Staff General John de Chastelain. The Airborne had had a successful deployment to Rwanda but reports of regimental shenanigans had taken a toll. The Airborne colours were laid up at a solemn ceremony at Canadian Forces Base Petawawa. Most of the members of the regiment were returned to their home regiments and incorporated into "jump companies" of the regimental light battalions. For a while those paratroopers were not even allowed to wear their maroon berets because of government fears that the conduct of the defunct unit be recalled by the public. Although the complete disbandment of the Airborne was an extreme measure that was interpreted by many soldiers as a blow to Canadian regimental tradition, much good emerged from the Somalia Affair as the subsequent decade brought a revolution in leadership education and training to the Canadian Forces and prepared Canada's soldiers for a trial no one could have anticipated.

—ɯ—

BY THE EARLY 1990S the word *soldier* in Canada had been replaced by *peacekeeper*. Press reports might proclaim: "a Canadian peacekeeper was wounded in Cyprus today when he stepped on a landmine." No mention of *soldier* would be made. There were two reasons for this unhistorical view of the Canadian military. First, the vast majority of Canadian Forces (CF) personnel were training and preparing for the next war, for when the Cold War turned hot, for when Soviet and NATO forces clashed in Europe. But no one really thought that would happen, so almost no one—except other soldiers, and their families—paid any attention to them. Neither the Canadian press nor Canadians generally were especially excited about the annual fall exercise in Germany or the anti-submarine patrolling by Canadian ships in the North Atlantic. But *peacekeeping* missions were different. They sent Canadian troops to exotic trouble spots such as the Congo, West Irian, or Namibia. Occasionally someone even got hurt there! Second, although most Canadian troops were preparing for war, the men and women who donned the blue berets or helmets of peacekeeping reinforced the image—which Canadian governments have tried to burnish since the mid-1960s—of Canada as a "kinder, gentler" nation that does not make war, unlike the Americans, who resort to war all the time.

In the early 1990s the end of the Cold War brought profound changes to U.N.-style peacekeeping. No longer was there any need to place blue-helmet buffers between clients of "the West" and the "Soviet bloc" in global trouble spots. It became very apparent to the Canadian military—especially the army—that the old and relatively leisurely peacekeeping once done between Arabs and Israelis in the Sinai or Greeks and Turks on Cyprus was a thing of the past. The present was the disintegrating republic of Yugoslavia, which began to come apart in the latter half of 1991. Civil war broke out there almost as soon as the different political components of Yugoslavia began to secede, starting with Slovenia in 1991. There was especially heavy fighting in both Croatia and Bosnia, and Canadian "peacekeepers"—sent there to monitor an early ceasefire in Croatia—found themselves smack in the middle of it, with one battle group (reinforced battalion) in Croatia and another in Bosnia.

Canadian Brigadier-General Lewis MacKenzie commanded U.N. troops in the region of Sarajevo, the capital of Bosnia, in the spring of

1992. The forces under MacKenzie, a former Queen's Own re-badged to the PPCLI, included a Canadian battle group made up primarily of the 1st Battalion of the Van Doos. In early July 1992, after weeks of intensive negotiations, the two armies battling each other for control of Sarajevo—the largely Muslim Bosnian army and the army of the Bosnian Serbs—finally agreed to allow the United Nations to occupy the Sarajevo airport. The airport was the only way to get supplies into the beleaguered capital, and MacKenzie wanted the Canadians there. But the Van Doos, coming by road from Croatia, had to contend with rebellious local commanders who did not want to let them through. After his troops finally arrived, Colonel Michel Jones, then the commander of 1 R22ᵉR, related the story to MacKenzie of how he got by a drunken Serbian commander:

> He wouldn't let us through. . . . So we pulled back about 28 kilometres and waited for the rest of the battalion to catch up to us. This morning I thought we'd give it another try. The same guy was in charge and sober now, but he still wouldn't let us through. He threatened to shoot if we tried to continue. There was the odd bit of sniper fire in the air, so I deployed our TOW system (anti-armour rockets), mortars, and our own snipers and told him that if we were fired at, we would fire back. He cooled down a bit but started to reinforce his position. I told him "if you reinforce with one more person, I'm driving through." Well, he did, so we drove straight through to Sarajevo. All I can say is, it's a good thing he didn't fire at us, because we had a lot of firepower facing in his direction.

—w—

IN SEPTEMBER 1993 a Canadian battle group formed around the 3rd Battalion of the PPCLI, under the command of Lieutenant-Colonel

Jim Calvin, was deployed in the Krajina region of southern Croatia—an area known as the Medak Pocket—with orders to protect the Serb minority in the region when the Croatian army launched a full-scale offensive to take the area over. The local Serb forces fought back, a ceasefire was called, and the Croatians agreed to withdraw. The Patricias were supposed to monitor the ceasefire and the withdrawal. But suddenly the Croatians attacked and the PPCLI returned fire. The Battle of the Medak Pocket, as it was called, lasted barely a day, on September 15, 1993, but it was the first time Canadians had engaged in action with an opposing force since Korea.

As the civil war continued, so did attacks on Canadian soldiers. They were supposed to be peacekeepers, but there was no peace to keep in the former Yugoslavia. On the night of July 15–16, 1994, Sergeant Tom Hoppe of Lord Strathcona's Horse and his troop of M113 armoured personnel carriers with TOW (wire-guided anti-tank) missiles were positioned between Bosnian and Serb forces at Charlie One, a small forward base about 3 kilometres from the main Canadian position, near the town of Visoko. Hoppe was in charge of the M113s parked above the Bosnian trenches. A U.N. flag was flying, illuminated by a spotlight. Corporal Darren Magas had just dismounted from one of the vehicles at about 11:30 PM and had entered a tent to begin his break: "The Serbs opened up machine gun fire just over top of the tents. . . . This was about 150, 200 rounds . . . it was just non-stop. I was in the tent beside another guy trying to slap the old boots on really quick. You are screaming at him and you can't hear what he is saying, that's how loud it was." Phil Ward was outside the tents when the shooting began. He yelled at the men inside to stay down, then dashed around the corner of the position: "I could see a muzzle blast from just behind the tree line, this went on for about five or six minutes but I couldn't get a clear view of the guy so I didn't return fire." Ward then climbed into one of the APCs and got the engine started. With the bullets cracking around him, he waited for someone to get the other two moving.

The machine-gun fire intensified as the Bosnians began to shoot back at the Serb positions. Both sides poured fire into the Strathconas at Charlie One. Trooper Jason Skilliter ran out of his tent, grabbed his machine gun, and sprawled on the ground facing a Bosnian bunker. Then he opened up at the bunker's firing slit. When the shooting from the bunker stopped for a moment, he and Sergeant Hoppe ran to the other two APCs, got them started, then started to move them back out of the line of fire. With Ward's APC as rearguard, Hoppe and Skilliter then led the troop off the hill and out of danger. Hoppe and Skilliter were later decorated for their bravery.

The civil war in the Balkans ended in 1995 with a U.S.-brokered ceasefire enforced by NATO. Canada contributed battle groups to the NATO force, which was first known as IFOR—International Security Assistance Force, then SFOR Stabilization Force—and was responsible for the northwestern corner of Bosnia next to the Croatian border. Every six months for eight years a new Canadian battle group formed around a permanent-force regiment or battalion would take over responsibility for Canadian operations in that region. Because of an acute shortage of infantry due to deep budget cuts in Canada, battle groups were sometime based on the Canadian Armoured Corps and Horse Artillery. Most soldiers rotated to Bosnia at least twice and some went three times as the ceasefire held and Bosnia returned to some sort of normalcy. Many of the soldiers who served in the Balkans, both before and after the ceasefire, were reservists from militia regiments who had volunteered to serve for up to a year, including pre-deployment training, the deployment itself, and the post-deployment decompression period. It has been estimated that up to 40 percent of Colonel Calvin's soldiers at the Medak Pocket were reservists. In 1996 the Special Commission on the Restructuring of the Reserves recommended that army reserve units in Canada be reorganized into brigades and that they be allowed to send formed units—platoons, troops, even companies—on active operation, but to date reservists—who now usually constitute some 20 percent of every deployment—continue their service abroad as individuals augmenting regular-force units.

Canadian army service in the Balkans in the 1990s was a dramatic sign that, for Canada at least, "blue helmet" peacekeeping was rapidly becoming an activity of the past. Few Canadians took notice. When the government decided to redesign the backs of most of Canada's paper currency, the new five-dollar bill depicted both a peacekeeper with binoculars and traditional veterans' symbols such as the cenotaph in Ottawa and poppies. The message was clear: Canadians had fought valiantly in the past, but fighting was not an activity that Canada's army might be called upon to do any time soon. In the aftermath of the Somalia Affair, and with the army shrinking rapidly after deep cuts in the defence budget beginning in 1993, Canada's soldiers seemed to turn inwards, and so did their regiments. The regimental tradition seemed to be wavering, even among the reserves, which appeared aimless and rudderless as the government and the defence establishment dithered about their future. All that ended very suddenly on a clear morning in early September 2001.

Chapter Seventeen

THE LATEST WAR: THE ARMY IN AFGHANISTAN

I remember an RPG fly[ing] right over my head. If I hadn't stepped down
in a ditch, it would have hit me in the face.

     —Lieutenant Jeremy Hiltz, Operation Medusa, September 3, 2006

IT WAS A COOL, BLUSTERY DAY in Edmonton on March 17, 2007, as members of the Princess Patricia's Canadian Light Infantry family gathered in the large indoor convention centre at the Mayfield Inn on the south side of Edmonton. March 17 is a special day for the PPCLI: the birthday of Princess Patricia, which is still celebrated by all the PPCLI battalions as one of the regiment's two most important milestones. The other is August 17—the day in 1914 when Princess Patricia first presented the regimental colour to the PPCLI, at Lansdowne Park in Ottawa. But this Saturday was both special and historic. For only the second time in the history of this storied regiment, a new colonel-in-chief (the PPCLI's term for colonel commandant) was about to be installed—the PPCLI's third and, unlike the previous two, a Canadian—the Right Honourable Adrienne Clarkson, former Governor General of Canada. The Patricias' first two colonels-in-chief—Princess Patricia herself (known after her marriage in February 1919 as Lady Patricia Ramsay) and her successor, Lady Patricia, Countess Mountbatten of Burma, who had been appointed colonel-in-chief on the death of Princess Patricia on June 15,

1974 (she was a cousin and goddaughter of the Princess)—were both members of the Royal Family. The appointment of Adrienne Clarkson was a departure for the PPCLI, for Canada's regular-force regiments, and for the nation. Henceforth the titular head of this regiment would be a distinguished Canadian, and no doubt all of Canada's regular-force regiments will in time follow suit.

The appointment of a colonel-in-chief is reserved for Canada's regular-force regiments. Reserve or militia regiments have honorary colonels, while smaller but still stand-alone formations have honorary lieutenant-colonels. For more than a hundred years regular-force Canadian regiments have sought their colonels-in-chief from the Royal Family—a tangible link between Canadian and British regimental traditions. The colonel-in-chief is "the guardian of Regimental traditions [and] history and promotes the Regiment's identity and ethos." As such, colonels-in-chief travel extensively each year to visit their regiments at home, on exercises and ceremonial occasions, and in the field, sometimes even in battle zones. In the case of the PPCLI, the Regimental Guard—composed of both serving and retired senior · officers of all three regular-force Patricia battalions and the regimental sergeant major—decided in 1997 that should Her Majesty Queen Elizabeth give her permission, a Canadian might be appointed to succeed Lady Mountbatten. When Lady Mountbatten indicated in June 2006 that she wished to retire because she felt "she would soon be unable to perform her duties effectively," former Governor General Clarkson was selected.

Lady Mountbatten and Madame Clarkson both attended the handing-over ceremony on March 17, and the whole afternoon was rich with regimental tradition. All three regular-force PPCLI battalions—the 1st and 3rd, from CFB Edmonton, and the 2nd, from CFB Shilo—as well as the 4th Battalion, which is actually the Loyal Edmonton Regiment (a reserve battalion), were represented by guard contingents. All wore the traditional PPCLI Wolseley-pattern foreign service helmets, or topi, introduced by the British army in the late nineteenth century and used throughout the Boer War. All were resplendent in their scarlet jackets and dark blue red-striped trousers, black boots brilliantly gleaming. After the troops were all in place, the regimental colours were paraded onto the arena floor and the PPCLI band played the regimental marches and the marches of each of the four battalions. A table and chairs were brought out as Lady Mountbatten officially resigned her commission and Madame Clarkson took up hers. Then it was three cheers for Lady Mountbatten before the troops marched off and the ceremony ended. The chain of tradition was intact; a ninety-three-year-old regimental heritage continued. In an age of unspeakable acts of terrorism, attacks on the world's democracies, and Canadian troops serving and being killed on a "thin red line" in far-off Afghanistan, the regimental tradition was alive and well. Or was it?

—⸻—

CANADA AND CANADIANS were directly affected by the 9/11 attacks carried out by al Qaeda against New York City and Washington. Although the attacks were wholly directed at the United States, some two dozen Canadians working in the World Trade Center were killed. The Canadian economy was crippled by the immediate grounding of all civil air traffic over North America and by the virtual closing of the Canada–U.S. border. Canadians were dumbfounded and horror-stricken by the special effects–like images on their TV screens of airliners crashing into the World Trade Center, of dust-covered rescue workers scrambling over the ruins looking for survivors, of relatives trying to cope with the sudden and inexplicable loss of loved ones. Canadians were angry and demanded that Canada play a role in whatever military response the U.S. was about to lead.

The tone for Canada's participation was established by Minister of Foreign Affairs John Manley on September 16, when he declared that Canada would "unambiguously" join U.S. military action to strike back at terrorism. "Canada is at war against terrorism," Manley told reporters, and would stand "shoulder to shoulder" with the U.S., adding that if the Americans needed Canadian military help, "they should simply let us know." When asked if Canada was prepared to put Canadian lives on the line in this campaign, Manley replied: "Let's remember that we have already lost Canadian lives . . . we have Canadian victims of the attack."

The first tangible sign that Canadians would participate in whatever military campaign the U.S. might launch came on September 20, when Minister of National Defence Art Eggleton authorized more than a hundred Canadian Forces personnel then serving on exchange programs with the U.S. military to participate in operations in response to 9/11. But it was not until October 7, almost four weeks after the attacks, that Prime Minister Jean Chrétien finally announced commencement of Operation Apollo—the Canadian military contribution to the war against terror in Afghanistan. Chrétien told the nation that Canada would contribute land, sea, or air forces to the gathering international force led by the United States, which was on that very day starting air attacks against Taliban airfields and radar installations and al Qaeda training camps in Afghanistan. The sea and air contingents were sent almost immediately, as was a group of Canada's highly secret special forces, JTF 2 (JTF stands for Joint Task Force). But regular ground forces were another matter. The Canadian public clamoured to send "boots on the ground," but whose boots? And where to send them? Given the state of the army after eight years of budget cuts, the answers were not simple.

On November 14 Chrétien and defence minister Art Eggleton announced that Canada's Immediate Reaction Force (Land) would deploy to Afghanistan, possibly within forty-eight hours, as the Canadian contribution to an international force. Once again the Patricias would be first in the field—Canada's Immediate Reaction Force in the fall of 2001 was the 3rd Battalion of the PPCLI, based at CFB Edmonton. The 3 PPCLI battle group would be augmented by a rifle company from 2 PPCLI, based in Shilo, Manitoba, as well as a small engineer squadron, a battalion headquarters, a combat support company, and an administration company. They would be accompanied by a squadron of Lord Strathcona's Horse (Royal Canadians) equipped with twelve of Canada's state-of-the-art Coyote armoured reconnaissance vehicles.

The commanding officer of 3 PPCLI in November 2001 was Lieutenant-Colonel Patrick B. Stogran, a twenty-one-year career soldier born in 1958 in La Sarre, Quebec, who had graduated from the Royal Military College with a degree in electrical engineering in 1980. After leaving RMC he was posted to 3 PPCLI, then in Victoria, B.C., where he was a rifle platoon commander, mortar platoon commander, and operations captain in succession. Few of Stogran's soldiers were surprised by the announcement that they were heading for Afghanistan. They were Canada's NATO standby force, and NATO had resolved within days of 9/11 that the attack against the United States was deemed to be an attack against all of NATO. One twenty-four-year-old private from Nova Scotia had told his mother that the 9/11 attack was likely to have some impact on his life, "but we thought we were going to Bosnia or Kosovo to replace the Americans. We weren't expecting this." Dwayne Kohl had been hunting south of Calgary when he heard the news over the radio: "I called my boss and he said to get my butt back to town. . . . I knew in my own mind all along I'd be going, so I was preparing myself and my family. But I don't think it's really sunk in yet." "You never know what to expect," declared Sergeant Robert Vanouwerkirk. "This is different from, say, Rwanda. This time we're going into ground zero, right into the zone."

The Patricias quickly began full-scale training for the mission while the government searched for a suitable role for the troops. The prime minister preferred to commit the Canadians to the newly established U.N. force—the International Security Assistance Force—led by Britain. The ISAF was beginning to occupy the Afghan capital of Kabul, which had fallen within weeks of the start of the campaign when the anti-Taliban Northern Alliance, backed by U.S. and coalition special forces and airpower, surrounded the city. But the British did not want so many Canadian infantry in the ISAF, preferring a much smaller force of Canadians, primarily specialists such as engineers, communications troops, or supply and logistics technicians. New Year's came and went. Then, on January 7, defence minister Eggleton held a press conference along with Chief of the Defence Staff General Ray Henault at National Defence Headquarters in Ottawa. His announcement stunned the nation: "After consulting with our allies and closely examining the military situation on the ground, we have decided to provide a battle group to support the US operation in the Kandahar area. The Canadian land force contingent will deploy to this area and will work with a United States combat team." The 3 PPCLI battle group would be going to Afghanistan after all; eventually the group would total some 880 soldiers.

The new Patricia mission was to replace a battalion of the U.S. 101st Airborne Division and serve under American operational command. The Patricias would help clear the last remnants of Taliban and al Qaeda fighters still holding out in southeastern Afghanistan, secure the Kandahar airport, and pacify the surrounding countryside. For the first time since the end of the conflict in Korea, the Canadian army was going abroad not to keep the peace but to fight a war.

The next few weeks were busy ones. As the soldiers took to the training areas at CFB Wainwright for round-the-clock live-fire training, the Patricias' Rear Party began to prepare programs and facilities to support the families of the deployed soldiers after they had departed Edmonton. This is a normal part of any unit deployment in a Canadian army regiment; when the spouses are away on long-term rotation, the families they leave behind work with the Rear Party to establish support facilities such as drop-in centres and a variety of activities designed to keep the families together and in good spirits. There would be family days, regular updates on the mission, trips, children's activities, movies, potluck dinners, babysitting, and briefings on home security.

At CFB Edmonton's huge warehouses, supply centres, vehicle parks, and mechanical facilities, the immense job of packing a battle group's supplies and equipment went on day and night. Vehicles had to be painted in desert camouflage and made ready for airlift. Thousands of items, from toilet paper to rations to belt buckles to blankets and assault rifle magazines, had to be packed in cargo pallets for loading onto aircraft. Personal gear was inspected and packed. The press made much of the predominantly dark green "CadPat" (Canadian Pattern) camouflage uniforms the men would be wearing in the high desert of Afghanistan, but few of the men dwelt on the issue. They were no doubt thinking far more about the mission confronting them and the long stretch their families would face without their support and presence than they were about the usual small problems that plague any deployment. Besides, Canadian soldiers are old hands at "making do."

On Thursday, January 31, 2002, the first flight of troops bound for Kandahar left Edmonton aboard giant C-5 transports of the United States Air Force. They flew to Frankfurt, where they were transferred to C-17s for the long flight to Afghanistan. The first plane landed early, at 4:30 AM local time in near-freezing weather two days later. One of the first Coyotes unloaded bore the painted words "I love New York" on its back door. Stogran, who had arrived several days earlier, was in his bunk when the first plane landed. He gathered the seventy soldiers from the first two aircraft to remind them that this mission was unlike any they had ever undertaken and to warn them to be very careful. As usual, Stogran minced no words and, as usual, his soldiers appreciated his straightforward attitude. "He's a tough man—aggressive but thoughtful, considerate and deliberate in his decisions," Sergeant Mike Gauley told a reporter. "He's the right man to lead us."

Captain Sean Davis of the 101st Airborne quickly briefed the Patricias on the security rules for their new home: "We are in an area where there are still mines. . . . Your number one concern is your personal security. . . . Everyone is a fighter, [you] are warriors first and cooks second." Soldiers were required to carry personal weapons at all times, even when doing their morning fitness runs around the base. No one went anywhere alone, even to the latrines. The fine dust that blew around constantly made it necessary for everyone to clean their weapons several times a day. And Davis pointed out that terrorists weren't the only threats to their safety. There were pygmy vipers, scorpions, and poisonous spiders too: "Watch out when you even turn over a rock."

On February 11 the Canadian flag was formally raised at the base; more than two-thirds of the Canadians had set up shop. At first the Strathcona Coyotes patrolled the base perimeter within the outer defensive wire, but when the Canadian battle group went operational by mid-month, they began to leave the base to aid in reconnoitering possible approaches to it. The Patricias mostly used American Humvees (also called Hummers) for patrol duty. Mounting heavy machine guns, they were ideal for covering ground in the bleak high-desert country. CBC Radio reporter Mike Smith, a former member of the Canadian Airborne Regiment, arrived at the Canadian base in late March to cover the story. He described the countryside this way: "There is nothing. It is where water goes to die; a plant's concept of hell. Baked-hard mud littered with rocks is the only flora here. Beetles and snakes the only daytime fauna." Every day began and ended the same way, with the mornings "bright and crisp, not a cloud in the sky and the temperature around eight degrees . . . the nights . . . just as spectacular as the mornings—cool breezes under a blanket of stars." When the men were not on patrols or combat missions, the day began early as they arose from their canvas cots for the morning run. There were no huts, just tents, and rations and water that had been run through so many purification procedures it was "stripped of its natural goodness." There was no running water and almost no electricity; outhouses and latrines dotted the base. Each day grew hotter as winter ended, and the fine sand sifted into everything.

The Patricias first went into action in an American-led attack to clear a mountainous and cave-ridden area near Gardez, about 150 kilometres south of Kabul, at the end of February. Operation Anaconda involved coalition forces from six countries alongside some 1,500 local Afghani fighters. In the first part of the operation six Patricia snipers accompanied troops from two separate battalions of the 101st Airborne, who advanced under fire along a series of ridgelines as American B-52s wheeled high over the Shah-e-Kot mountain range, dropping heavy bombs into caves and defiles. At one point early in the advance the PPCLI snipers were almost shot up by a U.S. helicopter, but as the attack progressed they provided lethal fire support for the Americans, helping to extract a number of their men who were trapped by enemy mortar and machine-gun fire. At several points the snipers too came under enemy fire, as one master corporal later told a reporter: "They were bracketing us, walking them in. . . . We'd move and they'd adjust fire. Eventually they ran out of rounds or just gave up. . . . You could hear the fins (of the mortar rounds) rotating as they came in. . . . It's a sound I'll never forget." Whatever misgivings these men may have had as they shot down the enemy while watching their faces in the crossed hairs of their sniper scopes melted away when they thought of why they had come to Afghanistan. As Mike Smith put it, "I asked a few of them how they feel about the killing they did. . . . With every shot taken, they felt that lives were being saved in terms of soldiers fighting on the ground and people around the world who deserve to live without terrorism."

The largest number of Patricias taking part in the campaign to clear the area south of Gardez were involved in Operation Harpoon, under Stogran's command. Five hundred Patricias and a hundred Americans began the attack on Wednesday, March 13, when they were airlifted into a mountainous region by large U.S. Chinook helicopters from an airbase at Bagram, fifty-five minutes away. The troops had been told that between sixty and eighty al Qaeda fighters were holed up in caves, bunkers, and mortar positions on the 3,500-metre Tergul Ghar, a mountain that the soldiers dubbed the Whale's Back. The Whale's Back was 7 by 3 kilometres at the base, rocky, rugged, covered with loose shale, and high. Much of it had been blasted and cratered by American bombs, and unexploded ordnance lay everywhere. The mountain posed almost as much of a physical challenge to men carrying packs of 25 to 45 kilos as did the dangers of al Qaeda guns. The position was formidable; it had stymied American attempts to bypass it or capture it during the first stages of Operation Anaconda.

The troops advanced cautiously, watching every step, guarding against mines or slipping down the steep, shale-covered slopes. On the second day of the operation, the lightly armed Patricia reconnaissance platoon led by Captain Ryan Latinovich discovered an intact al Qaeda gun position that appeared to be manned by enemy fighters. The Patricias guided in a nearby company of more heavily armed American assault troops, then planned an attack with the U.S. commanders. The Americans began by firing antitank missiles into the bunker; everyone then opened up with automatic weapons fire. The position was destroyed and at least two enemy bodies were discovered.

Harpoon lasted four days; the only Canadian casualties were broken bones and sprained ankles—most of the enemy had evacuated their positions. But the attack did destroy more than thirty caves and bunkers along with weapons and ammunition, and turned up valuable intelligence data. Most importantly for the men, they had come prepared to fight and perhaps to pay the ultimate price, and they had come through with pride in a mission well done: As Corporal Ed Morin told a CBC TV reporter, "There's always some fear and apprehension, but it's taken over big time by excitement. I've been training for over 16 years, and this is my first combat mission."

—⚏—

TWO CANADIAN SOLDIERS LAY ON THEIR BACKS on the hard, dusty ground of a designated training area some 15 kilometres south of their base at the Kandahar airport and stared up at the stars early in the morning of April 18, 2002. Corporal Chris Kopp and Corporal Ainsworth Dyer were on a break during a night live-fire exercise with Alpha Company of 3 PPCLI. Live-fire training, day or night, is a necessary part of a soldier's life in a combat zone. Constant training keeps the edge on, especially when live rounds are fired. There is always the danger of a horrible accident, but in a war zone all risks are calculated. On this night the troops were practising mock assaults. They were in a well-known training area and had taken the usual precautions of informing their coalition partners, especially American ground and air forces, where they were going to be, what they were going to be doing, and when they would begin and end the exercise. Flying over them in the dark, in the wrong place and at the wrong time, an American fighter pilot saw the tracer fire and ricochets in the darkness below and reported that he was under enemy fire. No one yet knows exactly what happened next, except that in a ghastly mistake the pilot dropped a laser-guided bomb. Kopp lived; Dyer was killed along with three others. Master Corporal Stan Clark was thrown down a 6-metre hill by the blast. "I saw a big orange flash," he later told reporter Stephen Thorne. "All I recall is it felt like I got slammed in the chest." Company commander Major Sean Hackett no doubt spoke for most of the Patricias when he reflected: "You can't fill the void they left behind. But we should all realize they died doing what they loved to do and they were doing it with the guys they loved. We can honour them best by finishing the job we set out to do." They were honoured instead by the government's announcement on May 21, 2002, that they would pull out of Afghanistan as soon as their initial six-month deployment ended—air, sea, and JTF 2 would remain. In August the Patricias came home, the job of fighting the Taliban in Kandahar Province—the homeland of the jihadi fighters—still incomplete; that would now be a job for Americans, Poles, and others.

But the four Patricias who died on April 18, 2002, were only the first Canadians killed in action in Afghanistan. In February 2003, as the United States was preparing to make war on Saddam Hussein—a campaign that Canada had indicated it would participate in by sending a battalion of some eight hundred soldiers—Prime Minister Jean Chrétien suddenly denounced the Iraq campaign and announced that Canada would play no part in it. Several days later Minister of National Defence John McCallum announced instead that Canada would send a contingent of one thousand soldiers to Kabul in the fall of that year to become the lead nation in the U.N. ISAF mission. Canada did take over the mission in mid-July with 1,800 stationed at Camp Julien, a major base constructed especially for them. The ISAF's multinational brigade was, however, taken over by NATO—though still under U.N. sanction—in August. Three Canadian soldiers were killed in this period, two when their light Jeep was blown to pieces in a land-mine explosion and the third by a suicide bomber.

The government shifted course once again in the spring of 2005, when Minister of National Defence Bill Graham announced on May 17 that Canada's presence in Afghanistan would be shifted to Kandahar Province and particularly Kandahar City, where they would take over from American troops who were needed elsewhere. The new mission would be threefold: Canada would establish a provincial reconstruction team (PRT) in Kandahar to help the local population get back on their feet after years of warfare; a contingent of Canadian soldiers known as the Operational Mentoring and Liaison Team (OMLT) would train members of the Afghan national army; and a battle group would provide security in Kandahar Province as part of an ISAF presence expanding from the Kabul region to all of Afghanistan. In early August 2005, the Canadians in Kabul began to move to Kandahar Airfield, where they were to be based along with other ISAF troops. Once established, the PRT began its work and Canadians began to patrol the countryside and establish forward operating bases (FOBs) at key strategic locations.

Kandahar City was the birthplace of the Taliban movement—the Taliban consider the province to be their home turf and know every cave, dry riverbed, and hiding place. Like classical guerrillas, they hide in broad daylight alongside their Pashtun countrymen. The Pashtun are one of many ethnic groups in Afghanistan—in fact the largest in Afghanistan. They speak Pashto and live by the code of Pashtunwali, which combines Islamic sharia law with Pashtun tribal customs dating back at least a thousand years. They are proud, tough, and resilient and they have a strong aversion to foreigners. The Pashtun who dominate southern and eastern Afghanistan consider themselves part of the larger Pashtun people who live in both Afghanistan and the western and northwestern regions of Pakistan. Not all Pashtun are Taliban—Afghan President Hamid Karzai is himself a Pashtun—but most Taliban are Pashtun. The Taliban campaign in southern Afghanistan is aimed at taking back the city and the province as a preliminary step in retaking control of the country. With its border hard up against Pakistan, Kandahar Province is a major crossing point for arms and Taliban fighters coming in from Pakistan. It is also the centre of the opium culture, which provides the Taliban with large illicit profits that allow them to carry on their war.

Southern Afghanistan is a soldier's nightmare. It is rough, dusty, criss-crossed by dry riverbeds, and dotted with mud-walled villages that have been baked hard by the sun. The poppies grow tall and the marijuana plants grow taller, so tall that they can hide almost anything. Aside from narcotics, the main crop is grapes, grown on low walls at least a metre high and a metre apart that provide easy protection for ambushers. Grape-drying huts add to the dangers. In summer, daytime temperatures hover around 50 degrees Celsius or more. Virtually all the roads are dirt and very easy to mine.

It wasn't long after the Canadians took over responsibility from the Americans that more Canadians began to die there. The very first Canadian to be killed by enemy action was ironically not a soldier but a diplomat, Glyn Berry, who had come to Kandahar to run the Provincial Reconstruction Team; he was killed in a suicide attack on his convoy on January 15, 2006.

The first rotation (or "roto," as the army calls it) into Kandahar was the 1st Battalion of Princess Patricia's Canadian Light Infantry, part of Task Force Orion. Almost as soon as they arrived the Taliban began to ramp up their attacks on the troops. Testing a new rotation is standard procedure for an enemy, and the Taliban wanted to know what this new batch of ISAF forces was made of. In April 2006 the Taliban offensive began. Its aim was to seize the road from Quetta, in Pakistan, to Kandahar and the main highway connecting Kandahar to the rest of the country. On April 1 a Canadian convoy was attacked and two district centres were taken; evidence was mounting that the Taliban were attempting to take control of large swaths of territory near Kandahar City. The Canadians struck back on May 17 with an offensive of their own, aimed at seizing control of the Panjwai District to the west of Kandahar and expunging the Taliban from the area. Captain Nichola Goddard, a forward observation officer from A Battery, 1st Regiment, Royal Canadian Horse Artillery, was killed in the very first day of the attack when her light armoured vehicle (LAV) was hit by a rocket-propelled grenade (RPG). She was the first Canadian female soldier ever to be killed in combat operations. Her death caused shock waves in Canada; although the government and the chief of the defence staff, General Rick Hillier, had warned Canadians that the mission in Kandahar was going to be very dangerous and that casualties should be expected, not many had paid attention. Now, with the fighting in Kandahar raging almost daily in the spring of 2006, people were apparently shocked to realize that Canada was in a war and taking casualties.

It was a strange type of war, as Captain Andrew Charchuk noted in a very long email sent to friends in Canada just after his first baptism by fire, on July 7, 2006. Charchuk was Goddard's replacement. On that particular day he took part in what the Canadians have since called the First Battle of Panjwai, an attack on Taliban entrenched in the small town of Pashmul:

> As we arrived closer to the objective we saw women and children pouring out of the town . . . not a good sign. We pushed on and about 3 kilometres from our intended line of departure to start the operation we were ambushed by Taliban fighters. At around 0030 hrs (12:30 AM), I had my head out of the turret . . . commanding my light armoured vehicle (LAV) with my night vision monocular on. Two rocket propelled grenade (RPG) rounds thundered into the ground about 75 m from my LAV. For about half a second I stared at them and thought "Huh,

so that's what an RPG looks like." The sound of an adversary's 7.62 mm fire cracking all around the convoy snapped me back to reality and I quickly got down in the turret and we immediately began scanning for the enemy. They were on both sides of us adding to the "fog of war." We eventually figured out where all of our friendlies were, and where to begin engaging. . . . We let off bursts from our 25 mm cannon and 7.62 mm machine gun. During the fight I went to jump up on the pintle-mounted machine gun, but as I stuck my head out of the LAV I realized the bad guys were still shooting at us and that the Canadian engineer LAV beside us was firing 25 mm rounds from their cannon right over our front deck. I quickly popped back down realizing that was probably one of the stupider ideas I have had in my life.

That first contact lasted two hours; the fight for Pashmul lasted the rest of the day and began again the next morning. One Canadian soldier was killed on the morning of July 9.

In late July 2006 the Patricia-led Task Force Orion was replaced in Kandahar by Task Force Kandahar, built around the 1st Battalion of the Royal Canadian Regiment. It wasn't long before the Taliban began to test the RCR's mettle—nine members of the battle group had been killed by the end of August. Canadian General David Fraser, commander of the ISAF forces in the region, decided to launch a major attack on the Taliban. The assault was dubbed Operation Medusa; it involved soldiers from four NATO countries—Canada, the United States, Denmark, and Holland—and it eventually proved to be the largest NATO battle in history up to that point. The objective was to root out the Taliban who had settled into an area north of the Arghandab River. The river itself was dry but the riverbed was several hundred metres across. On its north side lay marijuana fields bordered by hard earthen berms, mud huts, walled compounds, and an abandoned white schoolhouse that had been turned into a fortified position by the Taliban. It had been the scene of fighting several times before in previous months. On the morning of September 3, 2006, the RCR LAVs joined the artillery in shooting up the fields and compounds north of the river to give cover fire for the infantry assault. Lieutenant Jeremy Hiltz, commander of 8 Platoon, Charles Company, 1 RCR, later remembered: "You could see it, a lot of the younger guys, they were apprehensive and it was something completely new to them. . . . They knew that once they were done shooting . . . then the next step would be to go across."

Charlie Company's three platoons—7, 8, and 9—descended to the riverbed while chain-gun and artillery shells flew over their heads. The Taliban did not return fire. By 9:00 AM all three platoons and their LAVs were across the riverbed and into the marijuana fields. The lush, thick plants obscured their vision. Company commander Major Matthew Sprague later recalled, "you couldn't see more than two feet in front of you . . . it was very bizarre." As 7 Platoon approached within 50 metres of the white schoolhouse, a Taliban flare shot into the sky, and then "it was complete chaos all the way around," Hiltz remembers. The Taliban launched a coordinated attack from ahead of the Canadians and from both flanks using RPGs, recoilless rifles, machine guns, and Kalashnikov assault rifles. A Canadian G-Wagon (Jeep-type vehicle) was hit immediately and 7 Platoon Warrant Officer Rick Nolan, thirty-nine, from Mount Pearl, Newfoundland, was killed. Then an LAV was hit, killing Sergeant Shane Stachnik of Waskatenau, Alberta. Sprague recalls both hits: "it's not like you see in a movie, where a rocket hits a vehicle and it explodes in a giant ball of flame. There's a puff of smoke and the vehicle stops."

When the Taliban started firing, Hiltz grabbed his radio, jumped down from his LAV, and ran up the line of marijuana plants trying to organize his platoon. "I remember an RPG fly[ing] right over my head" he recalls. "If I hadn't stepped down in a ditch, it would have hit me in the face. It singed the top of my helmet. That was kind of a slow-motion thing I remember." Because Hiltz was carrying a radio, it was obvious he was a commander of sorts, and the Taliban tried hard to kill him. He would later tell a reporter: "Back in Canada, we do it with blanks. With this, if you make a mistake, you don't just get failed, you get killed. There's nothing I can do about that. It's luck, fate, God, whatever you want to call it." Sprague called in air cover to hit the Taliban, but it was too late for Warrant Officer Frank Mellish, thirty-eight, of Truro, Nova Scotia, and Private Will Cushley, twenty-one, of Port Lambton, Ontario, who were killed by a Taliban round as they tended to the wounded at the casualty collection point near the riverbed. Finally Sprague ordered a withdrawal across the river; by 3:00 PM Charles Company was back where it had started. Early the next morning Charles Company was hit again—this time by an American A-10 attack aircraft, which mistook a trash fire in the company locale for the Taliban in the white schoolhouse and made a strafing run. One Canadian—Private Mark Anthony Graham—was killed and thirty-four were wounded, thirteen so seriously that they had to be returned to Canada. Operation Medusa officially ended two weeks after it started, on September 17, 2006. The next day four Canadians were killed by a suicide bomber as they conducted a security patrol. Three more had been killed by the time the 1 RCR Battle Group left Afghanistan in February 2007.

—∞—

THE WAR IN AFGHANISTAN CONTINUES. As of this writing two Canadian battle groups have rotated through Kandahar since February 2007, and two more are scheduled to go before February 2009. But the odds are that Canadian soldiers will be in Afghanistan for at least another two years after that, if not longer. To anyone in Canada on September 10, 2001, the notion that Canadians would be fighting and dying in Afghanistan in 2008 would have seemed a form of madness. And yet, as General Dwight D. Eisenhower declared in *Crusade in Europe,* his memoir of the Second World War, war always comes as a shocking surprise to democracies. Canadians especially seem to have little appreciation of their country's interests and how intricately the fate of Canada is now tied to so many faraway places in this globalized world. Some Canadians object vehemently to the very idea that Canada would actually fight a war in some faraway land when not a square metre of Canadian soil appears to be threatened. Other Canadians have become resigned to the reality that the post–Cold War world is in its own way as dangerous as the Cold War ever was. No one can tell where our fighting regiments will be deployed in future, but given the history of Canada and war over the past three centuries, it would be a foolish prophecy indeed for anyone to predict that Afghanistan will be the last war for Canada.

The war in Afghanistan has had a strange impact on the Canadian regimental tradition. On the one hand, wars provide the very soil out of which regimental traditions grow. It is battle honours that most tellingly mark the twists and turns of regimental history and that weigh so heavily in regimental tradition. In battle, soldiers bond as they never could in peacetime. And whether or not a particular regimental tradition affords them greater opportunity to seek succour from their fellow soldiers, it is the regiment that brings them to battle and that will accompany them from the battlefield—and, in some cases, through the rest of their lives. Many former soldiers will declare, "Once a Patricia, always a Patricia," or "Once a Strathcona, always a Strathcona." And that is true enough. But although battle may well provide the glue that keeps a regiment alive, the strain of war often forces regiments to put inculcation of regimental tradition aside as they scramble to put soldiers in the field. The war in Afghanistan caught the Canadian army—and the rest of the Canadian Forces—by surprise. After the deep budget cuts of the early 1990s, the army was only just beginning to struggle back when the twin towers and the Pentagon were attacked on September 11, 2001. There simply weren't sufficient soldiers or enough up-to-date equipment to fight a war in such a faraway place.

The army was better prepared when it went back to Kabul in the late summer of 2003, but the entire defence establishment continued to strain because both Liberal and Conservative governments were seeking to fight a war, modernize the military, expand the Canadian Forces, and ready the CF for other possible assignments at home and abroad—all at the same time. As a result, Canada's regular-force regiments were forced to cut back on teaching regimental heritage, trips to regimental museums, days to study regimental history, and mess dinners and other important regimental celebrations. They were forced instead to look to the next six to twelve months, when they would have to contribute a battalion, or a company, or a headquarters, or some other necessary element, to a battle group bound for Afghanistan. At the same time, ironically, the regimental tradition thrived in Canada's reserve or militia regiments, who challenged themselves to send their best members to serve with the battle groups. Perhaps it has always been that way—the regimental tradition may thrive on war, but war itself causes Regular Force regiments to deal with the nuts and bolts of force generation while the militia upholds regimental tradition. That was certainly the case in both world wars that Canada fought in the twentieth century. But even so, the regimental tradition is now so deeply ingrained in the very soul of the Canadian army that its demise will come only when men and women truly "beat their swords into plowshares."

Conclusion

REGIMENTS FOREVER

AN UNBROKEN LINE OF TRADITION stretching back five hundred years connects Lieutenant Jeremy Hiltz (as of this writing, Captain Hiltz) and his comrades-in-arms in Afghanistan to the aboriginal warriors of the Huron or Iroquois in the St. Lawrence lowlands of the fifteenth century. They are, and were, fighting men who pledged their lives in the service of the people they were defending. The Iroquois warrior might not have put it quite the same way, but he, like Jeremy Hiltz, entered into an agreement with the society he defended to offer it his "unlimited liability" in return for society's succour and protection in times of peace. The unlimited liability of a warrior, then and now, is the liability of offering up his (or her) life, if necessary, to complete the mission. No one else in society bears such a heavy responsibility, not even police or firefighters. Warriors do what no one else in society does: they offer up their lives and go into harm's way—deliberately, at great risk—in the middle of the chaos of battle, and they undertake to kill other people—their enemies—at the behest of the political authorities who sent them.

This is true even of the small number of women who have entered combat roles in the Canadian army since the mid-1990s. A decision by the Canadian Human Rights Tribunal in 1989 obligated the Canadian Forces to lift all quotas on the employment of women except aboard submarines. Thus women who can meet the physical requirements of naval service, pilot training, or service in the land forces are allowed every opportunity to advance. Today more than 15 percent of the regular and reserve land forces are women, but the great majority serve in support units such as service battalions. A small number have found their way into combat units. One, Captain Nichola Goddard, twenty-six, was killed in action on May 17, 2006, while acting as a forward observation officer with Task Force Orion in Kandahar Province in southern Afghanistan. For the most part these unique individuals appear to have been fully accepted into the once completely male world of combat, in effect being treated as "one of the boys." But there are very few, and it remains to be seen what impact large numbers of women combat soldiers might have on regimental cohesion, should that ever become a reality.

War and killing sets these people apart. And because they are apart, they cling to rituals, lore, history, traditions, and religious or quasi-religious practices that are unique to them. Anthropologists today study the military just as they study other distinct cultures. The military culture is unique and it likely always has been, far into the distant past. Although the aboriginal warriors of Champlain's day, and even before, did not strictly speaking form regiments to steady and to nurture them as they approached the horror and chaos of combat, they did nonetheless have special rituals and symbols that set them apart in wartime, and sometimes even in peacetime.

The French regiments that came to New France in the seventeenth and eighteenth centuries were formed bodies of regular troops that had already started to develop distinctions among themselves based on their places of origin, their sponsors, their founders and commanders, or their specific battle tasks. They followed traditions designed to create and sustain cohesion in the ranks that were established at least as far back as the Roman legions. Put a group of fighters together, give them a special standard and distinctive accoutrements, tell them the history of their legion or regiment with both its glorious victories and its tragic last stands, and then challenge them to live up to their heritage. That may not be enough to prevail without inspiring leadership, good weapons, brilliant tactics, and a good bit of fortune with the weather, the quality of the enemy commander, the nature of the ground, and so on, but it will certainly help in a pinch. It has been well known for millennia that solidarity among fighters enhances their courage. When they are sharing their fate with hundreds, if not thousands, of others, there comes a comfort from that very act of sharing, as well as a desire not to shame oneself in front of one's closest comrades. In French, British, and now Canadian army tradition the regiment was the vehicle that allowed them to seek solace before battle, sustain them during it, and care for them afterward.

The British knew that and built it into their reformed army in the early seventeenth century, when the regimental system was adopted and standardized. When they conquered Canada in the 1760s, they brought the British regimental system with them. Not only were the imperial troops that fought the Americans in the War of Independence and the War of 1812–14 organized into regiments, so too were the colonial militia who fought beside them. In the War of 1812 can be seen the false dawn of a Canadian army. The fencible regiments raised from the men of the colony—who fought wherever they were sent in British North America alongside the British line regiments in defence of the imperial link—might have become the heart of a colonial army but were disbanded after the war, possibly because Britain's rulers were uncomfortable with the notion that colonial governments might nurture standing armies of their own. The War of 1812 was immeasurably important in stabilizing the regimental tradition in Canada.

The regimental system that exists in Canada today has its roots in the regiments established immediately prior to Confederation and immediately afterward. These were all militia regiments, but they formed the structure within which the regular regiments—the Royal Canadian Regiment, the Royal Canadian Dragoons, and the Royal Canadian Horse Artillery—emerged by the dawn of the twentieth century. The regimental tradition survived Sam Hughes's creation of numbered battalions in the First World War and formed the basis of mobilization of the Canadian army in the Second World War. It survived Korea, NATO duty, peacekeeping, and the Airborne debacle.

Never once did the Canadian army waver in its belief that the regimental system lies at its very heart. When the army published its basic field manual in 1998—*Canada's Army: We Stand on Guard for Thee*—it said this of the regimental system: "Institutionally, Canada's army is organized on a corps/branch and regimental basis commonly known as the regimental system. This is a time-proven method of military organization whose antecedents date back to the Roman legions and even earlier. The regimental system is of critical importance to the army as it is within the regiment or branch that the military ethos is most visibly embodied and practised."

And yet, the war in Afghanistan may well do what nothing else could—not the disbandment of the Airborne in the 1990s, not unification in the 1960s, not even the numbered battalions of Sam Hughes—erode the regimental system. The Canadian army was not prepared for combat in Afghanistan in the spring of 2002. When 3 PPCLI went to Kandahar as part of the U.S.-led coalition forces to hunt down al Qaeda and expel the Taliban, the soldiers were certainly well trained and well led, but 3 PPCLI was too small to sustain itself because the entire army had shrunk noticeably since 1993. To ensure that the full complement of a battle group was sent to Kandahar, the army was forced to augment 3 PPCLI with a rifle company from 2 PPCLI. That was not a radical augmentation, but it set the pattern for all the battle groups that have gone to Afghanistan thus far—they are all a mix-and-match from different regiments. It is now standard practice to mix two or more regiments together in one battle group. This is dictated largely by the strain the war is putting on Canada's very small army of fewer than twenty-five thousand men and women, in all ranks and all professions. As Lieutenant-Colonel (retired) David Pentney wrote in a recent article in *Canadian Army Journal,* the new system amounts to an "institutional undermining of cohesion and the regimental system." When combined with the weakening of the process of regimental indoctrination in regular-force regiments today—a weakening that is also rooted in the strain of the war—regimental cohesion is suffering.

It is hard to tell how badly it is suffering. Nor is it easy to predict whether or not Canada's eventual withdrawal from Afghanistan will allow the regimental tradition to revive to its former strength in the regular force. But chances are that it will. After all, men and women who go to war need to believe in something greater than themselves, even more than most human beings. Grizzled veterans will declare—and rightly so—that when the hot metal is flying, soldiers fight for their immediate comrades-in-arms—their section or their platoon. Their regimental identities may even be lost for a while as Taliban bullets whiz over their heads. But a section or a platoon does not have a history or a tradition, and the cohesion it inculcates can quickly disappear after its members move on in their military careers or back to civilian life. In most of those soldiers, however, the regimental spirit will soon after be reborn—if it ever really left them—and they will dwell within it for the rest of their lives. That has been the case in every war Canada has fought and it is unlikely to ever change. So it will be with the Canadian army. Born of the regimental tradition and built on the regimental system, it may have to forgo regimental purity for a while—or until the government channels sufficient resources to the military to allow the system to thrive in wartime—but most soldiers know it will revive eventually. There is too much blood invested in the Canadian regimental tradition for the Canadian army to ever allow it to die. Canada's fighting regiments will continue to fight as long as there is a Canada.

Acknowledgements

I AM GRATEFUL to Jim Gifford, senior editor, non-fiction, at HarperCollins for suggesting this subject to me and for having the patience to see it through a long gestation period. My agent, Linda McKnight, offered me both a firm hand and the TLC that she is so well known for. Thank you to Nancy Pearson Mackie for indexing the book. Thanks to Adam Lajeunesse for gathering pictures, regimental crests, and the list of regiments covered in this volume. Thanks also to Jack Granatstein for his comments and criticisms on the manuscript. I am especially grateful to Russ Benneweis, erstwhile grain farmer and now well on his way to a PhD in history for all his research help, for his conceptual ideas, and for helping me to select the regiments and the key events in the history of those regiments that form the core of this book. Russ also compiled the bibliography. I look forward to working with him as a co-author in the near future.

Appendix A

ACTIVE REGIMENTS

Note: R denotes a reserve regiment. RCA denotes Royal Canadian Artillery. RCAC denotes Royal Canadian Armoured Corps. All others are regular-force regiments.

Canadian Land Forces Northern Area
Canadian Rangers (Yellowknife)

Canadian Land Forces Atlantic Area
1st Field Artillery Regiment, RCA (Halifax–Dartmouth, NS) R
3rd Field Artillery Regiment, RCA (St. John's, NL) R
1 Nova Scotia Highlanders (Truro, NS) R
2 Nova Scotia Highlanders (Sydney, NS) R
Prince Edward Island Regiment (RCAC) (Charlottetown, PE) R
Princess Louise Fusiliers (Halifax, NS)
R 2 Royal Canadian Regiment (Oromocto, NS)
1 Royal New Brunswick Regiment (Fredericton, NB) R
2 Royal New Brunswick Regiment (Bathurst, NB) R
1 Royal Newfoundland Regiment (St. John's, NL) R
2 Royal Newfoundland Regiment (Corner Brook, NL) R
West Nova Scotia Regiment (Aldershot, NS) R

Canadian Land Forces Central Area (Ontario)
1st Air Defence Regiment (Pembroke) R
Algonquin Regiment (North Bay) R

Argyll and Sutherland Highlanders of Canada (Princess Louise's) (Hamilton) R

Brockville Rifles (Brockville) R

Cameron Highlanders of Ottawa (Ottawa) R

3 Canadian Rangers Patrol Group (Borden) R

2 Combat Engineer Regiment (Petawawa)

31 Combat Engineer Regiment (The Elgins) (St. Thomas) R

32 Combat Engineer Regiment (Toronto) R

33 Combat Engineer Regiment (Ottawa) R

Essex and Kent Scottish (Windsor) R

11th Field Artillery Regiment (Guelph) R

30th Field Artillery Regiment (Ottawa) R

49th Field Artillery Regiment, RCA (Sault Ste. Marie) R

56th Field Artillery Regiment, RCA (Brantford) R

Governor General's Foot Guards (Ottawa) R

Governor General's Horse Guards (Toronto) R

Grey and Simcoe Foresters (Owen Sound) R

Hastings and Prince Edward Regiment (Belleville) R

48th Highlanders of Canada (Toronto) R

1st Canadian Hussars (London) R

C Squadron, 1st Hussars (Sarnia) R

2 Irish Regiment of Canada (Sudbury) R

Lake Superior Scottish Regiment (Thunder Bay) R

Lincoln and Welland Regiment (St. Catharines) R

Lorne Scots (Peel, Dufferin and Halton Regiment) (Brampton) R

Ontario Regiment (RCAC) (Oshawa) R

Princess of Wales's Own Regiment (Kingston)

Queen's Own Rifles of Canada (Toronto) R

Queen's York Rangers (1st American Regiment) (RCAC) (Toronto) R

Royal Canadian Dragoons (Petawawa)

2 Royal Canadian Horse Artillery (Petawawa)

1 Royal Canadian Regiment (Petawawa)

3 Royal Canadian Regiment (Petawawa)

4 Royal Canadian Regiment (London) R

Royal Hamilton Light Infantry (Wentworth Regiment) (Hamilton) R

Royal Highland Fusiliers of Canada (Cambridge) R

Royal Regiment of Canada (Toronto) R

Stormont, Dundas and Glengarry Highlanders (Cornwall) R

7th Toronto Regiment, RCA (Toronto) R

Toronto Scottish Regiment (Toronto) R

Windsor Regiment (RCAC) (Windsor) R

Canadian Land Forces Quebec Area

Black Watch (Royal Highland Regiment) of Canada (Montreal) R

Canadian Grenadier Guards (Montreal) R

2 Canadian Rangers Patrol Group (Richelain) R

5 Combat Engineer Regiment (Courcelette)

34 Combat Engineer Regiment (Montreal) R

35 Combat Engineer Regiment (Quebec City) R

6th Field Artillery Regiment (Lévis) R

2nd Field Regiment, RCA (Montreal) R

62nd Field Regiment, RCA (Shawinigan) R

Fusiliers Mont-Royal (Montreal) R

Fusiliers du Saint-Laurent (Rimouski) R

Fusiliers de Sherbrooke (Sherbrooke) R

5ᵉ Régiment d'artillerie légère du Canada (Courcelette)

12ᵉ Régiment blindé du Canada (Courcelette)

Régiment de Hull (Gatineau) R

Régiment de la Chaudière (Lévis) R

Régiment de Maisonneuve (Montreal) R

Régiment du Saguenay (Chicoutimi) R

Royal Canadian Hussars (Montreal) R

Royal Montreal Regiment (Montreal) R

Royal 22ᵉ Régiment (Courcelette)

2 Royal 22ᵉ Régiment (Quebec City)

3 Royal 22ᵉ Régiment (Courcelette)

4 Royal 22ᵉ Régiment (Montreal) R

6 Royal 22ᵉ Régiment (Saint-Hyacinthe) R

Sherbrooke Hussars (Sherbrooke) R

Voltigeurs de Québec (Quebec City) R

Canadian Land Forces Western Area

18th Air Defence Regiment, RCA (Lethbridge, AB) R

British Columbia Dragoons (Kelowna, BC) R

British Columbia Regiment (Duke of Connaught's Own) (Vancouver, BC) R

Calgary Highlanders (Calgary, AB) R

4 Canadian Rangers Patrol Group (Victoria, BC) R

Canadian Scottish Regiment (Princess Mary's) (Victoria, BC) R

1 Combat Engineer Regiment (Edmonton, AB)

39 Combat Engineer Regiment (Vancouver, BC) R

41 Combat Engineer Regiment (Edmonton, AB) R

5th (British Columbia) Field Regiment, RCA (Victoria, BC) R

10th Field Artillery Regiment, RCA (Regina, SK) R

15th Field Artillery Regiment, RCA (Vancouver, BC) R

20th Field Artillery Regiment, RCA (Edmonton, AB) R

78th Battery, 20th Field Artillery Regiment, RCA (Red Deer, AB) R

26th Field Artillery Regiment, RCA (Brandon, MB) R

Fort Garry Horse (Winnipeg, MB) R

King's Own Calgary Regiment (Calgary, AB) R

Lord Strathcona's Horse (Royal Canadians) (Edmonton, AB)

Loyal Edmonton Regiment (4 Princess Patricia's Canadian Light Infantry)
    (Edmonton, AB) R

North Saskatchewan Regiment (Saskatoon, SK) R

B Company, North Saskatchewan Regiment (Prince Albert, SK) R

Princess Patricia's Canadian Light Infantry (Edmonton, AB)

2 Princess Patricia's Canadian Light Infantry (Shilo, MB)

3 Princess Patricia's Canadian Light Infantry (Edmonton, AB)

Queen's Own Cameron Highlanders of Canada (Winnipeg, MB) R

Rocky Mountain Rangers (Kamloops, BC) R

1st Regiment, Royal Canadian Horse Artillery (Shilo, MB)

Royal Regina Rifles (Regina, SK) R

Royal Westminster Regiment (New Westminster, BC) R

Royal Winnipeg Rifles (Winnipeg, MB) R

Saskatchewan Dragoons (Moose Jaw, SK) R

Seaforth Highlanders of Canada (Vancouver, BC) R

South Alberta Light Horse (RCAC) (Medicine Hat, AB) R

B Squadron, South Alberta Light Horse (RCAC) (Edmonton, AB) R

Appendix B

HISTORICAL REGIMENTS

Multi-region
Canadian Airborne Regiment
Canadian Guards
1st Special Service Force
Joint Task Force 2
Oxford Rifles
Prince of Wales's Leinster Regiment (Royal Canadians)
Royal Canadian Regiment

Arctic
Canadian Rangers
Dawson Rifles
Yukon Regiment

Maritimes
Annapolis Regiment
Cape Breton Highlanders
Carleton Light Infantry
Carleton and York Regiment
Colchester and Hants Regiment
Cumberland Highlanders
Halifax Rifles
King's New Brunswick Regiment
Lunenburg Regiment

New Brunswick Dragoons
New Brunswick Fencibles
New Brunswick Rangers
New Brunswick Regiment (Tank)
New Brunswick Regiment of Yeomanry Cavalry
New Brunswick Scottish
Newfoundland Militia
North Nova Scotia Highlanders
North Shore (New Brunswick) Regiment
Pictou Highlanders
Prince Edward Island Fencibles
Prince Edward Island Highlanders
Prince Edward Island Light Horse
Prince Edward Island Regiment
Prince Edward Volunteers
Princess Louise Fusiliers
Queen's County Regiment
Queen's County Provisional Battalion of Infantry
Royal New Brunswick Regiment
Royal Newfoundland Companies
Royal Newfoundland Fencibles
Royal Newfoundland Regiment
Royal Nova Scotia Regiment
Saint John Fusiliers
West Nova Scotia Regiment

Quebec
Black Watch (Royal Highland Regiment) of Canada
Canadian Grenadier Guards
Canadian Regiment of Fencible Infantry
Canadian Voltigeurs
Carabiniers Mont-Royal
Chasseurs Canadiens
Civil Service Rifle Regiment

Dorchester Provincial Light Dragoons

Eastern Townships Mounted Rifles

Frontenac Regiment

Fusiliers de Sherbrooke

Fusiliers du Saint-Laurent

Fusiliers Mont-Royal

Infantry School Corps

Irish Canadian Rangers

Lower Canada Sedentary Militia

Lower Canada Select Embodied Militia

Queen's Own Canadian Hussars

Quebec Volunteers

Régiment de Beauce

Régiment de Chateauguay

Régiment de Gaspé Bonaventure

Régiment de Hull (RCAC)

Régiment de Joliette

Régiment de la Chaudière

Régiment de Lévis

Régiment de Maisonneuve

Régiment de Montmagny

Régiment de Québec

Régiment de Sainte-Hyacinthe

Régiment de Trois-Rivières

Régiment du Saguenay

Royal 22ᵉ Régiment

Royal Canadian Artillery

Royal Canadian Hussars

Royal Guides

Royal Montreal Regiment

Sherbrooke Fusiliers Regiment

Sherbrooke Hussars

Sherbrooke Regiment

Temiscouata Provisional Battalion

Victoria Rifles of Canada
Voltigeurs de Québec Volunteer Militia Cavalry
1st Battalion Volunteer Militia Rifles of Canada

Ontario

Algonquin Regiment
Argyll and Sutherland Highlanders of Canada (Princess Louise's)
Argyll Light Infantry
Brockville Rifles
Cameron Highlanders of Ottawa
Canadian Fusiliers (City of London Regiment)
Canadian Mounted Rifles
Cavalry School Corps
Dufferin Rifles of Canada (Haldimand Rifles)
Dundas, Stormont and Glengarry Highlanders
Earl Grey's Own Rifles
Elgin Regiment
Essex and Kent Scottish Regiment
Essex Fusiliers
Essex Regiment
Essex Scottish Regiment
Glengarry Light Infantry Fencibles
Governor General's Bodyguard
Governor General's Foot Guards
Governor General's Horse Guards
Grenville Regiment
Grey and Simcoe Foresters
Grey Regiment
Halton Rifles
Hastings and Prince Edward Regiment
Highland Fusiliers of Canada
Highland Light Infantry of Canada
Huron Regiment
Incorporated Militia of Upper Canada

Irish Regiment of Canada
Kenora Light Infantry
Kent Regiment
Lake Superior Scottish Regiment
Lambton Regiment
Lanark and Renfrew Scottish Regiment
Lincoln and Welland Regiment
Lincoln Militia
Lincoln Regiment
London and Oxford Fusiliers
Lorne Rifles
Lorne Scots (Peel, Dufferin and Halton Regiment)
Loyal Essex Volunteers
Loyal Kent Volunteers
Loyal London Volunteers
Michigan Fencibles
Middlesex and Huron Regiment
Middlesex Light Infantry
Midland Provisional Battalion
Midland Regiment (Northumberland and Durham)
Mississauga Horse
Mississippi Volunteers
Niagara Light Dragoons
Nassau Militia
Norfolk Regiment of Canada
North Waterloo Regiment
Ottawa Highlanders
Ontario Mounted Rifles
Ontario Regiment
Perth and Waterloo Regiment (Highland Light Infantry of Canada)
Perth Regiment
Peterborough Rangers
Prince County Regiment
Prince County Provisional Battalion of Infantry

Prince of Wales Rangers (Peterborough Regiment)

Princess of Wales's Own Regiment

Queen's Own Rifles

Queen's Own Cameron Highlanders of Canada

Queen's Rangers

Queen's York Rangers (1st American Regiment)

Royal Canadian Dragoons

Royal Grenadiers

Royal Hamilton Light Infantry

Royal Highland Fusiliers of Canada

Royal Regiment of Canada

Sault Ste. Marie and Sudbury Regiment

Sault Ste. Marie Regiment

Scots Fusiliers of Canada

Stormont, Dundas and Glengarry Highlanders

Toronto Regiment

Toronto Scottish Regiment

Volunteer Militia Cavalry

Welland Militia

Wentworth Regiment (Royal Hamilton Light Infantry)

West Toronto Regiment

Windsor Regiment

York Rangers

York Regiment

Yorkton Regiment

Prairie Region

Alberta Mounted Rifles

Alberta Regiment

Assiniboia Regiment

Battleford Light Infantry

Border Horse

Calgary Highlanders

Calgary Regiment

Edmonton Fusiliers

Edmonton Regiment

Fort Garry Horse

King's Own Calgary Regiment (RCAC)

Manitoba Dragoons

Manitoba Horse

Manitoba Mounted Rifles

Manitoba Rangers

Manitoba Regiment

Prince Albert and Battleford Volunteers

Prince Albert Volunteers

Lord Strathcona's Horse (Royal Canadians)

Loyal Edmonton Regiment (4th Battalion, PPCLI)

North Alberta Regiment

North Saskatchewan Regiment

Princess Patricia's Canadian Light Infantry

Regina Rifle Regiment

Royal Canadian Horse Artillery

Royal Regina Rifles

Royal Rifles of Canada

Royal Winnipeg Rifles

Saskatchewan Border Regiment

Saskatchewan Dragoons

Saskatchewan Mounted Rifles

Saskatoon Light Infantry

South Alberta Horse

South Alberta Light Horse

South Alberta Regiment

South Saskatchewan Regiment

Weyburn Regiment

Winnipeg Grenadiers

Winnipeg Light Infantry

British Columbia

British Columbia Dragoons

British Columbia Hussars

British Columbia Regiment (Duke of Connaught's Own) (RCAC)

Canadian Scottish Regiment (Princess Mary's)

Irish Fusiliers of Canada

Kootenay Regiment

Kootenay Rifles

New Westminster Volunteer Rifles

North British Columbia Regiment

Pacific Coast Militia Rangers

Prince Rupert Regiment

Seaforth Highlanders of Canada

Vancouver Island Rifle Volunteers

Vancouver Regiment

Victoria and Halliburton Regiment

Victoria Provisional Battalion of Infantry Argyll Highlanders

Victoria Rifles of Canada

Westminster Regiment

Chapter Sources

Introduction: Battle Honours and Mess Dinners

Anthony Beevor, *Inside the British Army* (London: Corgi Books, 1991).

D.J. Bercuson, *Significant Incident: Canada's Army, the Airborne, and the Murder in Somalia* (Toronto: McClelland & Stewart, 1996).

Gordon Brown and Terry Copp, *Look to Your Front . . . Regina Rifles, A Regiment at War: 1944–45* (Waterloo, ON: Laurier Centre, 2001).

Department of National Defence, *Duty with Honour: The Profession of Arms in Canada* (Ottawa: DND, 2003).

John Hackett, *The Profession of Arms* (London: Sidgwick and Jackson, 1983).

Stewart A.G. Mien, *Up the Johns!: The Story of the Royal Regina Rifles* (North Battleford, SK: Royal Regina Rifles, 1992).

Michael M. O'Leary, "The Regimental System," www.regimentalrogue.com.

E.C. Russell, *Customs and Traditions of the Canadian Armed Forces* (Ottawa: Deneau & Greenberg, 1980).

C.P. Stacey, *Official History of the Canadian Army in the Second World War,* vol. 3, *The Victory Campaign* (Ottawa: DND, 1960).

Mark Zuehlke, *Juno Beach: Canada's D-Day Victory, June 6, 1944* (Vancouver: Douglas & McIntyre, 2004).

Chapter 1: First Regiments: The French in Early Canada

Jay Cassel, "The Troupes de la Marine in Canada, 1683–1760: Men and Materiel" (PhD diss., University of Toronto, 1987).

Alfred A. Cave, *The French and Indian War* (Westport, CT: Greenwood Press, 2004).

René Chartrand, *Canadian Military Heritage,* vol. 1, *1000–1754* (Montreal: Art Global, 1993).

John P. DuLong, "Carignan-Salières Regiment Lineage Chart," http://habitant. org/carignan.htm.

Donald Graves and Warren Sinclair, *A Sketch Account of Aboriginal Peoples in the Canadian Military* (Ottawa: Department of National Defence, 2004).

Bernd Horn, "Terror on the Frontier: The Role of Indians in the Struggle for North America, 1754–1760," in *Forging a Nation: Perspectives on the Canadian Military Experience,* ed. Bernd Horn (St. Catharines, ON: Vanwell Publishing, 2002).

D. Peter MacLeod, *The Canadian Iroquois and the Seven Years' War* (Toronto: Dundurn Press, 1996).

Daniel Marston, *The French-Indian War, 1754–1760* (New York: Routledge, 2002).

Desmond Morton, *A Military History of Canada* (Toronto: McClelland & Stewart, 1999).

William R. Nester, *The Great Frontier War: Britain, France and the Imperial Struggle for North America, 1607–1755* (Westport, CT: Praeger, 2000).

Stuart Reid, *Quebec 1759: The Battle That Won Canada* (Westport, CT: Praeger, 2005).

Daniel K. Richter, "War and Culture: The Iroquois Experience," *William and Mary Quarterly* 40, no. 4 (October 1983): 528–59.

G.F.G. Stanley, *Canada's Soldiers: The Military History of an Unmilitary People* (Toronto: Macmillan, 1960).

Bruce Vandervort, *Indian Wars of Mexico, Canada and the United States, 1812–1900* (New York: Routledge, 2006).

Jack Verney, *The Good Regiment: The Carignan-Salières Regiment in Canada, 1665–1668* (Montreal: McGill-Queen's University Press, 1991).

Chapter 2: The Redcoats: British Regiments of Foot and Canadian Militia

Beevor, *Inside the British Army.*

Bercuson, *Significant Incident.*

J.M. Brereton, *The British Soldier: A Social History from 1661 to the Present Day* (London: Bodley Head, 1986).

Stewart H. Bull, *The Queen's York Rangers: An Historic Regiment* (Erin, ON: Boston Mills Press, 1984).

Canadian Forces Headquarters, Directorate of History, Reports nos. 6 and 7, "Canadian Militia Prior to Confederation," 1966.

René Chartrand, *Canadian Military Heritage,* vol. 2, *1755–1871* (Montreal: Art Global, 1993).

Timothy Dubé, "Tommy Atkins, We Never Knew Ye: Documenting the British Soldier in Canada, 1759–1871; Military Organization and the Archival Record," *Canadian Military History* (Spring 1995): 113–20.

Hackett, *The Profession of Arms.*

Brian Hearn, "Soldiers of the Rock," *The Beaver,* December 1, 1995.

Nester, *The Great Frontier War.*

O'Leary, "The Regimental System."

Reid, *Quebec 1759.*

Russell, *Customs and Traditions.*

Stanley, *Canada's Soldiers.*

Chapter 3: The War of 1812: Saving Canada

Canadian Forces Headquarters, Directorate of History, Report no. 6, "Canadian Militia Prior to Confederation," June 30, 1966.

Chartrand, *Canadian Military Heritage,* vol. 2.

The Friends of Crysler's Farm Battlefield Memorial, "The Other November 11: The Battle That Saved Canada," http://www.cryslersfarm.com.

Mary Beacock Fryer, *Battlefields of Canada* (Toronto: Dundurn Press, 1986).

"The Glengarry Light Infantry Fencibles" http://glengarrylightinfantry.ca/.

J.L. Granatstein, *Canada's Army: Waging War and Keeping the Peace* (Toronto: University of Toronto Press, 2002).

Donald E. Graves, *Red Coats and Grey Jackets: The Battle of Chippawa, 5 July 1814* (Toronto: Dundurn Press, 1994).

John R. Grodzinski, "'They Really Conducted Themselves Remarkably Well': Canadian Soldiers and the Great War, 1783 to 1815," in *The Canadian Way of War: Serving the National Interest,* ed. Bernd Horn (Toronto: Dundurn Press, 2006).

Donald R. Hickey, *The War of 1812: A Forgotten Conflict* (Chicago and Urbana: University of Illinois Press, 1990).

MilitaryHeritage.com, "His Majesty's Canadian Regiment of Fencible Infantry, 1803–1816," http://www.warof1812.ca.

Stanley, *Canada's Soldiers.*

Jack L. Summers and René Chartrand, "History and Uniform of the 104th (New Brunswick) Regiment of Foot," http://www.warof1812.ca.

Summers and Chartrand, "History and Uniform of the Royal Newfoundland Regiment of Fencible Infantry," http://www.warof1812.ca.

War of 1812, "People and Stories," http://www.galafilm.com/1812.

Mark Zuehlke and C. Stuart Daniel, *The Canadian Military Atlas: The Nation's Battlefields from the French and Indian Wars to Kosovo* (Toronto: Stoddart, 2001).

Chapter 4: Britannia Departs: Canada's New Regiments Emerge

Army Historical Section, *The Regiments and Corps of the Canadian Army* (Ottawa: Minister of National Defence, 1964).

W.T. Barnard, *The Queen's Own Rifles of Canada, 1980–1960; One Hundred Years of Canada* (Toronto: Queen's Own Rifles of Canada, n.d.).

Ken Bell and C.P. Stacey, *100 Years: The Royal Canadian Regiment, 1883–1983* (Toronto: Royal Canadian Regiment Trust, 1983).

Kingsley Brown Sr., Kingsley Brown Jr., and Brereton Greenhous, *Semper Paratus: The History of the Royal Hamilton Light Infantry (Wentworth Regiment), 1862–1977* (Hamilton: RHLI Historical Association, 1977).

Ernest J. Chambers, *The Queen's Own Rifles of Canada* (Toronto: E.L. Ruddy, 1901).

A. Fortescue Duguid, *History of the Canadian Grenadier Guards, 1760–1964* (Montreal: Gazette Printing Company, 1965).

John R. Grodzinski, "A Modicum of Professionalism: The Canadian Militia in the Nineteenth Century," in *The Canadian Way of War: Serving the National Interest,* ed. Bernd Horn (Toronto: Dundurn Press, 2006).

Paul P. Hutchison, *Canada's Black Watch: The First Hundred Years, 1862–1962* (Montreal: Royal Highlanders of Canada Armoury Association, 1962).

Desmond Morton, *The Canadian General: Sir William Otter* (Toronto: Hakkert, 1974).

Morton, *Military History of Canada.*

Stanley, *Canada's Soldiers.*

Upper Canada Historical Arms Society, *The Military Arms of Canada* (Bloomfield, ON: Museum Restoration Service, 1963).

Chapter 5: Rebellion and War: Canada's Regiments in Saskatchewan and South Africa

David J. Bercuson and J.L. Granatstein, *Dictionary of Canadian Military History* (Toronto: Oxford University Press, 1992).

David J. Bercuson and J.L. Granatstein, *War and Peacekeeping: From South Africa to the Gulf—Canada's Limited Wars* (Toronto: Key Porter Books, 1991).

Charles A. Bolton, "Reminiscences of the North-West Rebellions" (Toronto, 1886), http://wsb.datapro.net/rebellions/index.html.

R. Cunliffe, *The Story of a Regiment* (Lord Strathcona's Horse [Royal Canadians] Regimental Society, 1995).

Fryer, *Battlefields of Canada*.

Lord Strathcona's Horse (Royal Canadians) Society, "History of a Regiment," http://www.strathconas.ca.

WarMuseum.ca, "Canada & the South African War, 1899–1902": "Battles," "Units," http://www.civilization.ca/cwm/boer/boerwarhistory_e.html.

Zuehlke and Daniel, *Canadian Military Atlas*.

Chapter 6: Ypres: The Patricias and the 10th Battalion

David J. Bercuson, *The Patricias: The Proud History of a Fighting Regiment* (Toronto: Stoddart, 2001).

Daniel G. Dancocks, *Gallant Canadians: The Story of the Tenth Canadian Infantry Battalion: 1914–1919* (Calgary: Calgary Highlanders Regimental Funds Foundation, 1990).

D.J. Goodspeed, *The Road Past Vimy: The Canadian Corps, 1914–1918* (Toronto: Macmillan, 1969).

Ronald G. Haycock, *Sam Hughes: The Public Career of a Controversial Canadian, 1885–1916* (Waterloo, ON: Wilfrid Laurier University Press, 1986).

G.W.L. Nicholson, *Canadian Expeditionary Force: 1914–1919: The Official History of the Canadian Army in the First World War* (Ottawa: Queen's Printer, 1962).

Chapter 7: St-Eloi and the Somme: The 28th Battalion and the Newfoundland Regiment

Graveyards of Gallipoli, "Royal Newfoundland Regiment at Gallipoli, 1915," www.diggerhistory2.info/graveyards/pages/units/newfoundland.htm.

G.E. Hewitt, "The Story of the Twenty-Eighth (North-West) Battalion, 1914–1917," www.nwbattalion.com/28thbattalion.html.

Mein, *Up the Johns!*

National Archives of the United Kingdom, "Report on Operations: First Day of the Battle of the Somme," Catalogue reference WO 158/327, www.nationalarchives.gov.uk/pathways/firstworldwar/transcripts/battles/.

Newfoundland and Labrador Heritage, "Newfoundland and the Great War," www.heritage.nf.ca/greatwar/articles/somme.html.

G.W.L. Nicholson, *The Fighting Newfoundlander: A History of the Royal Newfoundland Regiment* (Montreal: McGill-Queen's University Press, 2006).

Donald George Scott-Calder, "The History of the 28th (Northwest) Battalion, C.E.F. (October 1914–June 1919)," www.nwbattalion.com/28thbattalion.html.

C.P. Stacey, ed., *Introduction to the Study of Military History for Canadian Students* (Ottawa: Canadian Forces Headquarters, n.d.).

Terra Nova Greens, "Newfoundland's Military Heritage to 1920," www.infonet.st-johns.nf.ca/green/jing068.html.

Veterans Affairs Canada, "Beaumont-Hamel Newfoundland Memorial," www.vac-acc.gc.ca/remembers/sub.cfm?source=Memorials/ww1mem/beaumonthamel.

Chapter 8: Redemption: The Van Doos at Courcelette and the 85th Battalion at Vimy Ridge

Serge Bernier, *The Royal 22ᵉ Régiment: 1914–1999* (Montreal: Art Global, 2000).

Brereton Greenhous and Stephen J. Harris, *Canada and the Battle of Vimy Ridge: 9–12 April, 1917* (Montreal: Art Global, 1997).

Haycock, *Sam Hughes.*

Joseph Hayes, "The Eighty-Fifth Canadian Infantry Battalion, Nova Scotia Highlanders, in France and Flanders," 3.ns.sympatico.ca/sgowen/85chbook.html.

Library and Archives Canada, RG9, Records of the Department of Militia and Defence, War Diaries for the 22nd and 85th Battalions of the CEF and the Royal Canadian Regiment.

Jean Pariseau and Serge Bernier, *French Canadians and Bilingualism in the Canadian Armed Forces,* vol. 1, *1763–1969: The Fear of a Parallel Army* (Ottawa: Directorate of History, Department of National Defence, 1988).

"Story of the 22nd Battalion: September 15, 1916, The Capture of Courcelette," *Canadian Military History* 16, no. 2 (Spring 2007): 49–58.

Robert S. Williams, "The 85th Canadian Infantry Battalion and First Contact with the Enemy at Vimy Ridge, 9–14 April, 1917," *Canadian Army Journal* 8, no. 1 (Winter 2005): 73–82.

Chapter 9: Victory: The 58th Battalion at Passchendaele and the Royal Canadian Regiment at Cambrai

Bell and Stacey, *100 Years.*

R.C. Fetherstonhaugh, *The Royal Canadian Regiment: 1883–1933* (Fredericton: Royal Canadian Regiment, 1936).

J.F.B. Livesay, *Canada's Hundred Days: With the Canadian Corps from Amiens to Mons, Aug. 8—Nov. 11, 1918* (Toronto: Thomas Allen, 1919).

Library and Archives Canada, RG9, Records of the Department of Militia and Defence, War Diaries for the 58th Battalion of the CEF and the Royal Canadian Regiment.

Nicholson, *Canadian Expeditionary Force.*

Kevin R. Shackleton, *Second to None: The Fighting 58th Battalion of the Canadian Expeditionary Force* (Toronto: Dundurn Group, 2002).

W.G. Wurtele, "Cambrai 1918," *Pro Patria* 40 (July 1979).

Chapter 10: Disaster: The Winnipeg Grenadiers at Hong Kong and the Fusiliers Mont-Royal at Dieppe

Terry Copp, "The Defence of Hong Kong: December 1941," *Canadian Military History* 10, no. 4 (Autumn 2001): 5–20.

Ted Ferguson, *Desperate Siege: The Battle of Hong Kong* (Toronto: Doubleday Canada, 1980).

Brereton Greenhous, *"C" Force to Hong Kong: A Canadian Catastrophe, 1941–1945* (Toronto: Dundurn Press, 1997).

Library and Archives Canada, Historical Section Army Headquarters, Reports nos. 89, 98, and 108 Concerning Operation Jubilee, the Raid on Dieppe, August 19, 1942.

Oliver Lindsay, *The Lasting Honour: The Fall of Hong Kong 1941* (London: Hamish Hamilton, 1978).

Sherry McNair, *Soldiers All!* (North Battleford, SK: Turner-Warner Publications, 1994).

John Mellor, *Forgotten Heroes: The Canadians at Dieppe* (Toronto: Methuen, 1975).

Robin Neillands, *The Dieppe Raid: The Story of the Disastrous 1942 Expedition* (London: Aurum Press, 2005).

Pariseau and Bernier, *French Canadians.*

Cameron Pulsifer, "John Robert Osborn: Canada's Hong Kong VC," *Canadian Military History* 6, no. 2 (Autumn 1997): 79–89.

Reader's Digest, *The Canadians at War 1939/45,* vol. 1 (Reader's Digest Association, 1969).

Terence Robertson, *Dieppe: The Shame and the Glory* (Toronto: McClelland & Stewart, 1962).

C.P. Stacey, *Official History of the Canadian Army in the Second World War,* vol. 2, *Six Years of War: The Army in Canada, Britain and the Pacific* (Ottawa: Queen's Printer, 1955).

George Trist, "Report on the Part Played by the Winnipeg Grenadiers in the Defence of Hong Kong," *Canadian Military History* 10, no. 4 (Autumn 2001): 21–26.

Denis Whitaker and Sheila Whitaker, *Dieppe: Tragedy to Triumph* (Toronto: McGraw-Hill Ryerson, 1992).

Chapter 11: The Forgotten Campaign: The Hasty Ps in Sicily and the Loyal Eddies at Ortona

David J. Bercuson, *Maple Leaf Against the Axis: Canada's Second World War* (Toronto: Stoddart, 1995).

Shaun R.G. Brown, "'The Rock of Accomplishment': The Loyal Edmonton Regiment at Ortona," *Canadian Military History* 2, no. 2 (Autumn 1993): 10–23.

A.R. Campbell and N.R. Waugh, "The Hasty Pees in Sicily," *Canadian Military History* 12, no. 3 (Summer 2003): 65–73.

Dan Dancocks, *The D-Day Dodgers: The Canadians in Italy, 1943–1945* (Toronto: McClelland & Stewart, 1991).

Geoffrey Hayes, "The Canadians in Sicily Sixty Years On," *Canadian Military History* 12, no. 3 (Summer 2003): 5–18.

Farley Mowat, *The Regiment* (Toronto: McClelland & Stewart, 1955).

G.W.L. Nicholson, *The Canadians in Italy, 1943–45* (Ottawa: Queen's Printer, 1956).

G.R. Stevens, *A City Goes to War* (Brampton, ON: Charters Publishing for the Edmonton Regiment Associates, 1964).

Mark Zuehlke, *Ortona: Canada's Epic World War II Battle* (Toronto: Stoddart, 1999).

Chapter 12: Bloody Fighting: The Gee-Gees in the Liri Valley and the Sherbrookes in Normandy

Dancocks, *D-Day Dodgers*.

Department of National Defence, "History of the (Sherbrooke) Regiment," www.army.dnd.ca/sherbrooke_hussars/.

Roman Johann Jarymowycz, "The Quest for Operational Maneuver in the Normandy Campaign," (PhD diss., McGill University, 1997).

John Marteinson, *The Governor General's Horse Guards: Second to None* (Toronto: Governor General's Horse Guards Foundation, 2002).

John Marteinson and Michael R. McNorgan, *The Royal Canadian Armoured Corps: An Illustrated History* (Ottawa: Royal Canadian Armoured Corps Association, 2000).

Nicholson, *Canadians in Italy*.

Jean E. Portugal, *We Were There: The Army, a Record for Canada* (Royal Canadian Military Institute Heritage Society, 1998).

Mark Zuehlke, *Juno Beach*.

Mark Zuehlke, *The Liri Valley: Canada's World War II Breakthrough to Rome* (Toronto: Stoddart, 2001).

Chapter 13: Hard Victory: The Black Watch at Verrières Ridge and the Essex Scottish in the Rhineland

Sandy Antal and Kevin R. Shackleton, *Duty Nobly Done: The Official History of the Essex and Kent Scottish Regiment* (Windsor: Scottish Borderers Foundation, 2006).

Bercuson, *Maple Leaf Against the Axis*.

Black Watch Regimental Archives, "Letters from War," www.blackwatchcanada.com.

Terry Copp, *The Brigade: The Fifth Canadian Infantry Brigade, 1939–1945* (Stoney Creek, ON: Fortress Publications, 1992).

Terry Copp, *Cinderella Army: The Canadians in Northwest Europe, 1944–1945* (Toronto: University of Toronto Press, 2006).

Terry Copp, *Fields of Fire: The Canadians in Normandy.* The 1998 Joanne Goodman Lectures (Toronto: University of Toronto Press, 2003).

Library and Archives Canada, Historical Section, Canadian Military Headquarters, "Operation 'BLOCKBUSTER': The Canadian Offensive West of the Rhine, 26 Feb–23 Mar 45 (Preliminary Report)."

C.P. Stacey, *Official History,* vol. 3, *Victory Campaign.*

Denis W. Whitaker and Shelagh Whitaker, *Rhineland: The Battle to End the War* (Toronto: Stoddart, 1989).

Whitaker and Whitaker, *Tug of War: The Canadian Victory That Opened Antwerp* (Toronto: Stoddart, 1984).

Jeffery Williams, *The Long Left Flank: The Hard-Fought Way to the Reich, 1944–1945* (Toronto: Stoddart, 1988).

Chapter 14: Kap'yong: The Patricias in Korea

David Bercuson, *Blood on the Hills: The Canadian Army in the Korean War* (Toronto: University of Toronto Press, 2002).

Bercuson, *True Patriot: The Life of Brooke Claxton, 1898–1960* (Toronto: University of Toronto Press, 1993).

Pierre Berton, "Corporal Dunphy's War," *Maclean's,* June 1, 1951.

Clay Blair, *The Forgotten War: America in Korea, 1950–1953* (New York: Times Books, 1987).

Hub Gray, *Beyond the Danger Close: The Korean Experience Revealed, 2nd Battalion Princess Patricia's Canadian Light Infantry* (Calgary: Bunker to Bunker Publishing, 2003).

Michael G. McKeown, *Kapyong Remembered: Anecdotes from Korea* (Calgary: PPCLI Archives, n.d.).

John Melady, *Korea: Canada's Forgotten War* (Toronto: McClelland & Stewart, 1983).

Denis Stairs, *The Diplomacy of Constraint: Canada, the Korean War, and the United States* (Toronto: University of Toronto Press, 1974).

G.R. Stevens, *Princess Patricia's Canadian Light Infantry: 1919–1957*, vol. 3
(Griesbach, AB: Historical Committee of the Regiment, n.d.).

James R. Stone and Jacques Castonguay, *Korea: 1951, Two Canadian Battles*
(Ottawa: Canadian War Museum, 1988).

Brent Byron Watson, "From Calgary to Kap'yong: The Second Battalion
Princess Patricia's Canadian Light Infantry's Preparation for Battle in Korea,
August 1950 to April 1951" (MA thesis, University of Victoria, 1993).

Chapter 15: Stalemate: The Van Doos and the RCR on the Jamestown Line

Jean V. Allard with Serge Bernier, *The Memoirs of Jean V. Allard* (Vancouver:
University of British Columbia Press, 1988).

A.J. Barker, *Fortune Favours the Brave: The Hook, Korea, 1953* (London: Leo
Cooper, 1974).

Christopher Doary, "'Miniature Set-Piece Battles': Infantry Patrolling
Operations in Korea, May–June 1952," *Canadian Military History* 6, no. 1
(Spring 1997): 20–33.

T.R. Fehrenbach, *This Kind of War* (Washington: Brassey's, 1963).

Roy K. Flint, Peter W. Kozumplik, and Thomas J. Waraska, *The Arab-Israeli
Wars, the Chinese Civil War, and the Korean War* (West Point, NY: United
States Military Academy, 1987).

John Gardam, *Korea Volunteer: An Oral History from Those Who Were There*
(Burnstown, ON: General Store Publishing, 1994).

Alexander L. George, *The Chinese Communist Army in Action: The Korean War
and Its Aftermath* (New York: Columbia University Press, 1967).

Jeffrey Grey, *The Commonwealth Armies and the Korean War* (Manchester:
Manchester University Press, 1988).

Max Hastings, *The Korean War* (London: Michael Joseph, 1987).

Robert Leckie, *Conflict: The History of the Korean War* (New York: Da Capo
Press, 1996).

Robert S. Peacock, *Kim-chi, Asahi and Rum: A Platoon Commander Remembers
Korea* (Toronto: Lugus, 1994).

Les Peate, "No Pay—No Uniforms—No Glory," *Esprit de Corps* 5, no. 5: 28–29.

Peate, "Food for Thought," *Esprit de Corps* 5, no. 9: 16–17.

David Rees, *Korea: The Limited War* (New York: St. Martin's Press, 1964).

Herbert Fairlie Wood, *Strange Battleground: Official History of the Canadian Army in Korea* (Ottawa: Queen's Printer, 1966).

Chapter 16: Soldiers and Peacekeepers: The Cold War

Bercuson, *Significant Incident.*

Bercuson, *The Patricias.*

John Hasek, *The Disarming of Canada* (Toronto: Key Porter Books, 1987).

Lewis MacKenzie, *Peacekeeper: The Road to Sarajevo* (Vancouver: Douglas & McIntyre, 1993).

John Marteinson, *We Stand on Guard: An Illustrated History of the Canadian Army* (Montreal: Ovale Publications, 1992).

William J. Patterson, *A Regiment Worthy of Its Hire: The Canadian Guards, 1953–1970* (Canadian Guards Regimental Association, 1997).

Tamara A. Sherwin, "From Total War to Total Force: Civil Military Relations and the Canadian Army Reserve (Militia), 1945–1995" (MA thesis, University of New Brunswick, 1997).

Chapter 17: The Latest War: The Army in Afghanistan

Gary M. Bowman, "Operation Medusa: Coalition Operations in Kandahar Province, Afghanistan, September 2006" (unpublished manuscript).

Steve Buist, *Hamilton Spectator,* September 1, 2007.

Calgary Herald, March 19, 2002.

Canadian Broadcasting Corporation, "Mike Smith's Notes from Afghanistan," various dates, http://www.cbc.ca.

Andrew Charchuk, "'Contact C': A Forward Observation Officer with Task Force Orion," *Canadian Army Journal* 10, no. 2 (Summer 2007): 25–35.

Edmonton Journal, November 16, 2001; February 3, 2002.

Globe and Mail, October 8, 2001.

National Post, September 17, 2001; February 4, 2002; April 22, 2002; May 7, 2002.

Ottawa Citizen, January 8, 2002.

PPCLI Regimental Headquarters, Princess Patricia Memorial Service, April 28, 2002.

Times Colonist (Victoria), September 21, 2001.

Conclusion: Regiments Forever

Department of National Defence, *Canada's Army: We Stand on Guard for Thee* (Ottawa: Department of National Defence, 1998).

David Pentney, "Managed Readiness—Flawed Assumptions, Poor Deductions and Unintended Consequences," *Canadian Army Journal* 10, no. 1 (Spring 2007): 24–33.

BIBLIOGRAPHY

Primary Sources

Library and Archives Canada. RG9, Records of the Department of Militia and
Defence. War Diaries for the 22nd, 58th, and 85th Battalions of the CEF
and the Royal Canadian Regiment.

———. Historical Section Army Headquarters. Reports nos. 89, 98, and 108
Concerning Operation Jubilee, the Raid on Dieppe, 1942.

———. Historical Section, Canadian Military Headquarters. "Operation
'BLOCKBUSTER': The Canadian Offensive West of the Rhine, 26 Feb–23
Mar 45 (Preliminary Report)."

Government Sources (print)

Canada. Canadian Army, Historical Section. *The Canadian Army List.* Ottawa:
Queen's Printer, 1964.

———. Department of National Defence. *Canada's Army: We Stand on Guard
for Thee.* Ottawa: Department of National Defence, 1998.

Canadian Forces Headquarters, Directorate of History. Reports nos. 6 and 7
—Canadian Militia Prior to Confederation, 1966.

Secondary Sources

Allard, Jean V., and Serge Bernier. *The Memoirs of General Jean V. Allard.*
Vancouver: University of British Columbia Press, 1988.

Anderson, Edward J., Upper Canada Historical Arms Society, and Museum
Restoration Service. *The Military Arms of Canada.* Historical Arms Series 1.
West Hill, ON: Museum Restoration Service, 1963.

Antal, Sandy, and Kevin R. Shackleton. *Duty Nobly Done: The Official History of the Essex and Kent Scottish Regiment.* Windsor, ON: Walkerville Publishing, 2006.

Barker, A.J. *Fortune Favours the Brave: The Battle of the Hook, Korea, 1953.* London: Cooper, 1974.

Barnard, W.T. *The Queen's Own Rifles of Canada, 1860–1960: One Hundred Years of Canada.* Don Mills, ON: Ontario Publishing, 1960.

Beevor, Anthony. *Inside the British Army.* London: Corgi, 1991.

Bercuson, David J. *Maple Leaf Against the Axis: Canada's Second World War.* Don Mills, ON: Stoddart, 1995.

———. *The Patricias: The Proud History of a Fighting Regiment.* Toronto: Stoddart, 2001.

———. *Significant Incident: Canada's Army, the Airborne, and the Murder in Somalia.* Toronto: McClelland & Stewart, 1996.

———. *True Patriot: The Life of Brooke Claxton, 1898–1960.* Toronto: University of Toronto Press, 1993.

Bercuson, David J. and J.L. Granatstein. *Dictionary of Canadian Military History.* Toronto: Oxford University Press, 1992.

Bernier, Serge. *The Royal 22ᵉ Régiment, 1914–1999.* Montreal: Art Global, 2000.

Berton, Pierre. "Corporal Dunphy's War." *Maclean's,* June 1, 1951.

Black Watch Regimental Archives. "Letters from War." www.blackwatchcanada.com.

Blair, Clay. *The Forgotten War: America in Korea, 1950–1953.* New York: Times Books, 1987.

Bolton, Charles A. "Reminiscences of the North-West Rebellions." http://wsb.datapro.net/rebellions/index.html.

Bowman, Gary M. "Operation Medusa: Coalition Operations in Kandahar Province, Afghanistan, September 2006." Unpublished manuscript.

Brereton, J.M. *The British Soldier: A Social History from 1661 to the Present Day.* London: Bodley Head, 1986.

Brown, Gordon, and Terry Copp. *Look to Your Front . . . Regina Rifles, A Regiment at War: 1944–45.* Waterloo, ON: Laurier Centre, 2001.

Brown, Kingsley, Sr., Kingsley Brown Jr., Brereton Greenhous, and R.H.L.I. Historical Association. Semper Paratus: *The History of the Royal Hamilton*

Light Infantry (Wentworth Regiment), 1862–1977. Hamilton, ON: Royal Hamilton Light Infantry Historical Association, 1977.

Brown, Shaun R.G. "'The Rock of Accomplishment': The Loyal Edmonton Regiment at Ortona." *Canadian Military History* 2, no. 2 (Autumn 1993): 10–23.

Buist, Steve. "One Bloody Weekend." *Hamilton Spectator,* September 1, 2007.

Bull, Stewart H. *The Queen's York Rangers: An Historic Regiment.* Erin, ON: Boston Mills Press, 1984.

Calgary Herald. March 19, 2002.

Campbell, A.R., and N.R. Waugh. "The Hasty Pees in Sicily." *Canadian Military History* 12, no. 3 (Summer 2003): 65–73.

Cassel, Jay. "The Troupes de la Marine in Canada, 1683–1760: Men and Materiel." PhD diss. University of Toronto, 1987.

Cave, Alfred A. *The French and Indian War.* Greenwood Guides to Historic Events, 1500–1900. Westport, CT: Greenwood Press, 2004.

Chambers, Ernest J. *The Queen's Own Rifles of Canada: A History of a Splendid Regiment's Origin, Development and Services, Including a Story of Patriotic Duties Well Performed in Three Campaigns.* Toronto: E.L. Ruddy, 1901.

Charchuk, Andrew. "'Contact C'—A Forward Observation Officer with Task Force Orion." *Canadian Army Journal* 10, no. 2 (Summer 2007): 25–35.

Chartrand, René, and Serge Bernier. *Canadian Military Heritage.* Vol. 1, *1000–1754.* Montreal: Art Global, 1993.

———. *Canadian Military Heritage.* Vol. 2, *1755–1871.* Montreal: Art Global, 1993.

Cook, Tim. "Literary Memorials: The Great War Regimental Histories, 1919–1939." *Journal of the Canadian Historical Association* 13, no.1 (2002):167–190.

Copp, Terry. *The Brigade: The Fifth Canadian Infantry Brigade, 1939–45.* Stoney Creek, ON: Fortress Publications, 1992.

———. *Cinderella Army: The Canadians in Northwest Europe, 1944–1945.* Toronto: University of Toronto Press, 2006.

———. "The Defence of Hong Kong: December 1941." *Canadian Military History* 10, no. 4 (Autumn 2001): 5–20.

———. *Fields of Fire: The Canadians in Normandy.* Joanne Goodman Lectures, 1998. Toronto: University of Toronto Press, 2003.

Copp, Terry, and Robert Vogel. *Maple Leaf Route: Caen.* Alma, ON: Maple Leaf Route, 1983.

Cuniffe, Richard. *The Story of a Regiment: Lord Strathcona's Horse (Royal Canadians).* Calgary: Lord Strathcona's Horse (Royal Canadians) Regimental Society, 1995.

Dancocks, Daniel G. *The D-Day Dodgers: The Canadians in Italy, 1943–1945.* Toronto: McClelland & Stewart, 1991.

————. *Gallant Canadians: The Story of the Tenth Canadian Infantry Battalion, 1914–1919.* Calgary: Calgary Highlanders Regimental Funds Foundation, 1990.

Department of National Defence. "History of the (Sherbrooke) Regiment." www.army.dnd.ca/sherbrooke_hussars/history.

Doary, Christopher. "'Miniature Set-Piece Battles': Infantry Patrolling Operations in Korea, May–June 1952." *Canadian Military History* 6, no. 1 (Spring 1997): 20–33.

Dubé, Timothy. "'Tommy Atkins, We Never Knew Ye': Documenting the British Soldier in Canada, 1759–1871. Military Organization and the Archival Record." *Canadian Military History* 4, no.1 (Spring 1995): 113–120.

Duguid, A. Fortescue. *History of the Canadian Grenadier Guards, 1760–1964.* Montreal: Gazette Printing, 1965.

DuLong, John P. "Carignan-Salières Regiment Lineage Chart." http://habitant. org/carignan.htm.

Edmonton Journal. November 16, 2001; February 3, 2002.

Fehrenbach, T.R. *This Kind of War: A Study in Unpreparedness.* New York: Macmillan, 1963.

Ferguson, Ted. *Desperate Siege: The Battle of Hong Kong.* Toronto: Doubleday Canada, 1980.

Fetherstonhaugh, R.C. *The Royal Canadian Regiment, 1883–1933.* Montreal: Gazette Printing, 1936.

The Friends of Crysler's Farm Battlefield Memorial. "The Other November 11: The Battle That Saved Canada." http://www.cryslersfarm.com.

Fryer, Mary Beacock. *Battlefields of Canada.* Toronto: Dundurn Press, 1986.

Gardam, John. *Korea Volunteer: An Oral History from Those Who Were There.* Burnstown, ON: General Store Publishing, 1994.

George, Alexander L. *The Chinese Communist Army in Action: The Korean War and Its Aftermath.* N.p., 1967.

"The Glengarry Light Infantry Fencibles." http://glengarrylightinfantry.ca/.

Goodspeed, D.J. *The Road Past Vimy: The Canadian Corps, 1914–1918.* Toronto: Macmillan, 1969.

Granatstein, J.L. *Canada's Army: Waging War and Keeping the Peace.* Toronto: University of Toronto Press, 2002.

Granatstein, J.L., and David Jay Bercuson. *War and Peacekeeping: From South Africa to the Gulf—Canada's Limited Wars.* Toronto: Key Porter, 1991.

Graves, Donald E. *Red Coats and Grey Jackets: The Battle of Chippawa, 5 July 1814.* Toronto: Dundurn Press, 1994.

Graves, Donald, and Warren Sinclair. *A Sketch Account of Aboriginal Peoples in the Canadian Military.* Ottawa: Department of National Defence, 2004.

Graveyards of Gallipoli. "Royal Newfoundland Regiment at Gallipoli, 1915." www.diggerhistory2.info/graveyards/pages/units/newfoundland.htm.

Gray, Hub, and Grania Litwin. *Beyond the Danger Close: The Korean Experience Revealed: 2nd Battalion Princess Patricia's Canadian Light Infantry.* Calgary: Bunker to Bunker, 2003.

Greenhous, Brereton. *"C" Force to Hong Kong: A Canadian Catastrophe, 1941–1945.* Toronto: Dundurn Press, 1997.

Greenhous, Brereton, et al., *Canada and the Battle of Vimy Ridge, 9–12 April 1917.* Ottawa: Department of National Defence, Directorate of History, 1992.

Grey, Jeffrey. *The Commonwealth Armies and the Korean War: An Alliance Study.* War, Armed Forces, and Society. Manchester: Manchester University Press, 1988.

Griess, Thomas E. *Atlas of the Arab-Israeli Wars, the Chinese Civil War, and the Korean War.* West Point Military History Series. Wayne, NJ: Avery Publishing, 1986.

Grodzinski, John R., "'They Really Conducted Themselves Remarkably Well': Canadian Soldiers and the Great War, 1783 to 1815." In *The Canadian Way of War: Serving the National Interest,* edited by Bernd Horn. Toronto: Dundurn Press, 2006.

Hackett, John Winthrop. *The Profession of Arms.* London: Sidgwick & Jackson, 1983.

Hasek, John. *The Disarming of Canada.* Toronto: Key Porter Books, 1987.

Hastings, Max. *The Korean War*. London: M. Joseph, 1987.

Haycock, Ronald Graham. *Sam Hughes: The Public Career of a Controversial Canadian*. Waterloo, ON: Wilfrid Laurier University Press, 1986.

Hayes, Geoffrey. "The Canadians in Sicily Sixty Years On." *Canadian Military History* 12, no. 3 (Summer 2003): 5–18.

Hayes, Joseph. "The Eighty-Fifth Canadian Infantry Battalion, Nova Scotia Highlanders, in France and Flanders." www3.ns.sympatico.ca/sgowen/85chbook.html.

Hearn, Brian. "Soldiers of the Rock: The Royal Newfoundland Regiment Remembers 200 Years of History." *The Beaver* (December 1995): 37.

Hewitt, G.E. "The Story of the Twenty-Eighth (North-West) Battalion, 1914–1917." www.nwbattalion.com/28thbattalion.html.

Hickey, Donald R. *The War of 1812: A Forgotten Conflict*. Urbana: University of Illinois Press, 1989.

Horn, Bernd. "Terror on the Frontier: The Role of Indians in the Struggle for North America, 1754–1760." In *Forging a Nation: Perspectives on the Canadian Military Experience,* edited by Bernd Horn. Toronto: Vanwell Publishing, 2002.

Hutchison, Paul P., Black Watch of Canada, and Museum Restoration Service. *Canada's Black Watch: The First Hundred Years, 1862–1962*. Montreal: Black Watch R.H.R. of Canada, 1962.

Jarymowycz, Roman Johann. "The Quest for Operational Maneuver in the Normandy Campaign." PhD diss., McGill University, 1997.

Leckie, Robert. *Conflict: The History of the Korean War, 1950–53*. New York: Da Capo Press, 1996.

Lindsay, Oliver. *The Lasting Honour: The Fall of Hong Kong, 1941*. London: Hamish Hamilton, 1978.

Livesay, John Frederick Bligh. *Canada's Hundred Days: With the Canadian Corps from Amiens to Mons, Aug. 8–Nov. 11, 1918*. Toronto: Thomas Allen, 1919.

MacKenzie, Lewis. *Peacekeeper: The Road to Sarajevo*. Vancouver: Douglas & McIntyre, 1993.

MacLeod, D. Peter. *The Canadian Iroquois and the Seven Years' War*. Canadian War Museum Historical Publication 29. Toronto: Dundurn Press, 1996.

Marston, Daniel. *The French-Indian War, 1754–1760*. Essential Histories. New York: Routledge, 2003.

Marteinson, J.K. *We Stand on Guard: An Illustrated History of the Canadian Army.* Montreal: Ovale Publications, 1992.

Marteinson, J.K., and Scott Duncan. *The Governor General's Horse Guards: Second to None.* Toronto: Robin Brass Studio, 2002.

Marteinson, J.K., and Michael R. McNorgan. *The Royal Canadian Armoured Corps: An Illustrated History.* Toronto: Royal Canadian Armoured Corps Association, in cooperation with the Canadian War Museum, 2000.

McKeown, Michael G. *Kapyong Remembered: Anecdotes from Korea.* PPCLI Archives.

McNair, Sherry. *Soldiers All!* North Battleford, SK: Turner-Warwick Publications, 1994.

Mein, Stewart A.G., and Royal Regina Rifle Regiment. *Up the Johns!: The Story of the Royal Regina Rifles.* Regina: Senate of the Royal Regina Rifles, 1992.

Melady, John. *Korea: Canada's Forgotten War.* Toronto: Macmillan, 1983.

Mellor, John. *Forgotten Heroes: The Canadians at Dieppe.* Toronto: Methuen, 1975.

"Mike Smith's Notes from Afghanistan." *Globe and Mail.* October 8, 2001.

MilitaryHeritage.com. "His Majesty's Canadian Regiment of Fencible Infantry, 1803–1816." http://www.warof1812.ca.

National Post. September 17, 2001; February 4, 2002; April 22, 2002; May 7, 2002.

Morton, Desmond. *A Military History of Canada: From Champlain to Kosovo.* 4th rev. ed. Toronto: McClelland & Stewart, 1999.

———. *The Canadian General Sir William Otter.* Canadian War Museum Historical Publication 9. Toronto: Hakkert, 1974.

Mowat, Farley. *The Regiment.* Toronto: McClelland & Stewart, 1955.

National Archives of the United Kingdom. "Report on Operations: First Day of the Battle of the Somme." WO 158/327. www.nationalarchives.gov.uk/pathways/firstworldwar/transcripts/battles/.

Neillands, Robin. *The Dieppe Raid: The Story of the Disastrous 1942 Expedition.* London: Aurum, 2005.

Nester, William R. *The Great Frontier War: Britain, France, and the Imperial Struggle for North America, 1607–1755.* Westport, CT: Praeger, 2000.

Newfoundland and Labrador Heritage. "Newfoundland and the Great War." www.heritage.nf.ca/greatwar/articles/somme.html.

Nicholson, Gerald W.L. *Canadian Expeditionary Force, 1914–1919.* Official History of the Canadian Army in the First World War. Ottawa: Queen's Printer, 1964.

———. *The Canadians in Italy.* Ottawa: Queen's Printer, 1956.

———. *The Fighting Newfoundlander: A History of the Royal Newfoundland Regiment.* St. John's: Government of Newfoundland, 1964.

O'Leary, Michael M. "The Regimental System." www.regimentalrogue.com.

Ottawa Citizen, January 8, 2002.

Pariseau, Jean, Serge Bernier, and Department of National Defence, Directorate of History. *French Canadians and Bilingualism in the Canadian Armed Forces.* Socio-Military Series 2, no. 4. Ottawa: Department of National Defence, Directorate of History, 1988.

Patterson, William John, and Canadian Guards Association. *A Regiment Worthy of Its Hire: The Canadian Guards, 1953–1970.* Ottawa: Canadian Guards Association, 1997.

Peacock, Robert S. *Kim-Chi, Asahi and Rum: A Platoon Commander Remembers Korea, 1952–1953.* Toronto: Lugus, 1994.

Peate, Les. "Food for Thought." *Esprit de Corps* 5, no. 9: 16–17.

———. "No Pay—No Uniforms—No Glory." *Esprit de Corps* 5, no. 5: 28–29.

Pentney, David. "Managed Readiness—Flawed Assumptions, Poor Deductions and Unintended Consequences." *Canadian Army Journal* 10, no. 1 (Spring 2007): 24–33.

Portugal, Jean E. *We Were There: A Record for Canada.* Shelburne, ON: Royal Canadian Military Institute Heritage Society, 1998.

PPCLI Regimental Headquarters. Princess Patricia Memorial Service, 2002.

Reader's Digest Association (Canada). *The Canadians at War, 1939/45.* Montreal: Reader's Digest Association Canada, 1969.

Rees, David. *Korea: The Limited War.* London: Macmillan, 1964.

Reid, Stuart. *Quebec, 1759: The Battle That Won Canada.* Praeger Illustrated Military History. Westport, CT: Praeger, 2005.

Richter, Daniel K. "War and Culture: The Iroquois Experience." *William and Mary Quarterly* 40, no. 4 (1983): 528–59.

Robertson, Terence. *Dieppe: The Shame and the Glory.* Boston: Little, Brown, 1962.

Russell, E.C., and Secretary of State, Canada. *Customs and Traditions of the Canadian Armed Forces.* Ottawa: Deneau & Greenberg, 1980.

Scott-Calder, Donald G. "The History of the 28th (Northwest) Battalion, C.E.F." www.nwbattalion.com/28thbattalion.html.

Shackleton, Kevin R. *Second to None: The Fighting 58th Battalion of the Canadian Expeditionary Force.* Toronto, ON: Dundurn Press, 2002.

Sherwin, Tamara A. "From Total War to Total Force: Civil Military Relations and the Canadian Army Reserve (Militia), 1945–1995." MA thesis, University of New Brunswick, 1997.

Stacey, C.P. *Introduction to the Study of Military History for Canadian Students.* Ottawa: Canadian Forces Headquarters, Directorate of Training, 1973.

———. *Official History of the Canadian Army in the Second World War.* Vol. 1, *Six Years of War: The Army in Canada, Britain and the Pacific.* Ottawa: Queen's Printer, 1955.

———. *Official History of the Canadian Army in the Second World War.* Vol. 3, *The Victory Campaign: The Operations in North-West Europe, 1944–1945.* Ottawa: Queen's Printer, 1960.

Stacey, C.P., and Ken Bell. *100 Years: The Royal Canadian Regiment, 1883–1983.* Don Mills, ON: Collier-Macmillan, 1983.

Stairs, Denis. *The Diplomacy of Constraint: Canada, the Korean War, and the United States.* Toronto: University of Toronto Press, 1974.

Stanley, George Francis Gilman, H.M. Jackson, and C.C.J. Bond. *Canada's Soldiers: The Military History of an Unmilitary People.* Toronto: Macmillan, 1960.

Stevens, George Roy. *A City Goes to War.* Brampton, ON: Edmonton Regiment Associates, Charters Publishing, 1964.

Stevens, George Roy, and Ralph Wilfred Hodder-Williams. *Princess Patricia's Canadian Light Infantry, 1919–1957.* Griesbach, AB: Historical Committee of the Regiment, 1959.

Stone, James R., and Jacques Castonguay. *Korea, 1951: Two Canadian Battles.* Canadian Battle Series 6. Ottawa: Balmuir Book Publishing, 1988.

"Story of the 22nd Battalion, September 15, 1916, the Capture of Courcelette." *Canadian Military History* 16, no. 2 (Spring 2007): 49–58.

Summers, J.L. and René Chartrand. "History and Uniform of the 104th (New Brunswick) Regiment of Foot." http://www.warof1812.ca.

————. "History and Uniform of the Royal Newfoundland Regiment of
    Fencible Infantry." http://www.warof1812.ca.

Terra Nova Greens. "Newfoundland's Military Heritage to 1920."
    www.infonet.st-johns.nf.ca/green/jing068.html.

Times Colonist (Victoria). September 21, 2001.

Trist, George. "Report on the Part Played by the Winnipeg Grenadiers in the
    Defence of Hong Kong." *Canadian Military History* 10, no. 4 (Autumn 2001):
    21–26.

Vandervort, Bruce. *Indian Wars of Mexico, Canada and the United States,
    1812–1900.* Warfare and History. New York: Routledge, 2006.

Verney, Jack. *The Good Regiment: The Carignan-Salières Regiment in Canada,
    1665–1668.* Montreal: McGill-Queen's University Press, 1991.

Veterans Affairs Canada. "Beaumont-Hamel Newfoundland Memorial." www.
    vac-acc.gc.ca/remembers/sub.cfm?source=Memorials/ww1mem/beaumonthamel.

WarMuseum.ca. "Canada & the South African War, 1899–1902." "Battles."
    "Units." http://www.civilization.ca/cwm/boer/boerwarhistory_e.html.

War of 1812. "People and Stories." http://www.galafilm.com/1812.

Watson, Brent Byron. "From Calgary to Kap'Yong: The Second Battalion
    Princess Patricia's Canadian Light Infantry's Preparation for Battle in Korea,
    August 1950 to April 1951." MA thesis, University of Victoria, 1993.

Whitaker, W. Denis, and Shelagh Whitaker. *Dieppe: Tragedy to Triumph.*
    Toronto: McGraw-Hill Ryerson, 1992.

————. *Rhineland: The Battle to End the War.* Toronto: Stoddart, 1989.

————. *Tug of War: The Canadian Victory That Opened Antwerp.* Toronto:
    Stoddart, 1984.

Williams, Jeffery. *The Long Left Flank: The Hard Fought Way to the Reich,
    1944–1945.* Toronto: Stoddart, 1988.

Williams, Lieutenant-Colonel Robert S. "The 85th Canadian Infantry Brigade
    and First Contact with the Enemy at Vimy Ridge, 9–14 April, 1917."
    Canadian Army Journal 8, no. 1 (Winter 2005): 73–82.

Wood, Herbert Fairlie. *Strange Battleground: The Operations in Korea and Their
    Effects on the Defence Policy of Canada.* Ottawa: Queen's Printer, 1966.

Wurtele, Lieutenant-Colonel W.G. "Cambrai 1918." *Pro Patria: The Royal
    Canadian Regiment,* no. 40 (July 1979) : 34–36.

Zuehlke, Mark. *Juno Beach: Canada's D-Day Victory, June 6, 1944*. Vancouver: Douglas & McIntyre, 2004.

———. *The Liri Valley: Canada's World War II Breakthrough to Rome*. Toronto: Stoddart, 2001.

———. *Ortona: Canada's Epic World War II Battle*. Toronto: Stoddart, 1999.

Zuehlke, Mark, and C. Stuart Daniel. *The Canadian Military Atlas: The Nation's Battlefields from the French and Indian Wars to Kosovo*. Toronto: Stoddart, 2001.

INDEX